Gender and Economics in Muslim Communities

Bringing together feminist analyses of economic processes and outcomes with feminist critiques of Orientalism, this book examines the diverse economic realities facing women in a range of Muslim communities. This approach pays special attention to the role of Islam in economic analyses of gender equality and women's well-being in Muslim communities, while at the same time challenging biased and inaccurate accounts that essentialize Islam.

Nuanced case studies conducted in Bangladesh, Iran, Israel, Nigeria, and Turkey illustrate the historical and institutional diversity of Muslim communities and draw vivid pictures of the everyday economic lives of Muslim women in these communities. These studies are complemented by quantitative analyses that extend beyond inserting Islam as a dummy variable. The contributions represent a wide range of disciplines, including anthropology, economics, gender studies, political science, psychology, and sociology.

By placing critiques of Orientalist scholarship in direct dialogue with scholarship on economic development in Muslim contexts, this diverse collection illustrates how different methods and frameworks can work together to provide a better understanding of gender equality and women's well-being in Muslim contexts. In doing so, the authors aim to facilitate conversations among feminist scholars across disciplines in order to provide a more nuanced picture of the situation facing women in Muslim communities.

This book was originally published as a special issue of *Feminist Economics*.

Ebru Kongar is Associate Professor of Economics at Dickinson College, Carlisle, PA, USA. Her research focuses on the gendered time-use and labor market outcomes of macroeconomic developments, such as deindustrialization, offshoring, and the Great Recession in the US economy. She is Research Associate at Levy Economics Institute's Gender Equality and the Economy Program and an Associate Editor of *Feminist Economics*.

Jennifer C. Olmsted is Professor of Economics and Director of Middle East Studies at Drew University, Madison, NJ, USA, with experience as well in the policy arena, including as the gender advisor at the UN Population Fund. Much of her research has focused on gender, economics, and the Middle East. Her publications have appeared in various journals, including *World Development*, *Industrial Relations*, the *Journal of Development Studies*, *Feminist Economics*, *Women's Studies International Forum*, and the *Journal of Middle East Women's Studies*, as well as numerous book volumes.

Elora Shehabuddin is Associate Professor of Humanities and Political Science at Rice University, Houston, TX, USA. Her publications include *Reshaping the Holy: Democracy, Development, and Muslim Women in Bangladesh* (Columbia University Press, 2008). She is an Associate Editor of the *Encyclopedia of Women and Islamic Cultures* (Brill). Her current book project is tentatively titled "Visions of Progress: Feminism, Empire, and Muslim Women."

Gender and Economics in Muslim Communities
Critical Feminist and Postcolonial Analyses

Edited by
Ebru Kongar, Jennifer C. Olmsted, and Elora Shehabuddin

LONDON AND NEW YORK

First published 2018
by Routledge
2 Park Square, Milton Park, Abingdon, Oxon, OX14 4RN, UK

and by Routledge
711 Third Avenue, New York, NY 10017, USA

Routledge is an imprint of the Taylor & Francis Group, an informa business

© 2018 International Association for Feminist Economics

All rights reserved. No part of this book may be reprinted or reproduced or utilised in any form or by any electronic, mechanical, or other means, now known or hereafter invented, including photocopying and recording, or in any information storage or retrieval system, without permission in writing from the publishers.

Trademark notice: Product or corporate names may be trademarks or registered trademarks, and are used only for identification and explanation without intent to infringe.

British Library Cataloguing in Publication Data
A catalogue record for this book is available from the British Library

ISBN 13: 978-0-415-78384-2 (hbk)
ISBN 13: 978-0-415-78387-3 (pbk)

Typeset in Baskerville
by RefineCatch Limited, Bungay, Suffolk

Publisher's Note
The publisher accepts responsibility for any inconsistencies that may have arisen during the conversion of this book from journal articles to book chapters, namely the possible inclusion of journal terminology.

Disclaimer
Every effort has been made to contact copyright holders for their permission to reprint material in this book. The publishers would be grateful to hear from any copyright holder who is not here acknowledged and will undertake to rectify any errors or omissions in future editions of this book.

"A groundbreaking volume that takes seriously the economic lives of women in Muslim communities and reveals the political economies and histories of their misrepresentation. Superb and diverse case studies show the way forward – theorizing the relationship between micro and macro, resisting the lure of Orientalism, and demonstrating once and for all that Islam should not be used as the 'dummy variable'."

Lila Abu-Lughod, Joseph L. Buttenweiser Professor of Social Science, Columbia University, and author of *Do Muslim Women Need Saving?*

"An exciting collection of papers on key issues of gender and economics in Muslim societies within the context of global inequalities and power relations. In particular, it provides interdisciplinary and methodologically rich analyses of whether and how gender norms are evolving across a great diversity of countries, and it projects feminist visions toward gender equality."

Lourdes Benería, Professor Emerita, Cornell University

"An outstanding comprehensive volume which situates the status of Muslim women in larger global economic structures and processes. The volume is illuminating and insightful! Definitely a must-read for students of gender studies and economics and feminism more broadly."

Amaney A. Jamal, Edwards S. Sanford Professor of Politics, Princeton University

"Moving beyond culturalist interpretations and operating at both macro and micro levels, this special issue engages with the full complexity of questions pertaining to gender and economics in Muslim communities. A timely and welcome addition to ongoing debates in gender and development."

Deniz Kandiyoti, Emeritus Professor, Development Studies, School of Oriental and African Studies

"This much-awaited collection of essays on women's economic realities in a diverse group of Muslim communities gives insight into the complex ways in which political, social, and economic conditions intersect and shape – and are shaped by – women's economic choices. Sophisticated in methodology, interdisciplinary in approach, and nuanced in analysis, *Gender and Economics in Muslim Communities* is a must read."

Ziba Mir-Hosseini, School of Oriental and African Studies, Legal Anthropologist and cofounder of Musawah

"This is a timely book that presents the diversity and complexities of the Muslim world and analyzes how women navigate the constraints and challenges and claim the opportunities. Each chapter reveals a different dimension of women's experiences and the choices they can and do make. Written by economists, political scientists, sociologists, and scholars of international relations and of religion, each chapter contributes to providing a rich tapestry of the lives of Muslim women."

Abena Oduro, Professor of Economics, University of Ghana

"A fascinating read! Challenging resurgent Orientalism and anti-Islamic rhetoric, and building on the subtle nuances that mark Muslim women's realities in different countries, this book provides rich description, a thoughtful critique, and fresh understanding."

Gita Sen, Distinguished Professor and Director, Ramalingaswami Centre on Equity and Social Determinants of Health, Public Health Foundation of India

Contents

Citation Information	ix
Notes on Contributors	xi
Acknowledgments	xv

Foreword xvii
Inderpal Grewal

Introduction – Gender and Economics in Muslim Communities:
A Critical Feminist and Postcolonial Analysis   1
Ebru Kongar, Jennifer C. Olmsted, and Elora Shehabuddin

1. Moving Beyond Culturalism and Formalism: Islam, Women,
   and Political Unrest in the Middle East   33
   Gamze Çavdar and Yavuz Yaşar

2. Patriarchy versus Islam: Gender and Religion in Economic Growth   58
   Elissa Braunstein

3. The Influence of Patriarchal Norms, Institutions, and
   Household Composition on Women's Employment in
   Twenty-Eight Muslim-Majority Countries   87
   Niels Spierings

4. Unilateral Divorce for Women and Labor Supply in the Middle
   East and North Africa: The Effect of Khul Reform   113
   Lena Hassani-Nezhad and Anna Sjögren

5. Diverging Stories of "Missing Women" in South Asia: Is Son
   Preference Weakening in Bangladesh?   138
   Naila Kabeer, Lopita Huq, and Simeen Mahmud

6. Funding Pain: Bedouin Women and Political Economy in the
   Naqab/Negev   164
   *Nadera Shalhoub-Kevorkian, Antonina Griecci Woodsum,
   Himmat Zu'bi, and Rachel Busbridge*

CONTENTS

7. Peace in the Household: Gender, Agency, and Villagers'
Measures of Marital Quality in Bangladesh   187
Fauzia Erfan Ahmed

8. "Just Like Prophet Mohammad Preached": Labor, Piety, and
Charity in Contemporary Turkey   212
Damla Isik

9. Entrepreneurial Subjectivities and Gendered Complexities:
Neoliberal Citizenship in Turkey   235
Özlem Altan-Olcay

10. Choice and Constraint in Paid Work: Women from Low-Income
Households in Tehran   260
Roksana Bahramitash and Jennifer C. Olmsted

11. Agency through Development: Hausa Women's NGOs and
CBOs in Kano, Nigeria   281
Adryan Wallace

Index   307

Citation Information

The chapters in this book were originally published in *Feminist Economics*, volume 20, issue 4 (October 2014). When citing this material, please use the original page numbering for each article, as follows:

Introduction
Gender and Economics in Muslim Communities: A Critical Feminist and Postcolonial Analysis
Ebru Kongar, Jennifer C. Olmsted, and Elora Shehabuddin
Feminist Economics, volume 20, issue 4 (October 2014) pp. 1–32

Chapter 1
Moving Beyond Culturalism and Formalism: Islam, Women, and Political Unrest in the Middle East
Gamze Çavdar and Yavuz Yaşar
Feminist Economics, volume 20, issue 4 (October 2014) pp. 33–57

Chapter 2
Patriarchy versus Islam: Gender and Religion in Economic Growth
Elissa Braunstein
Feminist Economics, volume 20, issue 4 (October 2014) pp. 58–86

Chapter 3
The Influence of Patriarchal Norms, Institutions, and Household Composition on Women's Employment in Twenty-Eight Muslim-Majority Countries
Niels Spierings
Feminist Economics, volume 20, issue 4 (October 2014) pp. 87–112

Chapter 4
Unilateral Divorce for Women and Labor Supply in the Middle East and North Africa: The Effect of Khul Reform
Lena Hassani-Nezhad and Anna Sjögren
Feminist Economics, volume 20, issue 4 (October 2014) pp. 113–137

CITATION INFORMATION

Chapter 5
Diverging Stories of "Missing Women" in South Asia: Is Son Preference Weakening in Bangladesh?
Naila Kabeer, Lopita Huq, and Simeen Mahmud
Feminist Economics, volume 20, issue 4 (October 2014) pp. 138–163

Chapter 6
Funding Pain: Bedouin Women and Political Economy in the Naqab/Negev
Nadera Shalhoub-Kevorkian, Antonina Griecci Woodsum, Himmat Zu'bi, and Rachel Busbridge
Feminist Economics, volume 20, issue 4 (October 2014) pp. 164–186

Chapter 7
Peace in the Household: Gender, Agency, and Villagers' Measures of Marital Quality in Bangladesh
Fauzia Erfan Ahmed
Feminist Economics, volume 20, issue 4 (October 2014) pp. 187–211

Chapter 8
"Just Like Prophet Mohammad Preached": Labor, Piety, and Charity in Contemporary Turkey
Damla Isik
Feminist Economics, volume 20, issue 4 (October 2014) pp. 212–234

Chapter 9
Entrepreneurial Subjectivities and Gendered Complexities: Neoliberal Citizenship in Turkey
Özlem Altan-Olcay
Feminist Economics, volume 20, issue 4 (October 2014) pp. 235–259

Chapter 10
Choice and Constraint in Paid Work: Women from Low-Income Households in Tehran
Roksana Bahramitash and Jennifer C. Olmsted
Feminist Economics, volume 20, issue 4 (October 2014) pp. 260–280

Chapter 11
Agency through Development: Hausa Women's NGOs and CBOs in Kano, Nigeria
Adryan Wallace
Feminist Economics, volume 20, issue 4 (October 2014) pp. 281–305

For any permission-related enquiries please visit:
http://www.tandfonline.com/page/help/permissions

Notes on Contributors

Fauzia Erfan Ahmed is Associate Professor in the Department of Sociology and Gerontology at Miami University, Ohio, USA. Her academic interests focus on gender and development, ranging from masculinity and Islam to gender, labor, and globalization. Her work has appeared in *Feminist Economics, Perspectives on Global Development and Technology, Feminist Formations,* and *The Muslim World.*

Özlem Altan-Olcay is Associate Professor of Political Science at Koç University, Istanbul, Turkey. She has published articles in *Citizenship Studies, Ethnic and Racial Studies, Geoforum, Social Politics,* and *Sociology,* among others. Her research interests include transnational class formations, politics of expertise, gender and citizenship, elite networks, and inequality. Her current research focuses on tensions between discourses of cultural difference and women's socioeconomic rights.

Roksana Bahramitash is a graduate of the Sociology Department at McGill University, Canada, and is the author of numerous books and articles, including *Veiled Employment: Islamism and the Political Economy of Women's Employment in Iran* (with Hadi Salehi Esfahani, 2011), *Gender and Entrepreneurship in Iran: Microenterprise and the Informal Sector* (2013), and *Islamist Women and Social Economy in Iran* (forthcoming).

Elissa Braunstein is Associate Professor of Economics at Colorado State University, USA, and editor of *Feminist Economics.* She is currently on leave from her university, working at the Division on Globalization and Development Strategies for the UN Conference on Trade and Development. Her work uses a feminist lens to better understand macroeconomic and international economic processes and outcomes, with particular emphasis on issues of economic development, growth, and gender equality.

Rachel Busbridge is a Research Associate of the *Thesis Eleven* Centre for Cultural Sociology, La Trobe University, Melbourne, Australia. Her main research interests are the politics of recognition and reconciliation;

NOTES ON CONTRIBUTORS

postcolonialism and colonial legacies; and nation, identity, and culture, all of which she explores in the contexts of Australian multiculturalism and Israel-Palestine.

Gamze Çavdar is Associate Professor of Political Science at Colorado State University, USA. Her research interests are nonviolent Islamist groups in the Middle East, and gender in North Africa and the Middle East. Her essays have appeared in *Political Science Quarterly, PS: Political Science and Politics, Religion and Politics, Journal of South Asian and Middle Eastern Studies,* and *Middle East Policy,* among others.

Lena Hassani-Nezhad is a Ph.D. candidate in the Department of Economics at Royal Holloway University, London, UK. She has a Master's degree in Economics from Uppsala University, Sweden. Her research interests are in the fields of labor economics and the economics of the family.

Lopita Huq is a Research Fellow at the Centre for Gender and Social Transformation at BRAC Institute of Governance and Development (BIGD), BRAC University, Bangladesh. Her main areas of interest include qualitative research on social norms, attitudes, and practices related to women's work, marriage, dowry, education, and adolescence. Her interests also include NGO strategies and practices around mobilization, and citizenship and rights.

Damla Isik is Associate Professor of Anthropology at Regis University, Denver, USA. She is interested in the increasingly important role of charitable civil society organizations in Turkey's society and economy within the context of globalization, neoliberalization policies, and local economic conditions. She is currently doing research on the gendered ethics of poverty alleviation projects in charitable associations in Turkey.

Naila Kabeer is Professor of Gender and Development at the London School of Economics, UK. Her research focuses on gender, poverty, social exclusion, labour markets and livelihoods, social protection, and citizenship, with particular focus on South and South East Asia. Recent books include *The Power to Choose: Bangladeshi Women and Labour Supply Decisions in London and Dhaka* (2000) and *Organizing Women Workers in the Informal Economy: Beyond the Weapons of the Weak* (2013).

Ebru Kongar is Associate Professor of Economics at Dickinson College, Carlisle, PA, USA. Her research focuses on the gendered time-use and labor market outcomes of macroeconomic developments, such as deindustrialization, offshoring, and the Great Recession in the US economy. She is Research Associate at Levy Economics Institute's Gender Equality and the Economy Program and an Associate Editor of *Feminist Economics.*

NOTES ON CONTRIBUTORS

Simeen Mahmud is Lead Researcher on Deepening Democracy at the BRAC Development Institute in Dhaka, Bangladesh, and a member of the Citizenship DRC. Her research focuses on citizenship and participation, education and gender, and women's work and empowerment in Bangladesh. She is working on health and education policy; the construction of citizen identity and practice in difficult environments; and the effect of health- and micro-credit interventions on women's well-being.

Jennifer C. Olmsted is Professor of Economics and Director of Middle East Studies at Drew University, Madison, NJ, USA, with experience as well in the policy arena, including as the gender advisor at the UN Population Fund. Much of her research has focused on gender, economics, and the Middle East. Her publications have appeared in various journals, including *World Development, Industrial Relations,* the *Journal of Development Studies, Feminist Economics, Women's Studies International Forum,* and the *Journal of Middle East Women's Studies,* as well as numerous book volumes.

Nadera Shalhoub-Kevorkian is Director of the Gender Studies Program and Chair in Law at the Institute of Criminology at the Hebrew University of Jerusalem, Israel. She is also a native Palestinian and a longtime anti-violence and feminist activist and scholar. Her research focuses on femicide and other forms of gendered violence, abuse of power in settler colonial contexts, surveillance, securitization, and trauma in militarized and colonized zones. She is the author of *Security Theology, Surveillance, and the Politics of Fear* (2015).

Elora Shehabuddin is Associate Professor of Humanities and Political Science at Rice University, Houston, TX, USA. Her publications include *Reshaping the Holy: Democracy, Development, and Muslim Women in Bangladesh* (Columbia University Press, 2008). She is an Associate Editor of the *Encyclopedia of Women and Islamic Cultures* (Brill). Her current book project is tentatively titled "Visions of Progress: Feminism, Empire, and Muslim Women."

Anna Sjögren is Associate Professor at the Institute for Evaluation of Labour Market and Education Policy and the Uppsala Centre for Labour Studies, Uppsala University, Sweden. Her research focuses on education, human capital, family economics, and the labor market. She is currently researching the importance of school and family policies for child health and human capital development, and long-run changes in men's and women's opportunities to combine family and career.

Niels Spierings is Assistant Professor of Sociology at Radboud University, The Netherlands. His research interests include economic and political participation, Islam, economic and political development, social science research methods, gender and inequality, and migration. He

NOTES ON CONTRIBUTORS

has published in journals such as *Journal of Marriage and Family, Electoral Studies, Review of Religious Research, Electoral Behavior, Politics & Religion,* and *European Journal of Women's Studies.*

Adryan Wallace is Assistant Professor in the Department of Politics and Government at the University of Hartford, USA. Her research interests include gender, political economy, Islam, and the dynamic interactions of politics and culture on political institutions. The majority of her work focuses on how Muslim women in West Africa are able to articulate their development interests within the context of Sharia law and secular political institutions.

Antonina Griecci Woodsum is a Ph.D. student in the Department of History at Columbia University, USA. She has a Master of Science degree in Labor Studies from the University of Massachusetts Amherst. Her research focuses on questions of settler colonialism, indigenous politics, and labor histories.

Yavuz Yaşar is Associate Professor in the Department of Economics at the University of Denver. His research focuses on health economics, social policy, and development, with an emphasis on healthcare and pension systems. His research has been published in *Review of Radical Political Economics, Cambridge Journal of Economics, Journal of Economics Issues, Social Science Journal,* and *International Journal of Health Services,* among others.

Himmat Zu'bi, a Palestinian researcher and feminist activist, is a Ph.D. candidate in the Department of Sociology and Anthropology at Ben-Gurion University of the Negev, Israel. She is writing her dissertation on surveillance discipline and urban indigenous people in settler colonial society. She has contributed to the *Journal of Palestine Studies* and co-authored *Palestinian Women in Israel: Annotated Bibliography: 1948–2006.* Her academic interests focus on settler colonialism, indigenous cultures, historical sociology, and gender.

Acknowledgments

This book was previously published in October 2014 as a special issue of *Feminist Economics*, the official journal of the International Association for Feminist Economics (IAFFE). All contributions have been subjected to the journal's rigorous peer review process and comply with the journal's editorial policies, as overseen by the editors, Günseli Berik and Diana Strassmann, and the journal's editorial team, including the associate editors, the editorial board, numerous volunteer reviewers, and the journal's in-house editorial staff and style editors. The special issue and book have been made possible by the very generous financial support of the Swedish International Development Cooperation Agency (Sida), Rice University, and the University of Utah.

Foreword

This collection is long overdue. And of course it is only to be expected that feminist scholars, especially those invested in postcolonial, transnational, and intersectional approaches, would take on the crucial task of asking how to critically understand women in Muslim communities as a category in development and economics. At the same time, the authors of this issue examine how a variety of women in these communities are engaged in economic activities, they work to disaggregate and reveal the heterogeneity of the category "Muslim women," and ask questions about the hegemonic project of imperialism in this new century. As the "war on terror" catches more and more Muslims in its net, producing Islamophobia and racism in Europe and North America, and as conditions in the Middle East deteriorate, the task of suggesting the heterogeneity of women in Muslim communities remains as difficult as that of disaggregating the unitary global woman who is the product of so many development and human rights projects. This volume shoulders the work with the tools necessary: an interdisciplinary, postcolonial, and anti-imperialist methodology that sees the category "Muslim women" as the product of power, and the topic of "women in Muslim communities" as a project consisting of widely divergent histories, but also of connected, lived, and experienced material, social, and cultural formations.

How are we in this situation where, at the end of the twentieth century and the beginning of the twenty-first, the "Muslim woman" remains a colonial trope and object of rescue and surveillance? She has, of course, also become the subject of development and neoliberal processes. It is the legacy of European colonialism that religion continues to be seen as the main identity for billions of people marked as Muslims, even as a great majority of them are economically disenfranchised under a variety of conditions across the globe. What we see now is that the heterogeneity of Islam as it is practiced across the globe is being reduced by global and regional powers, licit and illicit, all of them violent, and this power needs to be interrogated through different tools. The study of the relationships between women in Muslim communities and economic activity thus must

FOREWORD

engage with consideration of representations that continue to produce "Muslim women" as victims to be rescued or threats to be removed. These representations are intimately connected to the projects of late-capitalist authoritarian patriarchies of various kinds, including those within Muslim communities. Such projects manifest at national and transnational scales, as different groups of Muslims have been thrown together by migrations, wars, and rearticulations of borders and national boundaries. When "Muslim women" are homogenized, or when they are considered as encompassed by non-Western institutions and processes, depends on both the projects of empire and a variety of political, social, and economic contexts.

"Muslim women" is an identity category mobilized by a variety of agents and groups, and inhabited in heterogeneous and intersectional ways. This subject is a product of Western imperialism whose classification systems assumed that particular groups of people – non-Western, non-Christian, nonmodern – were controlled by religion, while religion was not central to the lives of modern Westerners. As Talal Asad (1993) has argued, we must begin "unpacking the comprehensive concept which he or she translates as 'religion' into heterogeneous elements according to its historical character." Because the category of religion itself is part of the history of empire, to attribute causality to it in relation to women's economic activities must always be a fraught enterprise, as the essays in this collection reveal. Yet as religion is instrumentalized by power, the work that any articulation of a religion or religious tradition does may not be contained only by this colonial genealogy. The scholars in this volume take on the difficult task of unpacking and understanding the historical complexity of the category of religion as informing, but not encompassing, the economic.

Thus, the study of women in Muslim communities must be seen as both impacted by empire and race, and also as a powerful mode of inhabiting empire. Muslim-majority nations are so widely divergent that they may powerfully resist the work of empire and its allies to reduce them to a single formation, even as they create new projects of masculine state authority (Moallem 2005).[1] Muslim-minority nations, as in India, use the language of decolonization alongside the project of the US-sponsored war on terror to produce new Islamophobic projects that not only discriminate and violate constitutional rights, but also further affect the economic well-being of an already economically disempowered minority. Religion becomes identity, imposed and resisted in relation to the state. Geographies still matter, as borders and boundaries make lives sustainable or impossible, a matter as important as critiquing the dominant international relations notion of nation-states as bounded and territorialized entities. Thomas Blom Hansen and Finn Stepputat (2005) argue that international-relations scholars have produced a normative idea of the state that is increasingly out of touch with the kinds of dispersed sovereignty and governance regimes that currently

FOREWORD

operate beyond the state. Economic regimes certainly operate within and beyond the state, and are both territorialized and deterritorialized.

This volume then resists the simplistic relation between religion, gender, and economic activity as causing inequality or disempowerment, especially with regard to Islam. There is no evidence that in all of Islam and all Muslim communities across time and space, women are economically subordinated. Positing Islam as a cause of gender inequality means ignoring an entire body of literature that has suggested the underpinnings of capitalism through Christian genealogies, for instance in the history of Protestant Christianity in Europe that Max Weber (2001) laid out. On the other hand, how any religion may be connected to economic activity is anything but straightforward, certainly those considerations will resist the production of Islam as the "dummy variable," as the editors of this volume succinctly phrase it. They insist we pay attention to history and method. While nation-states and their citizens and noncitizens comprise different polities and relations, gender – of masculinities and femininities and many other combinations of these – cannot be attributed solely to religion, or to a singular and modern notion of religion, or even to the way that economic activity is defined.

An important aspect of globalization at the end of the twentieth century was the emergence of what has been termed "neoliberalism" as a manifestation of a new phase of capitalism. In the 1970s, the International Monetary Fund began using structural adjustment programs in what were then labeled developing and postcolonial nations; these programs can now be seen as neoliberal laboratories that formed policies that were used in other regions. Such programs disproportionately reduced state welfare and support for women and children, who tended to use state subsidies more than men (Harrison 1997). Over time, these processes moved to other states through transnational finance networks and global banking systems, creating ever more precarious lives for people. States and ordinary citizens became delinked because of such precarities, even as global flows connected experts, authorities, knowledges, and technologies.

In some countries, neoliberal policies that reduced state welfare shifted it to religious and community organizations in which much of the work was done by women on a voluntary and lower-paid basis in many Muslim communities. These policies privatized public goods and lands, increased inequality based on religion (of religious minorities, in particular), nationality, and citizenship status, and made the self-improving entrepreneurial subject the target of development.

Much of the writing about neoliberalism assumes a uniformity of processes and a teleology that, even as it critiques economic processes that produce inequality and immiseration, dispossession, and accumulation, homogenizes economic activity. For example, David Harvey (2005) has defined neoliberalism in terms of an altered relation between public and

xix

FOREWORD

private in which contemporary capitalism accumulates by dispossession and eliminates the commons. Gender, the family, and sexuality appear as superstructural, as consequences of globalization's new mode of production. Such a singular definition of what must be thought of as a set of heterogeneous and linked processes of capitalist accumulation poses problems for scholars working on such disparate sites as Bangladesh, Palestine, and Iran. The Gulf region has its own particularities, and the wars in the Middle East have now created a wholly different set of problems of state and imperial power. The nature of the state–citizen tie, enabled by local and transnational structures of power, was historically different in each state, so that the guises in which neoliberalism could be accommodated or selectively appropriated or resisted were also different. The developmental state was not reduced in many cases, and in many places the welfare state was not wholly replaced by a security state that protected privatized accumulation by a capitalist class. The neoliberal entrepreneurial subject also appeared in different guises, sometimes as the Muslim humanitarian, or as the recipient of microcredit, as dispossessed labor, or as the newly empowered entrepreneur. The dominance of NGOs in Bangladesh produced another set of female subjects of neoliberal development policy, while the Gulf region foregrounded citizenship and indentured labor as lines of demarcation of economic subjectivity. Yet, as these essays show, neoliberalism is not the logic of all these different processes of dispossession or of empowerment; sometimes it is colonial power that works by expulsion and dispossession, as in Palestine. The ties between empowerment and employment, especially with regard to gender in Muslim communities, as this volume shows, are tenuous, and what is defined as economic activity is only a part of the story of gender and economics.

This volume thus has the important task of revealing not simply how neoliberalism manifests differentially, as some of its processes and ideologies are incorporated into a variety of projects of development, but also whether neoliberalism is the most important approach to understanding the lives of heterogeneous groups of women in both Muslim-majority and Muslim-minority countries. There are desires for authority, power, and pleasure that may not be wholly explained by neoliberalism, but may be produced by gender, sexuality, caste, race, identities, and emergent political movements. Further, the matter of gender is not simply of attention to women or patriarchy. Masculinities and sexualities also produce gendered projects of power and inequality, and an uneven picture of gendered power and subordination may emerge as a result.

Yet it is to the credit of the editors and contributors that the question of methodologies and approaches remains at the forefront of the achievement of this volume. The stakes of analysis are important: where does a feminist postcolonial, intersectional, and transnational project take us? And the answer emerges in the importance of combining approaches

FOREWORD

that bring together the scales of the global, imperial, nation, community, family, and household. The terms are critical: how do we understand the historical notion of "religion" (and the "economic") as an imperial and overdetermined category? The forms of power are also crucial: colonialism, empire, neoliberalism, patriarchy. And finally, what are the projects of gendering – homogenizing, universalizing, nationalizing, and community-making – that are ongoing through the economics of Western hegemony and in Muslim communities? The answers lie in the excellent introduction and in this collection of essays.

Inderpal Grewal
Professor of Women's, Gender, and Sexuality Studies
Yale University
New Haven, Connecticut
United States

NOTES

[1] A second concern about the category is the work done outside the West but in re-action to it. Minoo Moallem (2005) writes of Islamist movements in Iran that also homogenized Muslim women in the 1979 revolution. For that project, the notion of a unified Muslim world was also a project of power. Moallem reveals that *ummat* was a "new imagined community in Iran" defined as "transnational ethnicity positioned oppositionally in relation to the global hegemony of the West." While this *ummat* "was represented as uniquely Islamic . . . it was fashioned from identities borrowed from the Western imaginary."

REFERENCES

Asad, Talal. 1993. *Genealogies of Religion: Discipline and Reasons of Power in Christianity and Islam.* 1st ed., Baltimore: Johns Hopkins University Press.

Blom Hansen, Thomas and Finn Stepputat, eds. 2005. *Sovereign Bodies: Citizens, Migrants, and States in the Postcolonial World.* New Jersey: Princeton University Press.

Harrison, Faye V. 1997. "The Gendered Politics and Violence of Structural Adjustment: A View from Jamaica." In *Situated Lives: Gender and Culture in Everyday Life,* edited by Louise Lamphere, Helena Ragoné, and Patricia Zavella, 451–68. New York: Routledge.

Harvey, David. 2005. *A Brief History of Neoliberalism.* New York: Oxford University Press.

Moallem, Minoo. 2005. *Between Warrior Brother and Veiled Sister: Islamic Fundamentalism and the Politics of Patriarchy in Iran.* 1st paperback ed., Berkeley: University of California Press.

Weber, Max. 2001 (1930). *The Protestant Ethic and the Spirit of Capitalism.* Translated by Talcott Parsons. Abingdon, UK: Routledge.

GENDER AND ECONOMICS IN MUSLIM COMMUNITIES: A CRITICAL FEMINIST AND POSTCOLONIAL ANALYSIS

Ebru Kongar, Jennifer C. Olmsted, and Elora Shehabuddin

ABSTRACT

This contribution seeks to delineate the broad contours of a transnational, anti-imperial feminist perspective on gender and economics in Muslim communities by bringing together feminist analyses of Orientalist tropes, development discourses and policies, and macro- and microeconomic trends. The goal is to facilitate conversations among scholars who have tended to work within their respective disciplinary and methodological silos despite shared interests. This approach pays special attention to intersectionality, historicity, and structural constraints by focusing on the diversity of the experiences of women and men by religion, location, citizenship, class, age, ethnicity, race, marital status, and other factors. It recognizes the complex relationships between the economic, political, cultural, and religious spheres and the role of local and transnational histories, economies, and politics in shaping people's lives. Finally, it emphasizes that openness to different methodological approaches can shed clearer light on the question of how various structural factors shape women's economic realities.

INTRODUCTION

Why a special issue devoted to gender and economics in *Muslim* communities?[1] We have grappled with this question at length, finding ourselves in the odd position of critiquing scholarship that assumes Islamic exceptionalism, yet arguing for attention to gender norms and economic processes in Muslim communities around the world. We believe that questions of gender and economics in Muslim communities merit special attention, not because Islam holds special explanatory power, but because of the long history of problematic Euro-American knowledge production about Muslims in general, and Muslim women in particular, within the context of global political and economic inequalities and power relations.

GENDER AND ECONOMICS IN MUSLIM COMMUNITIES

The studies in this special issue affirm that Islam *per se* cannot explain either the successes or the challenges facing Muslim men and women. Like members of any other community, Muslims are diverse across the countries and communities in which they live, love, and labor. The opportunities and constraints they face are far from unique and are better understood with serious attention to the complex ways that religion intersects with local and global socioeconomic and political structures to circumscribe Muslim women and men's lives, decisions, and activisms.

In the wake of the 9/11 terrorist attacks, a particularly pernicious kind of scholarship and popular writing about Islam, Muslims, and the special status of women and gender in these discussions has reemerged (miriam cooke 2002; Lila Abu-Lughod 2013). With much of the recent anti-Muslim rhetoric focused on the Arab world, Gamze Çavdar and Yavuz Yaşar note: "Highly ethnocentric and frustratingly resilient culturalism is again dominating public debates and the popular media, giving Middle East specialists a *déjà vu* feeling coupled with an 'I-thought-this-was-resolved-30-years-ago' disbelief" (2014:259; this volume).[2] Dramatic political, social, and economic changes worldwide since 9/11 have added urgency to the need for thoughtful scholarly research on the subject of gender, economics, and Muslim communities.

A main objective of this contribution, and of this special issue more broadly, is to advocate for an approach that challenges ethnocentric and culturalist accounts of gender equality and women's well-being in Muslim communities and highlights the limitations of attributing gender inequalities to the black box of Islam. By providing nuanced quantitative and qualitative analyses of women's economic realities in a diverse group of Muslim communities, the studies in this volume expand our understanding of how political, social, and economic conditions at both the micro and macro levels shape and are shaped by women's economic decisions and conditions. They also provide insights into broader questions that center on gender and development and important input into how research can inform the policy arena in more productive ways. What emerges is a vivid picture of the complex ways that Islam interacts with social, economic, and political factors in women's lives, decision making, and economic realities.

The contributions in this special issue advance our knowledge of gender and economics in Muslim communities in three ways. First, by making use of a variety of methodological approaches, the studies illustrate how different methods are complementary and work together to provide a better understanding of the problems and struggles of communities in which Muslims live. Second, we bring together scholars – among the guest editors as well as the authors – with a range of disciplinary backgrounds, including anthropology, economics, gender studies, political science, psychology, and sociology. This diversity of disciplines allows us to place critiques of Orientalist scholarship in more direct dialogue with scholarship

2

GENDER AND ECONOMICS IN MUSLIM COMMUNITIES

on economic development in Muslim contexts. Finally, the special issue comprises a close textual analysis that provides examples of ongoing Orientalism, several quantitative studies that challenge the notion of Islam as a dummy variable, and detailed studies conducted in Bangladesh, Iran, Israel, Nigeria, and Turkey. Taken together, they illustrate the historical and institutional heterogeneity of Muslim communities and allow us to address the question, what do the everyday economic lives of Muslim women actually look like?

In this introductory essay, we bring together feminist analyses of Orientalist tropes, development discourses and policies, *and* macro- and microeconomic trends to facilitate conversations among scholars who have tended to work within their respective disciplinary and methodological silos despite shared interests. We do so in an effort to delineate the broad contours of a transnational, anti-imperial feminist perspective on gender and economics in communities of Muslims. This perspective rejects simplistic approaches that decontexualize Islam, in favor of those where attention to religion in general, and Islam in particular, is embedded in an analysis that takes into account intersectionality, historicity, and structural constraints through a focus on differences in the experiences of girls and boys, women and men by location, citizenship, class, age, caste, ethnicity, race, sexuality, and so on. This approach also recognizes the complex relationships between the economic, political, cultural, and religious spheres and the role of local and transnational histories, economies, and politics, in shaping people's lives. Finally, we emphasize that obtaining a nuanced picture of how Muslim women live their lives requires openness to learning from different methodological approaches such as ethnographic work, quantitative data analyses, and historical and rhetorical analyses. This openness can shed clearer light on the question of how various structural factors shape women's economic realities.

FEMINIST APPROACHES AND ORIENTALISM

In his canonical 1978 text *Orientalism*, Edward Said expanded on Michel Foucault's insights on discourse to argue that Orientalism, essentialist portrayals of the non-West by Western scholars, both built on and enabled European imperial ambitions in many parts of world. Said directed his critique not only to the Orientalist scholars of the nineteenth century, but also to the modernization theorists of the Cold War era, whose influence in the policy arena has been substantial. Contemporary examples include Raphael Patai, whose 1973 book (republished in 2002 in the wake of 9/11) furthers various stereotypes about Islam and is regarded as "essential reading" for officers at Fort Bragg, a large military base in Texas (Malini Johar Schueller 2007: 57). As Seymour M. Hersh (2004) reported, the book, for example, propagates "the notion that Arabs are particularly vulnerable to sexual humiliation," an assumption that underlay the torture revealed at Abu Ghraib.

Our discussion of gender and economics in Muslim communities highlights two aspects of current popular and scholarly discussions about Muslim women's lives that draw on Orientalist tropes that have been the object of postcolonial critique. The first is the figure of the oppressed Eastern woman, who is presented as the binary opposite of the liberated Western woman, itself a constructed figure.[3] This idea came to play a central role in the so-called civilizing mission of colonial powers such as Britain and France, which justified their imperial presence in countries around the world by pointing to the need to save local women from their oppressed existence. The second idea is that of the unchanging East that can be rescued from its state of torpor only by the catalytic presence of (male) Western political, social, and economic ingenuity (Meyda Yeğenoglu 1998). One need only remember the instrumental use of the figure of the helpless burqa-clad woman of Afghanistan to help justify the 2001 US invasion of that country to appreciate the continued salience of Orientalist ideas (Malini Johar Schueller 2011). A similar strategy was used to justify US intervention in Iraq after 9/11, despite the fact that there was no evidence that Iraq bore any responsibility for that attack. As Nadje al-Ali and Nicola Pratt point out: "[b]y highlighting the plight of female victims in far away lands, US officials not only provided a pretext for military invasion, but also restored the image of the US as the strong hero, rather than the victim of terrorist attacks" (2009: 83).

Feminist critiques of Eurocentric representations of women in the Global South[4] emerged as early as 1984, when Chandra T. Mohanty noted that contemporary development discourse and Western feminist scholarship had come together to produce the "average third world woman," who

> leads an essentially truncated life based on her feminine gender (read: sexually constrained) and being 'third world' (read: ignorant, poor, uneducated, tradition-bound, domestic, family-oriented, victimized, etc.). This, I argue, is in contrast to the (implicit) self-representation of Western women as educated, modern, as having control over their own bodies and sexualities, and the freedom to make their own decisions. (1984: 337)

The interventions of scholars such as Mohanty, Gayatri Spivak (1985), Inderpal Grewal and Caren Kaplan (1994), and Uma Narayan (1997) have transformed certain strands of scholarship about the Global South over the last thirty years by underscoring the continued relevance of colonial histories, as they intersect with factors such as class, geographic location, state policies, and local and global cultural practices and policies.

GENDER AND ECONOMICS IN MUSLIM COMMUNITIES

On the subject of Muslims and Muslim communities, this approach has meant an acknowledgement that there is not a monolithic, unchanging construct known as Islam that can be easily theorized, quantified, operationalized, or considered independently of the history, politics, and economics of that particular context. Yet there persists a desire to "save Muslim women," whether through development and modernization projects, war and occupation, corporate outsourcing, or corporeal liberation (Jennifer L. Fluri 2009; Dina Siddiqi 2009; Abu-Lughod 2013). Scholars have pointed to the particularly shameful use of a new form of Orientalism to advance the objectives of neoliberalism and empire, including by segments of the US feminist movement that supported the US invasions of Afghanistan and Iraq (Lori Jo Marso 2007; Saba Mahmood 2008; Elora Shehabuddin 2011). Like the old Orientalism of the eighteenth and nineteenth centuries, the new Orientalism of scholarship, popular culture, and policymaking takes to be inevitable, natural, and universal what are often in fact uniquely Western ideas or experiences; it generalizes across the vast Muslim population of the world, regarding all Muslim women as oppressed and as oppressed specifically by Islam, and thus, the polar opposite of allegedly liberated, modern, Western women.

Given the size of the world's Muslim population and the intricate diversity of this population, there is of course no single Muslim position or voice, just as there is no single explanation for the very real problems that women in Muslim communities face, and no single solution. Recognizing the complexities of these societies is an important step toward assuring that future policies do not oversimplify the situation facing women in various Muslim communities.

THE DIVERSITY OF MUSLIM COMMUNITIES AROUND THE GLOBE

Muslims constitute about 23 percent of the world's population and one-third of the population in the Global South, but importantly, the average percentage of Muslims in countries that are categorized as highly indebted poor countries (HIPC) is 38, suggesting that in terms of global inequalities, Muslims are overrepresented among the poor, a point we return to later.[5] Forty-nine countries are considered Muslim majority, while seventy-two countries have more than a million Muslim inhabitants, and this number is expected to rise to seventy-nine by 2030, if current trends in immigration and fertility continue (Pew Forum 2011b). Despite the common erroneous conflation of Arabs, Muslims, and the Middle East, only one-fifth of the global Muslim population are Arabs. Since Turkey and Iran, after Egypt, are the two largest countries in this geographic area, most Middle Eastern Muslims are non-Arab. The largest concentration of Muslims is and will remain in Southeast and South Asia, most notably in

Indonesia, India, Pakistan, and Bangladesh, followed by the Middle East and Africa, where the most populous country is Nigeria.[6] Muslim minorities also make up substantial and growing proportions of the population of several countries in Europe and North America, with Pew Forum (2011b) predicting that by 2030 over 10 percent of the French population will be Muslim, while in Canada, the numbers will rise from 3 to over 6 percent of the population over the next twenty years.

Considerable diversity exists both within and across Muslim minority and majority communities in terms of the practice and interpretation of Islam, as well as the role of Islam in legal institutions.[7] The coexistence of numerous sects and schools of law, as well as Islam's interactions with local, preexisting cultures and traditions, has contributed to the development of varied local forms of practice. In rural Bangladesh, for example, Fauzia Erfan Ahmed (2014; this volume) shows how beliefs and practices have emerged from the intermingling of Muslim, Hindu, Buddhist, and other local traditions over the centuries, with this amalgam of beliefs in turn shaping villagers' understandings of masculinity, femininity, and marriage.

A great deal of variation exists also in the extent to and the manner in which religion shapes legal systems in both Muslim and non-Muslim contexts.[8] In countries in the Global South, legal traditions were in many instances codified by colonial powers, in some cases eliminated only to be reintroduced, and/or reformed, by modern postcolonial states in response to grassroots activism or by executive decree (Abdullahi An-Naim 2002). In South Asia, for example, the Orientalist assumptions and imperial needs of the British colonial administration worked together to lead it to rely selectively on Muslim and Hindu religious texts rather than the more fluid existing practices in establishing "modern" religious laws; while some of the legal changes worked in women's favor, not all did (Elisa Giunchi 2010). Personal status laws – laws governing marriage, divorce, child custody, and inheritance – therefore vary across Muslim communities and change over time. Today, theological and legal activists in Muslim communities continue to reinterpret and debate key elements in Islamic doctrine in order to empower women to fight more conservative reinterpretations of gender roles within marriage and in communities (Amina Wadud 2006).

The degree to which national governments self-identify as religious, as well as the legal frameworks they rely upon in civil, criminal, and family matters, differs greatly. Considerable ambiguity around the separation of religion and the state exists in each of the countries discussed in depth in this volume. For instance, Bangladesh was established in 1971 as a secular republic but formally recognized Islam as its state religion in 1988. Iran has been a theocracy since the 1979 revolution, yet numerous political shifts and reinterpretations have occurred in the period following the revolution (Roksana Bahramitash 2004; Roksana Bahramitash and Jennifer

GENDER AND ECONOMICS IN MUSLIM COMMUNITIES

Olmsted 2014; this volume). Israel was founded as a Jewish state, and family law there is largely adjudicated through religious courts (Jennifer Olmsted 2002). The Turkish and Nigerian constitutions reject the notion of a state religion yet, as in other parts of the world (including non-Muslim contexts), struggles exist between those in favor of closer ties between religion and the state and those who are against. For example, Turkey is currently governed by a party that self-identifies as Islamist, and strict forms of Islamic law are in effect in northern Nigeria. An examination of both secular and religious, Muslim and non-Muslim countries in fact suggests that male-biased legal structures persist in many contexts. Elissa Braunstein and Nancy Folbre (2001), for example, explore the institutionalization of what they label as patriarchal property rights in the context of the US and UK historically.[9] Family law in Turkey, while based mostly on secular sources, discriminates against women – not unlike legal systems that claim to be built on Christian, Muslim, or Jewish law (Valentine M. Moghadam 2003; Yesim Arat 2010). Similarly, divorce laws in Israel heavily favor men (Ruth Halperin-Kadderi 2004). Divorce laws in Arab countries have also historically favored men, but reforms in a number of countries have in recent years made such laws more egalitarian (Lena Hassani-Nezhad and Anna Sjögren 2014; this volume).

Countries also differ in terms of their globalization experiences, including the manner, degree to which, and when they were affected by colonialism, the Cold War, structural adjustment, and neoliberalism, all of which have shaped the gendering of their economies. Given their differing political histories and resource bases, today Muslims live in countries that fall along a broad spectrum in terms of national income levels, poverty rates, and social safety nets. Consider, at one end, the Gulf emirates, which have among the highest per capita income levels in the world and, at the other, countries such as Niger, which has a per capita income that is one-hundredth the size. Just among the countries discussed in the special issue, per capita income figures (GNI Atlas Method 2014 US$) range from $840 in Bangladesh and $1,440 in Nigeria to $4,290 in Iran, $10,830 in Turkey, and $28,380 in Israel (World Bank n.d.a).

Poverty rates vary considerably across the countries included in this special issue, as do average life expectancy figures, maternal mortality, and women's labor force participation rates. In general, poorer countries have lower life expectancy rates and higher poverty and maternal mortality rates, although among the countries included in the special issue, Bangladesh is performing better than Nigeria in terms of its life expectancy rate (70 versus 52 years), poverty rate (43 versus 68 percent living on less than US$1.25 a day), and maternal mortality rate (240 versus 630 per 100,000), illustrating the degree to which other factors, including policy differences, can be as important as national income in determining socioeconomic outcomes (World Bank n.d.a). While the examples of Bangladesh and Nigeria underscore the limits of simplistically linking low national income and higher poverty, higher per capita income is generally associated with lower absolute poverty rates. For example, Turkey and Iran are both categorized as middle-income countries with only 1.3 (2010) and 1.5 (2005) percent of their populations, respectively, living on less than US$1.25 a day, and with similar life expectancy rates (75 and 73, respectively; World Bank n.d.b). Categorized as a high-income country, Israel has no official absolute poverty, and an average life expectancy of 82, although statistics indicate that the Arab population in Israel has a considerably lower (by four years) average life expectancy rate (Siham Badarneh 2009) and that the Bedouin in particular have extremely high poverty rates – six to seven times higher than the Jewish population (Suleiman Abu-Bader and Daniel Gottlieb 2009). More generally, as Nadera Shalhoub-Kevorkian, Nina Griecci, Himmat Zubi, and Rachel Busbridge (2014; this volume) illustrate, the Bedouin community remains extremely marginalized within the context of the larger Israeli economy.

Women's labor force participation rates in Muslim communities, including the countries covered in this issue, also vary considerably, with Iran having the lowest official rate, while Bangladesh has the highest, in part due to the high rates of women contributing to agricultural production and the global apparel industry.[10] Fertility rates, another key variable for assessing women's relative unpaid work burden, also vary, with 2009–13 total fertility rate estimates for Bangladesh, Iran, Israel, Nigeria, and Turkey being 2.2, 1.9, 3.0, 6.0, and 2.1, respectively (World Bank n.d.a).

Several factors have played a role in shaping the way and the degree to which countries have been integrated into the global economy. Among the countries in our special issue, Bangladesh has had a more typical globalization experience to the extent that, by the 1980s, it was providing a cheap labor pool for transnational corporations, particularly the garment industry, which over time has increased demand for women's labor. As Naila Kabeer, Lopita Huq, and Simeen Mahmud (2014; this volume) point out, women's growing employment opportunities, as well as households' increasing recognition of the value of women's paid *and* unpaid work, have played an important role in reducing son preference in some communities in South Asia. As oil exporters, Nigeria and Iran have had rather different globalization trajectories, with export earnings coming primarily from extractive industries rather than manufacturing. Iran, moreover, has faced tightening international sanctions in recent years, contributing further to a particularly challenging globalization experience. It is therefore in a larger context of very different macroeconomic conditions and global political dynamics that we must situate and understand gendered processes and globalization generally, and the economic analyses included in this special issue.

GENDER AND ECONOMICS IN MUSLIM COMMUNITIES

"DEVELOPING" WOMEN

Since World War II, relations between the Global North and South, the latter including the Muslim-majority countries, have been studied and understood primarily through the lens of development and modernization.[11] Articulated and propagated systematically starting in the 1950s (with clear colonial antecedents), modernization theory defined progress and development to be marked by a transition from an agrarian to an industrially based economy, with modernity being characterized in terms of increased education, urbanization, secularization, and technological innovation, which in turn was seen as increasing economic well-being (Isabella Bakker 1999). While economists generally emphasized the importance of income growth, anthropologists, political scientists, and sociologists focused on modern democratic institutions and the evolution of so-called modern political, social, and cultural traits and values among groups and individuals. In the post–Bretton Woods era, the emergence and formal institutionalization of development thought strengthened the resolve to address the socioeconomic problems of so-called developing countries.

Starting in the 1960s, Marxist and dependency theory critics of modernization theory drew attention to the role of the capitalist system in polarizing the world into the core or center of wealthy countries and the periphery or satellite of poor countries. According to these approaches, the core exploited the raw materials, labor, and consumers of the periphery, and as a result the periphery remained dependent on the center, particularly for inputs, technical expertise, and markets, enriching the core at the expense of the periphery. In other words, the development of the core was portrayed as directly responsible for the underdevelopment of the periphery and, crucially, vice versa. Scholars such as Arturo Escobar (1984) built on the work of Foucault, Said, and others, merging it with Marxist and dependency theories to develop a postcolonial critique within developmentalist studies of the Global South.

The vast majority of Muslims in fact today live in the Global South, whereas the countries that make up the wealthy core predominantly have a Christian majority, and, as noted earlier, while a number of Christian-majority countries are among those categorized as HIPC, Muslim-majority countries are overrepresented among HIPC. Furthermore, an analysis of the relative deprivation experienced by Muslims both in contexts where they are a minority population, as well as globally (through a comparison of Muslim-majority and non-Muslim countries), reveals that Muslims are less well off than their counterparts, at both a national and a global level (Frances Stewart 2013). When taken in combination with a critique that frames these findings in the context of the legacy of colonialism and the ongoing hegemony of Western economic models, these contemporary data raise important questions about the links between Muslim grievances and global inequality.

The link between gender norms and persistent inequalities received little attention in early discussions of development, modernization, and dependency theories (Irene Tinker 1990).[12] In the 1970s and 1980s, researchers and policymakers began realizing the need to better integrate women into existing development processes, with a particular emphasis on agricultural productivity, as well as the need to design better-targeted incentives and opportunities for women, in what later became known as the Women in Development (WID) approach (Ester Boserup 1970; Bakker 1999). Although by 1979 the General Assembly had adopted a document that later became known as CEDAW (UN Women n.d.), early meetings to discuss the challenge of gender equality were already marked by tension and conflict between participants from North and South. To highlight awareness of the exploitative conditions under which many women from the Global South were working (and the role of the North in creating and maintaining such conditions), a feminist critique of the women in/and development literatures emerged. Building on dependency theory, this approach formulated an argument regarding the inequalities between women and men, pointing out that "[w]ithin an inegalitarian world order, so-called development could not release women from oppressive social, economic and political institutions" (Naila Kabeer 1994: 46–7). Unlike WID scholars, dependency feminists, many of whom became associated with the Women and Development approach (WAD), saw gender inequalities as part of the "larger systems of inequality, created by and essential to capitalist processes of accumulation" (49).

In response to what Southern participants saw as Northern dominance and a lack of attention to global inequality and imperialism in the early conferences, women from the South established new networks to better address their concerns, such as Development Alternatives for Women for a New Era (DAWN) in 1984, which was based in the Caribbean and with active branches in Latin America and South Asia (Gita Sen and Caren Grown 1987). Eventually, as feminists increasingly recognized that focusing on women was not sufficient, a third framework emerged known as the Gender and Development (GAD) perspective, which stressed the need for policymakers to tackle gender norms, male attitudes, patriarchal institutions, and class inequalities that contribute to widespread gender inequalities (Frédérique Apffel-Marglin and Suzanne L. Simon 1994; Lourdes Benería, Günseli Berik, and Maria Floro forthcoming).

With neoliberal economic policies in ascendance worldwide in the 1980s, feminist scholars across disciplines in particular turned their attention to the gendered implications of structural adjustment policies (SAPs), the shrinking state, and the growing nongovernmental organization

GENDER AND ECONOMICS IN MUSLIM COMMUNITIES

(NGO) sector. Some studied household dynamics in the context of rising neoliberalism and broader institutional structures that perpetuated inequalities. Others focused on the two-way relationships between gender inequalities and macroeconomic policies and outcomes in the post–oil crisis period (Kabeer 1994; Diane Elson 1995; Stephanie Seguino 2000; Lourdes Benería 2008).

Neoliberal policies reducing government spending and regulations on trade and finance mobility were initially required in the Philippines and Mexico but eventually also in many other countries, including some of those discussed in this special issue (Turkey, Bangladesh, and Nigeria). More generally, the spread of neoliberalism has been linked with a withdrawal of the state in certain key sectors, including in Iran and Israel, which, while not mandated to carry out SAPs by the International Monetary Fund, also introduced austerity measures in response to internal and global pressures (Bahramitash 2004; Orly Benjamin 2008).

Much of the early analysis that informed the gendered outcomes of SAPs focused on Latin America and Southeast Asia. As empirical studies were undertaken in new contexts, including some Muslim-majority economies, a more nuanced view of neoliberalism emerged. For example, whereas previously it had been assumed that neoliberalism and the feminization of the manufacturing workforce went hand in hand, Günseli Berik and Nilüfer Çağatay (1991) and Ragui Assaad (2005) found little evidence of this in Turkey and Egypt, respectively.

Feminist research has also identified the complex causal relationships between gender inequality and macroeconomic outcomes, such as economic growth and export competitiveness, in a neoliberal environment. Using a composite index of "patriarchal dominance" that encompasses gender inequalities in civil liberties, ownership rights, physical integrity, and family code, Elissa Braunstein (2014; this volume) contributes to this literature by arguing that patriarchal rent, defined as economic gains that accrue to men as a result of gender inequalities, rather than Islam, is the source of slow economic growth in a number of Muslim *and* non-Muslim-majority countries.

Considerable gaps remain in our understanding of how women in various Muslim-majority contexts have fared in the context of neoliberalism and the degree to which women's experiences in Latin America and Southeast Asia can be generalized to Muslim-majority contexts. Given the need for an interdisciplinary feminist perspective, it is not surprising that existing studies of gender and economic processes and outcomes in Muslim communities have been undertaken not only by economists but also by scholars in other disciplines, including anthropology, geography, political science, sociology, and women's, gender, and sexuality studies (Jennifer Olmsted 2003; Azza Basaruddin 2013; Amaney Jamal and Vickie Langohr 2013; Robina Mohammad 2013; Rachel Rinaldo 2013a).

GENDER AND ECONOMICS IN MUSLIM COMMUNITIES

The vexed relationship between NGOs, the state, and local elites in the transformation of women's lives in various contexts has received much critical attention in recent years (Elora Shehabuddin 2008; Manal Jamal 2012; Victoria Bernal and Inderpal Grewal 2014), as has the central role of women factory workers in the global apparel industry (Siddiqi 2009). In their discussion of these trends in Bangladesh, Kabeer, Huq, and Mahmud (2014) explore the potential role of institutional structures (including religion and an active NGO sector) and macroeconomic conditions in improving women's economic opportunities and in the emergence of different patterns in Bangladesh and India.

Whereas Kabeer, Huq, and Mahmud view NGOs as relatively positive forces in terms of furthering gender norm change, Özlem Altan-Olcay (2014; this volume), Damla Işık (2014; this volume), and Shalhoub-Kevorkian et al. (2014; this volume), complicate our views of NGOs by illustrating the degree to which such institutions can be instruments of capitalism and/or the state. Shalhoub-Kevorkian et al. in particular are critical of the role that Israeli NGOs play in reinforcing state power and further marginalizing the Bedouin community in Israel. Işık and Altan-Olcay also provide explicit examples of how, within the context of neoliberal development, which rejects the notion of a strong welfare state tasked with the role of redistribution and the provision of a safety net, NGOs play an increasing role in the delivery of services and the shaping of discussions around gender norms and policies more generally.

Finally, in her study of Hausa women's NGOs in Kano, Nigeria, Adryan Wallace (2014; this volume) provides insights into how women who lead various religiously based NGOs view potential funding sources. The leaders of the NGOs with whom Wallace worked articulated concerns about both funding sources and objectives and were conscious of the need to resist being manipulated by funders. Interestingly none of these NGOs were recipients of *zakat* funding (tithing by Muslims that has been institutionalized to provide development assistance), although all grounded their work in the context of Islam. These women were also leery of receiving funds from Western donors because they did not want to compromise their missions. By grounding her analysis in women's own voices, Wallace shows how women navigate the complex terrain in which development policies are playing out in the context of state and non-state, as well as religious and non-religious, actors, shedding light on the degree to which women leaders working in the field of development are mindful of the dilemmas brought out by analysts such as Narayan (1997).

FEMINIST POLICY SOLUTIONS

Feminists concerned with the rapid embrace of neoliberalism at the development policy level have identified various alternative ways of

GENDER AND ECONOMICS IN MUSLIM COMMUNITIES

framing development challenges. One challenge to neoliberalism is the capabilities approach developed by Amartya K. Sen and Martha C. Nussbaum, who define development as the expansion of people's capabilities, providing the concept of capabilities as an alternative to subjective measures (such as utility) and income-based measures (such as GDP) for evaluating well-being. Sen (1993), Nussbaum (2000), and Ingrid Robeyns (2003) distinguish between capabilities (what people can achieve) and functionings (what people actually achieve) and argue that the political goal is capability, not functioning. While Amartya K. Sen (2004) has resisted the idea of a fixed list of central capabilities, Martha C. Nussbaum has proposed a particular list, arguing for "an account, for political purposes of what the central human capabilities are, even if we know that this account will always be contested and remade" (2003: 56).

In many ways complementary to the capabilities framework, scholars have also focused on developing a framework to assess the effectiveness of particular policies in addressing human rights. In arguing for the need for careful analyses of government spending patterns, Radhika Balakrishnan and Diane Elson (2011) emphasize the need to hold governments accountable within the context of their compliance with human rights treaties and the norms, standards, responsibilities, and procedures that have been developed around them.

Both these approaches provide frameworks that not only identify the importance of addressing deprivations in general, and gender inequality in particular, but also the central importance of collective action and institutions to assure that capabilities are achieved. The human rights–based approach puts a particularly heavy emphasis on the importance of the state, while Martha C. Nussbaum identifies a broader set of actors, including transnational corporations, who should be assigned "certain responsibilities for promoting human capabilities" (2004: 15).

There is disagreement about the degree to which such approaches directly address the key concerns of feminists who focus on the link between Orientalism, global inequalities, and historical and contemporary power asymmetries. Alison Jaggar (2006) and S. Charusheela (2008), for example, raise concerns related to the challenge of addressing issues of structural power, as well as the feasibility of achieving universal capabilities in the context of capitalism. Nilüfer Çağatay and Korkut Ertürt (2004) also address the challenge of global inequality, through an approach that is explicitly critical of capitalism and global power relations, arguing for the need for gender-sensitive policies – such as gender-sensitive budgets, gender-equitable macroeconomic policies, and democratization of macroeconomic policymaking – that address both national and global inequalities, a recommendation that, if properly implemented, would be particularly valuable to impoverished Muslim women.

13

GENDER AND ECONOMICS IN MUSLIM COMMUNITIES

The studies in this special issue illustrate the value of both multiple methodological and theoretical approaches to challenging the ways neoliberalism intersects with gender norms and religion in the context of Muslim communities. Building on the work of feminist economists who have previously advocated for methodological diversity (Michèle Pujol 1997), we argue that the persistence of Orientalism as well as the very real material consequences that an Orientalist framing can have are best unraveled through studies that examine the way certain scholarship frames Islam (Gamze Çavdar and Yavuz Yaşar 2014); through multiple methodological approaches (Kabeer, Huq, and Mahmud 2014) as well as through broader macroeconomic analyses that involve challenging simplistic assumptions that Islam (Braunstein 2014; Hassani-Nezhad and Sjögren 2014; Niels Spierings 2014), or for that matter any other religion, can be measured through the insertion of a dummy variable; or alternatively through in-depth analyses of particular Muslim communities (Ahmed 2014; Altan-Olcay 2014; Bahramitash and Olmsted 2014; Işık 2014; Shalhoub-Kevorkian et al. 2014; Wallace 2014) in order to illustrate the diversity of Muslim women and men's experiences.

GENDER, INSTITUTIONS, AND DECISION MAKING

Key to any nuanced microeconomic analysis is that it be framed within a macroeconomic context. A number of authors in the special issue frame their microanalysis within the context of a macroeconomic critique of neoliberal development policies. Altan-Olcay (2014), for example, examines how these policies lead to the somewhat contradictory gendered construction of neoliberal subjects: low-income women are encouraged to become individualistic entrepreneurs, but at the same time are expected to continue to play the role of nurturing, self-sacrificing mothers. Altan-Olcay's analysis adds to feminist critiques of the neoliberal development agenda that favors the replacement of the role of state by the market and of the growing emphasis on entrepreneurship as the solution to gender inequality.

While many studies – some feminist, some not – begin from the premise that low rates of labor force participation are problematic, implicitly setting up women's gainful employment as a desirable goal and a proxy for women's economic empowerment, other scholars question the facile link between women's employment and their empowerment as they point out the role played by a multiplicity of factors including class, age, location, and reasons for entry into paid employment (Kanchana N. Ruwanpura and Jane Humphries 2004; Jennifer Olmsted 2005; Cecilia Menjívar 2006). Moreover, feminist economists have made particularly important contributions through their focus on the often unequal burden of both unpaid and total work on women, the link between unpaid work and

GENDER AND ECONOMICS IN MUSLIM COMMUNITIES

women's (lack of) access to and control over economic resources (land, microcredit, and others) and social safety nets, among other issues (Bina Agarwal 1997; Günseli Berik and Ebru Kongar 2013; Seçil A. Kaya Bahçe and Emel Memiş 2013).

Time-use data have now been collected for several Muslim-majority countries, but in-depth analysis of women's unpaid work in most Muslim communities remains limited (Olmsted 2005).[13] Still, a number of studies in this special issue provide insights into women's concerns when it comes to the double burden and the challenge of balancing paid and unpaid work. Işık (2014), for instance, addresses issues related to how women understand the concept of work. Through her focus on pious women in Istanbul, who make sense of their daily routines by framing their experiences in the context of their spiritual understanding, Işık concludes that women's work means more than exploitation, but also that "pious conduct" is conducive to increasing transnational competition. In other words, Işık finds that while many of the women she studied are subject to the double burden and are also economically vulnerable due to paid work conditions that may involve low wages and/or earnings and uncertainty, their religious views help them to cope with and make sense of the harsh realities they face.

Feminist economists have also analyzed and challenged the male-breadwinner norm that confines women to their reproductive roles as wives and mothers and restricts their access to paid employment (Nancy Folbre and Julie A. Nelson 2000). This scholarship is concerned with gaining a better understanding of issues related to paid employment, including the determinants of women's labor force participation and earnings, as well as broader questions around the conditions of paid work (Elson 1995). Thus, it is perhaps not surprising that six studies in this special issue investigate questions related to women's labor force participation rate and employment. For instance, through his examination of women's labor force participation in twenty-eight countries with majority-Muslim populations, Spierings (2014) challenges the attribution of low levels of women's labor force participation in these economies to Islam, which is often used as a proxy for patriarchy. Spierings' findings are consistent with previous studies that have illustrated the degree to which household dynamics shape women's participation in paid employment. Specifically, Spierings finds that women with child- and eldercare responsibilities at home are less likely to participate in the labor market, unless there are other women in the household; the presence of a male breadwinner in the household lowers women's labor force participation; the effect is weaker in countries with a greater gender gap in higher education.

Feminist scholars focusing on the household have also often emphasized the key role that household bargaining can play in terms of shaping women's well-being. The studies by Işık (2014) and Bahramitash and

Olmsted (2014) add to our understanding of women's bargaining position through their emphasis not only on the role that control of material goods can play in shifting household dynamics, but also on how ideology and particularly religion may be either invoked by women to reduce their work burden or on the other hand become internalized in a manner that leads to women not questioning the economic conditions they face. These authors also help illustrate the visceral importance of spirituality to many women's lives and the limits of approaches to well-being that do not include a focus on women's non-material concerns.

The more standard approach to household bargaining of course focuses on the importance of women's access to and control over economic resources to strengthen women's relative bargaining power (Agarwal 1997; Ramzi Mabsout and Irene van Staveren 2010), with these in turn being shaped by legal structures. Within the context of understanding household dynamics and bargaining power, family law is therefore one important factor to consider. For this reason, divorce laws have been the focus of considerable research among feminist scholars in both Muslim and non-Muslim majority communities (Mary Ann Glendon 1997; Sameena Nazir and Leigh Tomppert 2005; Srimati Basu 2012). By regulating a woman's ability to exit a marriage, such laws play an important role in shaping and/or limiting women's economic well-being. Hassani-Nezhad and Sjögren (2014) build on existing empirical research through an examination of the impact of changes in divorce laws on women's labor force participation, focusing on the introduction of *khul* divorce (divorce initiated by women) between 1984 and 2006 in a number of Arab Muslim-majority countries. Upon investigating whether countries where legal changes have given women the right to divorce unilaterally have seen an increase in women's labor force participation rate, they find this to be true primarily among younger women.

Marriage, rather than divorce, is at the center of the study by Ahmed (2014). Weaving together the narratives of villagers in Bangladesh, Ahmed challenges game-theoretic approaches that focus on women's empowerment as being narrowly associated with their ability to exit from marriages. Among the women she interviewed, Ahmed found a strong consensus that achieving marital harmony and household peace are highly valued. The women also had a firm understanding of what qualities constitute their notions of ideal masculinity.

An analysis of whether and how gender norms are evolving is also key to assuring the progress toward gender equality. This analysis is at the center of the study by Kabeer, Huq, and Mahmud (2014), who focus on son preference in Bangladesh, with some comparative discussion of India. Concerned about male-biased sex ratios in a number of communities in the region, the authors illustrate that, in Bangladesh, sex ratios are becoming less skewed. Combining quantitative findings with interviews with parents,

GENDER AND ECONOMICS IN MUSLIM COMMUNITIES

the authors find that daughters are increasingly valued in Bangladesh, and they see this as evidence that son preference is on the decline.

More generally, feminist scholars, including economists, have long argued to deconstruct binary categories, such as masculine versus feminine, male versus female, and have called for nuanced analyses that take into account intersectionalities when it comes to different aspects of women and men's identity (Kimberlé Crenshaw 1991). In the case of Muslim communities, this is particularly important, given that Muslim women have often been reduced to stereotypes. Through their analysis of the intersection of age and gender, a number of authors in this volume shine light on the complex identities of women in Muslim communities. Bahramitash and Olmsted (2014), for instance, uncover empirical evidence of a generational shift in gender norms in Iran, with older women more wedded to the male-breadwinner model than their younger counterparts. Drawing on interviews and participant observation, they argue that women's preferences in terms of the degree to which women wish to combine paid and unpaid work vary by age, class, type of employment, and marital status. And through their analysis of *khul* reform in a number of Arab countries, Hassani-Nezhad and Sjögren (2014) also implicitly provide evidence of norm change, since legal changes themselves can often be emblematic of societal norm shifts. Age in particular emerges as an important lens through which women's employment patterns should be examined, with the authors finding that younger mothers' labor force participation changes more than older women's, which they in turn suggest is related to the particular ways that the legal reforms have been carried out. More generally, it is key of course to not only examine the links between gender and age, but also other aspects of identity, such as class, geographic location, sexuality, marital status, education level, and other factors.

BEYOND ORIENTALISM

Despite a growing body of scholarship in several disciplines that provides much-needed nuance, the image of oppressed Arab/Muslim/Eastern women, popularized anew post-9/11, continues to hold sway today in certain segments of feminist and development scholarship, as noted, for instance, by Jennifer Olmsted (2002, 2004), Fida Adely (2009), and Frances Hasso (2009).[14] Orientalism is of pressing concern not just because of the way Muslim women are stripped of their agency, but also because such narratives influence development and policy decisions, with often devastating consequences for women's lives. Through both the theoretical and methodological frames they opt to utilize, the studies in this special issue challenge the Orientalism that continues to reduce Muslim women to caricatures.

The problem of Orientalism is partly one of disciplinary methodology. Economists in particular rely predominantly on statistical methods and thus pay less attention to historical and political processes that are difficult to capture quantitatively. A related shortcoming of primarily quantitative analysis is the lack of focus not just on context, but also on process (Berik 1997; Jennifer Olmsted 1997, 2002). This raises questions about whether statistical or econometric analysis can provide the degree of nuance needed to unpack Orientalist stereotypes, a challenge a number of feminist economists and some of the authors in this special issue take on and effectively address. For instance, building on the work of Stephanie Seguino (2011), who uses statistical analysis to challenge the view that Muslims have less gender-equitable views than other religions, Braunstein (2014), Hassani-Nezhad and Sjögren (2014), and Spierings (2014) undertake nuanced cross-country analyses that avoid the trap of reducing Islam to a dummy variable.

Orientalism poses a challenge also because of the underlying assumption in economics of modernism and of a unilinear path of development. Two postcolonial feminist economics scholars who have been particularly concerned with the hegemony of modernist discourse in shaping development economics are S. Charusheela and Eiman Zein-Elabdin (2004; see also Charusheela [2008]), who argue that existing theoretical frames often privilege Western experiences and understandings of women's well-being and opportunity at the expense of others. Moreover, they show how the mainstream development literature has ignored the complex causal linkages between economic development, colonial history, and gender relations, depending instead on notions of unchanging, backward gender norms or traditional culture to explain the lack of economic development in many countries. The tendency to fall back on a cultural explanation has been particularly true in discussions of Muslim-majority countries.

Another important contribution of the studies in this special issue is to incorporate religiosity, specifically that of Muslim women, into feminist economic inquiry. For many women around the world, Muslim and non-Muslim alike, material and spiritual needs are intertwined and difficult to disentangle. A Pew poll carried out in 2008 for example, found that in seventeen out of twenty-three countries surveyed, religion was considered to be somewhat or very important by the majority of respondents (Pew Forum 2008), and this was true in Muslim and non-Muslim contexts alike. While religion is often manipulated both by patriarchs and capitalists to serve their own interests, the Pew study also indicates that women are more likely to identify religion as important, compared to men, in all but the poorest country contexts (where religion was considered as important by almost all men and women surveyed). Therefore it is not surprising that building on work by Lara Deeb (2006), Elora Shehabuddin (2008), and

GENDER AND ECONOMICS IN MUSLIM COMMUNITIES

Rachel Rinaldo (2013b), a number of studies included in this special issue provide examples of women who state that religion is important for them and who also (re)interpret religion as a liberating force or as a source of self-esteem.

Feminist scholars need to question ethnocentric and class-biased understandings of terms such as empowerment, agency, liberation, family, and motherhood that are often promoted by scholars and policymakers. For instance, as noted earlier, some of the earlier feminist studies have overemphasized the significance of paid employment outside the home in women's empowerment, taking it to be an overwhelmingly positive development, when women in a variety of contexts, not only in Muslim communities, may think very differently, or at least ambivalently, about paid work.[15] In addition, as noted earlier, across Western scholarship and popular culture, there has been a tendency to *assume* that Islam is the villain rather than to *interrogate* other factors, including the role of the West itself in creating or facilitating the difficult conditions in which many Muslim women and men find themselves. To move forward, it is crucial to address not only the concerns over male and market biases in economic scholarship that feminist economists have already long been critiquing very productively, but also incorporate into that an awareness of white bias and privilege (Peggy McIntosh 1988; Rose M. Brewer, Cecilia A. Conrad, and Mary C. King 2002) and Western bias and privilege (Charusheela and Zein-Elabdin 2004; Nitasha Kaul 2004; Olmsted 2004). More generally, given the role of gender, race, geography, *and* religion in both national and international inequalities, it is crucial that greater attention be paid to intersectionality.

Doing so requires not only a focus on macroeconomic conditions and policies, but also assuring that women's own voices are heard. This calls for finely grained microanalyses and methodological diversity. The econometric analysis by Hassani-Nezhad and Sjögren (2014), for example, suggests that pushing for more flexible divorce laws should be a main policy priority. Ahmed's (2014) ethnographic analysis, however, complicates this conclusion, suggesting the need for a more comprehensive approach to women's well-being and empowerment that incorporates multiple perspectives, so that women who prioritize improving their marriage over seeking a divorce have that option. More generally, this special issue illustrates the key importance of making space for multiple methodological approaches and sufficiently flexible policy solutions that reflect the diversity of women's concerns.

Indeed, feminist scholars have grappled with the challenge of policy responses to changing social norms and practices in the past, both in terms of sifting through empirical evidence, as well as by providing theoretical frameworks within which such questions can be assessed in a more comprehensive fashion. Nancy Fraser (1994: 591), for example, lays out the various ways that nation-states have addressed the "crumbling of the old gender order" that had been "centered around the ideal of the family wage." Her insights are particularly relevant to several of the Muslim communities represented in this special issue, in which women's labor force participation rates have been on the rise and where it is clear that a new social contract is emerging, in part due to neoliberalism, but also due to changes in norms associated with marriage, fertility, among others (Olmsted 2005).

In analyzing how nation states have responded to changing social realities related to household structure, Fraser (1994) contrasts the "Universal Breadwinner Model" with the "Caregiver Parity Model." Under the former, women and men are equally engaged in paid employment, while the state/market absorbs much of the responsibility of care labor (particularly child- and eldercare.) The disadvantage of this model, Fraser argues, is that it "valorizes men's traditional sphere – employment," and it does not lead to leisure time equality (1994: 605), since not all unpaid work responsibilities of women can be replaced by the state or the market. The Caregiver Parity Model, which Western Europe has largely followed, gives care labor adequate recognition though it remains primarily female and reduces women's economic vulnerability through a combination of part-time work and state-sponsored safety nets. This model, Fraser points out, continues to marginalize women by assuming they should maintain the primary responsibility for reproduction. Fraser suggests not only that both these models are "highly utopian visions of a postindustrial welfare state" and have not yet been realized in most of the world (1994: 59),[16] but that assuring gender equality requires a "deconstructive" model where both men and women work part time in paid labor and part time in the unpaid sector.

The analysis in a number of the studies in this special issue suggests that Muslim women are demanding that they have meaningful work, in the broadest sense of the term and that their material and spiritual needs are met. The solutions being proposed to resolve the problem of assuring material well-being as well as reproductive labor needs are as contested as elsewhere. Feminist scholars and policymakers need to think creatively about how to attain Fraser's ideal model, and attention must also be given to the problem of global inequalities that have certainly disproportionately affected women and, as we argue in this essay, Muslim women in particular.

DIRECTIONS FOR FUTURE RESEARCH

In addition to the clear need for more analysis of global inequalities and their intersection with colonial histories and ongoing Orientalism, other significant empirical gaps remain when it comes to studies of gender and economics in Muslim communities. For example, basic microeconomic studies that provide detailed analyses of wage structures, women's vulnerability to poverty, and existing or proposed social safety net structures are missing for a large number of Muslim communities, especially in Sub-Saharan Africa. Unfortunately, the gaps are often largest in countries suffering from the most acute levels of poverty, in part given the correlation between high rates of poverty and weak data availability, but also between high levels of economic deprivation and violent unrest and conflict, which can further complicate the ability to collect and analyze data.

Another gap pertains to the situation of Muslim women in Muslim-minority contexts. While Kabeer, Huq, and Mahmud (2014) include some discussion of the Muslim minority in India, and Shalhoub-Kevorkian et al. (2014) focus on the Bedouin community in Israel,[17] we unfortunately received no submissions that address the unique challenges that arise in the context of communities where Muslims are a minority, as a result of recent global migratory trends. As tensions over migration persist, the situation facing Muslims in the Global North, particularly in Europe, for example warrants further research (Pew Forum 2011b). Muslim minorities face discrimination, hate crimes, and, in certain contexts, the passage of various controversial types of legislation. Feminist scholars have expressed concern, for example, about the negative stereotypes associated with Muslim youth (Caitlin Killian 2007/2008) and the headscarf controversy that emerged in France in 2004, with the implementation of a law restricting French schoolchildren from wearing religious dress (Joan C. Scott 2010). While the French law was couched in language that potentially targeted several groups, including Orthodox Jewish and Sikh boys, feminist scholars generally concur that a primary aim of that law was to prevent Muslim girls from wearing head coverings. Aside from the unintended consequences of likely reducing girls' access to school in France, Scott (2010) argues that as the law was being debated, the girls themselves were denied a voice and were portrayed primarily as victims requiring protection.

More generally, since we issued our call for papers for this special issue in 2010, a number of events have brought home the degree to which global and local institutions, religious and secular, are (re)shaping political and economic outcomes, which in turn are both being shaped by and shaping prevailing gender norms. The series of Arab uprisings that began in 2010 is a particularly compelling example. A number of scholars have examined the political changes that occurred between 2010 to 2013. Deniz Kandiyoti (2013) emphasizes the challenge of addressing violence against women, while Valentine M. Moghadam (2013) examines whether these revolutions/movements have led to patriarchal or egalitarian outcomes. Moghadam suggests that the direction taken depended on preexisting gender roles and inequalities, women's legal status and social positions prior to the political change, the degree of women's mobilization, the new government's political positions, its capacity and will to mobilize resources for rights-based development, as well as various external factors, again illustrating the value of taking into account particular historical antecedents and using a case-study approach to understand women's economic and political gains and losses.

Other recent historical events also illustrate how religious institutions and beliefs interact with states and markets in diverse ways and require considerably more research. This is true in the context of Islam, as well as Christianity, Hinduism, Judaism, and other religions, with increasing tensions emerging between groups that disagree on the nature of the relationship between religious institutions and the state. An important issue being debated in both national and global contexts is the right to access to contraceptives and safe abortions. One example is the June 2014 ruling by the US Supreme Court on the significance of a family-owned corporation's religious sensibilities in determining whether its insurance policy will cover all types of contraceptives needed by its women employees (Adam Liptak 2014). In the context of Turkey, similarly, access to family planning has been undermined through a restrictive 2012 abortion law, reduced budgets, and various disincentives to doctors (Sebnem Arsu 2012). Also noteworthy is the fact that in the global arena, US-based conservative Christian NGOs have been instrumental in creating a coalition of conservative religious groups to mobilize against the expansion of sexual and reproductive rights in various UN documents (NORAD 2013).

More generally, the emergence of the Tea Party in the US; the popularity of Islamist parties in the aftermath of the so-called Arab spring; tensions between Israeli Jews and Palestinian Christians and Muslims, which have culminated, to date, in three extremely lopsided military confrontations between Hamas and the Israeli government, in 2004, 2011, and 2014; the *Gezi* Protests in Turkey in opposition to the Islamist *Adalet ve Kalkınma Party* (AKP); the victory of Hindu nationalists in India in the 2014 elections; the emergence of Boko Haram in Nigeria; and increased anti-Muslim immigrant sentiments in Europe, are all instances where tensions within and among various groups are being shaped by religion and have gendered political and economic implications.[18]

Muslim women around the world have been actively involved in responding to and contesting religious politics and interpretations of religion that discriminate against women. They have also protested discriminatory secular codes, debilitating sanctions, authoritarian rulers (many of whom, like Hosni Mubarak of Egypt, were openly supported by Western powers), and unfair elections (as happened with the Green Movement that followed the 2009 elections in Iran). Sufficient energy, however, has not been devoted to exploring women's active participation in various contested political spaces. Muslim women's rights activists, like

GENDER AND ECONOMICS IN MUSLIM COMMUNITIES

women's rights activists elsewhere, are divided over what rights to fight for and in what order of priority, what questions and arguments to focus on (theological or political, social, and economic), within what framework (Quranic or universal). As in much of the formerly colonized world, the very term "feminist" is contested and often seen as an imperial imposition (Narayan 1997; Valentine M. Moghadam 2002); yet many prominent women's rights activists, such as Omaima Abou-Bakr (2001) of Egypt, embrace the term.

The studies in this special issue illustrate the complexity of analyzing the intersection between religion, economics, and politics, particularly when it comes to deepening feminists' understanding of the factors that determine women's empowerment. They also point to the need to combine multiple approaches to provide nuanced analyses to determine how various institutions further, or not, the goals of gender equality. The state, for example, is an institution that feminists realize they must engage with, but also one that is clearly far from free of patriarchal influences that may be imposed on women through both religious and secular means. Similarly, NGOs may be both institutions that women shape and make use of to further gender empowerment, but may also be co-opted to further the neoliberal agenda. Paid employment can help improve women's well-being, but often also contributes to the exploitation experienced by women. While nuanced analyses of micro-level outcomes are needed, so too is a focus on meta-level influences and power dynamics, particularly in the context of global neo- and postcolonial policy dynamics. Finally, religion itself is dynamic and contested, which is why it can play both a positive and a negative role in shaping women's lives, as the studies in this special issue illustrate.

ACKNOWLEDGMENTS

This special issue was made possible by the generous support of the Swedish International Development Cooperation Agency (Sida), Rice University, and the University of Utah. The funding allowed us to organize a GEMC workshop in June 2012 in Barcelona, Spain, in conjunction with the annual IAFFE conference there. The workshop was attended by the authors included in this volume and a number of other experts on gender and economics in Muslim communities. We all benefited greatly from these discussions. We wish to thank the experts at the workshop and the reviewers who contributed their time and expertise to assist us in selecting the most novel and high quality articles in this volume. Following the workshop, the Sida grant allowed us to work with FE Co-Editor Günseli Berik to develop a mentoring process in which an established contributor to *Feminist Economics* and other highly-ranked journals "pairs" with a scholar less familiar with FE.

We are grateful to Heba Khan and Gemini Wahhaj of the FE office at Rice University for the initial impetus for a special issue focused on the

GENDER AND ECONOMICS IN MUSLIM COMMUNITIES

links between gender, economic well-being, and the varying influences of religion and, specifically, on the need to close the gaps caused by gender-blind analyses and unexplored assumptions and generalizations regarding Muslim women's experiences. We wish to acknowledge with deep appreciation the careful constructive feedback that we received on this introduction from the FE Editors, Diana Strassmann and Günseli Berik. For the support and infinite patience of the FE staff throughout the four-year process of producing this special issue, many thanks to Becky Byron, Christine Cox, Anne Dayton, Heba Khan, Polly Morrice, as well as the undergraduate interns and graduate fellows who worked on various aspects of special issue logistics and manuscript preparation.

NOTES

[1] A note on terminology: in assembling this special issue, we opted for the term "Muslim communities" because it allows us to consider both Muslim-majority and Muslim-minority contexts. Moreover, we deemed that "Islam" suggests a narrow focus on the impact of Islam on women's lives (presuming that this is even possible to study), and we would fall into the very trap that we were trying to challenge, the notion that Muslim women's lives are shaped solely by Islam. We also decided against the terms "Muslim world" and "Islamic world." Both terms suggest a closed, monolithic community with defined boundaries, when in fact Muslims live in a variety of legal, political, and economic contexts, with a wide range of gendered implications for the choices, constraints, and opportunities available to them. Finally, while mindful of the assumptions embedded in data that try to identify whether a country is a Muslim-, Christian- or Hindu-majority country, since the degree to which the population actually adheres to (any) religion in practice is difficult to discern, we use the term "Muslim-majority" to refer to countries where at least 50 percent of the population identifies as culturally Muslim.

[2] Çavdar and Yaşar focus on scholarship about the Middle East because of the intensive focus placed on the Arab world, but research on non-Arab Muslim communities, for example, focusing on Afghanistan, Nigeria, and Pakistan, is also fraught with similar problems.

[3] Identifying Muslim communities as Eastern and Judeo-Christian ones as Western sets up these religions as oppositional, when in fact they emerged from the same geographic region and build on the same sacred texts, with Islam viewing Jewish and Christian texts as sacred. We have, however, retained the East/West distinction when discussing Orientalist images, particularly of the nineteenth and early twentieth centuries, since that was the binary in use at the time. It is worth noting also that the figure of the oppressed Eastern woman encompassed non-Muslim women in the Arab world as well as India, China, and elsewhere in Asia and Africa.

[4] Whereas much of the early literature set up East/West as a binary, later literature focused on North/South as the key geographic divide. Rather than choosing one over the other, we have used the terms that align with the terminology generally accepted within particular contexts.

[5] Authors' calculations using Pew 2010 data (Pew Forum 2011a) and World Bank (n.d.c) list of HIPC countries.

25

GENDER AND ECONOMICS IN MUSLIM COMMUNITIES

6 The use of the very term "Middle East" is itself emblematic of the colonial power dynamics since the region has come to be known in relation to Europe, rather than in terms of the continent on which it sits. The UN uses "West Asia," but we have opted for the term "Middle East" because it will be more familiar to the readers.

7 This is true not only in the case of Muslim immigrants to the Global North, but also in the case of countries such as India and many countries in Africa, with Ethiopia and Tanzania being two examples.

8 See for example a recent analysis of the US (Bruce Ledewitz 2011), as well as some comparative work focusing on Turkey, the US, and France (Ahmet Kuru 2009).

9 The UK is generally not defined as a secular state, due to the Church of England's involvement in governance.

10 Feminist scholars have also contested the degree to which women's labor force participation is accurately measured (Margaret Coleman 1999).

11 The term "developing" is highly contested, particularly when it comes to a focus on individual women, but also more generally in the context of larger questions of economic well-being (Naila Kabeer 1999; Amartya Sen 1999).

12 One notable exception was the arena of population control, which targeted women in the Global South directly. As early as the 1950s, Western and local efforts to "control" the world's population focused on women from the Global South (Matthew Connelly 2008). These efforts were focused on reducing births with scant attention to women's general health and well-being or to the larger national and global structural factors behind poverty and the important links between poverty, conflict, and environmental degradation (Betsy Hartmann and Elizabeth Barajas-Román 2011).

13 According to UN Department of Economic and Social Affairs (n.d.), as of 2014, at least one time-use survey had been collected for the following Muslim majority countries: Albania, Algeria, Chad, Djibouti, Indonesia, Iraq, Malaysia, Morocco, Nigeria, Oman, Pakistan, Palestine, Tanzania, and Turkey. Additionally time-use data are available in a number of countries that have large Muslim minorities, such as Benin, Ghana, India, Israel, Macedonia, and Mauritius.

14 Of the few feminist economic analyses that have focused explicitly on the relationship between Islam and women's well-being, some have fallen into the trap of essentializing Islam and, by association, also essentializing Muslim women (for example, Barbara Bergmann [1995]; see also Shoshona Grossbard-Schechtman and Shoshona Neuman [1998], to which Sondra Hale [1995] and Olmsted [2002] responded, respectively).

15 See, for example, a discussion of this subject in the context of Japan (Corinne Boyles and Aiko Shibata 2009).

16 Fraser argues that both models assume certain conditions, such as "major political-economic restructuring, including significant public control over corporations, the capacity to direct investment to create high-quality permanent jobs, and the ability to tax profits and wealth at rates sufficient to fund expanded high-quality social programs" (1994: 610).

17 Before 1948, the Bedouin were an ethnic minority within the larger predominantly Arab and Muslim community of Palestine. In 1948, the state of Israel was created and the vast majority of Palestinians, including most Bedouin, fled or were expelled, and thus Muslims became the minority within Israel, with the Bedouin continuing as a subminority within the larger Muslim population (Josh Raisher 2014).

18 A recent Pew Forum report (2008) suggests that support for more radical strands of Islam has never been high and is currently on the decline among Muslims. But such reports also raise questions about why a particular emphasis is placed on examining Muslims' support for violence that is carried out in the name of religion, when similar surveys are not conducted to explore the degree to which violence is being condoned in other religious contexts.

REFERENCES

Abou-Bakr, Omaima. 2001. "Islamic Feminism: What is in a Name? Preliminary Reflections." *Middle East Women's Studies Review* 15–16: 1–4.

Abu-Bader, Suleiman and Daniel Gottlieb. 2009. "Poverty, Education and Employment in the Arab-Bedouin Society: A Comparative View." ECINEQ Working Paper 2009-137. http://www.ecineq.org/milano/WP/ECINEQ2009-137.pdf.

Abu-Lughod, Lila. 2013. *Do Muslim Women Need Saving?* Cambridge, MA: Harvard University Press.

Adely, Fida. 2009. "Educating Women for Development: *The Arab Human Development Report 2005* and the Problem with Women's Choices." *International Journal of Middle East Studies* 41(1): 105–22.

Agarwal, Bina. 1997. "'Bargaining' and Gender Relations: Within and Beyond the Household." *Feminist Economics* 3(1): 1–51.

Ahmed, Fauzia Erfan. 2014. "Peace in the Household: Gender, Agency, and Villagers' Measures of Marital Quality in Bangladesh." *Feminist Economics* 20(4): 397–421.

al-Ali, Nadje and Nicola Pratt. 2009. *What Kind of Liberation: Women and the Occupation of Iraq.* Berkeley: University of California Press.

Altan-Olcay, Özlem. 2014. "Entrepreneurial Subjectivities and Gendered Complexities: Neoliberal Citizenship in Turkey." *Feminist Economics* 20(4): 445–69.

an-Naim, Abdullahi. 2002. *Islamic Family Law in a Changing World.* London: Zed Books.

Apffel-Marglin, Frédérique and Suzanne L. Simon. 1994. "Feminist Orientalism and Development." In *Feminist Perspectives on Sustainable Development,* edited by Wendy Harcourt, 26–45. London: Zed Books.

Arat, Yesim. 2010. "Women's Rights and Islam in Turkish Politics: The Civil Code Amendment." *Middle East Journal* 64(2): 235–51.

Arsu, Sebnem. 2012. "Premier of Turkey Seeks Limits on Abortions." *New York Times,* May 29.

Assaad, Ragui. 2005. "Informalization and Defeminization: Explaining the Unusual Pattern in Egypt." In *Rethinking Informalization: Precarious Jobs, Poverty and Social Protection,* edited by Neema Kudva and Lourdes Benería, 86–102. http://hdl.handle.net/1813/3716.

Badarneh, Siham. 2009. *Health Discrimination: The Right to Health of the Palestinian Arab Minority in Israel: A Status Report.* Arab Association for Human Rights, Nazareth, Israel. http://www.arabhra.org/HraAdmin/UserImages/Files/Health%20Discrimination-%20English.pdf.

Bahçe, Seçil A. Kaya and Emel Memiş. 2013. "Estimating the Impact of the 2008–09 Economic Crisis on Work Time in Turkey." *Feminist Economics* 19(3): 181–207.

Bahramitash, Roksana. 2004. "Market Fundamentalism versus Religious Fundamentalism: Women's Employment in Iran." *Critique: Critical Middle Eastern Studies* 13(1): 33–46.

Bahramitash, Roksana and Jennifer Olmsted. 2014. "Choice and Constraint in Paid Work: Women from Low-Income Households in Tehran." *Feminist Economics* 20(4): 470–90.

Bakker Isabella. 1999. "Development Policies." In *The Elgar Companion to Feminist Economics,* edited by Janice Peterson and Margaret Lewis, 83–94. Cheltenham, UK: Edward Elgar.

Balakrishnan, Radhika and Diane Elson. 2011. "Introduction: Economic Policies and Human Rights Obligations." In *Economic Policy and Human Rights,* edited by Radhika Balakrishnan and Diane Elson, 1–27. New York: Zed Books.

Basaruddin, Azza. 2013. "Anthropology." In *Women and Islamic Cultures: Disciplinary Paradigms and Approaches 2003–2013,* edited by Suad Joseph, 21–36. Leiden: Brill.

GENDER AND ECONOMICS IN MUSLIM COMMUNITIES

Basu, Srimati. 2012. "Judges of Normality: Mediating Marriage in the Family Courts of Kolkata, India." *Signs* 37(2): 469–92.

Benería, Lourdes. 2008. "The Crisis of Care, International Migration, and Public Policy." *Feminist Economics* 14(3): 1–21.

Benería, Lourdes, Günseli Berik, and Maria Floro. Forthcoming. *Gender, Development and Globalization*, 2nd ed. London: Routledge.

Benjamin, Orly. 2008. "Roots of the Neoliberal Takeover in Israel." *Challenge* 110, July/August. http://www.challenge-mag.com/en/article_224/roots_of_the_neo liberal_takeover_in_israel.

Bergmann, Barbara. 1995. "Becker's Theory of the Family: Preposterous Conclusions." *Feminist Economics* 1(1): 141–50.

Berik, Günseli. 1997. "The Need for Crossing the Method Boundaries in Economics Research." *Feminist Economics* 3(2): 121–5.

Berik, Günseli and Nilüfer Çağatay. 1991. "Transition to Export-led Growth in Turkey: Is There a Feminization of Employment?" *Review of Radical Political Economics* 22(1): 115–34.

Berik, Günseli and Ebru Kongar. 2013. "Time Allocation of Married Mothers and Fathers in Hard Times: The 2007–09 US Recession." *Feminist Economics* 19(3): 208–37.

Bernal, Victoria and Inderpal Grewal, eds. 2014. *Theorizing NGOs: States, Feminisms, and Neoliberalism*. Durham: Duke University Press.

Boserup, Ester. 1970. *Woman's Role in Economic Development*. New York: St. Martin's Press.

Boyles, Corinne and Aiko Shibata. 2009. "Job Satisfaction, Work Time, and Well-Being Among Married Women in Japan." *Feminist Economics* 15(1): 57–84.

Braunstein, Elissa. 2014. "Patriarchy versus Islam: Gender and Religion in Economic Growth." *Feminist Economics* 20(4): 268–96.

Braunstein, Elissa and Nancy Folbre. 2001. "To Honor and Obey: Efficiency, Inequality, and Patriarchal Property Rights." *Feminist Economics* 7(1): 25–44.

Brewer, Rose M., Cecilia A. Conrad, and Mary C. King. 2002. "The Complexities and Potential of Theorizing Gender, Caste, Race, and Class." *Feminist Economics* 8(2): 3–18.

Çağatay, Nilüfer and Korkut Ertürk. 2004. *Gender and Globalization: A Macroeconomic Perspective*. ILO Working Paper 19. http://www.ilo.int/wcmsp5/groups/public/—dgreports/—integration/documents/publication/wcms_079097.pdf.

Çavdar, Gamze and Yavuz Yaşar. 2014. "Moving Beyond Culturalism and Formalism: Islam, Women, and Political Unrest in the Middle East." *Feminist Economics* 20(4): 243–67.

Charusheela, S. 2008. "Social Analysis and the Capabilities Approach: A Limit to Martha Nussbaum's Universalist Ethics." *Cambridge Journal of Economics* 33(6): 1135–52.

Charusheela, S. and Eiman Zein-Elabdin. 2004. *Postcolonialism Meets Economics*. London: Routledge.

Coleman, Margaret. 1999. "Labor Force Participation." In *The Elgar Companion to Feminist Economics*, edited by Janice Peterson and Margaret Lewis, 500–5. Cheltenham, UK: Edward Elgar.

Connelly, Matthew. 2008. *Fatal Misconception: The Struggle to Control World Population*. Cambridge, MA: Belknap Press.

cooke, miriam. 2002. "Islamic Feminism Before and After September 11th." *Duke Journal of Gender Law and Policy* 9: 227–35.

Crenshaw, Kimberlé. 1991. "Mapping the Margins: Intersectionality, Identity Politics, and Violence Against Women of Color." *Stanford Law Review* 43(6): 1241–99.

Deeb, Lara. 2006. *An Enchanted Modern: Gender and Public Piety in Shi'i Lebanon*. Princeton, NJ: Princeton University Press.

Elson, Diane, ed. 1995. *Male Bias in the Development Process*. Manchester: Manchester University Press.

Escobar, Arturo. 1984. "Discourse and Power in Development and the Relevance of His Work to the Third World." *Alternatives* 10(3): 377–400.

Fluri, Jennifer L. 2009. "The Beautiful 'Other': A Critical Examination of 'Western' Representations of Afghan Feminine Corporeal Modernity." *Gender, Place and Culture: A Journal of Feminist Geography* 16(3): 241–57.

Folbre, Nancy and Julie A. Nelson. 2000. "For Love or Money – Or Both?" *Journal of Economic Perspectives* 14(4): 123–40.

Fraser, Nancy. 1994. "After The Family Wage: Gender Equity and the Welfare State." *Political Theory* 22(4): 591–618.

Giunchi, Elisa. 2010. "The Reinvention of Shari'a under the British Raj: In Search of Authenticity and Certainty." *Journal of Asian Studies* 69(4): 1119–42.

Glendon, Mary Ann. 1997. *The Transformation of Family Law: State, Law, and Family in the United States and Western Europe.* Chicago: University of Chicago Press.

Grewal, Inderpal and Caren Kaplan. 1994. "Introduction: Transnational Feminist Practices and Questions of Postmodernity." In *Scattered Hegemonies: Postmodernity and Transnational Feminist Practices*, edited by Inderpal Grewal and Caren Kaplan, 1–33. Minneapolis: University of Minnesota Press.

Grossbard-Shechtman, Shoshona and Shoshona Neuman. 1998. "The Extra Burden of Moslem Wives: Clues from Israeli Women's Labor Supply." *Economic Development and Cultural Change* 46(3): 491–517.

Hale, Sondra. 1995. "Gender and Economics: Islam and Polygamy – A Question of Causality." *Feminist Economics* 1(2): 67–79.

Halperin-Kadderi, Ruth. 2004. *Women in Israel: A State of Their Own.* Philadelphia: University of Pennsylvania Press.

Hartmann, Betsy and Elizabeth Barajas-Román. 2011. "The Population Bomb is Back – with a Global Warming Twist." In *The Women, Gender and Development Reader*, edited by Nalini Visvanathan, Lynn Duggan, Nan Wiegersma, and Laurie Nisonoff, 327–33. London: Zed Books.

Hassani-Nezhad, Lena and Anna Sjögren. 2014. "Unilateral Divorce for Women and Labor Supply in the Middle East and North Africa: The Effect of Khul Reform." *Feminist Economics* 20(4): 323–47.

Hasso, Frances. 2009. "Empowering Governmentalities Rather Than Women: The *Arab Human Development Report 2005* and Western Development Logics." *International Journal of Middle East Studies* 41(1): 63–82.

Hersh, Seymour M. 2004. "The Gray Zone: How a Secret Pentagon Program Came to Abu Ghraib." *New Yorker*, May 24.

Işık, Damla. 2014. "'Just Like Prophet Muhammad Preached': Labor, Piety, and Charity in Contemporary Turkey." *Feminist Economics* 20(4): 422–44.

Jaggar, Alison. 2006. "Reasoning About Well-Being: Nussbaum's Methods of Justifying the Capabilities." *Journal of Political Philosophy* 14(3): 301–22.

Jamal, Amaney and Vickie Langohr. 2013. "Political Science." In *Women and Islamic Cultures: Disciplinary Paradigms and Approaches 2003–2013*, edited by Suad Joseph, 269–82. Leiden: Brill.

Jamal, Manal. 2012. "Democracy Promotion, Civil Society Building, and the Primacy of Politics." *Comparative Political Studies* 45(1): 3–31.

Kabeer, Naila. 1994. *Reversed Realities: Gender Hierarchies in Development Thought.* New York: Verso.

———. 1999. "Resources, Agency, Achievements: Reflections on the Measurement of Women's Empowerment." *Development and Change* 30(3): 435–64.

Kabeer, Naila, Lopita Huq, and Simeen Mahmud. 2014. "Diverging Stories of 'Missing Women' in South Asia: Is Son Preference Weakening in Bangladesh?." *Feminist Economics* 20(4): 348–73.

GENDER AND ECONOMICS IN MUSLIM COMMUNITIES

Kandiyoti, Deniz. 2013. "Fear and Fury: Women and Post-Revolutionary Violence." *Open Democracy 50.50*, January 10. https://www.opendemocracy.net/5050/deniz-kandiyoti/fear-and-fury-women-and-post-revolutionary-violence.

Kaul, Nitasha. 2004. "Writing Economic Theory an*Other* Way." In *Postcolonialism Meets Economics*, edited by S. Charusheela and Eiman Zein-Elabdin, 183–200. London: Routledge.

Killian, Caitlin. 2007/2008. "Covered Girls and Savage Boys: Representations of Muslim Youth in France." *Journal of Social and Ecological Boundaries* 3(1): 69–90.

Kuru, Ahmet. 2009. *Secularism and State Policies toward Religion: The United States, France, and Turkey*. Cambridge: Cambridge University Press.

Ledewitz, Bruce. 2011. *Church, State, and the Crisis in American Secularism*. Bloomington: Indiana University Press.

Liptak, Adam. 2014. "Court Limits Birth Control Rule." *New York Times*, July 1.

Mabsout, Ramzi and Irene van Staveren. 2010. "Disentangling Bargaining Power from Individual and Household Level to Institutions: Evidence on Women's Position in Ethiopia." *World Development* 38(5): 783–96.

Mahmood, Saba. 2008. "Feminism, Democracy, and Empire: Islam and the War of Terror." In *Women's Studies on the Edge*, edited by Joan Scott, 81–114. Durham, NC: Duke University Press.

Marso, Lori Jo. 2007. "Feminism and the Complications of Freeing the Women of Afghanistan and Iraq." In *W Stands for Women: How the George W. Bush Presidency Shaped a New Politics of Gender*, edited by Michaele L. Ferguson and Lori Jo Marso, 221–43. Durham, NC: Duke University Press.

McIntosh, Peggy. 1988. "White Privilege: Unpacking the Invisible Knapsack." *Peace and Freedom* (July/August): 9–10.

Menjívar Cecilia. 2006. "Global Processes and Local Lives: Guatemalan Women's Work and Gender Relations at Home and Abroad." *International Labor and Working-Class History* 70(1): 86–105.

Moghadam, Valentine M. 2002. "Islamic Feminism and its Discontents: Toward a Resolution of the Debate." *Signs* 27(4): 1135–70.

———. 2003. *Modernizing Women: Gender and Social Change in the Middle East*. Boulder, CO: Lynne Rienner Publications.

———. 2013. "What is Democracy? Promises and Perils of the Arab Spring." *Current Sociology* 61(4): 393–408.

Mohammad, Robina. 2013. "Geography." In *Women and Islamic Cultures: Disciplinary Paradigms and Approaches 2003–2013*, edited by Suad Joseph, 103–26. Leiden: Brill.

Mohanty, Chandra T. 1984. "Under Western Eyes: Feminist Scholarship and Colonial Discourses." *boundary 2* 12(3): 333–58.

Narayan, Uma. 1997. *Dislocating Cultures: Identities, Traditions, and Third World Feminism*. New York: Routledge.

Nazir, Sameena and Leigh Tomppert. 2005. *Women's Rights in the Middle East and North Africa: Citizenship and Justice*. Lanham: Rowman & Littlefield.

NORAD. 2013. *Lobbying for Faith and Family: A Study of Religious NGOs at the United Nationso*. http://www.norad.no/no/resultater/publikasjoner/norads-rapportserie/publikasjon/_attachment/401798?_download=true&_ts=13d91dd065b.

Nussbaum, Martha C. 2000. *Women and Human Development: The Capabilities Approach*. New York: Cambridge University Press.

———. 2003. "Capabilities as Fundamental Entitlements: Sen and Social Justice." *Feminist Economics* 9(2–3): 33–59.

———. 2004. "Beyond the Social Contract: Capabilities and Global Justice. An Olaf Palme Lecture, Delivered in Oxford on 19 June 2003." *Oxford Development Studies* 32(1): 3–18.

GENDER AND ECONOMICS IN MUSLIM COMMUNITIES

Olmsted, Jennifer. 1997. "Telling Palestinian Women's Economic Stories." *Feminist Economics* 3(2): 141–51.

———. 2002. "Assessing Religion's Impact on Gender Status – A Comment on 'The Extra Burden of Moslem Wives: Clues from Israeli Women's Labor Supply'." *Feminist Economics* 8(3): 99–111.

———. 2003. "Economics." In *Encyclopedia of Women and Islamic Cultures*, Vol. 1: *Methodologies, Paradigms and Sources*, edited by Suad Joseph, 165–82. Leiden: Brill.

———. 2004. "Orientalism and Economic Methods: (Re)reading Feminist Economic Texts." In *Postcolonialism Meets Economics*, edited by S. Charusheela and Eiman Zein-Elabdin, 162–82. London: Routledge.

———. 2005. "Is Paid Work the (Only) Answer? Neoliberalism, Arab Women's Well-Being, and the Social Contract." *Journal of Middle East Women's Studies* 2(1): 112–39.

Pew Forum. 2008. "Unfavorable Views of Jews and Muslims on the Increase in Europe." http://www.pewglobal.org/files/2008/09/Pew-2008-Pew-Global-Attitudes-Report-3-September-17-2pm.pdf.

———. 2011a. "Table: Muslim Population by Country." http://www.pewforum.org/2011/01/27/table-muslim-population-by-country/#.

———. 2011b. "The Future of the Global Muslim Population." http://www.pewforum.org/2011/01/27/the-future-of-the-global-muslim-population/.

Pujol, Michèle, ed. 1997. "Explorations – A Special Explorations on Field Work and Methodology." Special Issue, *Feminist Economics* 3(2): 119–51.

Raisher, Josh. 2014. "The State Doesn't Exist for You." *Foreign Policy* 206, May–June. http://www.foreignpolicy.com/articles/2014/05/01/the_state_doesnt_exist_for_you_israel_palestine_bedouin.

Rinaldo, Rachel. 2013a. "Sociology." In *Women and Islamic Cultures: Disciplinary Paradigms and Approaches 2003–2013*, edited by Suad Joseph, 339–60. Leiden: Brill.

———. 2013b. *Mobilizing Piety: Islam and Feminism in Indonesia*. New York: Oxford University Press.

Robeyns, Ingrid. 2003. "Sen's Capability Approach and Gender Inequality: Selecting Relevant Capabilities." *Feminist Economics* 9(2–3): 61–92.

Ruwanpura, Kanchana N. and Jane Humphries. 2004. "Mundane Heroines: Conflict, Ethnicity, Gender, and Female Headship in Eastern Sri Lanka." *Feminist Economics* 10(2): 173–205.

Said, Edward. 1978. *Orientalism*. New York: Vintage Books.

Scott, Joan C. 2010. *The Politics of the Veil*. Princeton, NJ: Princeton University Press.

Schueller, Malini Johar. 2007. "Area Studies and Multicultural Imperialism: The Project of Decolonizing Knowledge." *Social Text* 25(1): 41–62.

———. 2011. "Cross-Cultural Identification, Neoliberal Feminism, and Afghan Women." *Genders Online Journal* 53. http://www.genders.org/g53/g53_schueller.html.

Seguino, Stephanie. 2000. "Accounting for Gender in Asian Economic Growth." *Feminist Economics* 6(3): 27–58.

———. 2011. "Help or Hindrance? Religion's Impact on Gender Inequality in Attitudes and Outcomes." *World Development* 39(8): 1308–21.

Sen, Amartya K. 1993. "Capability and Well-Being." In *The Quality of Life*, edited by Martha Nussbaum and Amartya K. Sen, 30–53. New York: Oxford University Press.

———. 1999. *Development as Freedom* New York: Knopf.

———. 2004. "Capabilities, Lists, and Public Reason: Continuing the Conversation." *Feminist Economics* 10(3): 77–80.

Sen, Gita and Caren Grown. 1987. *Development, Crises and Alternative Visions: Third World Women's Perspectives*. London: Earthscan.

GENDER AND ECONOMICS IN MUSLIM COMMUNITIES

Shalhoub-Kevorkian, Nadera, Nina Griecci, Himmat Zubi, and Rachel Busbridge. 2014. "Funding Pain: Bedouin Women and Political Economy in the Naqab/Negev." *Feminist Economics* 20(4): 374–96.

Shehabuddin, Elora. 2008. *Reshaping the Holy: Development, Democracy, and Muslim Women in Bangladesh.* New York: Columbia University Press.

———. 2011. "Gender and the Figure of the 'Moderate Muslim': Feminism in the 21st Century." In *The Question of Gender: Engagements with Joan W. Scott's Critical Feminism,* edited by Judith Butler and Elizabeth Weed, 102–42. Bloomington: Indiana University Press.

Siddiqi, Dina. 2009. "Do Bangladeshi Factory Workers Need Saving? Sisterhood in the Post-Sweatshop Era." *Feminist Review* 91: 154–74.

Spierings, Niels. 2014. "The Influence of Patriarchal Norms, Institutions, and Household Composition on Women's Employment in Twenty-Eight Muslim-Majority Countries." *Feminist Economics* 20(4): 297–322.

Spivak, Gayatri. 1985. "Can the Subaltern Speak? Speculations on Widow Sacrifice." *Wedge* 7/8 (Winter/Spring): 120–30.

Stewart, Frances. 2013. "Global Horizontal (or Social) Inequalities." Leontief Prize Lecture, Tufts University. http://www.ase.tufts.edu/gdae/about_us/leontief/Stewart Lecture2013.pdf.

Tinker, Irene, ed. 1990. *Persistent Inequalities: Women and World Development.* New York: Oxford University Press.

UN Women. n.d. "Short History of CEDAW Convention." http://www.un.org/womenwa tch/daw/cedaw/history.htm (accessed August 2014).

UN Department of Economic and Social Affairs. n.d. "Allocation of Time and Time Use." http://unstats.un.org/unsd/demographic/sconcerns/tuse/ (accessed August 2014).

Wadud, Amina. 2006. *Inside the Gender Jihad: Women's Reform in Islam.* Oxford: Oneworld Press.

Wallace, Adryan. 2014. "Agency through Development: Hausa Women's NGOs and CBOs in Kano, Nigeria." *Feminist Economics* 20(4): 491–515.

World Bank. n.d.a. "DataBank." http://databank.worldbank.org/data/ (accessed July 2014).

———. n.d.b. "Poverty Statistics." http://povertydata.worldbank.org/poverty/cou ntry/IRN (accessed July 2014).

———. n.d.c. "Heavily Indebted Poor Countries (39 countries)." http://web.worldbank. org/WBSITE/EXTERNAL/TOPICS/EXTDEBTDEPT/0,,contentMDK:20260049~me nuPK:528655~pagePK:64166689~piPK:64166646~theSitePK:469043,00.html (accessed July 2014).

Yeğenoglu, Meyda. 1998. *Colonial Fantasies: Towards a Feminist Reading of Orientalism.* Cambridge: Cambridge University Press.

Moving Beyond Culturalism And Formalism: Islam, Women, And Political Unrest In The Middle East

Gamze Çavdar and Yavuz Yaşar

ABSTRACT

Scenes of political unrest throughout the Middle East are often coupled with media reports and public debates in the United States that have a recurring theme: the relationship between women and Islam. After discussing the culturalist accounts that portray women as being in grave danger from Islam and in need of Western protection and supervision, this contribution examines an emerging trend in political science developed under the influence of the formalism of neoclassical economics. The study argues that despite ostensibly universal assumptions about human behavior and alleged objectivity, the theoretical foundations of neoclassical economics and its methodological formalism fall short in providing an alternative to culturalism, and, instead, reinforce the misperceptions and misunderstandings about the region.

INTRODUCTION

Since December 2010, after the self-immolation of a Tunisian vegetable seller sparked waves of protests, the Middle East region has witnessed unprecedented political activism.[1] The uprisings eventually led to the ousters of presidents and a possible emergence of new regimes in Tunisia, Egypt, and Libya, and have posed significant challenges to the existing authoritarian governments in Bahrain, Yemen, and Syria, among others. Scenes of the ongoing political unrest are often coupled with media reports and public debates in the United States that have a recurring theme: women threatened by Islam. These accounts repeatedly express concerns about a likely eradication of women's rights under the newly emerging regimes, and they imply Western protection.

GENDER AND ECONOMICS IN MUSLIM COMMUNITIES

While the issue of gender inequality in Muslim societies is indeed challenging and persistent, the remarkable characteristic of these accounts is a highly ethnocentric and paternalistic stance toward women, who are portrayed as being in grave danger from Islam, with the West depicted as savior.[2] A large body of scholarship has long criticized such culturalist explanations, arguing that Islam is neither more nor less patriarchal than the other Abrahamic religions and urging the use of other conceptual tools to understand Muslim women (Deniz Kandiyoti 1991; Valentine M. Moghadam 2001). The impact of this literature on public debates, however, has been minor, as similar characterizations of Islam tend to emerge repeatedly, especially in times of political crisis.

As an alternative to such culturalist accounts, a new scholarly trend has emerged recently in political science scholarship and its application to Middle East studies. This development is the use of the theoretical foundations of neoclassical theory and its methodological formalism, which has been the focus of feminist economic critiques as well as internal critiques within economics (see, for example, Julie Nelson 1995; Roger E. Backhouse 1998). Starting from universal assumptions that individuals are rational, autonomous, and self-interested, and relying on methodological formalism that consists of axiomatization, mathematization, and empirical testing, this approach has been advocated as a scientific and objective alternative to the specificity of Islam presented by culturalism (see the discussion on the hostility against area studies below). Although not yet applied to the Middle East uprisings, our research, discussed below, has revealed that this perspective represents the most prevalent framework being used to examine the Middle East in disciplinary and sub-disciplinary political science journals. An analysis of this trend illustrates the influence of neoclassical economics and its methodological formalism on the discipline and illuminates some of the common and persistent problems that emanate from it.

The main objective of this contribution is to criticize formalism emerging in Middle East studies especially under the influence of neoclassical theory. The study does so by first discussing the culturalist accounts of the Middle East, which formalism claims to oppose. Then, it examines two examples of formalist analyses (M. Steven Fish 2002; Lisa Blaydes and Drew A. Linzer 2008). The aim is to demonstrate that the use of formalism under the influence of neoclassical theory in Middle East studies has not only failed to provide an alternative to culturalism, but has also reinforced previous misconceptions about women and Islam. The study further argues that a better understanding of Middle Eastern women requires analytical tools used in a comparative, contextualized, and interdisciplinary fashion instead of an exclusive focus on the methods that give attention only to outcomes.

GENDER AND ECONOMICS IN MUSLIM COMMUNITIES

POPULAR UPRISINGS IN THE MIDDLE EAST: THE REINVENTION OF CULTURALISM

The peoples of the Middle East have been conceptualized as *sui generis* in some European and American scholarship, a practice that is rooted in colonialism:

> According to Lord Cromer, author of the 1908 pseudo-history *Modern Egypt*, their progress was "arrested" by the very fact of their being Muslim, by virtue of which their minds were as "strange" to that of a modern Western man "as would be the mind of an inhabitant of Saturn." (Mark LeVine 2011)

Others (Samuel P. Huntington 1993; Bernard Lewis 1993; Elie Kedourie 1994; Adrian Karatnycky 2002) also identified Islam as the villain: "Islam's democracy and freedom deficits .... appear to have something to do with the nature of Islam itself" (Charles K. Rowley and Nathanael Smith 2009: 298). In fact, these authors often argued, Middle Eastern societies lack almost everything required for modern politics:

> [T]here is no state, but only a ruler; no court, but only a judge. There is not even a city with defined powers, limits, and functions, but only an assemblage of neighborhoods, mostly defined by family, tribal, ethnic, or religious criteria, and governed by officials, usually military, appointed by the sovereign. (Lewis 1993: 94)

For these authors, Western supervision, control, and promotion of democracy offered the only hope for the development of liberal institutions and democracy and the emancipation of women, because "the small-scale autocracy of the home, especially the upper-class home, founded on polygamy, concubinage, and slavery, was preparation of an adult life of domination and acquiescence, and a barrier to the entry of liberal ideas" (Bernard Lewis 1996: 96). If democratic movements existed at all, they were "a consequence of the growing impact of the U.S. democracy and of American popular culture" (Lewis 1993: 91). After all, liberal democracy, "a product of the Judeo-Christian West," was alien to these "Islamic lands" (Lewis 1993: 93).[3]

Middle East experts from various disciplines have produced an impressive body of scholarship over the last three decades disputing the above-mentioned culturalist accounts that have been prevalent in some Western scholarship and the US popular media. Some have emphasized the roles of institutions, instead of culture, in shaping women's lives. Kandiyoti (1991) argued that women's lives vary greatly across Muslim societies, and their roles cannot be understood without understanding the political roles played by nation-states. Some experts demonstrated that even Islamist groups and parties are not uniform in their treatment of women, as their policies are shaped by women's activism and their relationship with the states that solidify reforms (Janine Astrid Clark and Jillian Schwedler 2003; Janine Astrid Clark 2006; Janine Astrid Clark and Amy E. Young 2008). Others criticized culturalism from a political economy perspective by demonstrating how neoliberal policies imposed by the International Monetary Fund (IMF) contribute to patriarchal structures (Nilüfer Çağatay and Günseli Berik 1994; Mervat Hatem 1994; Eleanor Abdella Doumato and Marsha Pripstein Posusney 2003; Valentine M. Moghadam 2005). Valentine M. Moghadam (2003) provided one of the most comprehensive and nuanced frameworks for understanding women's status in Muslim societies. Moghadam argued that a framework that takes into account class, the gender system, economic development, and state policies, instead of Islam, better explains Muslim women's status.

Among these responses, postcolonial studies have provided the most detailed criticism to culturalism. Following in the footsteps of Edward W. Said (1978), postcolonial scholarship has focused on demonstrating that the knowledge produced in some Western scholarship demonizes Middle Eastern people and justifies Western foreign policy objectives, such as colonialism and imperialism, while conveniently blaming local culture for all problems. Leila Ahmed (1993) criticized the commonly held conviction that Islamic societies are inherently oppressive to women by demonstrating the historical evolution of women's status in the Middle East. Lila Abu-Lughod (2002) argued that Muslim women do not need saving in her discussion on the "War on Terrorism." Elora Shehabuddin (2011) demonstrated that the "moderate Muslim" is a concept rooted in colonialism and is now used to justify some foreign policy objectives, and Frances S. Hasso (2009) criticized some global indicators, such as the Human Development Index, arguing that it is "part and parcel of transnational feminist governmentalities, which manage, normalize, and even constitute a range of inequalities among women" (68). Lila Abu-Lughod (2009) and Fida J. Adely (2009) similarly criticized the United Nation Development Programme's (UNDP) *Arab Development Report of 2005* for understating or ignoring the role of the West in the region's problems. The emphasis of postcolonial studies on the region's own cultural heritage has paved the way for Islamic feminism, a form of feminism rooted in the Islamic tradition. The West does not have the monopoly over women's empowerment and feminism, the Islamic feminists argue. By reinterpreting Islamic texts and the tradition, they aim to demonstrate that Islam and feminism are fully compatible (Leila Ahmed 1993, 2011; Margot Badran 1999, 2001, 2011; Isobel Coleman 2010).

Although critics of the culturalist accounts have reached no consensus about the exact determinants of women's lives, by adopting different theoretical approaches, they have provided examples of analyses that move

GENDER AND ECONOMICS IN MUSLIM COMMUNITIES

away from focusing on Islam to providing alternative frameworks of analysis and highlighting complexity and diversity. Their work remains sensitive to domestic contexts through ethnographic fieldwork, interviews, observation, and personal experience, all relying on regional languages.

The impact of this rich body of scholarship on public debates seems to be limited or absent, however, especially during times of political crisis. During the recent uprisings in the region, US media comments once again echoed culturalist claims. A paternalistic tone toward women and the fear of the danger of Islam remerged among pundits and policymakers alike. In a NPR radio interview with Michele Kelemen on March 9, 2011, US Secretary of State, Hillary Clinton, offered help:

> [We] certainly try to ensure that [women's] concerns are heard by the new Egyptian Government, because it would be a shame, with all of the extraordinary change that's going on in Egypt, if women were somehow not given their opportunity to be part of bringing about the new Egypt.

Some, including the Israeli analyst Barry Rubin, writing in the *Christian Science Monitor*, openly urged the US to back the authoritarian regime: "Mubarak may go, but his regime is necessary for US and Israeli security, regional stability, and keeping at bay the Islamic extremists that would rise in its place. Obama must support it" (2011).

What we argue here is not that the above-mentioned concerns about the Middle East uprisings are baseless because the uprisings will smoothly lead to democratic regimes. On the contrary, as the editors of *Middle East Report* (2011) write, "History, of course, is littered with revolutions interrupted, diverted, stolen and betrayed," and the fate of the recent uprisings has not been different. Nor is the point that women will be better off once autocrats collapse. In many Latin American and East European countries where the authoritarian regimes collapsed in the face of mass mobilization, Georgina Waylen writes, "popular movements organizing around practical gender interests have become increasingly marginal as the transition continues," and democratization and economic liberalization have negatively influenced women's interests concerning "reproductive rights, child care, and women's roles in the private sphere" (1994: 353). Our point is also not to stand up for Islamist movements, as they, like other faith-based movements, call for control over women's bodies and encourage women's submission to patriarchal values (Badran 2001; Moghadam 2001; Gamze Çavdar 2010). Rather, the idea is that behind the recurring concerns about women and Islam lie highly motivated political goals that aim to justify Western imperialism, intervention, and supervision (Clare Midgley 1998; Abu-Lughod 2002; Dana L. Cloud 2004; Shehabuddin 2011), instead of a "genuine commitment to eradicating the oppression faced by women" (Krista Hunt 2002: 116).[4]

GENDER AND ECONOMICS IN MUSLIM COMMUNITIES

This "feminism as imperialism," as Katherine Viner labels it (2002), is particularly evident in the selection of the cases for which ostensible concerns about women are raised as well as their timing. For instance, like Lord Cromer, a British colonial administrator, who wrote that Egyptian women's only hope for emancipation was Western supervision (Viner 2002), then-US president George W. Bush, who can be accused of being many things but not of being a feminist, suddenly became concerned about the well-being of Afghani and Iraqi women right *before* the US invasions (Abu-Lughod 2002; Lori Jo Marso 2007; Shehabuddin 2011). However, Bush ignored the fact that some of the worst atrocities against women in Afghanistan were committed during the Islamist regime of the Mujahideen (1992–6), which had grown strong as a result of American assistance in their fight against the Soviet Union (Barnett Rubin 1995; Moghadam 2003). Neither did Bush mention that the women of Afghanistan and Iraq were not liberated by the invasions. Rather, thousands of them were either killed by "smart bombs" or subjected to unprecedented violence "due to the social dislocation, economic hardship, ethnic and sectarian tensions, and endemic corruption that characterize the country today" (Nadje Al-Ali and Nicole Pratt 2011: 34).

Similarly, while evincing concern about Middle Eastern women in their speeches both President Barack Obama and former US Secretary of State Hillary Clinton remained silent about the misery of millions of Palestinian women living in refugee camps and under Israeli occupation for decades. The timing of the US media's favorite stories is also unmistakably strategic: an Afghani woman whose nose was cut off was covered in a *Time Magazine* August 2010 story entitled, "What Happens if We Leave Afghanistan?" exactly *when* the possibility of American withdrawal from Afghanistan was on the agenda (Aryn Baker 2010). A Libyan woman who was allegedly raped by pro-Gaddafi soldiers became another favorite story while many were questioning the North Atlantic Treaty Organization's (NATO) air strike on Libya (David D. Kirkpatrick 2011). Hardly a day goes by without a US media report on the danger of the emerging Islamist governments in the region. But, questions such as the following ones are seldom addressed by US government officials and media: Didn't the US contribute to the region's decades-long authoritarianism? Why was the US concerned about working with the Tunisian Rebirth Party (*Hizb al-Nahda*) and the Egyptian Muslim Brotherhood (*Ikhwan Al-Muslimin*) while it has no problem being a staunch ally of Saudi Arabia, which promotes a highly conservative agenda for women?[5]

FORMALISM: A VIABLE ALTERNATIVE?

The culturalist accounts of the Middle East have lately been challenged by a trend in political science influenced by neoclassical economics. The field

GENDER AND ECONOMICS IN MUSLIM COMMUNITIES

of political science had long been impressed with the ostensibly scientific assertions of economics and wanted to imitate its methods, a tendency that began in the 1950s and accelerated in the 1990s:

> A curious and little-noted ideological development accompanied the end of the Cold War. Just as the United States was stridently proclaiming its 'victory' over the materialism of the former USSR, its academic political science establishment was endorsing a form of economic determinism that is more rigid and less insightful than the Marxism it had seemingly discredited. (Chalmers Johnson 1997: 170)

Johnson argues that this development was the beginning of the "colonization" of political science by neoclassical economics, as political scientists began to "envy the prestige attached to academic economics in contemporary Anglo-American political culture and [wished] to acquire a little of that aura of authority for themselves" (170). They did so by joining what Johnson calls the "we-too-can-be-economists fad" (171).

Striving to be objective and scientific, neoclassical economic theory assumes that individuals are rational, self-interested, and autonomous. Accordingly, individuals who are fully aware of their interests try to maximize their gains and minimize their losses. These individuals are assumed to have three additional characteristics, namely "*fully ordered preferences,*" "*complete information,*" and "a *perfect internal computer*" (Martin Hollis 1995: 116; emphasis in original). A mainstream economist thus begins research by constructing a utility function for the rational agent's underlying motivations. Since the axioms apply to any time and society, rational agents can be consumers, producers, the state, voters, or the whole nation, just as their underlying motivations may include buying, selling, being autocratic, marrying, voting, or making a decision about war or peace. What usually follows is the use of mathematics (such as set theory or topology) to prove the existence and uniqueness of equilibrium and optimization of results (for example, maximization of utility or profit). The results of theoretical constructs are usually demonstrated by comparative-statics exercises and tested by regression analyses. Such formalism has been the dominant, if not almost uniform, way of conducting science in economics in modern journals since the 1920s (Backhouse 1998).

Backhouse (1998) identifies three different methodological formalisms in economics: axiomatization, mathematization, and empirical testing. Axiomatization reduces the main matters of knowledge to a set of independent axioms on which it makes propositions according to well-defined logical rules. Mathematization simply utilizes mathematical techniques (such as geometry, algebra, set theory, topology, etc.) in economic arguments. The empirical testing is used to solve specific problems based on a set of methods that are determined by a common consent. Obvious examples are the increased use of optimizing models of behavior, probabilistic models (such as linear regression models), and hypothesis testing. Although formalism could potentially help with rigor, clarity, and unambiguous demonstration, it is not problem free (Backhouse 1998; Victoria Chick 1998). Its problems can be grouped into two categories: (1) those associated with axiomatic as well as mathematization aspects and (2) those associated with the empirical aspects of formalism. Regarding the former, the use of formal methods can alter original (economic or political) theories by turning them into pure analytical statements that are appropriate for scrutiny by the methods themselves.[6] In addition, mathematical models are necessarily mechanistic and deterministic, even if stochastic, since they lay out in advance what is to happen. This characteristic does not mean they have no value; rather, it means they can explain only a known or presumed facet of reality or of the phenomena in question. Moreover, a common practice in mathematical modeling is to demonstrate the impact of one independent variable (for example: quantity consumed) on the dependent one (for example: utility) while holding all other relevant variables constant. This comparative-statics method, however, ignores the role of time as well as the interaction between variables (Chick 1998).

The fascination of political science with the so-called value-free, objective, and scientific research began with the behavioralist revolution after the Second World War, in which "[q]uantification, whenever possible and plausible, assumed an important place in the discipline" and through which the discipline "became adept at using a vast array of increasingly sophisticated and empirical and quantitative techniques – questionnaires, interviews, sampling, regression analysis, factor analysis, rational modeling, and the like" (David Easton 1993: 295). As Easton, one of the pioneers of this approach, argued, the ideological underpinning of this development was that ideology came to an end in the 1950s and the 1960s in the US. However, Easton continues, "it is clear that ideology had not disappeared but only seemed to have ended, because mainstream, liberal-conservative ideology was dominant and unchallenged for the moment" (297).

The subsequent period, dominated by rational choice theories under the influence of neoclassical economics, transformed the political science discipline and further encouraged the use of formalism. Rational choice theory, a slightly revised version of neoclassical economics, shares the main assumptions: "(a) that individuals are selfish, (b) that interpersonal utility comparisons are impossible, (c) that tastes are exogenous to the theory and unchanging, and (d) that individuals are rational" (Paula England and Barbara Stanek Kilbourne 1990:160). The premise that voters and politicians are essentially the same utility and interest maximizers and that they face the same constraints, respond to the same incentives, and engage in the same strategic calculations appealed to political scientists who were keen on applying universal methods of analysis based on inference.

40

GENDER AND ECONOMICS IN MUSLIM COMMUNITIES

The 1990s' promotion of formalism, accompanied by hostility toward qualitative research, was best articulated by Robert Bates, then-president of the American Political Science Association. Bates accused the area specialists of having "defected from the social sciences into the camp of the humanists" (1996: 1). As evidence of this "defection," Bates offered "their commitment to the study of history, languages, and culture, as well as their engagement with interpretivist approaches to scholarship" and their lack of familiarity with mathematical approaches to the study of politics (1).

The net outcome of the hostility toward area studies has been their marginalization in top political science journals. Andrew Bennett, Aharon Barth, and Kenneth R. Rutherford (2003) found that qualitative or case study research in American politics has almost disappeared over time (comprising only 1 percent of articles in 1999–2000), and that *American Political Science Review*, the flagship publication of the American Political Science Association, published the fewest number of articles using qualitative and case study methods (375). As of 2000, formal modeling and statistics methods combined constituted more than 70 percent of all articles published among the seven top political science journals in all subfields.

EMERGING FORMALISM ON ISLAM AND THE MIDDLE EAST IN POLITICAL SCIENCE

Middle East studies long remained outside the discipline of political science because of the institutional separation from political science departments. Pursuing different questions and methods, Middle East studies have largely continued to be policy oriented and case-study based, grounded in fieldwork and qualitative data.[7] Middle East studies also include regional experts among political scientists, who have aimed to bridge the gap with the general political science discipline; they have already produced rich, nuanced analyses for a number of decades.

However, an examination of the top disciplinary and sub-disciplinary journals in political science suggests that an emerging formalist trend applied to the Middle East and the Muslim world tends to ignore the body of literature previously produced by regional experts.[8] Specifically, this body of literature either (1) relies on the concepts of neoclassical theory and clearly and explicitly uses its assumptions, which are later empirically tested (Mario Ferrero 2005; Michael Munger 2006; C. Christine Fair and Bryan Shepherd 2006; Claude Berrebi and Esteban F. Klor 2008; Blaydes and Linzer 2008); or (2) it relies only on empirical testing, which is one of the manifestations of methodological formalism (Christopher Clague, Suzanne Gleason, and Stephen Knack 2001; Fish 2002; Ronald Inglehart and Pippa Norris 2003a, Ronald Inglehart and Pippa Norris 2003b; John Anderson 2004; Rollin F. Tusalem 2009; Feryal M. Cherif 2010). Despite the variation in method, data, and the specifics of the researchers' arguments,

41

GENDER AND ECONOMICS IN MUSLIM COMMUNITIES

this body of literature takes Islam as the determining factor for the actions of its members in those societies, a feature of culturalism. Attention to the analyses of Islam, terrorism, and women[9] – especially the relationship between Islam and gender equality – constitutes an important point of focus in this literature (Fish 2002; Inglehart and Norris 2003a, 2003b; Blaydes and Linzer 2008; Cherif 2010). In what follows, two examples of this formalist trend as it applies to gender are examined in detail. The works by Fish (2002) and Blaydes and Linzer (2008) are selected for their representativeness of formalism. Both articles start out by making some universal assumptions about human behavior and utilizing quantitative techniques that aim to discover universal trends. However, they still draw similar conclusions with culturalism.

"ISLAM AND AUTHORITARIANISM," BY STEVEN FISH

Fish begins his article by asking, "Are predominantly Muslim societies distinctly disadvantaged in democratization?" (2002: 4). He particularly seeks "to establish empirically whether a democratic deficit really exists, [and] if so, how it can be explained" (5). After demonstrating this deficit in empirical terms, Fish argues that gender inequity is the root cause of authoritarianism in Muslim-dominated countries.

Fish's article is long and his argument takes a number of unexpected turns. The discussion below focuses on two grounds of Fish's argument: (1) variable selection and (2) regression results and discussions.

Variables

Fish leaves no doubt about his commitment to methodological formalism by making it clear at the outset that he chose only those variables "commonly regarded as structural and cultural variables, as well as several historical variables that *are amenable to coding in 'yes' or 'no' terms*" (2002: 5–6; emphasis added). Fish also adds that he tests "only hypotheses that are *tractable to quantitative analysis* and that are manifestly distinct from the dependent variable" (5–6; emphasis added). Thus, the trajectory of his study, which is to understand the causal relationship between Islam and regime type, is left to the mercy of binary quantifiable variables and quantitative testing, which exclusively focuses on the question of "how many" while leaving out the crucial question of "how" (Günseli Berik 1997; Jennifer C. Olmsted 1997). In addition, Fish treats each variable according to the principles of comparative statics, losing the richness of interactions and relations between the variables.

Following this data-driven variable selection criterion, Fish considers a set of variables that are commonly employed in similar empirical research.[10] Only two are examined here: democracy and Islam. For the democracy variable, Fish uses Dahl's electoral–procedural definition of democracy, which takes elections as the main indicators of democracy, and is apparently also adopted by Freedom House and Polity scores, the datasets that are frequently used to operationalize the democracy variable. Dahl's definition of democracy is extremely narrow and even misleading because it mainly considers elections as the defining characteristics of a democratic system.[11] Moreover, Fish's operationalization (for example, Freedom House ratings or the Polity scores) carries a significant degree of political bias (Charles Tilly 2007), a point admitted even by Paul Gottfried (2011), one of the leading conservatives in the US:

> It [Freedom House] is in sync with the liberal interventionism that has dominated American foreign policy since Woodrow Wilson. Not surprisingly, the foundation offers a culturally compatible view of the world. The good countries are the "liberal democracies" that look like us right now, and especially Western countries, which are under our hegemony. Therefore we needn't notice the appalling erosion of freedom that is going on in such countries, although we should be free to fault them for indulging fanatical Muslim minorities.

For Islam, the second variable, Fish defends his choice of using a dummy variable for "Islamic religious tradition" rather than a commonly used "percentage of Muslim" variable by arguing that the former has two advantages: overcoming the disparities in data and testing the hypothesis regarding the role of the predominance of Islam for democracy rather than "whether a society that is one-tenth Muslim is more or less likely to have an authoritarian regime than is a society that is one-eighth Muslim" (7). Whether Islam is measured as predominance or percentage of adherents among the population, its use as an explanatory variable is troubling. Such a variable would reflect only the quantity, in the form of either "predominance" or "percentage of Muslim" population, an operationalization that ignores the qualitative dimension of the variable, such as the way Islam is perceived and practiced from one society to another. As Berik (1997) argues, such data-driven research is unfortunately conducted at the expense of losing the subtleties of social phenomena and the opportunity to enrich the analysis accordingly.

Fish's regression results and discussions

In regression results, Fish finds a negative link between Islam and democracy that is "too stark and robust to ignore, neglect, or dismiss" (13). Next, he entertains "some plausible but unsatisfactory ideas" (such as those of Huntington) as to why a connection exists between Islam and authoritarianism (16). Fish identifies the possible arguments as "Islam being prone to political violence," "lack of interpersonal trust in Muslim countries," and "incompatibility of secularism and Islam" (16). He rejects the first two arguments on the basis of ANOVA tests and regression analyses comparing Catholic and Muslim countries. He uses a different strategy to discuss the last argument, which is to return to mostly theoretical and qualitative discussions in the literature in order to question "the usual association between secularism with democracy and religiosity with authoritarianism" (24). By providing examples from different societies and citing from the World Values Survey, Fish rejects this third argument as well.

After dismissing these explanations, Fish proposes an alternative account based on some "ethnographic research" and the "deep knowledge" of some scholars (24). From his selective reading of the literature, he concludes that Muslim societies exhibit an "unusual degree of subordination of women," which, he argues, "may affect life not only in the family and immediate community but also at higher levels as well" (24). To test this idea empirically, Fish operationalizes this "unusual degree of subordination of women" as the difference between men and women's literacy rates, the number of men per 100 women (sex ratio), women in government, and the Gender Empowerment Measure (GEM).

Here, Fish's analysis takes a more interesting turn. His new regression analysis finds a negative association between "Islamic religious tradition" and the Freedom House scores in the presence of each of these variables (19).[12] To explain these associations, Fish goes back to the literature and offers "some provisional theory" (29–33). First, he argues that the differentials between men and women's literacy rates and the sex ratio imbalances (two of the four variables above) are not only the characteristics of individuals, but also the characteristics of a family and a society as a whole.[13] Although Fish admits that this argument of "isomorphism between primary and social relations" is a culturalist one that is not supported empirically, he insists, "the possibility of connection should not be ignored" (30). Fish does not feel the need to provide further evidence to substantiate his claims.

Second, Fish contends that "extremely high sex ratios" have the potential to turn a regime into an authoritarian one, "especially in Muslim countries":

> They [high sex ratios] may create conditions under which young men are more likely to join militant groups and engage in threatening, anomic behavior that provokes official expression. Late marriages for males, who in some Muslim countries must by custom be economically capable of supporting wives who do not work, may contribute to male aggression and frustration, but sheer numbers exacerbate the problem. Countries with sex ratios that exceed 103/100 – which include Afghanistan, Iran, Jordan, Kuwait, Libya, Pakistan, Saudi Arabia, Somalia, Sudan, and Syria – are not bereft of mass social stress and movements of militant religious brotherhoods. (31–2)

Fish provides no evidence to support these two points – other than a parallel he constructs between high sex ratios and a Hollywood-style characterization of Muslim countries.[14]

This brief analysis of Fish's article suggests that Fish relied on three strategies to make his argument that gender inequity lies at the center of authoritarianism in Muslim countries. First, whenever convenient, Fish runs regression analyses and approves or rejects arguments on the basis of those results. He applies this strategy to test the arguments that Islam is the main cause of authoritarianism, is prone to political violence, and that Muslim countries lack interpersonal trust. In other cases, he adopts a second strategy to back his arguments, which is to simply cite literature in a highly selective way. In other cases, Fish uses a third strategy in which he provides no hard or soft evidence and cites no literature. Rather, he merely reiterates his own opinion and insists on its plausibility.

Fish's "provisional theory" belongs to the third category. He claims that only Muslim countries have an environment that is conducive to "extremely high sex ratios," which supposedly led to authoritarianism, despite the fact that other countries, such as India and China, show even higher trends in his data with respect to sex ratios, literacy gap, women in government, and the GEM (27). But, Fish insists:

> Finally, the findings presented in this article highlight a fundamental difference between two types of societies: on the one hand, those that have a reputation for male dominance and emphasis on clan and family honor but that nevertheless do not exhibit large sex disparities in basic indicators, and, on the other hand, those that do exhibit such disparities. (36)

Not surprisingly, Muslim countries belong to the former group.

What drives Fish's research, therefore, is the availability and quantifiability of his data as well as convenience and his own unsubstantiated convictions. Fish does not mind switching his methodology and/or arguments as long as they serve his own position well. In doing so, he proudly "saves" Islam from one culturalist view, criticizing Huntington's assertions with the help of other versions of culturalism by arguing that Islam is *sui generis* in oppressing women, and that Islam is a determining factor in women's lives.

"THE POLITICAL ECONOMY OF WOMEN'S SUPPORT FOR FUNDAMENTALIST ISLAM," BY LISA BLAYDES AND DREW LINZER

Blaydes and Linzer begin by asking why women adopt the values of "fundamentalist Islam" in Muslim countries (2008: 577).[15] Their answer is that women are offered "economic and social incentives" to choose

GENDER AND ECONOMICS IN MUSLIM COMMUNITIES

fundamentalist ideology over secularism (577). Specifically, although "Muslim women have a *choice* of whether or not to adopt and identify with fundamentalist belief systems" (580), "[w]omen with *limited economic opportunities* – whether due to unemployment, minimal formal education, or poverty – are more likely to take on *fundamentalist and traditionalist belief systems* that *enhance their value as potential marriage partners* . . . in *the marriage market*" (577–80; emphasis added). The authors test their hypothesis by employing latent class analysis and using data from the World Values Survey.

Blaydes and Linzer's study suffers from a number of problems. Only two sets of problems will be discussed here: (1) the rationality assumption; and (2) the study's data, variables, and methods. These problems are intertwined and compound one another.

The rationality assumption

The hypothesis represents a typical utility maximization problem of a rational individual operating in a market.[16] It is a type of problem that researchers know the answer to at the outset, even as they ask, "Why do individuals engage in seemingly nonrational behavior?" Since researchers – here, Blaydes and Linzer – assume all individuals are rational and will engage in strategic calculation as a way to maximize their gains and minimize their losses, the answer is meant only to reiterate this assumption and to demonstrate it in empirical terms. The answer, again, is similar: Muslim women, too, have the same utility maximization problem of whether to support or to refuse the ideology of Islamic fundamentalism (Blaydes and Linzer 2008). More specifically, these authors explain that Muslim women support "fundamentalist Islam" after calculating the costs and benefits of their individual actions in order to maximize their "material security" in a so-called "marriage market" (580).

Blaydes and Linzer claim that seeking financial security is a key determining factor for Muslim women and seem to assume that Muslim women are unique in this aim. They argue that only a few opportunities exist for "material security for women in the Muslim world," such as "gainful employment, marriage to a gainfully employed spouse, or some combination of the two" (583). In other words, women choose "fundamentalist Islam" because "personal piety and support for conservative, traditionalist gender norms have value in the marriage market and increase their marriageability" (583). Anomalies are treated the same way. When the authors discover that not all women fit into this category of deprivation, they provide an explanation for why "extremely well-educated" Muslim women also support "fundamentalist Islam." These women "may see opportunities for ... serving in a leadership capacity for the mass Islamist movement" (587).

Blaydes and Linzer's research adopts a typical game-like approach in which the researcher tirelessly addresses an imagined gap between what is an

GENDER AND ECONOMICS IN MUSLIM COMMUNITIES

expected human behavior, according to the market model's version of a rational human being, and what actually happens. This made-up puzzle is only meant to lend support to the theory's assumptions and hypotheses at the very end rather than to offer a research question that genuinely considers alternative explanations and/or makes modifications to the initial assumptions and hypotheses. Indeed, as is always the case, the reader who is urged to believe by the researcher at the outset that there is indeed an irrational/nonrational behavior (an anomaly) only discovers later on that the behavior is, in fact, rational (normal).

While seemingly flawless, this type of research presents a major problem – that is, the gap between what the theory assumes and the empirical world:

> The material about business behavior that students read about in economics textbooks, and almost all of the new theoretical material developed by mainstream professionals and published in the profession's leading journals, was composed by economists who sat down in their home or their office and .... simply made it up. (Barbara R. Bergman 2005: 55)

In other words, that initial, assumed gap between the expected and the actual exists only in the mind of a researcher who gives *a priori* consent to the theory's assumptions.[17] Therefore, even when we assume that Islamism does not serve women's interests, no puzzle begs to be solved because social phenomena are full of examples in which women (and men) engage in activities that are against their self-interests.

This type of scholarly endeavor comes with a price, which is the scant contribution of the research to the understanding of the actual political phenomenon examined – in this case, women's participation in Islamist movements. As Ian Shapiro writes, "If the problems posited are idiosyncratic artifacts of the researcher's theoretical priors, then they will seem tendentious, if not downright misleading, to everyone except those who are wedded to her priors" (2002: 561). This problem of method-driven research

> leads to self-serving construction of problems, misuse of data in various ways, and related pathologies summed up in the old adage that if the only tool you have is a hammer everything around you starts to look like a nail. Examples include collective action problems such as free riding that appear mysteriously to have been "solved" when perhaps it never occurred to anyone to free ride to begin with in many circumstances, or the concoction of elaborate explanations for why people "irrationally" vote, when perhaps it never occurred to most of them to think by reference to the individual costs and benefits of the voting act. (598)

GENDER AND ECONOMICS IN MUSLIM COMMUNITIES

Data, variables, and method

The origin of the data that Blaydes and Linzer use lies in the sociological theory of post-materialism originated by Ronald Inglehart, who created the Inglehart Index (World Values Survey).[18] Inglehart's main thesis is that technological change and economic growth result in changes in values, such as "traditional" and "modern," which, in turn, lead to "secular-rational and self-expression values." Such a binary and simplistic characterization of "traditional" and "modern" values is problematic, to say the least (Max Haller 2002). Nevertheless, Blaydes and Linzer often engage in sweeping generalizations containing references to "traditional," "Muslim," "fundamentalist," "secular," and the like. Moreover, what the authors consider to be characteristic of Muslim societies is hardly unique to Muslims: that the mother has a key role in the socialization of children, that women are expected to be pious and pure before marriage. Here, Muslims not only are assumed to be different from everyone else, but also are assumed to be homogenous, remaining the same across countries whether they are in Egypt, Tajikistan, Uzbekistan, Kazakhstan, the Balkans, or West Africa. This is because the authors have no problem with conducting "dozens of interviews" in Cairo and generalizing their results to all Egyptian women and even to the entire Muslim world.[19] Muslims, once again, appear to be aliens that exist outside the flow of history, remaining constant over time and place.

Blaydes and Linzer explain that they:

> operationalize fundamentalism as a composite belief system that spans two broad areas: preferences consistent with a traditionalist worldview that systematically favors men over women and personal piety and support for the confluence of politics and religion consistent with conservative Islamic values. (577)

While such an operationalization may be practical for the authors, since the authors rely on the quantitative data and have to operationalize their variables by using proxies, these variables do not measure "Islamic fundamentalism." How can patriarchy, personal piety, and marriage of politics and religion consistent with conservative religious values be the key qualifiers of fundamentalism? By these standards, a significant majority of the world's population in general (and Americans in particular) would be considered fundamentalist: a 2005 survey found that 62 percent of Americans consider religion "very important," and 37 percent support the notion that politics should reflect religious values.[20]

Blaydes and Linzer argue that the operationalization is valid because "debate over the status, roles, and rights of women in Islam" can be summarized as the tension between two opposite views; that is, the reinterpretation of the religious texts in a timely fashion versus the literal

GENDER AND ECONOMICS IN MUSLIM COMMUNITIES

interpretation of these texts (598). This understanding of Islamism defines the movement in theological terms, neglecting its social, economic, political, and organizational dimensions (Quintan Wiktorowicz 2004). The timing of Islamism's emergence, the rise and demise of Islamist groups' strength, and the vast variation among countries cannot be explained through theology, but rather through factors such as their relations with their respected states, the institutional structure within which they operate, the framing of their messages, and the organizational and financial advantages that the Islamists have (Wiktorowicz 2004).

The two articles discussed here exemplify the emerging trend in political science: to study the Middle East region through the lens of neoclassical assumptions and methods. The above discussion aims to demonstrate that the study of the Middle East through the lens of formalism, despite its seemingly alternative approach to culturalism, not only fails to explain the social phenomena at hand, but might lead to misleading conclusions.

CONCLUDING REMARKS

Claiming that Islam is the major explanatory variable for Muslim women's lives is a long-standing allegation, which can be disputed without mathematical and statistical analyses by simply applying common sense. First, "[a]dherence to Islamic precepts and the applications of Islamic legal codes differ throughout the Muslim world" (Moghadam 2003: 6). In the Middle East, Iran has a clerical rule, Turkey and Tunisia have secular civil codes, and the rest of the region (including Israel) follows religious laws with respect to personal status – an application that is also far from being uniform. Second, millions of Muslim women live in Muslim majority and non-Muslim majority countries, where secular laws and practices dominate and democracies operate, and Muslims find no contradiction with their faith. Third, in contrast to popular assumptions, Islam does not determine Muslims' political identities or dictate their lives. Muslims, like everyone else, are divided along the lines of gender, class, ethnicity, and the like. As a result, Muslim societies (just like others) do change over time and show great variation, illustrating that "the status of women in Muslim societies is neither uniform nor unchanging nor unique" (6). None of this means that Islam, or religion in general, is irrelevant to women's lives. Rather, it means that "[religion] is less central or problematical than it is often made out to be," once one takes into account the broader political, social, and economic contexts within which Islam is practiced, interpreted, and experienced (8).

With the rise of popular mobilizations across the Middle East, age-old culturalist accounts have emerged all over again. Highly ethnocentric and frustratingly resilient, culturalism is again dominating public debates and popular US media, giving Middle East specialists a feeling of *déjà vu* coupled with "I-thought-this-was-resolved-thirty-years-ago" disbelief. As the literature review above demonstrated, although a large body of area studies long ago refuted these claims and moved on, the new trend in political science scholarship, under the influence of neoclassical economics and its methodological formalism, is not capable of doing so. On the contrary, having belittled the cumulative knowledge of area studies as not being parsimonious, quantifiable, and scientific, this new trend has only reinforced and reproduced the persistent misconceptions about Muslim societies in general and the Middle East in particular.

The question of how we got here cannot be addressed without highlighting the intersection of academia and politics. The latest economic recession has revealed some of the chronic problems in the discipline of economics and the gap between what is assumed by neoclassical theory and the empirical world. As Paul Krugman (2009) once argued,

> economists, as a group, mistook beauty, clad in impressive-looking mathematics, for truth. [...] They turned a blind eye to the limitations of human rationality that often lead to bubbles and busts; to the problems of institutions that run amok; to the imperfections of markets – especially financial markets – that can cause the economy's operating system to undergo sudden, unpredictable crashes; and to the dangers created when regulators don't believe in regulation.

The obsession with formalism in the field of economics came at the expense of history and philosophy, which were banished during the 1960s and 1970s. This trend also manifested itself when leading economics journals stopped publishing philosophical and historical articles and history and philosophy were excluded from graduate and undergraduate curricula (Philip Mirowski 2010). No doubt this trend in scholarship developed hand in hand with the trend of neoliberalism advocated around the world.

Critics of formalism have to confront this problem in graduate programs first. As Peregrine Schwartz-Shea argues, adopting methodological pluralism and having "no *a priori* methodological commitments, only a commitment to addressing substantive questions using the conceptual and methodological resources," might be a good place to start (2003: 384). Furthermore, a dire need exists for a return to basics, such as requiring history, foreign language, and philosophy of science in the graduate curriculum across social science disciplines. Once we do that, perhaps economics and political science will not look like completely discrete disciplines, but will benefit from the cumulative knowledge produced by one another. Perhaps then the quest for dignity demanded all over the Middle East will not appear too alien to understand, but will become something everyone can relate to at a human level. And, perhaps then, too, as doctors of philosophy, we will deserve the "Ph" in our PhDs.

ACKNOWLEDGMENTS

An earlier version of this study was presented to the Annual Convention of the International Studies Association (ISA), March 17, 2011, Montreal, Canada. The research was supported by the 2011 Faculty Development Fund of the Liberal Arts College at Colorado State University. We thank the four anonymous reviewers and the editors of this special issue for their feedback and suggestions.

NOTES

[1] The Middle East is broadly defined here in a way to include the Middle East and North Africa.

[2] As used here, "the West" is a loose cultural, political, and economic entity characterized by advanced capitalism and liberal democracy.

[3] For similar points, see, for instance, Albert Howe Lybyer (1924) and Fauzi M. Najjar (1958).

[4] Our position here is not to reject any and every Western institution's intervention, but rather to criticize the manipulation of the concerns about women to justify foreign policy objectives.

GENDER AND ECONOMICS IN MUSLIM COMMUNITIES

5 See Edward W. Said (1981) and Elizabeth Poole (2002) for detailed criticism of the media's coverage of Islam.

6 For instance, formal methods could alter theories, as in the case of Adam Smith's famous invisible hand (Backhouse 1998). Smith originally suggested that individuals who can freely engage in any activity by pursuing their self-interest in a free society would advance the interest of society more effectively than "if they consciously sought to pursue the public interest" (Backhouse 1998: 1853). However, Smith's statement was not rigorous enough by the standards of modern mainstream economic theory. It was made more rigorous by turning agents into rational profit or utility maximizers who compete in "perfectly competitive" markets. According to Backhouse, such modifications changed the theory from "a proposition about the real world" to "a theorem about the properties of an abstract mathematical model: the theorem has become 'analytified' ... or 'de-empirized' ... Its empirical content has become (at least partially) lost" (1853).

7 Please see the *Journal of Middle East Studies* (the flagship journal of the Middle East Studies Association), *Middle East Journal, Middle East Studies, Middle East Policy,* and *Middle East Report,* among others.

8 We examined a total of 118 abstracts and 104 articles for the literature review. Our review particularly focused on journals identified by Gerardo L. Munk and Richard Snyder (2007) as disciplinary (*PS: Political Science, American Political Science Review,* and *American Journal of Political Science*) and sub-disciplinary journals (*Comparative Politics, World Politics, Comparative Political Studies,* and *International Studies Quarterly*) between 2005 and 2010.

9 Not every article published in political science journals exemplifies formalism or culturalism. For more nuanced analysis by political scientists who specialize in the Middle East, see Jamal A. Amaney (2007) and Augustus Richard Norton (2014). See also Michael L. Ross (2008), Niels Spierings, Jeroen Smits, and Mieke Verloo (2009), and Alice Kang (2009). For a critique of using Islam as the main explanatory variable for gender inequity, see Ross (2008).

10 Other variables are democracy, Islamic religious tradition, economic development, sociocultural division, economic performance, British colonial heritage, communist heritage, and natural resource abundance. Fish acknowledges that the variables of gross domestic product (GDP), per capita, and ethnolinguistic fractionalization scores are inadequate measures of economic development and sociocultural division within a society, respectively (2002: 14–6). However, his alternative measures (for example, the agrarian proportion of the population, ethnic homogeneity scores, etc.) still produce robust results. Fish also describes British colonial heritage as "the most empirically persuasive explanation for democracy in the developing world" (9).

11 This definition of democracy has long been criticized. See, for instance, Amartya Sen (2003).

12 To his credit, Fish admits "an obvious danger of bias due to endogeneity, particularly in the case of variables for women in government and the GEM" (2002: 29). But, having run two-stage least-squares regressions with almost identical results, he decides to use those variables despite the danger of endogeneity. In addition, one of the most reliable and often-used gender inequality measures, the GEM, is available for only fifty-four countries, of which only twenty are Muslim in Fish's regressions. This constraint not only reduces the overall sample size but more importantly excludes twenty-six other Muslim countries from the regression. However, this limitation does not seem to be a problem for the author.

13 This is commonly referred to in methodology as the fallacy of composition, or "arguing that because something is true of members of a group or collection, it is true of the group as a whole ... The fallacy of division is the converse fallacy of arguing that if something is true of a group, then it is also true of individuals belonging to it" (Simon

GENDER AND ECONOMICS IN MUSLIM COMMUNITIES

Blackburn 2008: 71). Fish also makes the latter mistake by constantly reducing Islam to a binary variable with the assumption that it is qualitatively the same religion for every Muslim country.

[14] Sex ratio measures the number of males for each female in population. Countries that have more males than females include China (119/100), India (108/100), Croatia (106/100), and the Czech Republic (106/100). For a discussion, see Naila Kabeer, Lopita Huq, and Simeen Mahmud (2013).

[15] Blaydes and Linzer use only the terms "Islamic fundamentalism" or "fundamentalist Islam." We will use these terms while discussing their research; however, we prefer to use the term "Islamism," as the former two terms fail to make a clear-cut distinction between religion and ideology.

[16] Neoclassical theory is adopted by political science with some modifications. The theory that mainly embraced neoclassical theory is rational choice theory. The basic assumptions of rational choice theory are: (1) ends/preferences are consistent and stable; (2) the selection of the means is a rational process; (3) actors pursue goals; (4) actors pursue their perceived self-interests; (5) behaviors result from conscious choice; and (6) actors possess extensive information on both the available alternatives and the likely consequences of their choices. According to rational choice theory, rationality applies to the means, not the ends. See Kristen Renwick Monroe (1991).

[17] For other critiques of the rationality assumption, see Monroe (1991), England and Kilbourne (1990), and Donald Green and Ian Shapiro (1994).

[18] The Index is based on Ronald Inglehart's (1997) book.

[19] The authors note that their observation about the significance of piousness in finding a marriage partner is based on interviews, but the article's empirical data are based on the World Values Survey.

[20] The polling was conducted by a private company for the Associated Press in the USA, Australia, Britain, Canada, France, Germany, South Korea, and Spain in 2005 (Ipsos-Public Affairs 2005)

REFERENCES

Abu-Lughod, Lila. 2002. "Do Muslim Women Really Need Saving? Anthropological Reflections on Cultural Relativism and Its Others." *American Anthropologies, New Series* 104(3): 783–90.

——. 2009. "Dialects of Women's Empowerment: The International Circuitry of the *Arab Human Development Report 2005*." *International Journal of Middle East Studies* 41(1): 83–103.

Adely, Fida J. 2009. "Educating Women for Development: *The Arab Human Development Report 2005* and the Problem with Women's Choices." *International Journal of Middle East Studies* 41(1): 105–22.

Ahmed, Leila. 1993. *Women and Gender in Islam: Historical Roots of a Modern Debate*. New Haven: Yale University Press.

——. 2011. *A Quiet Revolution: The Veil's Resurgence, from the Middle East to America*. New Haven: Yale University Press.

Al-Ali, Nadje and Nicole Pratt. 2011. "Conspiracy of Near Silence: Violence Against Iraqi Women." *Middle East Report* 41(258): 34–7.

Amaney, Jamal A. 2007. *Barriers to Democracy: The Other Side of Social Capital in Palestine and the Arab World*. Princeton, NJ: Princeton University Press.

Anderson, John. 2004. "Does God Matter? And If So, Whose God?" *Democratization* 11(4): 192–217.

GENDER AND ECONOMICS IN MUSLIM COMMUNITIES

Backhouse, Roger E. 1998. "If Mathematics is Informal, Then Perhaps We Should Accept That Economics Must Be Informal Too." *The Economic Journal* 108(451): 1848–58.

Badran, Margot. 1999. "Toward Islamic Feminisms: A Look at the Middle East." In *Hermeneutics and Honor: Negotiating Female "Public" Space in Islamic/ate Societies*, edited by Asma Afsaruddin, 159–88. Cambridge, MA: Harvard Center for Middle Eastern Studies.

———. 2001. "Understanding Islam, Islamism, and Islamic Feminism." *Journal of Women's History* 13(1): 47–52.

———. 2011. *Feminism in Islam: Secular and Religious Convergences*. Oxford: Oneworld Publications.

Baker, Aryn. 2010. "What Happens if We Leave Afghanistan?" *Time Magazine*, August 9.

Bates, Robert. 1996. "Letter from the President: Area Studies and the Discipline." *APSA-CP: Newsletter of the APSA Organized Section on Comparative Politics* 7(1): 1–2.

Bennett, Andrew, Aaron Barth, and Kenneth R. Rutherford. 2003. "Do We Preach What We Practice? A Survey of Methods in Political Science Journals and Curricula." *PS: Political Science and Politics* 36(3): 373–8.

Bergman, Barbara R. 2005. "The Current State of Economics: Needs Lots of Work." *Annals of the American Academy of Political and Social Science* 600: 52–67.

Berik, Günseli. 1997. "The Need for Crossing the Method Boundaries in Economics Research." *Feminist Economics* 3(2): 121–5.

Berrebi, Claude and Esteban F. Klor. 2008. "Are Voters Sensitive to Terrorism? Direct Evidence from the Israeli Electorate." *American Political Science Review* 102(3): 279–301.

Blackburn, Simon. 2008. *The Oxford Dictionary of Philosophy*. Oxford: Oxford University Press.

Blaydes, Lisa and Drew A. Linzer. 2008. "The Political Economy of Women's Support for Fundamentalist Islam." *World Politics* 60(4): 576–609.

Çağatay, Nilüfer and Günseli Berik. 1994. "What Has Export-Oriented Manufacturing Meant for Turkish Women?" In *Mortgaging Women's Lives: Feminist Critiques of Structural Adjustment*, edited by Pamela Sparr, 78–95. Totowa, NJ: Zed Books.

Çavdar, Gamze. 2010. "Islamist Moderation and the Resilience of Gender: Turkey's Persistence Paradox." *Totalitarian Movements and Political Religions* 11(3–4): 341–57.

Cherif, Feryal M. 2010. "Culture, Rights, and Norms: Women's Rights Reform in Muslim Countries." *Journal of Politics* 72(4): 1144–60.

Chick, Victoria. 1998. "On Knowing One's Place: The Role of Formalism in Economics." *The Economic Journal* 108(451): 1859–69.

Clague, Christopher, Suzanne Gleason, and Stephen Knack. 2001. "Determinants of Lasting Democracy in Poor Countries: Culture, Development, and Institutions." *Annals of the American Academy of Political and Social Science* 573: 16–41.

Clark, Janine Astrid. 2006. "The Conditions of Islamist Moderation: Unpacking Cross-Ideological Cooperation in Jordan." *International Journal of Middle East Studies* 38(4): 539–60.

Clark, Janine Astrid and Amy E. Young. 2008. "Islamism and Family Law Reform in Morocco and Jordan." *Mediterranean Politics* 13(3): 333–52.

Clark, Janine Astrid and Jillian Schwedler. 2003. "Who Opened the Window? Women's Activism in Islamist Parties." *Comparative Politics* 35(3): 293–312.

Cloud, Dana L. 2004. "'To Veil the Threat of Terror': Afghan Women and the Clash of Civilizations in the Imagery of the U.S. War on Terrorism." *Quarterly Journal of Speech* 90(3): 285–306.

Coleman, Isobel. 2010. *Paradise Beneath Her Feet: How Women Are Transforming the Middle East*. New York: Random House.

Doumato, Eleanor Abdella and Marsha Pripstein Posusney, eds. 2003. *Women and Globalization in the Arab Middle East: Gender, Economy and Society*. Boulder, CO: Lynne Rienner.

GENDER AND ECONOMICS IN MUSLIM COMMUNITIES

Easton, David. 1993. "Political Science in the United States: Past and Present." In *Discipline and History: Political Science in the United States,* edited by James Far and Raymond Siedelman, 291–308. Ann Arbor: University of Michigan Press.

England, Paula and Barbara Stanek Kilbourne. 1990. "Feminist Critiques of the Separative Model of Self." *Rationality and Society* 2(2): 156–71.

Fair, C. Christine and Bryan Shepherd. 2006. "Who Supports Terrorism? Evidence from Fourteen Muslim Countries." *Studies in Conflict and Terrorism* 29(1): 51–74.

Ferrero, Mario. 2005. "Radicalization as a Reaction to Failure: An Economic Model of Islamic Extremism." *Public Choice* 122(1/2): 199–220.

Fish, M. Steven. 2002. "Islam and Authoritarianism." *World Politics* 55(1): 4–37.

Gottfried, Paul. 2011. "Freedom House's Illiberal Democracies." *The American Conservative.* http://www.amconmag.com/blog/2011/02/21/freedom-houses-illiberal-democracies/

Green, Donald and Ian Shapiro. 1994. *Pathologies of Rational Choice Theory: A Critique of Applications in Critical Science.* London: Yale University Press.

Haller, Max. 2002. "Theory and Method in the Comparative Study of Values: Critique and Alternative to Inglehart." *European Sociological Review* 18(2): 139–58.

Hasso, Frances S. 2009. "Empowering Governmentalities Rather than Women: The *Arab Human Development Report 2005* and Western Development Logics." *International Journal of Middle East Studies* 41(1): 63–82.

Hatem, Mervat. 1994. "Privatization and the Demise of State Feminism in Egypt." In *Mortgaging Women's Lives: Feminist Critiques of Structural Adjustment,* edited by Pamela Sparr, 40–58. Totowa, NJ: Zed Books.

Hollis, Martin. 1995. *The Philosophy of Social Science: An Introduction.* New York: Cambridge University Press.

Hunt, Krista. 2002. "The Strategic Co-optation of Women's Rights." *International Feminist Journal of Politics* 4(1): 116–21.

Huntington, Samuel P. 1993. "Clash of Civilizations." *Foreign Affairs* 72(3): 22–49.

Inglehart, Ronald. 1997. *Modernization and Postmodernization: Cultural, Economic, and Political Change in 43 Societies.* Princeton, NJ: Princeton University Press.

Inglehart, Ronald and Pippa Norris. 2003a. "The True Clash of Civilizations." *Foreign Policy Magazine* 34(2): 67–74.

——. 2003b. *Rising Tide: Gender Equality and Cultural Change Around the World.* New York: Cambridge University Press.

Ipsos-Public Affairs. 2005. "Globus: International Affairs Polls." http://surveys.ap.org/data/Ipsos/international/Religion%20topline.pdf.

Johnson, Chalmers. 1997. "Preconception vs. Observation, or the Contributions of Rational Choice Theory and Area Studies to Comparative Political Science." *PS: Political Science and Politics* 30(2): 170–4.

Kabeer, Naila, Lopita Huq, and Simeen Mahmud. 2013. "Diverging Stories of 'Missing Women' in South Asia: Is Son Preference Weakening in Bangladesh?" *Feminist Economics.* DOI: 10.1080/13545701.2013.857423.

Kandiyoti, Deniz. 1991. *Women, Islam and the State.* Philadelphia: Temple University Press.

Kang, Alice. 2009. "Studying Oil, Islam, and Women as if Political Institutions Mattered." *Gender and Politics* 5(4): 560–8.

Karatnycky, Adrian. 2002. "Muslim Countries and the Democracy Gap." *Journal of Democracy* 13(1): 99–112.

Kedourie, Elie. 1994. *Democracy and Arab Political Culture.* London: Frank Cass.

Kirkpatrick, David D. 2011. "Libyan Woman Struggles to Tell Media of Her Rape." *New York Times,* March 26.

Krugman, Paul. 2009. "How Did Economists Get It So Wrong?" *New York Times,* September 2.

GENDER AND ECONOMICS IN MUSLIM COMMUNITIES

LeVine, Mark. 2011. "History's Shifting Sands." *Al-Jazeera*, February 26.

Lewis, Bernard. 1993. "Islam and Liberal Democracy." *The Atlantic Monthly*, February: 89–98.

———. 1996. "A Historical View." *Journal of Democracy* 7(2): 52–63.

Lybyer, Albert Howe. 1924. "Recent Political Changes in the Moslem World." *American Political Science Review* 18(3): 513–27.

Marso, Lori Jo. 2007. "Feminism and the Complications of Freeing the Women of Afghanistan and Iraq." In *W Stands For Women: How the George W. Bush Presidency Shaped a New Politics of Gender*, edited by Michaele L. Ferguson and Lori Jo Marso, 221–44. Durham, NC: Duke University Press.

Middle East Report. 2011. "Red-White-and-Black Valentine." http://www.merip.org/mero/mero021411.

Midgley, Clare. 1998. *Gender and Imperialism.* Manchester: Manchester University Press.

Mirowski, Philip. 2010. "The Great Mortification: Economists' Responses to the Crisis of 2007 (and Counting)." *The Hedgehog Review, Critical Reflections on Contemporary Culture.* 12(2): 28–41.

Moghadam, Valentine M. 2001. "Feminism and Islamic Fundamentalism: A Secularist Interpretation." *Journal of Women's History* 13(1): 42–5.

———. 2003. *Modernizing Women: Gender and Social Change in the Middle East.* London: Lynne Rienner.

———. 2005. "Women's Economic Participation in the Middle East: What Difference has the Neoliberal Policy Turn Made?" *Journal of Middle East Women's Studies* 1(1): 110–46.

Monroe, Kristen Renwick. 1991. "The Theory of Rational Action: What is It? How Useful is It for Political Science?" In *Political Science: Looking to the Future*, edited by William J. Crotty, 77–98. Evanston, IL: Northwestern University Press.

Munger, Michael. 2006. "Preference Modification vs. Incentive Manipulation as Tools of Terrorist Recruitment: The Role of Culture." *Public Choice* 128(1/2): 131–46.

Munk, Gerardo L. and Richard Snyder. 2007. "Debating the Direction of Comparative Politics: An Analysis of Leading Journals." *Comparative Political Studies* 40(1): 5–31.

Najjar, Fauzi M. 1958. "Islam and Modern Democracy." *The Review of Politics* 20(2): 164–80.

Nelson, Julie. 1995. "Feminism and Economics," *Journal of Economics Perspectives* 9(2):131–48.

Norton, Augustus Richard. 2014. *The Sunni-Shi'i Rift.* Princeton, NJ: Princeton University Press.

Olmsted, Jennifer C. 1997. "Telling Palestinian Women's Economic Stories." *Feminist Economics* 3(2): 141–51.

Poole, Elizabeth. 2002. *Reporting Islam: Media Representations of British Muslims.* New York: I. B. Tauris.

Ross, Michael L. 2008. "Oil, Islam, and Women." *American Political Science Review* 102(1): 107–23.

Rowley, Charles K. and Nathanael Smith. 2009. "Islam's Democracy Paradox: Muslims Claim to Like Democracy, So Why do They have So Little?" *Public Choice* 139(3/4): 273–99.

Rubin, Barnett. 1995. *The Fragmentation of Afghanistan.* New Haven, CT: Yale University Press.

Rubin, Barry. 2011. "Obama Must Back Egypt's Regime, or Face a Disaster like U.S. did in Iran." *Christian Science Monitor*, January 31.

Said, Edward W. 1978. *Orientalism.* New York: Vintage.

———. 1981. *Covering Islam: How the Media and the Experts Determine How We See the Rest of the World.* New York: Pantheon Books.

GENDER AND ECONOMICS IN MUSLIM COMMUNITIES

Schwartz-Shea, Peregrine. 2003. "Is This the Curriculum We Want? Doctoral Requirements and Offerings in Methods and Methodology." *PS: Political Science and Politics* 36(3): 379–86.

Sen, Amartya. 2003. "Democracy and Its Global Roots." *The New Republic* 29(14): 28–35.

Shapiro, Ian. 2002. "Problems, Methods, and Theories in the Study of Politics, or What's Wrong with Political Science and What to Do About It?" *Political Theory* 30(4): 596–619.

Shehabuddin, Elora. 2011. "Gender and the Figure of the 'Moderate Muslim': Feminism in the Twenty-First Century." In *The Question of Gender: Joan W. Scott's Critical Feminism*, edited by Judith Butler and Elizabeth Weed, 102–42. Bloomington: Indiana University Press.

Spierings, Niels, Jeroen Smits, and Mieke Verloo. 2009. "On the Compatibility of Islam and Gender Equality: Effects of Modernization, State Islamization, and Democracy on Women's Labor Market Participation in 45 Muslim Countries." *Social Indicators Research* 90(3): 503–22.

Tilly, Charles. 2007. *Democracy*. New York: Cambridge University Press.

Tusalem, Rollin F. 2009. "The Role of Protestantism in Democratic Consolidation Among Transitional States." *Comparative Political Studies* 42(7): 882–915.

Viner, Katharine. 2002. "Feminism as Imperialism: George Bush is Not the First Empire-Builder to Wage War in the Name of Women." *The Guardian*, September 20.

Waylen, Georgina. 1994. "Women and Democratization: Conceptualizing Gender Relations in Transition Politics." *World Politics* 46(3): 327–54.

Wiktorowicz, Quintan, ed. 2004. *Islamic Activism: A Social Movement Theory Approach.* Bloomington: Indiana University Press.

PATRIARCHY VERSUS ISLAM: GENDER AND RELIGION IN ECONOMIC GROWTH

Elissa Braunstein

ABSTRACT

This contribution evaluates whether affiliation with Islam is a theoretically and statistically robust proxy for patriarchal preferences when studying the relationship between gender inequality and economic growth. A cross-country endogenous growth analysis shows that direct measures of patriarchal institutions dominate a variety of religious affiliation variables and model specifications in explaining country growth rates, and that using religious affiliation, particularly Islam, as a control for culture produces misleading conclusions. This result is robust to the inclusion of measures of gender inequality in education and income, indicating that establishing and maintaining patriarchal institutions (a process this study calls "patriarchal rent-seeking") exact economic growth costs over and above those measured by standard gender inequality variables. One of the key contributions of this study is to draw on unique institutional data from the Organisation for Economic Co-operation and Development's Gender, Institutions and Development (GID) database to better understand the gendered dynamics of growth.

INTRODUCTION

This contribution evaluates whether affiliation with Islam is a good aggregate indicator of patriarchal preferences for studying the negative impact that gender inequality has on economic growth. "Good" is understood both from a statistical and theoretical perspective, though the analysis is grounded in an econometric framework that bridges the endogenous growth, gender inequality and growth, and gender inequality and religious affiliation literatures and methodologies.

GENDER AND ECONOMICS IN MUSLIM COMMUNITIES

A large subset of the econometric literature on gender inequality and development uses Islam as a proxy for traditional culture or as an exemplar of a "taste" for gender discrimination. This approach is a problem on at least two counts: first, it confirms Western stereotypes about Islam as exceptional relative to other religious affiliations, and second, it obscures the role of patriarchy as a system of male advantage that constrains economic growth and development. It is not that certain Islamic countries or societies are so closely wed to their (extremist) religious beliefs that they are willing to pay high economic costs to maintain them, but rather that patriarchal systems benefit a few at the expense of the many, a dynamic I term "patriarchal rent-seeking." Focusing on religion draws attention away from the sources and consequences of patriarchal power, centering it on misleadingly simplistic views of Muslim practice and culture.

I make this argument using regression analysis in a cross-country endogenous growth framework, utilizing the concept of patriarchal rent-seeking as a way to understand the economic costs of establishing and maintaining patriarchal institutions. The analysis shows that direct measures of patriarchal institutions dominate a variety of religious affiliation variables and model specifications. This result is also robust to the inclusion of measures of gender inequality in education and income, an outcome consistent with my contention that patriarchal rent-seeking is in and of itself economically costly.

PATRIARCHAL RENT-SEEKING AND GROWTH

The contention that gender inequality is economically costly is a common finding (and policy refrain) in empirical economic growth literature. The basic logic is that gender inequality and discrimination are inefficient because they do not maximize productive capacity. Selection-distortion effects in education and labor markets (where students or workers are chosen based on sex rather than aptitude) and imperfect capital, credit, and insurance markets prohibit women and men from making production- or profit-maximizing choices (David Dollar and Roberta Gatti 1999; Zafiris Tzannatos 1999; Stephen Klasen 1999; Stephen Klasen and Francesca Lamanna 2009). Lower fertility, increased investments in children, and less political corruption are also results of greater gender equality with positive externalities for growth (Klasen 1999; David Dollar, Raymond Fisman, and Roberta Gatti 2001; World Bank 2001). Contrary to these findings, Stephanie Seguino (2000) argues that gender-based wage gaps have actually contributed to growth among semi-industrialized countries by giving these economies a competitive advantage in global export markets. This research indicates it is important to specify types of inequality when considering questions of gender inequality and growth.

It is also likely that gender hierarchies exact other, less direct economic costs that are not adequately captured by the gender inequality variables typically used in these sorts of studies – namely, inequality in education or employment. After all, these variables capture how male bias gets manifested economically, as opposed to directly measuring the institutions that underlie these outcomes. Consider that patriarchy, a system of male advantage associated with a variety of institutions, rules, and norms, must be created and maintained. These efforts themselves exact an economic cost over and above those associated with gender inequality in education or labor markets. One way to conceptualize these activities economically is by thinking of them as patriarchal rent-seeking. Rent-seeking behavior, first termed so by Anne O. Krueger (1974), refers to economically wasteful efforts to claim unearned revenues. Rent-seeking is most typically applied to cases where government intervention in the economy creates artificial rents and where individuals waste resources in efforts to get the resultant revenue (Robert D. Tollison and Roger D. Congleton 1995). Krueger's early analysis applied to the efficiency losses from tariffs. But rent-seeking can also influence the organization of nonmarket institutions, as when patriarchal property rights create male advantage in capital markets, or when norms of violence against women maintain male dominance and privileged access to resources. Patriarchal rent-seeking can thus be thought of as socially wasteful efforts to establish and claim the economic rents associated with male privilege (see Elissa Braunstein [2008]).

This is a very different perspective from the one typically proffered in gender inequality and growth literature. Despite the centrality of inequality in these analyses, there is no sense in which economic actors exercise power or engage in collective action to create and maintain social norms and rules that are personally advantageous but socially costly, the kind of dynamic I identify as patriarchal rent-seeking. Perhaps it is the subliminal shadow of Adam Smith's invisible hand, but there is a persistent presumption that activities motivated by self-regard result in the greatest social good. In gender equality and growth literature, the curious persistence of gender discrimination despite its documented economic costs is often attributed to exogenous preferences, not to the economic self-interest of men (Dollar and Gatti 1999; Nancy Forsythe, Roberto Patricio Korzeniewicz, and Valerie Durrant 2000). Casting systems of male advantage as simply the harboring of economically costly tastes renders them irrational and existing outside the logic of the economic system. Thus patriarchal preferences take on a sort of invisibility – one that obscures how economically logical patriarchal systems can be (at least from the perspective of those at the top of the patriarchal hierarchy), and also one that draws others to the margins of the economically odd. Such is the case among studies that proxy for patriarchal preferences by including some measure of affiliation with Islam, an association that too frequently remains critically unexamined.

GENDER AND ECONOMICS IN MUSLIM COMMUNITIES
GENDER INEQUALITY, ISLAM, AND GROWTH

Empirical literature commonly uses religion – especially Islam – as a way to measure the limits that patriarchal preferences place on economic growth, or more frequently, as a way to explain the persistence of gender inequality with negative implications for growth. However, this literature rarely includes explicit discussion of the precise institutional practices that link particular religions with gender inequality, nor do these studies consider the diversity of religious and social practices across regions that are summarily categorized by one religious group or another (for example, Islam versus Christianity). In fact, that religion is used primarily as a proxy for patriarchal preferences or the pervasiveness of traditional culture is, even when it is discussed, too often an introductory aside or parenthetical point, lost in the discussion and ultimately contributing to the (mistaken) impression that Islam is not like other religions. This diverts focus away from patriarchy as a system that is socially costly and shifts it toward the more familiar terrain of "Orientalist" prejudice that still tends to dominate Western views of Islamic civilizations (Edward Said 1978).

One of the classic studies of gender and growth literature, Dollar and Gatti (1999), exemplifies this problematic use of religious affiliation. In this widely cited paper, Dollar and Gatti seek to explain both how growth affects gender inequality (measured by women versus men's educational achievements) and how gender inequality affects growth. Included in their analysis is a set of continuous variables for the percent of a country's population belonging to various religions. Dollar and Gatti find that Muslim and Hindu are (weakly) negatively correlated with women's secondary school achievement yet in contrast, Protestant religions are strongly positive. In the end, positing that religion affects economic growth only via its impact on gender inequalities in educational achievement, Dollar and Gatti use religion (and civil liberties) as instruments for women and men's education in the growth equations. Their interpretation of these results indicates how religion, particularly Islam, is used in empirical literature: "the fact that religion variables systematically explain differences in gender inequality suggests that some societies have a preference for inequality and are willing to pay a price for it" (Dollar and Gatti 1999: 3). They parenthetically add: "It would perhaps be more accurate to say that those who control resources in the society have a preference for gender inequality that they are willing to pay for" (3), a central point the implications of which are not considered again in their paper.

Other studies use Islam more explicitly as a proxy for patriarchal or traditional culture. In an article that assesses the impact of economic growth on women's status as measured by the UN's Gender Development Index (and a number of variants on it), Forsythe, Korzeniewicz, and Durrant (2000) measure what they term "patriarchal institutions" by including two dummy variables, one that reflects whether 50 percent or more of a country's population is Muslim and the second whether the country is in Latin America. The Muslim dummy is persistently negative and statistically (and economically) significant, though the Latin America fixed effect is not. Despite these statistically relevant findings, there is no discussion of what the authors think they might imply.

The majority of the empirical literature on gender that uses religion as a control variable is similarly vague. Tzannatos (1999) regresses women's labor force participation on the major religion of a country (if 50 percent or more of the population is affiliated with any one religion). Using data from the 1980s, Tzannatos finds that women's labor force participation rates in Muslim countries are, on average, 26 percentage points lower than the control group's, Christian (non-Catholic) and Jewish, with women's labor force participation in Roman Catholic countries 15 percentage points lower. Tzannatos concludes that religion is more effective at explaining gender differences in labor force participation than many of the standard economic variables (such as education, income, or economic structure) included in studies like these (1999: 555), but never considers why.

Mina Baliamoune-Lutz (2006) compares the impact of increased trade and economic growth on gender inequality in literacy in Sub-Saharan Africa (SSA) relative to other developing countries. One of the independent variables is a dummy for majority Islam, which is positively correlated with gender inequality in adult illiteracy for the full sample, negatively correlated with this sort of gender inequality in SSA (though the coefficient is much smaller than in the other regressions and not statistically significant), and positively correlated with gender inequality among non-SSA developing countries. With the exception of the SSA-only regressions, the Islam dummy coefficients are economically substantial, with about the same predictive power (though in the opposite direction) as income. Baliamoune-Lutz discusses specific institutional features of Islam that are discriminatory toward women, such as the strict interpretation of Sharia laws that may restrict women's rights to obtain a divorce. In a later co-authored study on the impact of gender inequality in literacy on economic growth in SSA and Arab countries, Baliamoune-Lutz shifts from using an Islam dummy to one for Arab culture, noting that culture, not religion, should be used in empirical analyses because Islam is the major religion in countries with a variety of gender relations (Mina Baliamoune-Lutz and Mark McGillivray 2009).

There have been explicit efforts to better understand the presumed relationship between Islam and patriarchy in the empirical literature, though these are not of the typical macroeconometric cross-country growth analyses that are the main consideration of this contribution. Peter Boone (1996) links religion with gender oppression and poverty, scoring the extent of gender oppression in particular countries based on Charles Humana's

GENDER AND ECONOMICS IN MUSLIM COMMUNITIES

(1992) rankings of a variety of human rights. Boone uses both Muslim and Christian dummy variables as predictors of gender and political oppression in a simple series of ordinary least squares (OLS) regressions (the star of his paper is the game theoretic modeling), with the Muslim dummy variable positively correlated with gender and political oppression, while the Christian dummy is not economically or statistically significant when regional fixed effects are included in the regressions (though the coefficient is positive). What is notable about Boone's study is that he goes to some lengths to specify why religion might be correlated with gender oppression – in particular, as a coordinating mechanism for patriarchal rent-seeking, though he does not call it that. Boone (1996) offers detailed discussion of the ways that certain religious practices and interpretations of historical texts, both in Islam and Christianity, have been used as tools of oppression as well as a foundation for equality under more liberal leadership such as that of Ataturk in Turkey. Still, however, the Islam dummy is used to explain gender oppression, a choice that ultimately contributes to the stereotype that Islam is uniquely linked with gender inequality.

In an empirical analysis of these issues, political scientist Michael L. Ross (2008) builds on the work of Valentine Moghadam (1998) and others to argue that women in the Middle East have made so little progress in terms of gender equality not because of Islam, but because oil production protects patriarchal norms and institutions from the counter-pressures of women's economic empowerment and collective action that women's rising labor force participation elicits. Ross includes the percent of a country's population that is Muslim, per capita oil rents, and a handful of other standard predictors as independent variables in panel data and cross-sectional analyses of women's labor force participation and the determinants of the share of women's seats in parliament and ministerial positions (the last two analyses are cross-sections only). Islam turns out not to be a good explanation of anything, while per capita oil rents are everywhere negative, large, and statistically significant. Ross's examination of whether Islam is a good explanation of gender inequality is compelling because it underscores how patriarchy should be understood as a distinct social system with varied sources of power of persistence – including economic ones.

It is important at this point to reference additional literature that links Islam with more conservative attitudes toward women. The issue here is one of proxies: if scholars can make a robust link between Islam and gender-biased preferences (rather than just presuming it), the relative availability of data on religious affiliation provides a strong argument for using it in this way. Here I refer to a set of studies that use the World Values Survey (WVS) to statistically connect attitudes toward gender equality with religious affiliation. Pippa Norris and Ronald Inglehart (2009) use the WVS to argue that the biggest gap between the Islamic and Western worlds is not political but rather social, especially as reflected in attitudes toward gender equality and sexual liberalization. After classifying cultural regions based on the primary religious identity within a country and controlling for a number of individual and country characteristics, they find that Islamic societies are the least supportive of gender equality, though the results for Orthodox societies seem statistically equivalent (Norris and Inglehart 2009). By contrast, Stephanie Seguino (2011) comes to a different conclusion in a similar analysis that uses an expanded set of WVS questions to capture attitudes toward gender equality. She concludes that while religiosity has a strong (negative) impact on gender equality attitudes, no major religion emerges as resulting in distinctively strong gender inequitable attitudes. In fact, Protestants, Buddhists, and Hindus stand out as having more gender inequitable attitudes relative to the nonreligious in four out of the nine questions considered, more than the other religious affiliations, including Islam. So there are inconsistencies in the literature connecting certain religions with more conservative attitudes toward women.

Luigi Guiso, Paola Sapienza, and Luigi Zingales (2003) also relate attitudes captured by the WVS to support for women's rights, but their analysis ultimately focuses on economic attitudes. Their results show that all religions are associated with more conservative attitudes toward women, but that the correlation is strongest for respondents who identify as Muslim (after controlling for a number of individual variables and country fixed effects). They also find that religious affiliation is associated with a number of economic attitudes that may affect growth, including opinions about government, laws, private ownership, markets, and the relationship between incentives and inequality. And herein lies another reason that we must be careful about using Islam as a proxy for gender bias in studies of growth: religious affiliation is potentially associated with attitudes or values that are not linked with gender but may have consequences for economic growth. A large qualitative and quantitative literature queries whether the commercial practices or political dynamics associated with Islam have constrained economic growth (see Deepak Lal [1998]; Bernard Lewis [2002]; Alan Heston [2003]; Timur Kuran [2003]; Marcus Noland [2005]). In empirical literature at least, there is little evidence that it has, particularly not in any way that distinguishes Islam from other religions (for instance, Robert J. Barro and Rachel McCleary [2003]; Xavier Sala-i-Martin, Gernot Doppelhofer, and Ronald I. Miller [2004]; Noland [2005]; Frederic L. Pryor [2007]).[1] Ultimately, we cannot presume that the correlations between religious affiliation and growth capture the effect of gendered preferences exclusively and may indeed incorporate attitudes or institutions that have (potentially) contradictory effects on growth.

GENDER AND ECONOMICS IN MUSLIM COMMUNITIES

EMPIRICAL SPECIFICATION AND DATA

I use a long-run (1960–2000) cross-country endogenous growth model as the basis of my analysis. The core of the model is given by Equation 1, where the dependent variable, the growth of real per capita GDP for country (i) between 1960 and 2000, depends on a vector of standard macroeconomic variables used in the endogenous growth literature, including measures of initial per capita GDP, investment and trade as shares of GDP, human capital, and institutional quality. Region captures regional fixed effects, with industrialized countries constituting their own regional group. To this basic framework, I add measures of religious affiliation and a variable I term "patriarchal dominance" (PD), a constructed index that measures the extent of patriarchal institutions. And finally, I add two measures of gender inequality that are common (in various guises) in the literature: one for educational inequality and a second for income.

$$g_i = \alpha + Z_i\beta + \text{Region}_i\,\delta + \varepsilon_i \quad i = 1,\ldots,N \tag{1}$$

In terms of data sources and empirical details, refer to Table 1 for a list of variables and associated statistics, and to Table 2 for regional groupings and country-specific values for the gender inequality variables.[2] A Supplementary Data Appendix with detailed information on variable definitions and sources is available on the publisher's website (http://dx.doi.org/10.1080/13545701.2014.934265). Data for per capita GDP and investment and trade as proportions of GDP, all in real purchasing power parity terms, were taken from Penn World Tables, version 6.2 (Alan Heston, Robert Summers, and Bettina Aten 2006). In the model, I use the natural log of per capita GDP in 1960 to control for convergence effects (wealthier countries tend to grow more slowly). For both investment and trade (imports plus exports) as proportions of GDP, I use the mean value over the period under consideration. Because my analysis is based on the idea that factors such as investment and trade are themselves the result of economic growth, I use an instrumental variable approach to control for the endogeneity of trade and investment. In addition to investment and trade as a share of GDP in 1960, these instruments include a dummy variable to control for location in the Southern hemisphere as an indicator of how geography shapes investment and trade (John Gallup, Jeffrey Sachs, and Andrew Mellinger 1999), and the predicted value of trade based exclusively on geography as calculated by Jeffrey Frankel and David Romer (1999; actual values taken from Dani Rodrik, Arvind Subramanian, and Francesco Trebbi [2004]). Since geography has direct effects on growth over and above its impact on investment and trade, I also include the percent of land area located in the tropics as an independent variable in the growth equation (Gallup, Sachs, and Mellinger 1999).[3]

GENDER AND ECONOMICS IN MUSLIM COMMUNITIES

Table 1 Data summary

Variable	Mean	SD	Minimum	Maximum
Per capita GDP (2000 $PPP)	US$4,711	US$5,935	US$99	US$34,365
Per capita GDP growth	2.29%	0.57%	0.55%	4.00%
Mean INV/GDP	0.18	0.08	0.03	0.33
Mean Trade/GDP	0.55	0.33	0.11	1.92
Average years of secondary education in the population older than age 15 in 1960 (syr)	0.76	0.82	0.01	3.33
Ratio of syr for women to men in 1960 (syrfm)	0.60	0.28	0.18	1.17
Rule of law	6.00	2.34	2.27	9.98
Patriarchal dominance (PD)	0.17	0.19	0.00	0.73
Female/male income (fmincome)	0.53	0.15	0.23	0.83
Percent Muslim	0.20	0.34	0.00	1.00
Percent Buddhist	0.04	0.18	0.00	0.95
Percent Hindu	0.01	0.10	0.00	0.81
Percent Catholic	0.37	0.38	0.00	0.97
Percent Orthodox	0.02	0.12	0.00	0.98
Percent Christian	0.20	0.25	0.00	0.98
All other religious affiliations, including none	0.16	0.18	0.00	0.82

Notes: This summary is based on the sixty-seven countries used in the regressions (for a list, see Table 2). SD stands for standard deviation. Explanations of the data and sources are provided in a Supplementary Data Appendix, available on the publisher's website (http://dx.doi.org/10.1080/13545701.2014.934265). Summary data for the following variables were taken as averages over the entire time period, 1960–2000: per capita GDP, INV/GDP, Trade/GDP, syr, and syrfm; per capita GDP growth refers to growth over the entire period, 1960–2000.

I measure the quality of public institutions by using Stephen Knack and Philip Keefer's (1995) rule of law index, an index that ranges between zero and 10 (a higher index means more institutional quality) and that is the sum of five subindices rating business attitudes toward government quality. Human capital is captured by average years of secondary education in the population age 15 and older, taken from Robert Barro and Jong-Wha Lee (2010). I also include the growth of this human capital measure to capture how improvements in education are correlated with GDP growth. Data on proportions of the population practicing various religions were taken from the *World Factbook* (Central Intelligence Agency [CIA] 2008). In a few cases with missing religious affiliation data, I drew on the *World Desk Reference.*

Turning to the gender inequality measures, educational inequality is figured from the Barro and Lee (2010) dataset as the female-to-male ratio of the average years of secondary schooling in the population age 15 and older. I use observations both at the beginning of the period in 1960 and

66

GENDER AND ECONOMICS IN MUSLIM COMMUNITIES

Table 2 Gender variable means by region and country

	PD	fmincome	syrfm1960	syrfm1960–2000
Asia				
Indonesia	0.17	0.45	0.41	0.27
India	0.50	0.31	0.23	0.83
Korea	0.02	0.46	0.30	1.00
Sri Lanka	0.14	0.42	0.66	0.40
Malaysia	0.24	0.36	0.30	1.13
Pakistan	0.73	0.29	0.22	0.75
Philippines	0.04	0.60	0.77	0.31
Thailand	0.04	0.59	0.42	0.71
Average	0.24	0.44	0.41	0.68
Sub-Saharan Africa (SSA)				
Cameroon	0.37	0.49	0.32	0.60
Ghana	0.41	0.71	0.25	0.93
Kenya	0.35	0.83	0.41	0.28
Mali	0.58	0.67	0.20	0.67
Mozambique	0.44	0.81	0.22	0.26
Malawi	0.34	0.73	0.18	0.89
Niger	0.60	0.57	0.31	0.08
Senegal	0.34	0.53	0.46	0.18
Togo	0.36	0.43	0.20	0.35
Tanzania	0.44	0.73	0.18	1.20
Uganda	0.47	0.7	0.18	1.14
South Africa	0.32	0.45	0.99	−0.02
Zambia	0.43	0.55	0.22	1.01
Zimbabwe	0.44	0.58	0.68	0.13
Côte d'Ivoire	0.28	0.32	0.37	0.19
Average	0.41	0.61	0.34	0.53
Latin America and the Caribbean (LAC)				
Argentina	0.03	0.53	0.87	0.21
Bolivia	0.10	0.57	0.65	0.22
Brazil	0.06	0.57	0.79	0.33
Chile	0.04	0.39	0.90	0.07
Colombia	0.04	0.58	0.82	0.19
Costa Rica	0.04	0.46	0.86	0.19
Dominican Republic	0.06	0.42	1.12	−0.02
Ecuador	0.03	0.55	0.75	0.30
Honduras	0.15	0.45	0.79	0.15
Mexico	0.03	0.39	0.72	0.24
Nicaragua	0.06	0.32	0.29	0.87
Panama	0.03	0.56	0.96	0.12
Peru	0.09	0.41	0.69	0.15

(*Continued*)

GENDER AND ECONOMICS IN MUSLIM COMMUNITIES

Table 2 Continued

	PD	fmincome	syrfm1960	syrfm1960–2000
Paraguay	0.03	0.41	0.59	0.44
El Salvador	0.05	0.43	0.81	0.12
Uruguay	0.04	0.55	0.94	0.06
Venezuela	0.05	0.51	0.65	0.52
Average	0.05	0.48	0.78	0.25
Middle East and North Africa (MENA)				
Algeria	0.31	0.33	0.42	0.53
Egypt	0.46	0.23	0.20	1.24
Jordan	0.40	0.3	0.31	0.92
Morocco	0.28	0.25	0.59	−0.05
Syria	0.36	0.33	0.30	1.13
Average	0.36	0.29	0.36	0.75
Industrialized Countries (IND)				
Australia	0.04	0.7	0.87	0.16
Austria	0.02	0.44	0.43	0.52
Belgium	0.02	0.63	0.77	0.20
Canada	0.02	0.63	1.07	−0.07
Switzerland	0.02	0.61	0.73	0.07
Denmark	0.02	0.73	0.61	0.36
Spain	0.02	0.5	0.58	0.50
Finland	0.04	0.71	0.85	0.08
France	0.02	0.64	0.85	0.08
United Kingdom	0.01	0.65	1.07	−0.01
Greece	0.04	0.55	0.70	0.25
Ireland	0.02	0.51	1.17	−0.13
Israel	0.12	0.64	0.79	0.27
Italy	0.04	0.46	0.66	0.31
Japan	0.06	0.44	0.58	0.44
Netherlands	0.02	0.63	0.68	0.30
Norway	0.02	0.75	0.67	0.32
New Zealand	0.03	0.7	0.98	−0.03
Portugal	0.03	0.59	0.53	0.63
Sweden	0.00	0.81	0.85	0.16
Turkey	0.11	0.35	0.37	0.51
United States	0.03	0.62	1.05	−0.04
Average	0.03	0.60	0.77	0.22

Notes: This list represents the sample used for the regression analysis. PD refers to patriarchal dominance; fmincome to the female share of GDP relative to the male share; syrfm1960 to the ratio of average years of secondary schooling among women older than age 15 to that of men, both in 1960; and syrfm1960–2000 to the growth of ratio over the period.

GENDER AND ECONOMICS IN MUSLIM COMMUNITIES

the percent change in the ratio between 1960 and 2000. Gender inequality in income is measured by the ratio of female-to-male income in purchasing power parity terms. I took these figures from Johannes Jutting, Christian Morrisson, Jeff Dayton-Johnson, and Denis Drechsler (2006), an estimation based on the ratio of female-to-male nonagricultural wages, female and male shares of the economically active population, total female and male population and per capita GDP, and the same methodology used to estimate these incomes for the Gender Empowerment Measure (GEM) in past United Nations Human Development Reports. The resulting variable measures relative shares of GDP, as opposed to wages, though it does use gender-based wage inequality as a basis for determining GDP shares. While it is certainly a crude measure of gender-based income inequality, both in terms of the underlying methodology and its potential endogeneity, I use this variable not in an effort to precisely estimate some correlation, but rather to see how it affects the results for the other gender and religion variables.

I calculated PD based on data from the GID database, a cross-national dataset from OECD that combines a number of different data sources (not all of them public) on women's relative status (Jutting et al. 2006). For the PD variable, I only included data on patriarchal social institutions, calculating an arithmetic average of four other GID indices, all of which range between zero (no male dominance) and 1 (complete male dominance). These four indices include: *family code* (based on the extent of early marriage for women, whether husbands have the legal right to unilaterally terminate their marriage through repudiation of the wife, acceptance of polygamy, whether parental authority is granted to mothers and fathers equally, and whether inheritance practices favor men); *physical integrity* (based on the prevalence of female genital mutilation, the existence of laws against domestic violence, sexual assault, or sexual harassment, and the number of missing women); *civil liberties* (based on women's freedom of movement and whether they are obligated to wear a veil in public); and finally *ownership rights* (based on women's access to land, bank loans, and property other than land). Table 3 lists more details on the components and scoring system.

Note that there is only one PD observation for the entire time period, and it is based on fairly recent information. If patriarchal institutions have changed a lot over the period, I have an errors-in-variables problem, which means that my estimates will be biased. However, I maintain that the particular institutions underlying PD are much more resistant to change than other measures of gender relations, such as income or education. PD was intentionally constructed not to proxy for gender inequality, but rather to measure the effect of the more extreme institutional practices associated with male dominance. It is in this sense that the model captures the deleterious effects of patriarchal rent-seeking. These dynamics may differ from the way we typically think about the economic aspects of gender inequality as limits on women's economic participation or labor market

Table 3 Components of patriarchal dominance (PD)

Subindex	Description	Range 0–1 on the following scales
Family code	An arithmetic average of the following five categories	0 = gender equal family code 1 = complete male dominance
Repudiation	Whether a husband can unilaterally terminate marriage via repudiation of his wife	0 = not possible 1 = legally binding practice
Early marriage	Percent of young women ages 15–19 who are currently married, divorced, or widowed	0 = no early marriage for women 1 = complete early marriage
Polygamy	Acceptance of polygamy	0 = none 1 = complete
Parental authority	Parental authority granted to father and mother equally	0 = yes 1 = no
Inheritance	Inheritance practices in favor of male heirs	0 = no 1 = yes
Physical integrity	An arithmetic average of the following three categories	0 = high physical integrity for women 1 = low physical integrity for women
Female genital mutilation	Share of women affected by female genital mutilation	0 = none 1 = all
Violence against women	Whether laws exist that prohibit the following: • domestic violence • sexual assault or rape • sexual harassment	0 = specific legislation is in place 0.25 = general legislation is in place 0.50 = specific legislation is being planned, drafted, or reviewed 0.75 = planned legislation is general 1.0 = no legislation
Missing women	Refers to the number of women that should be alive if there were gender equality relative to the number that actually are	Value of 1.0 was assigned to the country with greatest proportion (Afghanistan with 9.3%), and the rest indexed down to 0 from there

(Continued)

Table 3 Continued

Subindex	Description	Range 0–1 on the following scales
Civil liberties	An arithmetic average of the following two categories	0 = women have high civil liberties 1 = women have few civil liberties
Freedom of movement	Women can move freely outside the home	0 = none 1 = total
Obligation to wear a veil in public		0 = all women 1 = no women are obligated
Ownership rights	An arithmetic average of the following three categories	0 = gender equality 1 = women have few property rights
Women's access to land	Whether women can own land	0 = full 1 = impossible
Women's access to bank loans	Whether women have the right to secure bank loans	0 = full 1 = impossible
Women's access to property other than land	Whether women can own property other than land	0 = full 1 = impossible

Notes: Based on Jutting, Morrisson, Dayton-Johnson, and Drechsler (2006). The final PD variable varies between 0 (no PD) and 1 (full PD).

discrimination. For instance, Korea has a high degree of gender-based wage inequality but a low PD score (as reflected in Table 2 by the ratio of 0.46 for fmincome and 0.02 for PD). This figure is not a contradiction, but rather an indication of gender dynamics: in Korea, male dominance plays out in terms of gender bias in the labor market, as opposed to constraints on women's civil liberties or property rights. However, even if one accepts that the institutions captured by PD change only slowly, the changes that have occurred are likely to mean less patriarchal dominance at the end of the period than the beginning. From this perspective, my estimates underestimate the true relationship between PD and growth. Still, the potential endogeneity of PD, if, as is likely, economic growth affects patriarchal dominance (even if PD changes more slowly than other measures), would operate the other way. Ultimately, I have to utilize the data I have, and readers are cautioned to take these issues into account when interpreting the results.

As Table 1 indicates, the full sample mean of PD is 0.17, meaning that average male dominance in the sample is low, though the standard deviation is substantial by these terms, coming in at 0.19. To better understand how PD "behaves" relative to other variables of interest in the study, Table 4 provides an array of correlation coefficients with the religion variables as well as the regional controls. I include regional controls, which are sometimes understood to represent "culture," and a host of other characteristics shared by countries in the same geographical region (or with the same advanced industrial development). Consider first the explicitly gendered variables: PD, fmincome (the ratio of female-to-male income), and syrfm1960 (the average female-to-male ratio of years of secondary schooling in the population age 15 and older in 1960). The latter two indicators of gender equality, fmincome and syrfm1960, are negatively correlated with patriarchal dominance, though the relationship is much stronger for education, with a correlation coefficient of -0.67. This result is hardly surprising, given that patriarchal institutions will clearly result in unequal outcomes for women and men. Immediately, a question arises as to whether the correlation between these variables is too high, both in terms of what new information PD actually adds to the analysis and in terms of whether the regressors have a multicollinearity problem. This question is also the case when I consider the correlation between patriarchal dominance and the religious affiliation variables. Indeed, one might even suggest that percent Muslim or Catholic seem to be reasonable proxies for the extent of patriarchal dominance simply based on these coefficients, as many scholars discussed above have done (though few establish these relationships empirically beforehand).

However, we must be careful about what to deduce (and not to deduce) from simple correlation coefficients, as they are the statistically simple woman's indicator of collinearity, and whether it is a problem for the regression analysis. I will attempt to reassure readers on this point. First,

Table 4 Correlation coefficients

	PD	fmincome	syrfm1960	Muslim	Christian	Catholic	Orthodox	Buddhist	Hindu	Other
PD	1.00									
fmincome	−0.14	1.00								
syrfm1960	−0.67	0.07	1.00							
Muslim	0.62	−0.42	−0.53	1.00						
Christian	−0.03	0.57	0.09	−0.29	1.00					
Catholic	−0.54	−0.04	0.46	−0.51	−0.36	1.00				
Orthodox	−0.08	0.01	0.04	−0.05	−0.10	−0.13	1.00			
Buddhist	−0.13	−0.06	−0.07	−0.11	−0.15	−0.22	−0.03	1.00		
Hindu	0.21	−0.19	−0.16	−0.02	−0.09	−0.13	−0.02	0.01	1.00	
Other	0.08	0.26	0.02	−0.24	0.20	−0.30	−0.11	−0.05	−0.09	1.00
IND	−0.51	0.34	0.39	−0.27	0.30	0.00	0.18	0.00	−0.09	0.03
ASIA	0.03	−0.14	−0.13	0.06	−0.13	−0.29	−0.06	0.54	0.31	0.02
LAC	−0.37	−0.21	0.36	−0.34	−0.30	0.72	−0.08	−0.14	−0.08	−0.24
MENA	0.25	−0.39	−0.19	0.57	−0.20	−0.30	−0.02	−0.07	−0.04	−0.03
SSA	0.69	0.29	−0.50	0.16	0.26	−0.36	−0.07	−0.13	−0.07	0.34

Notes: Variable names, sources, and content detailed in a Supplementary Data Appendix, available on the publisher's website (http://dx.doi.org/10.1080/13545701.2014.934265). The religion variables refer to the percent of a country's population that is affiliated with that particular religion. Details on regional groupings can be found in Table 2.

GENDER AND ECONOMICS IN MUSLIM COMMUNITIES

correlation coefficients in the low 60 percent range are certainly substantial, but still far from the 0.8 or 0.9 that is considered to be perhaps "too high." Second, the symptoms of multicollinearity include large variances and consequent lack of statistical significance for the estimated coefficients because, essentially, the estimator will only use information that is unique to the two variables in the estimation. A typical result is high R-squares (meaning that the independent variables explain a large proportion of the dependent variable's variation), with no statistical significance on any of the coefficient estimates; I do not encounter this problem. For the statistically sophisticated, there are of course statistical tests to detect the presence of multicollinearity. I ran estimates for both the variance inflation factors and the condition number, neither of which indicated that collinearity is a problem.[4] Third, a close look at the correlation coefficients indicate that PD is measuring something other than religion: PD is positively correlated with both percent Muslim and the Sub-Saharan Africa region, but Muslim and Sub-Saharan Africa are not highly correlated with one another (the coefficient is 0.16). Finally, and perhaps most importantly, we need to depend on theory to structure and understand the data, not the other way around. Using the percent of the population practicing one religion or another does not explain much about gender inequality, as argued at length above. The robustness of the PD estimation results covered next support this assertion.

RESULTS

Tables 5 and 6 give the results for the basic model described by Equation 1, except for the addition of a variety of religious affiliation variables (Tables 5 and 6) and gender inequality in education and income (Table 6). Tables 7 and 8 reproduce the regression models of Tables 5 and 6 respectively, only with the addition of the PD variable. The dependent variable in all four tables is real per capita GDP growth between 1960 and 2000. Panel A presents two sets of results for each model specification, first the results for OLS, followed in the next column by two-stage least squares (2SLS) estimates. The 2SLS estimates use instrumental variable techniques to account for the endogeneity of investment and trade.[5] Standard errors in all the regressions are robust to control for heteroskedasticity across countries.

Looking at Table 5 first, column 1 gives the OLS results for the core model, with column 2 repeating the same model using 2SLS. The main difference between the two sets of results is that after controlling for the endogeneity of investment and trade, investment as a share of GDP becomes less important as a determinant of growth, decreasing substantially in terms of magnitude and losing statistical significance. This pattern is repeated throughout the various regression models in Tables 5–8, with little impact on the other coefficient estimates. As for trade, neither the OLS nor the 2SLS

GENDER AND ECONOMICS IN MUSLIM COMMUNITIES

Table 5 Per capita growth and religion, 1960–2000

	OLS (1)	2SLS (2)	OLS (3)	2SLS (4)	OLS (5)	2SLS (6)
Dependent variable is per capita GDP growth, 1960–2000						
ln per capita GDP1960	−0.552***	−0.528***	−0.572***	−0.543***	−0.589***	−0.547***
	(0.0871)	(0.0940)	(0.0858)	(0.0936)	(0.0910)	(0.0974)
Mean INV/GDP	2.018**	0.366	1.678*	−0.224	0.909	−0.842
	(0.865)	(0.980)	(0.896)	(0.987)	(0.985)	(1.045)
Mean Trade/GDP	0.0784	0.0914	0.0717	0.0187	0.0621	−0.0553
	(0.135)	(0.117)	(0.140)	(0.136)	(0.161)	(0.138)
syr1960	−0.0324	0.00264	−0.0420	−0.0100	−0.0357	−0.0142
	(0.0653)	(0.0670)	(0.0650)	(0.0662)	(0.0658)	(0.0672)
syr1960–2000	−0.144	−0.110	−0.135	−0.0859	−0.0871	−0.0134
	(0.0950)	(0.0907)	(0.101)	(0.100)	(0.101)	(0.0967)
Rule of law	0.133***	0.154***	0.128***	0.147***	0.152***	0.175***
	(0.0339)	(0.0366)	(0.0353)	(0.0377)	(0.0403)	(0.0413)
IND	−0.223	−0.270	−0.213	−0.264	−0.338	−0.450*
	(0.212)	(0.239)	(0.209)	(0.238)	(0.241)	(0.244)
MENA	−0.285	−0.365	−0.189	−0.216	−0.290	−0.326
	(0.220)	(0.244)	(0.224)	(0.240)	(0.232)	(0.239)
LAC	−0.146	−0.210	−0.216	−0.342*	−0.354*	−0.502**
	(0.164)	(0.170)	(0.179)	(0.206)	(0.215)	(0.228)
SSA	−0.924***	−1.102***	−0.972***	−1.190***	−1.146***	−1.377***
	(0.176)	(0.186)	(0.192)	(0.220)	(0.215)	(0.220)
TROPICAR	−0.321**	−0.328*	−0.342**	−0.336**	−0.384***	−0.369**
	(0.163)	(0.176)	(0.148)	(0.156)	(0.147)	(0.149)
Percent Muslim			−0.238	−0.355*	−0.542**	−0.633**
			(0.188)	(0.213)	(0.255)	(0.290)
Percent Christian					−0.411*	−0.373
					(0.241)	(0.276)
Percent Buddhist					−0.240	−0.114
					(0.257)	(0.299)
Percent Hindu					−1.081***	−1.411***
					(0.339)	(0.338)
Percent Orthodox					−0.0296	0.186
					(0.300)	(0.327)
Percent Catholic					−0.170	−0.151
					(0.236)	(0.261)
Observations	67	67	67	67	67	67
F statistic	15.17	13.05	14.96	11.69	16.47	12.56
R-squared	0.772	0.756	0.779	0.759	0.805	0.790
Overid test		Passed		Passed		Passed

Notes: Robust standard errors are in parentheses; ***, **, * denote statistical significance at the 1, 5, and 10 percent levels, respectively. "Passed" for overid test indicates that instruments are valid. Excluded region is Asia. Details on data definitions and sources are provided in the text and summarized in a Supplementary Data Appendix, available on the publisher's website (http://dx.doi.org/10.1080/13545701.2014.934265).

GENDER AND ECONOMICS IN MUSLIM COMMUNITIES

Table 6 Per capita growth and religion extended, 1960–2000

	OLS (1)	2SLS (2)	OLS (3)	2SLS (4)
Dependent variable is per capita GDP growth, 1960–2000				
ln per capita GDP1960	−0.651***	−0.614***	−0.632***	−0.613***
	(0.0877)	(0.0893)	(0.0864)	(0.0883)
Mean INV/GDP	1.649*	0.107	2.499***	1.095
	(0.955)	(1.056)	(0.830)	(0.972)
Mean Trade/GDP	−0.00430	−0.0499	−0.0109	0.0371
	(0.137)	(0.123)	(0.118)	(0.105)
syr1960	−0.0857	−0.0653	−0.0809	−0.0481
	(0.0589)	(0.0615)	(0.0607)	(0.0646)
syr1960–2000	−0.0944	−0.0355	−0.132	−0.104
	(0.0782)	(0.0801)	(0.0813)	(0.0811)
Rule of law	0.142***	0.163***	0.123***	0.142***
	(0.0363)	(0.0379)	(0.0324)	(0.0352)
IND	−0.192	−0.299	−0.101	−0.160
	(0.206)	(0.218)	(0.189)	(0.221)
MENA	−0.284	−0.324	−0.225	−0.299
	(0.218)	(0.225)	(0.207)	(0.231)
LAC	−0.371*	−0.463**	−0.270*	−0.299*
	(0.214)	(0.227)	(0.160)	(0.169)
SSA	−0.903***	−1.117***	−0.695***	−0.874***
	(0.218)	(0.242)	(0.190)	(0.214)
TROPICAR	−0.297**	−0.320**	−0.244*	−0.280*
	(0.123)	(0.132)	(0.136)	(0.153)
Percent Muslim	−0.418*	−0.504**		
	(0.218)	(0.251)		
Percent Christian	−0.437*	−0.448*		
	(0.223)	(0.258)		
Percent Buddhist	−0.304	−0.198		
	(0.220)	(0.260)		
Percent Hindu	−0.959***	−1.213***		
	(0.310)	(0.334)		
Percent Orthodox	−0.0742	0.0988		
	(0.241)	(0.273)		
Percent Catholic	−0.248	−0.248		
	(0.197)	(0.228)		
syrfm1960	0.982***	0.893***	1.078***	0.992***
	(0.228)	(0.258)	(0.239)	(0.250)
syrfm1960–2000	0.370**	0.340**	0.391**	0.369**
	(0.157)	(0.167)	(0.174)	(0.171)
fmincome	−0.346	−0.205	−0.445**	−0.298
	(0.269)	(0.294)	(0.223)	(0.250)
Observations	67	67	67	67

(*Continued*)

GENDER AND ECONOMICS IN MUSLIM COMMUNITIES

Table 6 Continued

	OLS (1)	2SLS (2)	OLS (3)	2SLS (4)
F statistic	26.78	24.17	23.40	20.32
R-squared	0.836	0.827	0.816	0.805
Overid test		Passed		Passed

Notes: See notes to Table 5.

models assign it much importance in terms of magnitude, and nowhere is it statistically significant.

Regarding the other coefficient estimates: first, the convergence effect as measured by the natural log of per capita GDP in 1960 is strongly negative across all of the models, as expected. Likewise, the results for rule of law and area in the tropics are as expected (positive in the first case and negative in the second) and stable across all of the models. The average number of years of secondary schooling in the population older than age 15 in 1960 (syr1960), and the growth of that measure between 1960 and 2000 (syr1960–2000) is not economically or statistically significant. Getting human capital variables to perform as expected in growth models is notoriously difficult. The 2SLS first-stage regression results for investment (not presented) suggest what may be part of the reason. In most of these models, both human capital measures are positive and statistically significant, which suggests that education affects economic growth via its positive impact on investment. In future iterations, it would be interesting to focus on these education variables; but for now, I just acknowledge that there is more going on here than my model structure uncovers. Turning to the regional controls, which are all measured relative to the Asian region, signs are as expected, though statistical significance increases as I add more variables.

Focusing on the religious affiliation and gender variables, starting with Table 5, column 4 repeats the same growth model as column 2, only with the addition of percent Muslim. The point here is to investigate how focusing exclusively on Muslim as a gendered institutional indicator compares to specifications that include all religious affiliations as well as direct measures of gender inequality. Column 6 adds all religious affiliations, excluding the "other" category. The results in Table 6 extend these models by adding measures of gender inequality in education (the female-to-male ratio of average years of secondary schooling in 1960, syrfm1960, and the growth of that ratio over the period, syrfm1960–2000) and income (fmincome). According to this set of results, percent Muslim is negatively correlated with per capita growth, with the largest coefficient estimate in column 6 of Table 5, when all religious affiliation variables are included but before adding any controls for gender inequality. To get a sense of magnitude, the

GENDER AND ECONOMICS IN MUSLIM COMMUNITIES

Table 7 Per capita growth, religion, and patriarchal dominance, 1960–2000

	OLS (1)	2SLS (2)	OLS (3)	2SLS (4)	OLS (5)	2SLS (6)
Dependent variable is per capita GDP growth, 1960–2000						
ln per capita GDP1960	−0.610***	−0.595***	−0.611***	−0.595***	−0.624***	−0.594***
	(0.0917)	(0.0967)	(0.0898)	(0.0961)	(0.0854)	(0.0912)
Mean INV/GDP	1.125	0.160	1.115	0.0750	0.873	−0.346
	(0.835)	(0.856)	(0.829)	(0.838)	(0.971)	(0.930)
Mean Trade/GDP	0.0381	−0.00259	0.0381	−0.0121	0.0579	−0.0295
	(0.140)	(0.115)	(0.140)	(0.121)	(0.152)	(0.134)
syr1960	−0.00373	0.0178	−0.00446	0.0154	−0.0150	0.000323
	(0.0630)	(0.0628)	(0.0646)	(0.0645)	(0.0698)	(0.0704)
syr1960–2000	−0.0881	−0.0580	−0.0881	−0.0555	−0.0814	−0.0289
	(0.0888)	(0.0843)	(0.0889)	(0.0847)	(0.101)	(0.0939)
Rule of law	0.127***	0.136***	0.127***	0.135***	0.140***	0.156***
	(0.0347)	(0.0366)	(0.0355)	(0.0374)	(0.0412)	(0.0412)
IND	−0.422**	−0.472***	−0.419**	−0.466***	−0.441*	−0.521**
	(0.170)	(0.178)	(0.172)	(0.180)	(0.225)	(0.228)
MENA	−0.257*	−0.290*	−0.253	−0.269	−0.302**	−0.327**
	(0.144)	(0.150)	(0.162)	(0.168)	(0.153)	(0.159)
LAC	−0.367*	−0.441**	−0.369*	−0.455**	−0.415*	−0.521**
	(0.189)	(0.198)	(0.193)	(0.210)	(0.236)	(0.249)
SSA	−0.754***	−0.835***	−0.758***	−0.855***	−0.873***	−1.032***
	(0.156)	(0.168)	(0.152)	(0.172)	(0.205)	(0.209)
TROPICAR	−0.445***	−0.446***	−0.445***	−0.444***	−0.452***	−0.441***
	(0.116)	(0.118)	(0.116)	(0.117)	(0.116)	(0.117)
Percent Muslim			−0.0123	−0.0546	−0.299	−0.359
			(0.160)	(0.174)	(0.260)	(0.281)
Percent Christian					−0.389	−0.359
					(0.261)	(0.280)
Percent Buddhist					−0.314	−0.226
					(0.262)	(0.283)
Percent Hindu					−0.598*	−0.824**
					(0.337)	(0.352)
Percent Orthodox					−0.0888	0.0628
					(0.303)	(0.304)
Percent Catholic					−0.191	−0.176
					(0.262)	(0.276)
PD	−1.437***	−1.594***	−1.426***	−1.553***	−1.249***	−1.262***
	(0.335)	(0.323)	(0.350)	(0.351)	(0.363)	(0.360)
Observations	67	67	67	67	67	67
F statistic	20.70	16.92	20.14	15.75	18.64	16.40
R-squared	0.818	0.813	0.818	0.812	0.829	0.822
Overid test		Passed		Passed		

Notes: See notes to Table 5.

GENDER AND ECONOMICS IN MUSLIM COMMUNITIES

Table 8 Per capita growth, religion, and patriarchal dominance extended, 1960–2000

	OLS (1)	2SLS (2)	OLS (3)	2SLS (4)
Dependent variable is per capita GDP growth, 1960–2000				
ln per capita GDP1960	−0.673***	−0.653***	−0.659***	−0.648***
	(0.0837)	(0.0870)	(0.0874)	(0.0905)
Mean INV/GDP	1.595*	0.693	1.688**	0.872
	(0.939)	(0.935)	(0.840)	(0.886)
Mean Trade/GDP	−0.0108	−0.0308	−0.0303	−0.0330
	(0.132)	(0.119)	(0.127)	(0.114)
syr1960	−0.0613	−0.0493	−0.0476	−0.0276
	(0.0608)	(0.0630)	(0.0577)	(0.0594)
syr1960–2000	−0.0992	−0.0660	−0.100	−0.0786
	(0.0800)	(0.0788)	(0.0771)	(0.0771)
Rule of law	0.134***	0.146***	0.122***	0.131***
	(0.0373)	(0.0371)	(0.0340)	(0.0358)
IND	−0.290	−0.351*	−0.269*	−0.319*
	(0.198)	(0.202)	(0.161)	(0.168)
MENA	−0.303**	−0.327**	−0.211	−0.244
	(0.147)	(0.153)	(0.151)	(0.156)
LAC	−0.412*	−0.462*	−0.420**	−0.461**
	(0.234)	(0.241)	(0.197)	(0.204)
SSA	−0.613***	−0.735***	−0.553***	−0.632***
	(0.186)	(0.196)	(0.160)	(0.170)
TROPICAR	−0.357***	−0.374***	−0.346***	−0.365***
	(0.0940)	(0.101)	(0.103)	(0.108)
Percent Muslim	−0.169	−0.218		
	(0.226)	(0.244)		
Percent Christian	−0.429*	−0.439*		
	(0.226)	(0.248)		
Percent Buddhist	−0.390*	−0.330		
	(0.217)	(0.240)		
Percent Hindu	−0.486*	−0.628**		
	(0.266)	(0.280)		
Percent Orthodox	−0.137	−0.0387		
	(0.250)	(0.258)		
Percent Catholic	−0.265	−0.267		
	(0.221)	(0.239)		
PD	−1.246***	−1.258***	−1.238***	−1.367***
	(0.327)	(0.328)	(0.329)	(0.325)
syrfm1960	0.967***	0.912***	0.880***	0.828***
	(0.241)	(0.255)	(0.236)	(0.249)
syrfm1960–2000	0.450***	0.431***	0.372**	0.366**
	(0.155)	(0.159)	(0.155)	(0.153)

(Continued)

GENDER AND ECONOMICS IN MUSLIM COMMUNITIES

Table 8 Continued

	OLS (1)	2SLS (2)	OLS (3)	2SLS (4)
fmincome	−0.365	−0.282	−0.498**	−0.426*
	(0.272)	(0.279)	(0.232)	(0.241)
Observations	67	67	67	67
F statistic	27.16	25.12	26.84	22.37
R-squared	0.859	0.856	0.847	0.844
Overid test		Passed		Passed

Notes: See notes to Table 5.

coefficient estimate here implies that an increase of one standard deviation from the mean – which translates to a shift from 20 percent Muslim to 54 percent Muslim – is associated with 0.51 percentage points lower per capita GDP growth, or 22 percent of growth over the period, which averaged 2.3 percent. (Recall that all of these effects are relative to the "other" category.) When only percent Muslim is included, as in column 4, the same change is associated with a 0.28 percentage point decline in growth, or 12 percent of the total.[6]

Muslim is not the only religious affiliation variable negatively correlated with growth. Percent Hindu is economically large and statistically significant, a result that persists across all of the specifications, though the magnitude declines as the gender variables are added. This result is driven by the fact that percent Hindu is essentially a fixed effect for India. Percent Christian also emerges as negatively correlated with growth, although its statistical significance is weak. Without any controls for gender inequality, as in Table 5's column 6, a one standard deviation increase in percent Christian (from 20 to 45 percent) is associated with a 0.09 percentage point decline in growth, about 4 percent of growth. Adding the gender inequality controls, as in Table 6's column 2, increases this effect to 11 percentage points, or 5 percent of growth.

After adding gender inequality in education and income in Table 6, the size of the coefficient estimates for the religious affiliation variables decline, (with the exception of percent Christian, which gets larger as just noted), but not by much. Likewise, comparing columns 2 and 4 in Table 6 indicates that dropping religious affiliation but maintaining measures of gender inequality in education and income does not substantially alter the latter's coefficient estimates. Both results are consistent with other findings in the gender and growth literature: educational quality is associated with more growth, and income equality with less.

Comparing Tables 5 and 6 with Tables 7 and 8, we see that adding PD does not change the coefficients for the core model regressors (all those besides

GENDER AND ECONOMICS IN MUSLIM COMMUNITIES

the religion or gender variables) much in terms of magnitudes and not at all in terms of signs, though there are some minor changes in statistical significance.[7] As a result, I will confine my detailed comments to the gender and religion variables.

Across the two sets of models, adding PD renders the estimated coefficients for percent Muslim much weaker and statistically no different from zero across all of the regression specifications. Setting aside the issue of statistical significance and taking the models that include all gender inequality controls and religious affiliation variables as a baseline (regression 2 in Tables 6 and 8), the effect of a one standard deviation change in percent Muslim declines from 0.40 (17.6) to 0.17 (7.6) percentage points (percent of growth).

The performance of the PD regressor is strong and robust across all the specifications in Tables 7 and 8: coefficient estimates are large, statistically significant, and remarkably stable, ranging from a low of -1.24 in regression 3 of Table 8 to a high of -1.59 in regression 2 of Table 7. This estimate puts the growth effect of a one standard deviation change in PD (from a score of 0.17 to 0.36) somewhere in the range of 0.23–0.30 percentage points, which amounts to between 10 and 13 percent of growth over the period. Alternatively, a country with the sample's maximum PD index, 0.73, would have between 0.91 and 1.16 percentage points lower growth relative to a country with no PD, which represents between 40 and 50 percent of real per capita GDP growth over the forty-year period – quite a substantial impact.[8]

The results for the gender inequality in education and income variables, as illustrated in Table 8, are not substantially changed by the inclusion of PD, though some of the magnitudes increase and fmincome gains statistical significance. According to the results in column 4 of Table 8, countries that started off in 1960 with a female-to-male education ratio (syrfm1960) one standard deviation below the mean (0.32 versus 0.60) experienced 0.23 percentage points in lower growth. Progress in achieving gender equality in education is also associated with higher economic growth over this period: if a country went from having the mean gender education ratio to full equality between women and men (implying a growth rate of 51 percent over the forty years), then economic growth is predicted to be 0.18 percentage points higher, or 8.2 percent of growth. The results on the female-to-male income ratio point in a different direction: a 15 percent increase in female income (the standard deviation) is associated with a 0.06 percentage point decline in growth. While these results are consistent with other studies of the impact of the gender wage gap on growth, they require further study (and better data) to fully understand.

Finally, it is customary at this point to say something about the robustness of the results. After reading Ross' (2008) study on oil, Islam, and women, I added oil rents as a percent of GDP (World Bank's "World Development

GENDER AND ECONOMICS IN MUSLIM COMMUNITIES

Indicators" database [2012]) to my regressions, with no changes here either (the coefficients on oil rents were negative). Dropping regional controls from the specification resulted in all of the 2SLS models failing the over-identification tests. Looking to the OLS results without regional controls, all of the religious affiliation variables lose magnitude and statistical significance, though all of the gender inequality variables become larger and gain statistical significance (including PD). In terms of the multicollinearity issue, I did not have the predicted problems of high R-squared but little statistical significance on the coefficients. I also considered how small changes in the sample affected my results, alternately dropping all of the industrialized countries and countries in the Middle East and North Africa region from the sample. Both PD and the other gender inequality variables are robust to these changes, though the religious affiliation variables lose all of their statistical significance. I also looked at the impact of dropping the countries with the five highest and five lowest PD scores to check for sensitivity of the results to sample outliers. PD coefficient estimates were similar in magnitude to the full sample's estimates, but standard errors were larger and thus the statistical significance of estimates declined. That the PD coefficient estimate, despite the many flaws of the underlying variable, was so stable across the variety of specifications tried, even after adding other gender inequality in education and income variables, fortifies my confidence in the overall approach and conclusions.

CONCLUDING REMARKS

Although gender inequality is now widely recognized as a major obstacle to economic development, our understanding of the institutional mechanisms behind its persistence is limited. In the econometric literature at least, a number of scholars use religious affiliation, particularly Islam, to proxy for patriarchal preferences, implicitly providing a noneconomic logic for the persistence of gender inequality. This literature covers a wide range of approaches, from direct analyses of growth to explanations of gender inequality and consequences for development accompanying more conservative attitudes toward women. My study utilizes an endogenous growth framework, with results that are broadly consistent with the gender and religious affiliation literature reviewed. Islam is found to be economically costly in that it is negatively correlated with growth, even after other religious affiliation and gender inequality in education and income variables are included. However, once I directly control for a variety of patriarchal institutions, the economic and statistical significance of Islam falls away.

I conclude that using affiliation with Islam as a control for patriarchal preferences in studies of growth and gender inequality is misleading

GENDER AND ECONOMICS IN MUSLIM COMMUNITIES

in multiple ways. First, it presumes an answer rather than critically investigating the question of what religious affiliation actually measures. This presumption is particularly problematic in the case of prevailing social and political stereotypes about Islam, which facilitate easy equivalences between Muslim communities and economic irrationality or gender bias. Second, it obscures the role of patriarchy as a system of male advantage, which incurs costs akin to those generated by rent-seeking activities. Therefore, it is likely that studies that use gender inequality outcomes, such as those in education, income, or the labor market, to capture the growth costs of gender bias are lower bound estimates. Incorporating direct measures of patriarchal institutions in studies of gender and growth, as I do in my measure of patriarchal dominance, adds more nuance and rigor to our understanding of the economic causes and consequences of gender systems.

ACKNOWLEDGMENTS

Many thanks to the anonymous reviewers and the guest editors for the time and care they took in giving constructive feedback on earlier versions of the article and to the participants in IAFFE and *Feminist Economics*' Gender and Economics in Muslim Communities workshop. All mistakes are, of course, my own.

NOTES

[1] One important exception is Rafael La Porta, Florencio Lopez-de-Silanes, Andrei Shleifer, and Robert Vishny, who empirically link percent Muslim (and percent Catholic) to poorer government performance, though these associations "generally become insignificant" once they control for per capita income and latitude (1999: 262).

[2] Note that because the GID database (from which I draw the gendered institutional variables) does not include economies with fewer than one million people, I do not include them in my analysis either.

GENDER AND ECONOMICS IN MUSLIM COMMUNITIES

[3] This specification stems from trying a number of geography variables as instruments. Area in the tropics consistently failed over-identification tests, so I came to include it in the growth regressions. I include the Frankel and Romer (1999) variable because it is widely accepted as a valid instrument for trade. I used location in the Southern hemisphere as an additional instrument because it was the only geography variable that had a marked impact on the 2SLS estimations, though primarily in terms of the overall fit of the first-stage regressions, as opposed to having much of a direct impact on the endogenous variables themselves.

[4] For instance, the variance inflation factor for patriarchal dominance when run with the other gender inequality and religion variables is 2.41 and the condition number is 24.7.

[5] First stage results are available from the author on request.

[6] Because some scholars use a Muslim dummy variable (which equals one if 50 percent or more of the population is Muslim and zero otherwise) to proxy for patriarchal preferences, I also ran the model with just a Muslim dummy variable for religious affiliation, but failed to get any statistical or economic significance. However, in a prior version of the paper, with a smaller sample of primarily Muslim countries, the Muslim dummy coefficient estimate was larger and statistically significant.

[7] Middle East and North Africa (MENA) does gain statistical significance, but this is primarily the result of a decline in standard errors rather than an increase in coefficients.

[8] Furthermore, the first stage regressions (not presented) indicate that there is a negative and statistically significant association between PD and investment, a correlation that does not manifest for any of the other gendered variables nor for percent Muslim.

REFERENCES

Baliamoune-Lutz, Mina. 2006. "Globalisation and Gender Inequality: Is Africa Different?" *Journal of African Economies* 16(2): 301–48.

Baliamoune-Lutz, Mina and Mark McGillivray. 2009. "Does Gender Inequality Reduce Growth in Sub-Saharan African and Arab Countries?" *African Development Review* 21(2): 224–42.

Barro, Robert and Jong-Wha Lee. 2010. "A New Data Set of Educational Attainment in the World, 1950–2010." Working Paper 15902, National Bureau of Economic Research (NBER), Cambridge, Massachusetts.

Barro, Robert J. and Rachel McCleary. 2003. "Religion and Economic Growth Across Countries." *American Sociological Review* 68(5): 760–81.

Boone, Peter. 1996. "Political and Gender Oppression as a Cause of Poverty." Centre for Economic Performance Discussion Paper 294. London School of Economics and Political Science.

Braunstein, Elissa. 2008. "The Feminist Political Economy of the Rent-Seeking Society." *Journal of Economic Issues* 42(4): 1–21.

Central Intelligence Agency (CIA). 2008. *The World Factbook 2008*. Washington, DC: CIA.

Dollar, David and Roberta Gatti. 1999. "Gender Inequality, Income, and Growth: Are Good Times Good for Women?" World Bank Policy Research Report Working Paper Series 1, Washington, DC.

Dollar, David, Raymond Fisman, and Roberta Gatti. 2001. "Are Women Really the 'Fairer' Sex? Corruption and Women in Government." *Journal of Economic Behavior and Organization* 46(4): 423–29.

GENDER AND ECONOMICS IN MUSLIM COMMUNITIES

Forsythe, Nancy, Roberto Patricio Korzeniewicz, and Valerie Durrant. 2000. "Gender Inequalities and Economic Growth: A Longitudinal Evaluation." *Economic Development and Cultural Change* 48(3): 573–617.

Frankel, Jeffrey and David Romer. 1999. "Does Trade Cause Growth?" *American Economic Review* 89(3): 379–99.

Gallup, John, Jeffrey Sachs, and Andrew Mellinger. 1999. "Geography and Economic Development." *International Regional Science Review* 22(2): 179–232.

Guiso, Luigi, Paola Sapienza, and Luigi Zingales. 2003. "People's Opium? Religion and Economic Attitudes." *Journal of Monetary Economics* 50(1): 225–82.

Heston, Alan. 2003. "Crusades and Jihads: A Long-Run Economic Perspective." *Annals of the Academy of Political and Social Science* 588(1): 112–35.

Heston, Alan, Robert Summers, and Bettina Aten. 2006. "Penn World Table Version 6.2." Center for International Comparisons of Production, Income and Prices, University of Pennsylvania.

Humana, Charles. 1992. *World Human Rights Guide*, 3rd ed. New York: Oxford University Press.

Jutting, Johannes, Christian Morrisson, Jeff Dayton-Johnson, and Denis Drechsler. 2006. "Measuring Gender (In)Equality: Introducing the Gender, Institutions and Development Data Base (GID)." OECD Development Centre Working Paper 247, Paris.

Klasen, Stephen. 1999. "Does Gender Inequality Reduce Growth and Development? Evidence from Cross-Country Regressions." Policy Research Report on Gender and Development, Working Paper Series 7, World Bank, Washington, DC.

Klasen, Stephen and Francesca Lamanna. 2009. "The Impact of Gender Inequality in Education and Employment on Economic Growth: New Evidence for a Panel of Countries." *Feminist Economics* 15(3): 91–132.

Knack, Stephen and Philip Keefer. 1995. "Institutions and Economic Performance: Cross-Country Tests Using Alternative Institutional Measures." *Economics and Politics* 7(3): 207–27.

Krueger, Anne O. 1974. "The Political Economy of the Rent-Seeking Society." *American Economic Review* 64(3): 291–303.

Kuran, Timur. 2003. "The Islamic Commercial Crisis: Institutional Roots of Economic Underdevelopment in the Middle East." *Journal of Economic History* 63(2): 414–46.

Lal, Deepak. 1998. *Unintended Consequences: The Impact of Factor Endowments, Culture, and Politics on Long-Run Economic Growth.* Cambridge: MIT Press.

La Porta, Rafael, Florencio Lopez-de-Silanes, Andrei Shleifer, and Robert Vishny. 1999. "The Quality of Government." *Journal of Law, Economics, and Organization* 15(1): 222–79.

Lewis, Bernard. 2002. *What Went Wrong? Western Impact and Middle Eastern Response.* New York: Oxford University Press.

Moghadam, Valentine. 1998. *Women, Work, and Economic Reform in the Middle East and North Africa.* Boulder, CO: Lynne Rienner Publishers.

Noland, Marcus. 2005. "Religion and Economic Performance." *World Development* 33(8): 1215–32.

Norris, Pippa and Ronald Inglehart. 2009. "Islamic Culture and Democracy: Testing the 'Clash of Civilizations' Thesis." In *New Frontiers in Comparative Sociology*, edited by Masamichi Sasaki, 221–49. Leiden: Koninklijke Brill NW.

Pryor, Frederic L. 2007. "The Economic Impact of Islam on Developing Countries." *World Development* 35(11): 1815–35.

Rodrik, Dani, Arvind Subramanian, and Francesco Trebbi. 2004. "Institutions Rule: The Primacy of Institutions Over Geography and Integration in Economic Development." *Journal of Economic Growth* 9(2): 131–65.

Ross, Michael L. 2008. "Oil, Islam, and Women." *American Political Science Review* 102(1): 107–23.

GENDER AND ECONOMICS IN MUSLIM COMMUNITIES

Said, Edward. 1978. *Orientalism.* New York: Pantheon Books.

Sala-i-Martin, Xavier, Gernot Doppelhofer, and Ronald I. Miller. 2004. "Determinants of Long-Term Growth: A Bayesian Averaging of Classical Estimates (BACE) Approach." *American Economic Review* 94(4): 813–35.

Seguino, Stephanie. 2000. "Gender Inequality and Economic Growth: A Cross-Country Analysis." *World Development* 28(7): 1211–30.

———. 2011. "Help or Hindrance? Religion's Impact on Gender Inequality in Attitudes and Outcomes." *World Development* 39(8): 1308–21.

Tollison, Robert D. and Roger D. Congleton. 1995. "Introduction." In *The Economic Analysis of Rent Seeking,* edited by Robert D. Tollison and Roger D. Congleton, xi–xix. Brookfield, VT: Edward Elgar.

Tzannatos, Zafiris. 1999. "Women and Labor Market Changes in the Global Economy: Growth Helps, Inequalities Hurt and Public Policy Matters." *World Development* 27(3): 551–69.

World Bank. 2001. *Engendering Development through Equality in Rights, Resources, and Voice.* New York: Oxford University Press.

———. 2012. "World Development Indicators." http://data.worldbank.org/data-catalog/world-development-indicators.

THE INFLUENCE OF PATRIARCHAL NORMS, INSTITUTIONS, AND HOUSEHOLD COMPOSITION ON WOMEN'S EMPLOYMENT IN TWENTY-EIGHT MUSLIM-MAJORITY COUNTRIES

Niels Spierings

ABSTRACT

The low level of women's employment in Muslim-majority countries is often explained by patriarchy, while disregarding variation among and within these countries. Using a new theoretical framework, this study translates patriarchy as a concept to macro- and micro-level explanations of employment. It formulates and tests hypotheses for societal norms and institutions and household composition, including how the latter's effects are context dependent. The study analyzes data from surveys (1997–2008) for twenty-eight countries, 383 districts, and 250,410 women and finds that men's public dominance over women decreases women's employment. Presence of – in particular non-foster – children and elderly people at home withholds women from labor market entrance. However, presence of other women in the household stimulates labor market entrance. Absence of a partner, male household head, or other adult men pushes women into the labor market, and thus, for example, male breadwinners' absence has a weaker negative effect in contexts of male public dominance.

INTRODUCTION

Patriarchy as an explanation for low levels of women's employment across countries with a Muslim-majority population is essentialist and ignores the diversity among and within these countries, both in terms of women's employment and patriarchy (examples of essentialist approaches: John C. Caldwell [1982]; Ronald Inglehart and Pippa Norris [2003]; Ephraim Yuchtman-Yaar and Yasmin Alkalay [2007]). Using data from twenty-eight countries, this study examines the relationships between patriarchal norms, institutions, household compositions, and women's nonagricultural paid employment. In other words, I apply a quantitative approach to "'the internal dynamics and plurality' of Muslim nations" (Nancy J. Davis and Robert V. Robinson 2006: 167).

While there is a vast literature on the concept of patriarchy and its different dimensions, forms, and manifestations (Sylvia Walby 1996, 2009; Georgia Duerst-Lahti 2008), two core elements recur: "gender inequality" and "systematicity" (Walby 1996: 20). Patriarchy is often conceptualized as a contract in which multiple parties are involved, creating gendered structures and norms that are then taken for granted (Liisa Rantalaiho 1993; Valentine M. Moghadam 1998; Carole Pateman 1998). These parties include women, other household members, and the state – all with their respective agendas. How these parties interact and how patriarchy takes shape (the patriarchal bargain) depends on the temporal and spatial context (Deniz Kandiyoti 1988). Studies examining patriarchy in relation to countries with predominantly Muslim populations (hereafter, Muslim-majority countries) often do so using the notion of "classic patriarchy," which centers on patrilineality and a strict male breadwinner/female homemaker model (Kandiyoti 1988). In this study, I argue that (1) this notion of patriarchy leads to internal differences in women's employment within Muslim-majority countries by the composition of the household in which these women live; (2) the importance of these dimensions of patriarchy varies across Muslim-majority countries, and I translate these differences into macro-levels hypotheses on the variation in women's employment in these countries; and (3) differences in the strength of patriarchal norms and policies at the macro level shape the impact of the household composition at the micro level.

I aim to enhance and nuance our understanding of the links between women's employment, household composition, and district-level norms and country-level laws and policies in Muslim-majority countries, leading to three important contributions to the literature. First, my framework shows that many more household composition characteristics are important as explanatory variables of women's employment than the presence of a partner (marital status) and children, which are central to existing studies (Sulayman S. Al-Qudsi 1998; Rebecca Miles 2002; Sajeda Amin and Nagah H. Al-Bassusi 2004; Ayse Gündüz-Hoşgör and Jeroen Smits 2008). I test hypotheses stating the number of adult women present in the household and a woman being head of household both lead to higher employment likelihoods, whereas the presence of more adult men, brothers, boys, and children biologically related to the head of household decreases women's employment likelihood, as is expected for being partner of the head of household as well.

Second, as (comparative) case studies on women's employment in Muslim-majority countries show, the degree to which societies are

GENDER AND ECONOMICS IN MUSLIM COMMUNITIES

patriarchal clearly differs across Muslim-majority countries (Barbara Callaway and Lucy Creevey 1994; Roksana Bahramitash 2002, 2003; Miles 2002; Valentine M. Moghadam 2003; Heba Nassar 2003). Still, most quantitative, cross-national studies tend to reinforce the dualistic approach by setting Muslim-majority countries apart with a dummy variable to capture the impact of "Islam's patriarchal nature."[1] The few studies that took a comparable perspective in the past included only district- (Ayse Gündüz-Hoşgör and Jeroen Smits 2007; Niels Spierings, Jeroen Smits, and Mieke Verloo 2010; Niels Spierings 2014) or country-level variables (Niels Spierings, Jeroen Smits, and Mieke Verloo 2009). This study presents a unique cross-sectional test among Muslim-majority countries on the impact of differences in patriarchy-informed norms and institutions at the country and district level.

The third contribution is found in linking the micro and macro levels. As I expect household composition will be important because of certain gendered contextual power relations, the effect of household composition should also be dependent on the strength of the patriarchal context. This interplay is largely ignored in the literature, but is theorized and tested in this study (Bina Agarwal, 1997; Becky Pettit and Jennifer Hook 2005; Spierings, Smits, and Verloo 2010).

Theoretically, I use the *needs, opportunities, and values* framework introduced by Spierings, Smits, and Verloo (2010) to conceptualize these relationships. I use data derived from the *Database Developing World* that collects and combines comparable and nationally representative households surveys including Demographic and Health Surveys (DHS), Pan Arab Project for Family Health (PAPFam), and Integrated Public Use Microdata Series (IPUMS; Database Developing World [DDW] 2010).[2] The sample includes over 250,000 women from 383 districts in twenty-eight Muslim-majority countries from the greater Middle East, Central Asia, Southeast Asia, and Sub-Saharan Africa. The surveys are mostly from between 2000 and 2008, with two exceptions (Kyrgyz Republic, 1997; Kazakhstan, 1999). Only including Muslim-majority countries allows for a focus on the diversity among them, instead of running the risk of overstressing the dualism with other countries (for example, Christian countries). Because I test hypotheses formulated at the micro, meso, and macro level as well as cross-level interactions, I use multilevel logistic regression models, which few studies have applied so far (Spierings, Smits, and Verloo 2009; Spierings 2014). Women's nonagricultural employment remunerated in cash is the dependent variable. I define employment rather strictly because agricultural and nonagricultural labors, as well as paid and unpaid employment, are influenced differently by the same explanatory factors. For instance, economic development reduces women's agricultural activities, and unpaid employment is often the result of having a family business (Fred C. Pampel and Kazuko Tanaka 1986; Debra Anne Donahoe 1999; Ester Boserup 1998).

I find significant differences in the odds of whether women are employed across households depending on the presence of adult women (+), adult men (-), elderly people (-), children not biologically related to the head of household (+), and on being head of the household (+). Also, more patriarchal norms and institutions regarding women's presence in the public sphere decrease employment likelihoods (contrary to norms and institutions of household power differentials). Finally, I found indications of context dependency for the impact of households' demands for income or care, which are smaller in more patriarchal environments, where all women are more restricted to the household.

THEORETICAL FRAMEWORK

Needs, opportunities, and values

The multilevel *needs, opportunities, and values* framework serves as an overarching structure that helps conceptualize the complexity and multitude of factors influencing women's employment in this study (Spierings, Smits, and Verloo 2010; Spierings 2014). Three of this study's core characteristics are important: (1) women live in different contexts – household, communities, and countries; (2) in each context, the magnitude of micro-level effects may differ; and (3) at these different levels, factors shaping women's *needs, opportunities, and values* influence women's employment. First, women's own characteristics (for instance, educational attainment) are important; their household characteristics (such as the composition) are important because many decisions are made at the household level (Agarwal 1997); and the larger context consists of a woman's country as well as the subnational level, the province or smaller community that is a woman's direct environment. This contextual level is particularly relevant for influences dependent on geographic proximity, such as societal norms and labor market opportunities. Second, effects of micro-level factors are embedded in the contextual levels as well and can thus differ according to characteristics of the context. Third, all influences on women's employment can be deduced from the *needs, opportunities, and values* of a woman and her environment. *Needs* refer to the micro-level material and care needs that can be met or threatened by paid employment. *Opportunities* focus on whether there are accessible jobs for women that are suitable to them according to societal norms. This depends on the labor market structure and the characteristics of the woman entering the marketplace, such as her human capital and resources. *Values* refer to whether it is deemed acceptable for women to work (or work in a certain occupation). These values can manifest themselves in societal norms (social

GENDER AND ECONOMICS IN MUSLIM COMMUNITIES

rules dictating that men and women should not mix socially in public life), policies (restrictions on driving a car), and individual attitudes (believing that a woman's primary task is running the household; Spierings, Smits, and Verloo [2010]). In addition, values shape which (micro-level) needs and opportunities become salient in influencing women's employment (Moghadam 2003). For instance, the impact of marriage on employment is grounded in the gendered division of household tasks in which a woman's primary role is considered to be the caregiver, while a man's primary role is considered to be the breadwinner. Value systems such as patriarchies are thus sources that determine which micro-level characteristics influence women's employment, and to what extent. I will apply this framework to theorize how patriarchy can influence women's employment in Muslim-majority countries.

Classic patriarchy

I treat the concept of patriarchy as a set of institutionalized, normalized, and internalized values (see above) that vary across Muslim-majority countries. Consistent with the long tradition of feminist and postcolonial studies (Leila Ahmed 1992; Lila Abu-Lughod 1998; Moghadam 2003), I challenge essentialist and dualistic conceptualizations that compare the "patriarchic Muslim world" with the "liberated West." I focus on the differences across and within different Muslim economies, understood by starting from the concept of classic patriarchy (Kandiyoti 1988). This focus should not be misconstrued to indicate Muslim exceptionalism. The particular patriarchal bargain focused on in this study is "ideal typical" (Kandiyoti 1988: 285); it is, by definition, nonexistent, and different communities at different times vary in how they measure up to this classic patriarchal bargain. Regarding this ideal type, Moghadam (2003: 1) speaks of the "patriarchal gender contract" in the greater Middle East, and Kandiyoti (1988) uses the term "classic patriarchy" for the Middle East and North Africa (MENA) and for south and east Asia. However, both authors conceptualize patriarchy as a variable that differs across countries and helps to explain differences between Muslim-majority countries. This study will be placed in that tradition.

The two core characteristics of classic patriarchy that are important for this study are: (1) the dominance of patrilineality and (2) a strict and traditional division of labor. With regard to the first, the typical household is characterized by patrilocality, meaning that senior men are first considered to be head of the household, status within the family is largely determined through the male line, women tend to live in their husband's households, sons are preferred over daughters, and women are generally subordinated to male household members (Kandiyoti 1988; Valentine M. Moghadam 2004; Gündüz-Hoşgör and Smits 2008). In the public domain, this translates to men being considered more suitable for positions of power. The second characteristic is a traditional division of labor; in other words, this means division of labor operates along the male breadwinner/female homemaker model (Kandiyoti 1988; Moghadam 1998; Miles 2002; Willy Jansen 2004). Adult men in the household are responsible for providing an income, while women's primary role is raising the children, caring for other household members, and housework. These tasks are mainly performed within the walls of the household, where women can maintain "their respectable and protected domestic roles," thus reserving the public domain for men (Kandiyoti 1988: 280).

The most straightforward way to derive hypotheses combining the *needs, opportunities, and values* framework with the notion of classic patriarchy is to focus on how these values (patrilineality and role division) translate differently to societal norms and institutions (Table 1 lists all hypotheses). First, I expect societal norms will be most relevant at the closer, subnational level. Stronger patrilineality manifests itself as a societal norm of a gendered power differential when the likelihood of women's employment is lower. Similarly, I expect that the stronger the norm when women have no public or income role, the lower women's employment likelihood will be. Second, these values can become institutionalized, hampering women's opportunities to find employment. For instance, women can be prohibited to travel without a *mahram* (male relative) or denied economic property and access to certain jobs, which is not the case in a substantial number of Muslim-majority countries, and the practice is not unique to or originating in Islam (Ahmed 1992; Asma Barlas 2002).[3] These laws and policies are mainly made at the national level. The more these institutions limit women's access to the public/monetary domain, the lower I expect women's employment likelihood will be. Also, the more strongly traditional household hierarchies are institutionalized, then the lower women's employment likelihood.

Household composition

The two core characteristics of classic patriarchy imply that households' configurations are important in determining the likelihood of women's employment. Highly gendered roles and power positions in the household determine how the balance in income and care's supply and demand is perceived. Consequently, more household compositions than just the two "classics" of micro-level studies – marital status and the presence of children – should be expected to impact employment (Peter Glick and David E. Sahn 1997; Al-Qudsi 1998; Miles 2002; Amin and Al-Bassusi 2004; Adebayo B. Aromolaran 2004).

Because within the household women are expected to supply care and men are expected to provide income, women will have lower incentives to

GENDER AND ECONOMICS IN MUSLIM COMMUNITIES

Table 1 Hypotheses

National level	
$H_n 1$	The more strongly policies restrict women's access of the public sphere, the lower women's employment likelihoods in that country
$H_n 2$	The more strongly policies reinforce traditional power differentials in households, the lower women's employment likelihoods in that country
Subnational level	
$H_{sn} 1$	The more traditional the norms on the access of the public sphere, the lower women's employment likelihoods in that country
$H_{sn} 2$	The more traditional the norms regarding household power differential, the lower women's employment likelihoods in that country
Household level	
$H_h 1$	Married women have a lower likelihood of employment than unmarried women
$H_h 2$	The more adult men present in a household, the lower the likelihood of employment of women in that household
$H_h 3$	Female heads of household are more likely to be employed than women who are not the head of household
$H_h 4$	The more adult women present in a household, the higher the employment likelihood of women in that household
$H_h 5$	Of the women who are not the head of the household, those who are married to of the head of household are less likely to be employed than other women
$H_h 6$	The higher the number of (young) children a woman has, the lower the employment likelihood of that woman
$H_h 7$	The higher the number of elderly people in a household, the lower the employment likelihood of women in that household
$H_h 8$	If the male:female ratio of children is higher in a household, then the lower the likelihood of employment for the women in that household
$H_h 9$	The larger the proportion of children who are non-biologically related to the head of household, the higher the likelihood that women in that household will be employed
$H_h 10$	The more brothers present in the household, the lower the likelihood of employment for a girl/woman in that household
Macro-micro cross-level	
$H_I 1$	The stronger the institutionalization of public seclusion values, the weaker the effects of the positive effects of economic needs
$H_I 2$	The stronger the institutionalization of traditional family values, the weaker the effects of the negative effects of household care needs

seek employment if men are present to provide an income. Thus, "marital status" is important, as the chances are higher that women without a spouse will have to raise an income themselves. In addition, other adult men in the household are more likely to provide an additional income first, as they face fewer obstacles and more incentives, given the patriarchal norms discussed above. Thus, I expect that women living in households with more adult men, even those who are not a spouse, have lower likelihoods of being employed (*ceteris paribus*). Moreover, in patrilineal households, the head of the household is considered the breadwinner. Therefore, I expect that female heads of household are more often employed than women who are not head of household (*ceteris paribus*).

For women, employment might often be problematic as this can be interpreted as neglecting their supposed primary task as caregiver (for which presence at home is considered necessary). However, if there are more potential care providers (adult women) in the household, the relative care burden for each of them is less. The presence of other women caregivers then increases women's probability of employment outside the home (Spierings, Smits, and Verloo 2010). Furthermore, being the partner of the head of household involves being responsible for provided care (Kandiyoti 1988). Therefore, I expect that the spouse of the head of household is less likely to be employed than the head of household or any other woman who is not the spouse to the male head of household (*ceteris paribus*).

Most studies (implicitly) present the demand for care by including the presence of (young) children (Glick and Sahn 1997; Al-Qudsi 1998; Miles 2002; Amin and Al-Bassusi 2004; Aromolaran 2004). The higher the number of young children present in the household, the greater the care duties and the lower women's employment probability. Whereas children might need the most care, they are not the only ones requiring care. Considering the prevalence of extended households, the presence of elderly people in households and the importance of age and respect for the elderly in patrilineal systems also affect household care duties. Women's employment is expected to decrease as the number of elderly individuals living in the household increases, thus increasing women's household care duties (Moghadam 2003; Jennifer Olmsted 2005; Andreas Kotsadam 2011).

The importance of patrilineality might also be reflected by the different perception of care needs for boys versus girls. Since it is important to have a son in this system, male children might require more attention and care and be restrictive for women who want, or need, employment. Besides being a boy, it is also important that a child is part of the hereditary line. While formal adoption is sometimes not allowed, is done in secret, or the foster child cannot receive inheritance, in about 3 percent of the households studied here, there is a child present in the household who is not a descendent of the household head (Nancy E. Riley and Krista E. Van Vleet 2012). In the Sub-Saharan African countries, this figure is generally higher, regularly being over 8 percent; in the Middle East it is generally much lower, regularly below 1 percent. Under these circumstances, children who are not biologically related to the head of household are not be considered fully part of the family; as a consequence, they might receive less care from the women and thus have less impact on women's employment (Glick and Sahn 1997).

Last, access to household resources (money, means of transport, contacts) that help women find a job can also depend on the household composition (Donahoe 1999; Moghadam 2003). Since employment is seen as more important for the male youth in the household (compared to the female youth), it is expected that household resources are mostly used to help boys find a job (Miles 2002). Consequently, there are fewer resources available when a girl has more brothers (*ceteris paribus*), and thus she might have lower chances of employment.

Contextualizing household composition

So far, I have treated the context-level and household-composition variables as separate influences on women's employment. However, if the contextual characteristics of patriarchy vary and embed micro-level relationships, the interaction of the two should be considered. I will discuss two ways in which the variation of system-level patriarchy might shape the effects of household compositions. Empirically, these forms of interrelatedness can be present simultaneously; they are disentangled for conceptual clarity.

First, I expect that income needs have less effect when the context is more restricting in terms of women entering the public sphere: if norms and policies stipulate that women do not work outside the home, the overriding economic reason to seek employment needs to be much stronger. Thus, when these contextual norms and policies are more prominent, only women experiencing really strong economic needs will enter the labor market; whereas areas with less strict norms and lower economic needs might lead women to seek employment. In statistical terms, this means that the absence of a partner, being head of the household, and the absence of other adult men can be expected to be (statistically) weaker in areas more hostile to women's public participation.

The second form of context dependency involves care tasks in a household and the strength of traditional family norms and policies. When the contextual pressure on women or households is stronger in terms of classical household roles, it can be expected that all women are supposed to stay at home and perform the care duties in a household (childcare and other housework). I expect that if the context becomes somewhat less strict, women who do not have children or elderly people to care for at home have the most freedom to seek employment. However, society will still expect women with children to stay at home and care for those children. Thus, the general negative effect of higher care needs (presence of children and elderly in the household and the absence of other adult women care providers) will be (statistically) weaker in more traditional areas.

GENDER AND ECONOMICS IN MUSLIM COMMUNITIES

DATA AND METHODS

Data

I used representative datasets from PAPFam, DHS, and IPUMS available through DDW (2010). When assessing the descriptive statistics, it should be taken into account that the datasets come from various years. For instance, if a worldwide recession took place in the late 2000s, this would affect all countries but only show up in the more recent surveys. The actual recession, however, had its main impact on these countries after 2008. For the explanatory analyses, I included random intercepts at the country level to correct for country-level differences. Since only one survey for each country is included, the random intercepts also capture year effects.

Each dataset includes women between the ages 15 and 49. In eight datasets, only ever-married women were included in the sample. To ensure the datasets are comparable across countries, I have selected only the ever-married in the other datasets.[4] In addition, I only include women who were neither in school nor disabled. After deleting the cases with missing values, 95.7 percent of women (250,410 of 261,728) from twenty-eight Middle Eastern, Sub-Saharan African, Central Asian and Southeast Asian Muslim-majority countries remained. Supplementary Appendix A provides an overview and detailed information on the datasets and is available on the publisher's website.[5]

For the district-level variables, I use the same data sources aggregating from the micro level. For the norms variables, caution should be taken in the interpretation as I had to use proxies for people's attitudes. Still, the usage of these district-level variables is an important step forward in the analyses of local norms' impact. For the country-level variables, external data were available: the Organisation for Economic Co-operation and Development's "Gender, Institutions and Development" (OECD GID) database on policies and praxis and data on the institutionalization of conservative Islam in the state (Spierings, Smits, and Verloo 2009).

Dependent variable and method

I use whether a woman was in paid employment in the nonagricultural sector (1 = Yes) as the dependent variable. For women who are either not employed or working in agriculture (both 0), seeking a nonagricultural job is a departure from the default option of staying at home (Spierings, Smits, and Verloo 2010). The use of household surveys to measure women's employment in developing economies has sometimes been criticized because respondents do not consider or strategically avoid labeling certain tasks as labor (Donahoe 1999; Jansen 2004; Ray Langstem

GENDER AND ECONOMICS IN MUSLIM COMMUNITIES

and Rania Salem 2008), and these biases might differ by country, thus problematizing comparisons. However, this mainly applies to women's agricultural, domestic, and informal labor. The dependent variable in this study is less compromised because women who are gainfully employed in the nonagricultural sector generally report their status as employed (Donahoe 1999; Langstem and Salem 2008).

The statistical analysis relies on logistic regression models (employed versus not employed). I use multilevel models (software: MLwiN 2.20, Centre for Multilevel Modelling, Bristol; estimation procedure: Markov chain Monte Carlo [MCMC]) to avoid biases toward finding statistically significant relationships for the household-, district-, and country-level variables, due to underestimated standard errors if the number of individual-level cases is used to calculate the country-level coefficients. MCMC estimations in MLwiN generally start from an estimation using the Iterative Generalized Least Squares (IGLS) procedure, as I do in this study. The data are weighed so the sample is representative within countries as well as for all countries combined (see Supplementary Appendix B, available on the publisher's website).

I used control variables for the most-used explanations of women's labor force participation and employment (Tanja van der Lippe and Liset van Dijk 2002; Spierings, Smits, and Verloo 2010). Since resources and opportunities stimulate employment, I include women's educational attainment, partner's occupation (to proxy socioeconomic status and network), and living in a city. I include three micro-level value proxies to tap into internalized and household values: age difference (−), age at birth of first child (+), and living in a polygynous household (−). At the district level, I control for the most important economic factors: economic development, urbanization, and the presence of a service sector and skilled manufacturing jobs. These are expected to increase employment. A fifth variable – unemployment among men in the district – generally decreases the odds of being employed. Moreover, the random intercepts of the model control for unmeasured differences among countries and among districts within countries.

Explanatory variables

Supplementary Appendix C provides detailed information on the variables and is available on the publisher's website. I measure the household-composition variables as follows. I distinguish *married* women (1) from widowed or divorced women (0). I measure the relative presence of *adult men* by dividing the number of men (age > 14) by the total number of household members (age > 14). The *household position* of women has three categories: household head; partner of household head (reference group); and other relationship to household head.[6] I measure the relative number of *adult women* by dividing the number of women in the same age range as the respondents (15–49) by the total number of household members. The number of *children* of a woman is included as well as a dummy if at least one child is under the age of 6. To estimate the presence of *elderly people,* I include the number of parents of the household head or his spouse(s) in a household (mostly grandparents of the respondent). The *male:female ratio of children* was measured by dividing the number of boys (age < 13) by the total number of children (age < 13) in a household. I also included the number of children not *biologically related* to the head of household divided by the total number of children of the head in the household. Finally, I measure the *number of brothers* for women who are a daughter of the head of household and include the boy:girl ratio of siblings (controlling for the number of siblings).[7]

At the district level, two variables besides the controls are included to represent patriarchal norms. Grounded in the idea of prescriptive norms (Joanne R. Smith and Winnifred R. Louis 2009), I measure district-level norms using behavioral indicators. For the "male dominance in the public sphere" variable, the percentage of men with secondary/tertiary education is divided by the percentage of women.[8] Similarly, this is done for nonagricultural employment, and the average of these two ratios is taken (Spierings, Smits, and Verloo 2010).[9] I created an index for the district-level norm on the household power differential and traditionalism using four common indicators (Raymond H. Wheeler and B.G. Hunter 1987; Carlos Varea 1993; Nicole H.W. Civettini and Jennifer Glass 2008): household size, polygynous households, the age differential between women and their partner, and the age of women at the birth of their first child.[10]

The degree of institutionalization of patriarchy in policies is measured at the country level. For the public seclusion dimension, I take the State Islamism variable introduced by Spierings, Smits, and Verloo (2009), which measures the incorporation of conservative Islam in the state structure and two indices from the OECD GID database (OECD GID 2012): "women's access to economic property (other than land or bank loans)," and "freedom in public movement."[11] Each of these three indicators is rescaled so that they run from 0 to 1, and the average was taken (higher equals more patriarchy).

For "private patriarchal institutions," the GID provides two indicators that nicely fit my theoretical concept: the measurement of household power differentials (based on polygyny, inheritance rights, and parental authority) and a scale on the preference for boys. The average of these two indices running from 0 to 1 is taken. Supplementary Appendix D illustrates the wide variety among Muslim-majority countries on the district- and country-level patriarchy scores and is available on the publisher's website.

GENDER AND ECONOMICS IN MUSLIM COMMUNITIES

RESULTS

Variation in employment and patriarchy

Among the twenty-eight countries included in this study, the nonagricultural paid employment rates vary from 3.6 percent in Yemen and 8.9 percent in Djibouti to 45.8 percent in Kazakhstan and 47.6 percent in Nigeria. The differences are even larger at the district level. In twenty-eight of the 383 districts, women's employment is higher than 50 percent, including areas in Burkina Faso, Chad, Indonesia, Kazakhstan, the Kyrgyz Republic, Malaysia, Mali, Nigeria, Senegal, Tunisia, and Zanzibar. The districts with the highest scores are often the capitals and highly urbanized areas. Employment falls below 5 percent in twenty-nine districts representing Algeria, Burkina Faso, Chad, Djibouti, Egypt, Mali, and Yemen. That three countries feature in both lists underscores the large differences within these countries. The household structure and patriarchal context-level factors also show high degrees of variation (see Supplementary Appendix C). Empirically, Muslim-majority countries and women are not one homogenous group.

Macro-level effects

After controlling for economic circumstances,[12] the strongest and most statistically significant effect on employment at the district level is found for the "male dominance public sphere" ($p < 0.001$; Table 2), which has also been found in Spierings, Smits, and Verloo (2010) for six Arab countries. One standard deviation higher score, as expected, lowers the odds of employment by 33 percent. Economically, this means that women are severely restricted in entering the labor market and face more obstacles in finding a job due to cultural norms, and these norms differ substantially within countries.

At the country level, the variable focusing on the policies regarding women's access to the public sphere was marginally significant ($p < 0.10$) and showed the expected lower employment in countries with more restrictions. Since only twenty-eight observations are made at the country level and because some other country-level comparative and single-case studies find similar results (Bahramitash 2002; Spierings, Smits, and Verloo 2009), I consider this outcome preliminarily supportive for the expectations formulated above. The effect of these policies is not very strong after the indirect effects are filtered out. Nevertheless, travel restrictions, *Shari'a* law, and fewer economic rights do seem to hinder women in finding a job. At the same time, the economic impact of public seclusion norms (which might partly explain the implementation of these policies) has more economic significance in these models. Contrary to

GENDER AND ECONOMICS IN MUSLIM COMMUNITIES

Table 2 Logistic regression results: women's odds of participation in gainful nonagricultural employment

	Log odds (β)	Std. error of β	Odds ratio [exp(β)]
MICRO: HOUSEHOLD COMPOSITION			
Married (ref = *No*)	− 0.724***	0.022	0.48
Adult men/adult household members	− 0.122**	0.047	0.89
Household position (ref = *Partner of head*)			
Head of household	0.203***	0.025	1.23
Other	− 0.053**	0.017	0.95
Adult women/household members	0.323***	0.077	1.38
Number of children	− 0.018***	0.005	0.98
Children below the age of 6 (ref = *No*)	− 0.075***	0.010	0.93
Number of parents household head and partner	− 0.044**	0.017	0.96
Boys/all children proportion	− 0.043*	0.017	0.96
Not biologically related/all children	0.244**	0.076	1.28
Number of siblings	− 0.003	0.009	1.00
Male:female sex ratio among siblings	− 0.045	0.076	0.96
DISTRICT: PATRIARCHAL NORMS			
Male dominance public sphere	− 2.484***	0.097	0.08
Traditionalist households	0.480	0.295	1.62
COUNTRY: PATRIARCHAL INSTITUTIONS			
Public seclusion	− 0.441[#]	0.253	0.64
Private sphere power differential	− 0.403	0.336	0.67
MICRO: CONTROL VARIABLES			
Age	0.164***	0.003	1.18
Age^2	− 0.002***	0.000	1.00
Education (ref = *No education*)			
At least some primary or some secondary	0.344***	0.017	1.41
Secondary completed	0.931***	0.021	2.54
At least some tertiary completed	2.160***	0.026	8.67
Living in city	0.608***	0.015	1.84
Partner's occupation (ref = *Blue collar*)			
Agriculture	− 0.737***	0.018	0.48
Lower white collar	− 0.013	0.017	0.99
Upper white collar	0.130***	0.018	1.14
Unemployed	0.014	0.037	1.01
Age difference (partner − woman)	− 0.007***	0.001	0.99
Age at birth first child	0.001	0.001	1.00

(*Continued*)

GENDER AND ECONOMICS IN MUSLIM COMMUNITIES

Table 2 Continued

	Log odds (β)	Std. error of β	Odds ratio $[exp(\beta)]$
Polygynous household (ref = *No*)	− 0.012	0.020	0.99
Instrumental variable *Not biologically related*	− 0.006	0.025	0.99
Instrumental variable *Boys/all children*	0.056***	0.020	1.06
DISTRICT: CONTROL VARIABLES			
Economic development	− 0.838***	0.137	0.43
Unemployment	− 2.131**	0.749	0.12
Labor market structure: service sector	1.318***	0.185	3.74
Labor market structure: skilled manufacturing	1.281***	0.351	3.60
Urbanization	− 0.240*	0.117	0.79
Model characteristics			
Intercept	− 2.360***	0.091	
Country-level variance	0.874***	0.268	
District-level variance	0.090***	0.016	
Household-level variance	0.206***	0.015	
Deviance	208,741.47		

Notes: ***, **, and * denote statistical significance at the 0.1, 1.0, and 5.0 percent levels, respectively, and [#] at the 10 percent level (only used for country-level variables).

$N_{Individuallevel} = 250,410$, $N_{Householdlevel} = 215,844$, $N_{Districtlevel} = 383$, $N_{Countrylevel} = 28$; sample only includes ever-married women, ages 15–49, who are neither in school nor disabled.

Sources: DHS, PAPFam, and IPUMS (DDW 2010); OECD GID (2012); Spierings, Smits and Verloo (2010).

expectations, at both the country and district levels, the private-sphere patriarchy variables show no statistically significant effect on employment.[13]

Household composition effects

At the micro level (Table 2), the control variables' effects are in line with previous studies (van der Lippe and van Dijk 2002; Spierings, Smits, and Verloo 2010).[14] Most of the household compositions show the expected relationship with women's employment and are economically significant.[15] Contrary to expectations, no statistically and economically significant relationships were found for the sex ratio among siblings and children.[16] The allocation of resources and care might be more determined by their status as child than their sex. Moreover, the difference between women who were married to of the head of household and other women who were not the head themselves showed a reverse relationship, but this was relatively small and economically less significant.

GENDER AND ECONOMICS IN MUSLIM COMMUNITIES

Regarding economic needs and in line with previous studies, married women have 52 percent lower odds of employment than widowed and divorced women, which is one of the strongest effects found and economically most significant (see Glick and Sahn [1997]; Gündüz-Hoşgör and Smits [2008]). In line with this, women who were head of the household had higher odds of nonagricultural employment then other women, and the presence of more adult men in the household lowers women's odds of employment. While this study is the first to include the presence of adult men as explanation and shows that it is relevant, its economic significance is limited given the relatively small impact.

For the care needs variables, a relatively large effect was found for the presence of other adult women in the household, as research has found for a pooled analysis of Algeria, Egypt, Jordan, Morocco, Syria, and Tunisia (Spierings, Smits, and Verloo 2010).[17] In terms of economic significance, for the average woman in an average household, the full possible impact of the presence of other women in the household on her probability of being gainfully employed is about 6 percentage points. Regarding the presence of the elderly, women's odds of employment are 4.3 percent lower for each additional elderly person, making it economically more significant than its absence from the current literature suggests. Kotsadam (2011) found a similar negative effect for European welfare states. Not surprisingly, each additional child decreases the odds of employment, but the mere 2 percent indicates that the economic impact of children is limited. The age of the children seems more relevant economically. If there are children present in the household below the age of 6, the odds of employment are on average 7.2 percent lower.

The patrilineal position of the children also seems to relate to women's employment (Glick and Sahn 1997). If, of all children present, a larger number is not biologically related to the head of household, women's employment likelihood increases, as was expected. The effect is economically limited but present. It might only apply to a fraction of the households (< 3 percent), but that includes over 13,000 households in the data used here, and for the women and children in those households, such an effect can make a discernible difference. In terms of causality, we should be careful interpreting this, but some anthropological work suggests a causal relationship. For instance, Betsy Udink (2006) describes a driver's child in Pakistan who lived in the household of his father's sister. He was considered an additional burden and had to assist his aunt in her work as a maid while his nephews and nieces (the uncle and aunt's biological children) were sent to school. There was a difference in how the children were valued and how they increased or decreased the care burden in the household. An alternative interpretation is that that the children in the data are servants, but that is unlikely given the demographic characteristics of the children.[18]

Table 3 Interaction coefficients of household composition with macro-level patriarchy variables

MACRO-LEVEL PATRIARCHY VARIABLES	Direction general effect	Country: Public seclusion		Country: Private sphere power differential		District: Male dominance public sphere		District: Traditionalist households	
		Log odds (β)	Std. error of β	Log odds (β)	Std. error of β	Log odds (β)	Std. error of β	Log odds (β)	Std. error of β
MICRO: HOUSEHOLD STRUCTURE VARIABLES									
Married (ref = *no*)	Neg	− 0.065	0.122			0.849***	0.092		
Adult men/adult household members	Neg	0.243	0.195			1.972***	0.161		
Household position (ref = *partner of head*)									
Head of household	Pos	− 0.576***	0.136			0.469***	0.120		
Other	Neg	− 0.592***	0.095			− 0.089	0.105		
Adult women/household members	Pos			2.231***	0.438			− 0.693	0.361
Number of children	Neg			0.075**	0.029			0.288***	0.025
Children below the age of 6 (ref = *No*)	Neg			0.300***	0.066			0.210	0.055
Number of parents household head and partner	Neg			− 0.030	0.123			− 0.252**	0.090

Notes: ***, **, and * denote statistical significance at the 0.1, 1.0, and 5.0 percent levels, respectively; all main coefficients can be found in Supplementary Appendix E, available on the publisher's website.

GENDER AND ECONOMICS IN MUSLIM COMMUNITIES

Patriarchy's macro/micro-level interactions

Table 3 presents the interactions coefficients. The other coefficients of this can be found in Supplementary Appendix E, available on the publisher's website. In a district in which men dominate the public sphere more, women's employment likelihood increases less if they become single and not married or when fewer men are present in the household; and the higher employment likelihood of women who are the head of the household is less pronounced in countries with more restrictive and excluding institutions. These three effects are in line with expectations, and the others are not statistically significant, with one exception: for being the head of the household, the interaction with the district-level variable is statistically significant and strengthening. Overall, I conclude that the expectation that the more exclusive the public sphere was, the weaker the impact of variables related to the presence of male breadwinners at the household level is preliminary supported.

Regarding the private sphere, it was expected that a more patriarchal environment would lead to weaker effects on the care needs variables because even with lower care relative needs, women are expected to stay at home. The four interaction terms on the effect of children's presence do indeed show this weakening effect. For the economic position of women this means that in more patriarchal districts or countries, women's employment likelihood is low throughout and decreases slightly as the number of children increases. In the less patriarchal districts and countries, women with many children have low employment likelihoods as well, but women with fewer children have considerably higher likelihoods of being employed. At the same time, of the other four interaction terms with care needs variables, two are not statistically significant and two show an effect contradicting my expectations. While the expectation is strongly supported for having children, further study seems appropriate in order to understand the more general mechanisms.

For now, the general economic significance of these results is mainly found in the realization that more patriarchal norms and institutions not only limit women in entering the labor market and finding a job, but also influence which women do so, creating economic inequalities among women.

CONCLUSION AND DISCUSSION

In this study of twenty-eight countries, 383 subnational districts, and about 250,000 women, an unpacked concept of patriarchy was applied to help understand what shapes women's employment differences across and within Muslim-majority countries. In particular, the study showed how the variation in variables tapping into patriarchal values (patrilineality and a strict gendered division of labor) influence women's employment.

GENDER AND ECONOMICS IN MUSLIM COMMUNITIES

The outcomes underscore the idea that patriarchy cannot be treated as a contextual constant, and they challenge an essentialized dualism of Muslim-majority countries opposing "the West" (Caldwell 1982; Inglehart and Norris 2003; Yuchtman-Yaar and Alkalay 2007). This study demonstrated that the differences in which macro-level policies and norms institutionalize the division of labor are important in explaining the variation in women's employment. In addition, it drew attention to the role household composition plays and how the impact of this composition depends on the variation in those (patriarchal) norms and policies.

Regarding household composition, this study pushed the frontier of micro-level research concerning Muslim-majority countries. Applying Spierings, Smits, and Verloo's (2010) framework to patriarchy, this study is one of the first to theorize and test how a wide range of household compositions influence women's employment as patriarchy shapes the needs, opportunities, and values informing women's employment decisions. Existing studies are often limited to a focus on marital status and having children (Al-Qudsi 1998; Miles 2002; Amin and Al-Bassusi 2004; Aromolaran 2004; Pettit and Hook 2005; Gündüz-Hoşgör and Smits 2008). This study focused on more and other aspects of household composition and showed that women who are heads of household and women in households with fewer adult men have higher likelihood of employment. Women in households with fewer adult women and more elderly people have lower employment likelihoods. Furthermore, when the children (all below the age of 13) in a household are not biologically related to the head of the household, women seem less restricted to enter the labor market and become employed. The presence of other adult women in the household was among the strongest influences on employment. It seems that the presence of an extra adult woman in the home decreases the care burden for the respondents, as these other women probably help in care provision and household management. These results are in line with the theoretical logic of economic and care needs. More qualitative research can help assess whether the found associations are indeed causal. As there is no evident alternative explanation that explains the collection of results in this paper, I conclude that the theoretical framework applied here is useful.

With regard to policy, the results imply that not only might childcare facilities foster employment; alleviating the care burden through care for the elderly can also do so. The shift to smaller households should be anticipated as well. If fewer male breadwinners are present, more women are pushed toward seeking employment, but the absence of other care providers (adult women) might withhold women from seeking said employment if no alternative sources of care are available. This shift makes the question for childcare facilities more salient.

Most macro-level studies on women's position in Muslim-majority countries are either case studies or large-scale comparisons with a strong

GENDER AND ECONOMICS IN MUSLIM COMMUNITIES

tendency to focus on what sets Muslim (or Arab) countries apart from other (often Western) countries (Roger Clark, Thomas W. Ramsbey, and Emily Stier Adler 1991; Inglehart and Norris 2003; Yuchtman-Yaar and Alkalay 2007; Jane Arnold Lincove 2008; Michael Ross 2008). This study has combined the more nuanced understanding of differences in patriarchal norms and institutions of the qualitative studies with the broad scope of the quantitative studies. Together with Michele Angrist's study (2012), this comparative study can be seen as a first step toward a new strand of quantitative comparative work on the position of women in Muslim communities. A second contribution to the literature is found in the inclusion of different dimensions of patriarchy at both the district and country levels. These are often collapsed in the above-mentioned comparative studies. This study indicates that whereas both patriarchal norms and policies advocating men's dominant presence in the public sphere decrease women's employment chances, similar norms and policies regarding power differentials in households do not seem to have such an effect. Future research would benefit greatly from comparative data on local-level gender norms. This study is one of the first to systematically assess the impact of these factors at the subnational level, but this study had to rely on proxy concepts. The conclusions should thus be treated with some caution, even though there are clear and strong results. Also, the results present average effects; it cannot be precluded that a power differential norm is relevant for some groups of women, such as women with lower levels of education (Spierings, Smits, and Verloo 2010).

Patriarchal policies and norms were also found to be important in shaping the effect of the household composition: (1) under more traditional circumstances, the presence of children has less impact, and similarly (2) men's stronger district-level dominance in the public sphere is related to a weaker influence from male breadwinners. In both cases, it seems that in more patriarchal environments, there is less room for choice for all women, regardless of the circumstances. These results underscore the role norms play in intrahousehold bargaining, as stressed by Agarwal (1997). However, Agarwal (1997) discusses (1) that norms limit what can be bargained about and thus favor some groups over others and (2) how norms determine the bargaining power of women as two separate points, whereas the analyses here showed that these aspects are two sides of the same coin.

More generally, the study of the context specificity of phenomena, as often argued for by feminist research, has led to an uneasy choice between diversity and generalizability (Shulamit Reinharz 1992). By applying cross-level interaction models, I have shown that it is possible to study which factors influence women's position across countries and simultaneously acknowledge that the influence of these factors is context dependent. This approach can create a better understanding of phenomena in many more

GENDER AND ECONOMICS IN MUSLIM COMMUNITIES

fields, but much theorizing is needed. I formulated two broad hypotheses: the results suggest that these hypotheses need to be refined further and, for instance, anthropological research can provide important insights in explaining unexpected results (some examples can be found in Jennifer Olmsted [2003, 2005]; Jansen [2004]; and Fida J. Adely [2009]).

Another avenue for further research would be applying this study's framework to a larger group of countries. This study was limited because it drew mostly from literature on patriarchal values dominant in Islam, Arab countries, or MENA. By drawing more from literature on, for instance Sub-Saharan Africa (Kandiyoti 1988) or Central Asia (Moghadam 1998; Barbara Wejnert and Almagul Djumabaeva 2004), new dimensions of patriarchy might be discerned leading to other new micro-level hypotheses. Similarly, the approach can be extended to include other regions of the world. For instance, Dante Contreras and Gonzalo Plaza's study (2010) on "Machista" attitudes in Chile suggests that one such dimension is "coupledom." If this is quantifiable for more countries, then it could be included in the theoretical and empirical model.

Finally, this study is in conversation with and advances the conceptual literature on patriarchy. I started from ideal type value patterns described as classical patriarchy (Kandiyoti 1988; Moghadam 1998; Olmsted 2005), focusing on the micro-level economic domain in terms of the phenomenon to be explained, but keeping the domain and manifestations open in terms of explaining concept(s). The latter showed how patriarchy manifests itself and how different aspects of it are related to one another. This study thus supports Kandiyoti when she argues that we need to "focus on more narrowly defined patriarchal bargains, rather than on an unqualified notion of patriarchy" (1988: 285). I would add, however, that narrowness does not preclude multilayered and multidimensional conceptualizations. It is important to understand the different dimensions and domains where this patriarchal bargain manifests itself, and I have shown how household composition, norms, and policies are interrelated. Additionally, if these norms and policies change, the household composition can also be expected to change (Kandiyoti 1988; Olmsted 2003, 2005), feeding back into the norms (see also Ross [2008]) and consequently shaping the household composition's effect as well. Moreover, norms might gradually change because of women entering the public sphere, but this does not have to be reflected immediately in policies regarding women's role in the public sphere, the institutional side of patriarchy. We should study these aspects and degrees of patriarchy not in isolation, but in interaction and relation to each other.

ACKNOWLEDGMENTS

I am very grateful to Mieke Verloo, Karen Anderson, the participants and organizers of the *Feminist Economics* workshop on "Gender and Economics in Muslim Communities," and the anonymous reviewers for the useful and inspiring suggestions on this study. I would also like to thank the participants of the Ninth International Conference of the Middle East Economics Association in Istanbul, Turkey, for commenting on an early draft of this article. The study is made possible by PAPFam and Measure DHS, whose data are used, and The Netherlands Organisation for Scientific Research (NWO) for providing a research grant (400-07-136).

NOTES

[1] Elissa Braunstein's (2014) contribution to this issue is a welcome exception.

[2] This database collects and merges large-scale representative household surveys conducted in developing countries (DDW 2010).

[3] In fourteen of the twenty-eight countries in this study, there are legal restrictions in public movement; and in twenty countries, women's economic access is limited (for example, individual entitlement to loans or bank accounts).

[4] The results cannot be generalized to never-married women and women of other ages. The label "not married" should thus not be read as being single in the never-married sense.

[5] The online Supplementary Appendix is available at http://dx.doi.org/10.1080/1354 5701.2014.963136.

[6] This variable and marital status are not multicollinear.

[7] The last three factors were not applicable to all women (for example, households without children). The missing values are replaced by the weighted average of the other women, and a variable was included to indicate no children were present (Paul D. Allison 2001).

[8] The variable cannot tap into women's own human capital, either, because all models are controlled for the individuals' educations.

[9] Using employment might seem problematic. However, theoretically the concept of prescriptive norms directs to the inclusion of the genderedness of employment, which shapes whether it is considered acceptable for women to have a job. Reversed causality is minimal, as the presence of a single woman will not substantially change the prescriptive norm. Methodologically, the bias can only be minimal: employment makes up only half of the district-level variable and is divided by men's employment,

GENDER AND ECONOMICS IN MUSLIM COMMUNITIES

making the figures relative, not absolute. Moreover, each district estimate is based on (on average) about a thousand women. A single woman accounts only for 0.1 percent of that aggregate. Finally, the models are controlled for women's educational attainment, as well as for the partners' occupation. The district-level variable cannot tap into that.

[10] In a factor analysis, these items load on one factor. The district-level average or proportion of these indicators is rescaled: maximum 1 (most patriarchal), minimum 0 (least patriarchal). The index is the mean of these four.

[11] The GID data are unique in presenting comparative data for Muslim-majority countries. Using the data to compare Muslim-majority countries with other countries is problematic because the chosen indicators focus on manifestations of gender inequality that are most prevalent in Muslim-majority countries (such as veiling; Mieke Verloo and Anna van der Vleuten [2009]).

[12] Areas with higher unemployment among men, fewer service and light manufacturing jobs, and more wealth have lower employment rates among women. The last, after control for other socioeconomic variables, might tap into the absence of a necessity to work.

[13] Models without the number of children non-biologically related to the head of household show largely similar results for the macro-level variables. Only the country-level public patriarchy variable showed a larger and more significant effect. Using a dummy for the presence of non-biologically related children delivers the same results.

[14] Statistically significant effects: higher education (+); living in a city (+); having a partner with an upper white-collar job (+), with an agriculture job (-), and who is older than the respondent (-); and age (inverted u-curve).

[15] Models without the number of children non-biologically related to the head of household show highly similar micro-level results. Using a dummy for the presence of non-biologically related children delivers the same results.

[16] The sex ratio among children was statistically significant, but not economically (0.3 percentage points in the average situation).

[17] This effect might seem a repetition of the marriage effect. That the other adult women in a household can help in care tasks might be related to the fact they these women are unmarried. Indeed, in the data used, 95 percent of the women in "single adult women households" are married; that percentage is between 86 percent and 90 percent for women in "multiple adult women households." This indicates that marriage plays a role in this relationship, but the observation that married women benefit from the presence of other (perhaps) unmarried women in the household is still in line with the theoretical reasoning on this variable.

[18] The age of these children is normally distributed around the teenage years, and they are roughly equally divided in boys and girls.

REFERENCES

Abu-Lughod, Lila, ed. 1998. *Remaking Women: Feminism and Modernity in the Middle East.* Princeton, NJ: Princeton University Press.

Adely, Fida J. 2009. "Educating Women for Development: The *Arab Human Development Report 2005* and the Problem with Women's Choices." *International Journal of Middle East Studies* 41(1): 105–22.

Agarwal, Bina. 1997. "'Bargaining' and Gender Relations: Within and Beyond the Household." *Feminist Economics* 3(1): 1–51.

GENDER AND ECONOMICS IN MUSLIM COMMUNITIES

Ahmed, Leila. 1992. *Women and Gender in Islam: Historical Roots of a Modern Debate.* London: Yale University Press.

Al-Qudsi, Sulayman S. 1998. "Labour Participation of Arab Women: Estimates of the Fertility to Labour Supply Link." *Applied Economics* 30(7): 931–41.

Allison, Paul D. 2001. *Missing Data.* London: Sage.

Amin, Sajeda and Nagah H. Al-Bassusi. 2004. "Education, Wage Work, and Marriage: Perspectives of Egyptian Working Women." *Journal of Marriage and Family* 66(5): 1287–99.

Angrist, Michele. 2012. "War, Resisting the West, and Women's Labor: Toward an Understanding of Arab Exceptionalism." *Politics & Gender* 8(1): 51–82.

Aromolaran, Adebayo B. 2004. "Female Schooling, Non-market Productivity, and Labor Market Participation in Nigeria." Economic Growth Center (EGC) Discussion Paper 879.

Bahramitash, Roksana. 2002. "Islamic Fundamentalism and Women's Employment in Indonesia." *International Journal of Politics, Culture, and Society* 16(2): 255–72.

———. 2003. "Revolution, Islamization, and Women's Employment in Iran." *Brown Journal of World Affairs* 9(2): 229–41.

Barlas, Asma. 2002. *"Believing Women" in Islam: Unreading Patriarchal Interpretations of the Qur'an.* Austin: University of Texas Press.

Boserup, Ester. 1998. *Woman's Role in Economic Development.* New York: Routledge.

Braunstein, Elissa. 2014. "Patriarchy versus Islam: Gender and Religion in Economic Growth."*Feminist Economics* 20(4).

Caldwell, John C. 1982. *Theory of Fertility Decline.* New York: Academic Press.

Callaway, Barbara and Lucy Creevey. 1994. *The Heritage of Islam: Women, Religion, and Politics in West Africa.* Boulder, CO: Lynne Rienner Publishers.

Civettini, Nicole H.W. and Jennifer Glass. 2008. "The Impact of Religious Conservatism on Men's Work and Family Involvement." *Gender and Society* 22(2): 172–93.

Clark, Roger, Thomas W. Ramsbey, and Emily Stier Adler. 1991. "Culture, Gender, and Labor Force Participation: A Cross-National Study." *Gender and Society* 5(1): 47–66.

Contreras, Dante and Gonzalo Plaza. 2010. "Cultural Factors in Women's Labor Force Participation in Chile." *Feminist Economics* 16(2): 27–46.

Database Developing World (DDW). 2010. "Datasets." http://www.databasedeveloping world.org.

Davis, Nancy J. and Robert V. Robinson. 2006. "The Egalitarian Face of Islamic Orthodoxy: Support for Islamic Law and Economic Justice in Seven Muslim-Majority Nations." *American Sociological Review* 71(2): 167–90.

Donahoe, Debra Anne. 1999. "Measuring Women's Work in Developing Countries." *Population and Development Review.* 25(3): 543–76.

Duerst-Lahti, Georgia. 2008. "Gender Ideology: Masculinism and Feminalism." In *Politics, Gender, and Concepts: Theory and Methodology,* edited by Gary Goertz and Amy G. Mazur, 159–92. Cambridge: Cambridge University Press.

Glick, Peter and David E. Sahn. 1997. "Gender and Education Impacts on Employment and Earnings in West Africa: Evidence from Guinea." *Economic Development and Cultural Change* 45(4): 793–823.

Gündüz-Hoşgör, Ayse and Jeroen Smits. 2007. "The Status of Rural Women in Turkey: What is the Role of Regional Differences." In *From Patriarchy to Empowerment: Women's Participation, Movements, and Rights in the Middle East, North Africa, and South Asia,* edited by Valentina M. Moghadam, 180–202. Syracuse: Syracuse University Press.

———. 2008. "Variation in Labor Market Participation of Married Women in Turkey." *Women's Studies International Forum* 31(2): 104–17.

Inglehart, Ronald and Pippa Norris. 2003. "The True Clash of Civilizations." *Foreign Policy Magazine* 34(2): 67–74.

GENDER AND ECONOMICS IN MUSLIM COMMUNITIES

Jansen, Willy. 2004. "The Economy of Religious Merit: Women and *Ajr* in Algeria." *The Journal of North African Studies* 9(4): 1–17.

Kandiyoti, Deniz. 1988. "Bargaining with Patriarchy." *Gender and Society* 2(3): 274–89.

Kotsadam, Andreas. 2011. "Does Informal Eldercare Impede Women's Employment? The Case of European Welfare States." *Feminist Economics* 17(2): 121–44.

Langstem, Ray and Rania Salem. 2008. "Two Approaches to Measuring Women's Work in Developing Countries: A Comparison of Survey Data from Egypt." *Population and Development Review* 34(2): 283–305.

Lincove, Jane Arnold. 2008. "Growth, Girls Education, and Female Labor: A Longitudinal Analysis." *Journal of Developing Areas* 41(2): 45–68.

Miles, Rebecca. 2002. "Employment and Unemployment in Jordan: The Importance of the Gender System." *World Development* 30(3): 413–27.

Moghadam, Valentine M. 1998. *Women, Work, and Economic Reform in the Middle East and North Africa.* Boulder, CO: Lynne Rienner.

———. 2003. *Modernizing Women: Gender and Social Change in the Middle East.* Boulder, CO: Lynne Rienner.

———. 2004. "Patriarchy in Transition: Women and the Changing Family in the Middle East." *Journal of Comparative Family Studies* 35(2): 137–62.

Nassar, Heba. 2003. "Egypt in Comparative Perspective." In *Women and Globalization in the Arab Middle East: Gender, Economy and Society*, edited by Eleanor Abdella Doumato and Marsha Pripstein Posusney, 95–118. Boulder, CO: Lynne Rienner.

OECD GID. 2012. "OECD.Statextracts. Gender, Institutions and Development Database 2009." http://stats.oecd.org/Index.aspx?DatasetCode=GID2.

Olmsted, Jennifer. 2003. "Reexamining the Fertility Puzzle in MENA." In *Women and Globalization in the Arab Middle East. Gender, Economy and Society*, edited by Eleanor Abdella Doumato and Marsha Pripstein Posusney, 73–94. Boulder, CO: Lynne Rienner.

———. 2005. "Gender, Aging, and the Evolving Arab Patriarchal Contract." *Feminist Economics* 11(2): 53–78.

Pampel, Fred C. and Kazuko Tanaka. 1986. "Economic Development and Female Labor Force Participation: A Reconsideration." *Social Forces* 64(3): 599–619.

Pateman, Carole. 1988. *The Sexual Contract.* Cambridge: Polity Press.

Pettit, Becky and Jennifer Hook. 2005. "The Structure of Women's Employment in Comparative Perspective." *Social Forces* 84(2): 779–801.

Rantalaiho, Liisa. 1993. *Reshaping the Gender Contract.* Paris: OECD.

Reinharz, Shulamit. 1992. *Feminist Methods in Social Research.* New York: Oxford University Press.

Riley, Nancy E. and Krista E. Van Vleet. 2012. *Making Families through Adoption.* Los Angeles: Sage.

Ross, Michael. 2008. "Oil, Islam, and Women." *American Political Science Review* 102(1): 107–23.

Smith, Joanne R. and Winnifred R. Louis. 2009. "Group Norms and the Attitude-behaviour Relationship." *Social and Personality Psychology Compass* 3(1): 19–35.

Spierings, Niels. 2014. "How Islam Influences Women's Paid Non-farm Employment: Evidence from 26 Indonesian and 37 Nigerian Provinces." *Review of Religious Research* (online publication first). (DOI 10.1007/s13644-014-0159-0).

Spierings, Niels, Jeroen Smits, and Mieke Verloo. 2009. "On the Compatibility of Islam and Gender Equality. Effects of Modernization, State Islamization, and Democracy on Women's Labor Market Participation in 45 Muslim-Majority Countries." *Social Indicators Research* 90(3): 503–22.

———. 2010. "Micro- and Macrolevel Determinants of Women's Employment in Six Arab Countries."*Journal of Marriage and Family* 72(5): 1391–407.

GENDER AND ECONOMICS IN MUSLIM COMMUNITIES

Udink, Betsy. 2006. *Allah & Eva*. Amsterdam: Uitgeverij Augustus.

van der Lippe, Tanja and Liset van Dijk. 2002. "Comparative Research on Women's Employment." *Annual Review of Sociology* 28(1): 221–41.

Varea, Carlos. 1993. "Marriage, Age at Last Birth and Fertility in a Traditional Moroccan Population." *Journal of Biosocial Science* 25(1): 1–15.

Verloo, Mieke and Anna van der Vleuten. 2009. "The Discursive Logic of Ranking and Benchmarking: Understanding Gender Equality Measures in the European Union." In *The Discursive Politics of Gender Equality: Stretching, Bending and Policymaking*, edited by Emanuela Lombardo, Petra Meier, and Mieke Verloo, 166–82. London: Routledge.

Walby, Sylvia. 1996. "The 'Declining Significance' or the 'Changing Forms' of Patriarchy?" In *Patriarchy and Development: Women's Positions at the End of Twentieth Century*, edited by Valentine M. Moghadam, 19–33. Oxford: Clarendon Press.

———. 2009. *Globalization and Inequalities: Complexities and Contested Modernities*. London: Sage.

Wejnert, Barbara and Almagul Djumabaeva. 2004. "From Patriarchy to Egalitarianism: Parenting Roles in Democratizing Poland and Kyrgyzstan." *Marriage and Family Review* 36(3/4): 147–71.

Wheeler, Raymond H. and B. G. Hunter. 1987. "Change in Spouse Age Difference at Marriage: A Challenge to Traditional Family and Sex Roles?" *Sociological Quarterly* 28(3): 411–21.

Yuchtman-Yaar, Ephraim and Yasmin Alkalay. 2007. "Religious Zones, Economic Development and Modern Value Orientations: Individual Versus Contextual Effects." *Social Science Research* 36(2): 789–807.

UNILATERAL DIVORCE FOR WOMEN AND LABOR SUPPLY IN THE MIDDLE EAST AND NORTH AFRICA: THE EFFECT OF KHUL REFORM

Lena Hassani-Nezhad and Anna Sjögren

ABSTRACT

This contribution investigates whether the introduction of Khul, Islamic unilateral divorce rights for women, helps to explain recent dramatic increases in women's labor supply in Middle Eastern and North African (MENA) countries over the 1980–2008 period. It shows, using data for eighteen countries, that Khul reform increased the labor force participation of women relative to men. Furthermore, we find evidence that the effect of Khul is larger for younger women (ages 24–34) compared to older women (ages 35–55). Younger women increased their labor force participation by 6 percent, which accounts for about 10 percent of the increase in their labor force participation from 1980 to 2008.

INTRODUCTION

Divorce laws have been shown to have implications for the balance of bargaining power between women and men in intrahousehold decision making. The introduction of unilateral, no-fault divorce in the United States is argued to have shifted power toward women and to have increased women's incentives to engage in market work and gain economic independence (Pierre-Andre Chiappori, Bernard Fortin and Guy Lacroix 2002; Betsey Stevenson and Justin Wolfers 2006; Betsey Stevenson 2008). Few or no studies have investigated the effect of divorce law changes on labor market decisions or empowerment of women in developing countries. There is, however, a growing literature on the importance of other forms of women's empowerment and control of resources for development in general, and child development and family health in particular (Duncan Thomas 1990; Esther Duflo 2003; Esther Duflo and Christopher Udry 2004). In spite of the lack of evidence, Esther Duflo (2012) is one of the most recent authors to assert that changing the legal institutions surrounding marriage is a potentially important policy tool to empower women. This contribution aims to provide some evidence on the importance of divorce legislation for women's labor force participation in developing countries by investigating the effects of introducing Khul, unilateral divorce for women in the Middle Eastern and North Africa (MENA).

In the MENA asymmetric divorce laws allowing men, but not women, to file for divorce, along with laws regulating custody over children, obedience laws and inheritance law have traditionally contributed to an imbalance of power in the household in the favor of men (Amira El-Azhari Sonbol 2003; Sameena Nazir 2005; Valentine M. Moghadam 2008; Sami Bibi and Mustapha K. Nabli 2010; Samar El-Masri 2012). Gender inequalities are manifested in women's labor force participation rates below 30 percent, which is well below other regions in the world. Household-survey data suggest that married women in this region are unlikely to work in comparison to other regions in the world (World Bank 2004).

Yet the labor force participation of women in the MENA increased by some 50 percent between 1980 and 2008, as shown in Figure 1. During this time period, many countries adopted Khul, which under Islamic law gives a woman the right to unilaterally petition for divorce in return for paying back her dower.[1] Divorce can be granted by decision of a judge, without the husband's consent. Prior to Khul, unilateral divorce existed only for men, and a woman petitioning for divorce needed the consent of the husband.

This paper investigates if the empowerment of women through the implementation of Khul reform has a role in explaining recent increases in labor force participation of women. This study thus extends our knowledge of the impact of the legal framework, and divorce legislation in particular, on women's labor force participation to a new set of countries. Analyzing the role of changing laws is of particular interest in a context where family and gender roles are often considered to be deeply rooted in patriarchal traditions and norms.

There are basically two mechanisms through which Khul reform may affect women's labor force participation. First, it is possible that the probability of divorce increases.[2] This raises a woman's incentive to secure a livelihood both within marriage and in the event of divorce. In marriage, the woman may want to prepare for the possibility of a life on her own by working and gaining attachment to the labor market. Following the divorce, the woman obviously has more incentives to work, since she cannot rely on the husband's earnings for her and her children's livelihood.

The second mechanism is that Khul reform increases women's bargaining power within the household by allowing women to end marriages. If it is

GENDER AND ECONOMICS IN MUSLIM COMMUNITIES

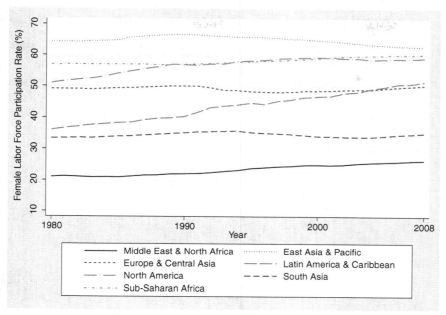

Figure 1 Regional women's labor force participation comparison
Sources: World Development Indicators Database/World Bank; ILO.

husbands' preferences that prevent women from working, then increasing the bargaining power of women may result in their increased labor force participation even if they do not act on their divorce threat. Indeed, Stevenson (2008) shows that US women, following the unilateral divorce law, increased their labor supply even if they stayed married.

The effect of Khul reform is not necessarily the same for all women. One important reason is that in most MENA countries, women risk losing legal custody of their older children if they divorce.[3] As a result, Khul may have limited impact on the woman's actual ability or willingness to file for divorce, and her bargaining power in the household may not change if the threat of losing the children is preventive. Khul may thus have less effect on mothers with older children compared to mothers with young children or non-mothers. We therefore expect and explore if younger women are more strongly affected by Khul reform than older women.

Another reason for expecting stronger effects on younger women is their longer time horizon. This implies that their incentives to invest in human capital and labor market attachment to insure themselves against divorce and future uncertainty are likely to be stronger. Older women have already invested in their marriages, and with a history of no labor market experience, they are likely to have a harder time finding employment.

GENDER AND ECONOMICS IN MUSLIM COMMUNITIES

We analyze the effects of Khul reform on the labor force participation of women in general, and in particular, on younger women (ages 24–34) by using cross-country variation in the timing of Khul reform between 1980 and 2008 in eighteen MENA countries. We use data on when countries have granted women the right to petition for divorce unilaterally under Khul collected by Lynn Welchman (2007). We further use aggregate data on labor force participation for men and women in different age groups from the International Labor Organization (ILO) Key Indicators of Labor Market. In addition, annual gross domestic product figures are taken from the World Bank World Development Indicators database. A difference-in-difference-in-differences estimator is used to study how the change in labor force participation of younger women affected by Khul reform differs from the change in labor force participation of older women (ages 35–55) as well as compared to the change in the labor force participation of men. We perform a number of robustness checks where we investigate the sensitivity of our results to the quality of data, and to OPEC membership.

In spite of the limited number of countries in the analysis, we find evidence that implementing Khul reform had a positive effect on labor force participation of younger women of the order of magnitude of 1.7 percentage points, or 6 percent. This implies that Khul reform accounts for about 10 percent of the increase in labor force participation of younger women. We also find that the effect on the labor force participation of younger women is stronger than the effect on older women, although the difference is only marginally significant.

We further show some descriptive evidence, for a smaller set of countries, that Khul reform does not seem to have affected the divorce rates. A possible interpretation of our results is, hence, that Khul reform shifts the household's bargaining power in favor of women within marriage and enables more women to participate in the labor market.

THE IMPLICATIONS OF KHUL ON LABOR FORCE PARTICIPATION OF WOMEN – BASED ON PREVIOUS LITERATURE

Gary S. Becker's (1973) analysis of marriage is based on the idea that people marry because there is something to gain by marrying.[4] Gains from marriage arise because marriage enables spouses to specialize. Minor differences in preference or comparative advantage in market versus household production are enough to generate specialization. Traditionally, women have specialized in household production, while men have specialized in market work.

The original Becker framework assumed that the preferences of the household were represented by a single utility function for the household. Mainstream and feminist economists have criticized the unitary framework

116

GENDER AND ECONOMICS IN MUSLIM COMMUNITIES

and proposed various bargaining models of the household (Marilyn Manser and Murray Brown 1980; Marjorie B. McElroy and Mary Jean Horney 1981; Amartya K. Sen 1990; Barbara Bergmann 1995; Elizabeth Katz 1997; Marianne A. Ferber and Julie A. Nelson 2003). Importantly, a single utility function of the household disregards the importance of individual preferences, and consequently does not show how power and individualistic behavior can affect the process of household decision making. It has also been stressed that the family is not only a production unit, but also an institution to promote consumption complementarities (Betsey Stevenson and Justin Wolfers 2007), and an institution of control and oppression (Heidi I. Hartmann 1981; Nancy Folbre 1994). Marriage contracts that stipulate asymmetric rights to claim divorce are an example of institutions that open up for abuse and oppression.

Khul reform in the MENA differs from the introduction of unilateral divorce in the US, as it is a unilateral divorce right extended to women. Men already had the right to unilaterally divorce their wives. Before Khul reform, a woman seeking divorce could, in theory, try to convince her husband to seek divorce by trying to reduce his value of staying in the marriage. Doing so would likely adventure the woman's well-being negatively, both if the husband refused divorce and in case of divorce because of the stigma. Khul reform allows women to dissolve the marriage unilaterally by paying back a sum of money equivalent to their dower. A judge decides on the amount in case of disagreement between spouses. In spite of coming at the high cost of losing their dower, the fact that divorce is now possible at all arguably makes the dissolution of marriage less costly for women.

Exit-threat bargaining models (for example, McElroy and Horney [1981]) predict that such a change results in higher probability of divorce initiated by women, since the reform implies redistribution of power toward women who want to leave the marriage. However, marriage models, assuming that spouses share a common utility function or separate-spheres bargaining models (Shelly Lundberg and Robert A. Pollack 1993), predict no increase in divorce rates due to such a redistribution of power.

Early US studies of how unilateral divorce laws affect divorce rates found either no effect (William R. Johnson and Jonathan Skinner 1986; H. Elizabeth Peters 1986) or an increase (Leora Friedberg 1998). Justin Wolfers (2006) reconciles the previous studies and argues that the initial increase in divorce rates found in Friedberg (1998) was reduced over time, resulting in little or no long-run effect.

Johnson and Skinner (1986) and Peters (1986) show that women increase their labor force participation in anticipation of a higher probability of divorce. This increase may be due to a reduction in their incentive to invest in their marriage-specific capital (Peters 1986) or due to incentives of women to self-insure against their reduced human capital during the marriage (Allen M. Parkman 1992).[5] In an early study of changed divorce laws in the US,

Jeffery S. Gray (1998) argued that the increase in participation of women in the labor market was limited to those states in which property rights were more in favor of women. However, Stevenson (2008) finds that the introduction of unilateral divorce increased labor force participation of married and unmarried women irrespective of property laws, and moreover, that the effect on labor force participation is weaker for women with long marriage durations. Similarly, Katie R. Genadek, Wendy A. Stock, and Christiana Stoddard (2007) find that responses of women with young children to change in divorce rights in the US are larger than for women with older children.[6] Stevenson (2008) argues that in a regime in which any party can exit at will, there is a greater incentive for wives (and husbands) to maintain and invest in their options outside of marriage. Women seeking both insurance against divorce and greater bargaining power within marriage are thus more likely to engage in market work.

Additional evidence that unilateral divorce changed the relative bargaining position of spouses in the household is presented in Stevenson and Wolfers (2006). They show that exposure to domestic violence dropped by 30 percent for both men and women, and that the number of women murdered by their husbands declined by 10 percent as a result of the changed divorce laws. Furthermore, there was an 8–10 percent decline in suicide among women. Hence, the ability to walk out of dysfunctional marriages appears to have significantly improved the situation, in particular for women, even if they in the long run appear to have stayed in their marriages to the same extent as before.

Although there are few or no studies of how divorce law changes affect labor market decisions of women in developing countries, the importance of women's empowerment and control of resources has received more attention (Duflo 2012). Control over assets and income has been shown to be important for child development and share of the household expenditure on food (Thomas 1990; Duflo 2003; Duflo and Udry 2004; Cheryl Doss 2005). These studies suggest that the distribution of bargaining power is affected by the distribution of income and assets, which in turn impacts household decision making.

In the MENA, not only is it expected of a wife to stay home, but this norm is institutionalized; in fact, the husband is entitled by law to prevent the wife from working. Recent reforms have granted women the right to work or the right to stipulate the right to work in the marriage contract (Sanja Kelly and Julia Breslin 2010).[7] However, many women fail to stipulate this right in the marriage contract. Moreover, judges mostly rule in favor of men when the issue is taken to the court (Sonbol 2003). Khul reform may empower women through their right to unilaterally petition for divorce, but is also likely to increase their bargaining power and influence over decisions in the household, such as their right to work. A woman can threaten to walk out of marriage if her husband opposes her wish to work outside the home. Market work also strengthens a woman's outside option. Without Khul reform, the husband can prevent his wife from working, leaving the wife without any outside option.

Nevertheless, the shift in bargaining power of women following the Khul reform is not the same for women with and without children or for women of different ages. There are several reasons. First, older women have had time to make more marriage-specific investments compared to younger women. For example, it is likely that they have spent more time specializing in household production and raising children. This increases the value of staying in the marriage and thus lowers divorce among older women compared to younger women. As a result, labor supply responses of older women to the changes in divorce laws are expected to be less strong compared to younger women. Second, women in most of the MENA countries lose custody of their older children following a divorce.[8] Hence, women with older children may be less inclined to leave a marriage and thus have less incentive to enter the labor market.[9]

Higher anticipated divorce rates may also affect how marriages are formed. Peters (1986) and Imran Rasul (2006) argue that anticipation of higher divorce rate may result in longer searches for better matches, which would reduce the marriage rate and raise the marriage age. Rasul (2006) points out that this may be a reason for why changed divorced laws need not impact long-run divorce rates, as was found in Wolfers (2006). Introducing unilateral divorce rights may hence in the long run lead to more efficient marriages (Niko Matouschek and Imran Rasul 2008). To the extent that Khul reform leads to increased marriage age, another mechanism through which Khul reform may affect women's labor supply is that women stay unmarried longer and therefore do not leave the labor force due to marriage as rapidly. This effect of Khul reform on marriage rates and thus labor force participation of women is, of course, relevant only for younger women, and is therefore another reason for why an increase in the labor force participation in response to Khul should be stronger for younger women than for older women.

Limitation to Khul

As pointed out in Duflo (2012), changing the legal conditions for women or empowering women in one dimension may be insufficient to influence the overall situation of women if there are enough other constraints on women's decision making that remain intact. In the MENA context studied here, this is very true, and there are a number of reasons for why Khul reform may fail to affect the situation of women. If social norms, religious or cultural, strongly discourage women's market work, then a change in divorce rights might not change labor force participation, because women accept the market work as a domain over which they cannot bargain (Kanchana N.

Ruwanpura 2007; Raquel Fernández and Alessandra Fogli 2009; Stephanie Seguino 2011). Furthermore, if divorce is a socially unacceptable outcome for women, then women are unlikely to use it as a threat. However, Bina Agarwal (1997) argues that although norms and perceptions affect the bargaining power, they can, themselves, be bargained over. Hence, whether Khul reform is able to change the situation for women is an empirical question.

So far in this paper we have discussed how Khul reform might lead to an increase in labor force participation of women without considering the further implications for the well-being of women in the MENA. To the extent that Khul redistributes power toward women, the consequences of such a reform are likely to be driven by the choices of women. Although short-run effects may be limited by the existence of social norms, in the long run, increased bargaining power for those women who are able to exercise their improved rights may contribute to changing norms toward divorce and women's market work.[10]

EMPIRICAL FRAMEWORK AND DATA

Variation in implementation of Khul reform across time and countries allows us to examine its effects on labor force participation of women in the MENA by exploring how the labor force participation of women in a given country changes as Khul reform is introduced and comparing this change to the development of women's labor force participation in a country without Khul reform. It is, however, important to recognize that there are different practices of Islam across countries in the MENA. Therefore, Khul may not have the same impact everywhere. Moreover, Khul reforms are unlikely to have the same impact on the non-Muslim population. However, to the extent that this variation in religious practice, as well as fractions of the population with different denominations remain relatively constant within each country during the study period, they pose no problem to identification of the effect of introducing unilateral divorce for women through Khul in these countries.

The econometric model

Theory predicts that Khul reform affects the labor supply of women, but not the labor supply of men (first hypothesis). Moreover, the effect of Khul is larger for younger women compared to older women (second hypothesis). Thus, labor force participation of men and labor force participation of older women can serve as comparisons allowing us to use a difference-in-difference-in-differences estimator in order to examine the first and the second hypotheses.

We use OLS estimation with three different specifications to investigate the validity of the stated hypotheses. In the first approach, we compare the

GENDER AND ECONOMICS IN MUSLIM COMMUNITIES

effect of Khul reform between women and men, in a given country over time, that is, controlling for country and year fixed effects. In the second approach, we include interactions of the effect of Khul reform with both gender and age to investigate age-specific reform effects. Third, we estimate the model separately for men and women in order to allow for gender-specific fixed effects and time trends. Because the education level of men and women and the general state of the economy are both likely to be important determinants of men's and women's labor force participation, we include controls for education of the considered populations groups in a given year, as well as GDP.

In practice, we estimate models of the following type:

$$L_{ijt} = \beta_0 + \beta_1 Khul_{jt} + \beta_2 Women^*_{ijt} Khul_{jt} + \beta_3 Women_{ijt}$$
$$+ \beta_4 Old_{ijt} + \beta_5 Women^* Old_{ijt} + Years\ of\ schooling_{ijt} + G_{jt}$$
$$+ Country_j + Year_t + Timetrend_j + \xi_{ijt} \tag{1}$$

In Equation 1, L_{ijt} corresponds to labor force participation of group i in country j in year t, where group is defined by gender and age: men and women, young (ages 25–34) and old (ages 35–54). $Khul_{jt}$ is a dummy variable equal to one if the country has adopted Khul reform at time t and 0 otherwise. The coefficient on $Khul_{jt}$, β_1, estimates the partial effect of the Khul reform on labor force participation of men in countries with implementation of Khul reform compared to women residing in the same countries. The coefficient on Women*Khul, β_2, reports the differential impact of Khul on labor force participation of women compared to men. This is the variable of interest. The coefficient on women, β_3, is expected to be negative as women on average have lower labor force participation compared to men. A dummy variable for Old captures the difference in labor force participation of older age groups compared to the younger age groups. The interaction term Women and Old is expected to have negative coefficient if younger women have higher labor force participation compared to older women (relative to the relation for men). A vector of country dummies controls for variation in labor force participation that differ across countries but are constant over time, including sociocultural beliefs. $Year_t$ are year fixed effects that capture changes in labor force participation that are common to all countries. We hold constant group-specific average years of schooling.

Country and year fixed effects, however, do not control for factors that change within groups or countries over time. We therefore also include linear country-specific time trends ($Timetrend_j$) to allow for such changes. There may be other country-specific, or country- and group-specific, factors influencing labor force participation that also change over time that are not captured by linear country-specific time trends or in the country fixed

GENDER AND ECONOMICS IN MUSLIM COMMUNITIES

effects. For example, the ILO uses one-year lag GDP growth to impute the missing values of labor force participation (ILO Global Employment Trends Unit 2010). We capture such influences that are not driven by Khul reform by controlling for average years of schooling in the relevant population group ($Years\ of\ schooling_{ijt}$) and for a one-year lag GDP growth (G_{jt}). ξ_{ijt} is the error term.

We cluster the standard errors at the country level in order to control for possible serial correlation in the error terms (Marianne Bertrand, Esther Duflo, and Sendhil Mullainathan 2004). Because the number of clusters is small, only eighteen when all countries are included and fifteen when we restrict the sample to countries for which there is education data, the clustered standard errors are likely to be underestimated. Hence, we use the bootstrap-based method, Wild cluster bootstrap-t, suggested in Colin A. Cameron, Jonah B. Gelbach, and Douglas L. Miller (2008) to compute improved critical values for the Wald statistics of interest. A table of critical values is presented in the Supplemental Online Appendix.[11]

The second hypothesis in this paper is that Khul reform has a larger impact on labor force participation of younger women compared to older women. In order to examine this hypothesis, we include interaction terms between Khul and old, and Khul and old women:

$$L_{ijt} = \beta_0 + \beta_1 Khul_{jt} + \beta_2 Women^*_{ijt} Khul_{jt} + \beta_3 Women^* Old^*_{ijt} Khul_{jt} + \beta_4 Old^*_{ijt} Khul$$

$$+ \beta_5 Women_{ijt} + \beta_6 Women^* Old_{ijt} + \beta_7 Old_{ijt} + Years\ of\ schooling_{ijt} + G_{jt}$$

$$+ Country_j + Year_t + Timetrend_j + \xi_{ijt} \qquad (2)$$

By adding these interaction terms to the model, we allow the effect of Khul reform to differ not only among women and men but also among younger and older age groups. The coefficient on Khul (β_1) represents the differential impact of Khul on labor force participation of younger men. The differential impact of Khul on older women, younger women, and younger men are captured respectively by β_2, β_3, and β_4. The other variables are the same as the previous model. As a robustness check, we also estimate the model separately for men and women. This implies that we allow coefficients on education, and GDP as well as year effects, country fixed effects, and time trends to differ for men and women. Because the labor market in many oil-producing countries is arguably very different, we also perform a robustness check allowing Khul reform effects to differ for OPEC countries.

Data

We base the empirical analysis on Welchman's (2007) dating for when a country implemented the Khul reform. During 1980 to 2008, the reform was implemented in 10 countries. Libya was the first country to restrict the husband's authority on divorce in 1984. Tunisia and Oman followed

GENDER AND ECONOMICS IN MUSLIM COMMUNITIES

suit. Egypt gave the wife the right to petition for divorce without consent of her husband in 2000. Note that the "Cairo court alone, only two months following the reform, received over 3,000 applications" (Abdullahi A. An-Na'im 2002: 159).[12] Following the reform in Egypt, Jordan, Morocco, Algeria, the United Arab Emirates, Palestine (West Bank and Gaza), and Qatar reformed Khul.

The implementation of Khul is summarized in Table 1. The first column in Table 1 reports the date of ratification of Khul reform, and the second column reports whether the divorce can be granted without consent of the husband or if the judge can grant the divorce when the husband persists in his refusal.[13]

There are some challenges to capturing the effects of Khul alone. The change in divorce laws in the MENA typically happened as parts of reform packages to family law. These reform packages in Algeria, Libya and UAE

Table 1 Khul reform and custody legislation

Country	*(1)* *Year of* *Khul reform*	*(2)* *Khul reform* *classification*	*(3)* *Custody legislation* *for mother*
Algeria	2005	Without consent of husband	Daughters until marriage, sons until age of 10[a]
Egypt	2000	Without consent of husband	Daughters until age of 12, sons until age of 10[b]
Jordan	2002	Without consent of husband	Daughters and sons up to age of puberty
Libya	1984	Restrictions on consent of husband	Daughter until marriage, sons until age of puberty
Morocco	2004	Judge can initiate the divorce (divorce for Shiqaq)	Mother gets the custody of children until age of 15[c]
Oman	1997	Judge can initiate the divorce	Daughters until puberty and sons until age of 11
Qatar	2006	Without consent of husband	Daughters until age of 15, Sons until age of 13[d]
Tunisia	1993	Right to divorce	Mothers first get the custody of children
UAE	2006	Judge can initiate the divorce	Daughters until age of 13 and sons until age of 10
Palestine (West Bank and Gaza)	2005	Judge can initiate the divorce	Daughters until age of 12 and sons until age of 10

Notes: [a]It is possible to extend the custody of son up to age 16. [b]It is possible to extend the custody of sons up to age 15 and daughters until marriage. [c]After age 15, the child can choose to live with father or mother. [d]After age 15 for girls and 13 for boys, either the judge or the children themselves decide about custody.

GENDER AND ECONOMICS IN MUSLIM COMMUNITIES

allowed women to stipulate the right to work in their marriage contract, and in Tunisia and Oman, women were granted the right to work without consent of the husband. This concurrency limits the ability of our estimations to capture only the effect of unilateral divorce. Instead, we are likely to also capture the additional impact of the right to work on labor force participation of women. It has, however, been argued that women typically fail to stipulate the right to work in their marriage contracts not only due to prevailing customs, but also because they are unaware of the existence of such a law and because their guardian – that is, father – is likely to play a major role in drawing up the marriage contract (Kelly and Breslin 2010).

The third column in Table 1 reports the legislation governing custody of children at the time of divorce reform.[14] For example, women residing in Algeria cannot get the custody of their sons ages 10 and older, and this is likely to affect their decisions over divorce or their bargaining power in the household.

The data on women's labor force participation – that is the ratio of women in the labor force to those in the relevant age group – are taken from the Key Indicators of Labor Market database (KILM) provided by the ILO. KILM provides data for labor force participation of both men and women in standard age groups: 15+, 15–24, 25–34, 35–54, 55–64, 65+ and in aggregate levels of 15–64 and 25–54. For the purpose of this study, we focus on men and women ages 24–55 and the two subgroups: younger ages 24–34 and older ages 35–55.

The data on years of schooling and fractions of the population with primary, secondary, or tertiary schooling are taken from Barro–Lee dataset disaggregated by sex and by 5-year age intervals (Robert Barro and Jong-Wha Lee 2013). We have constructed education measures for the age groups used in our study, taking the average of (25–29) and (30–34) age groups for the (25–34) age group; and the average of (35–39), (40–44), (45–49) and (50–54) for (35–54) age group. We have also imputed missing values using a linear model. Furthermore, we use data on GDP from the World Development Indicators.

There are two important limitations to the data. First, some observations in KILM are estimates rather than based on actual micro data. This is likely to limit our ability to find any effects of Khul on labor force participation of women (Jennifer C. Olmsted 2011). We address this data quality issue by performing a robustness check where we include a country by year specific dummy variable taking the value 0 if the data on labor force participation is estimated and 1 if the information is based on actual micro data. Second, due to large participation of women in the informal market in the MENA, the data regarding labor force participation of women tend to underestimate the true labor force participation of women. It has been pointed out in several studies that informal economy plays a major role in economic activity, and especially so for women (Nasra M. Shah and Sulayman

S. Al-Qudsi 1990; Lourdes Benería 1999; Fatemeh Etemad Moghadam 2011). Hence, if women who are trying to find a job following the Khul reform find employment disproportionally in the informal sector, then we are, if anything, likely to underestimate the effect of Khul on the true labor force participation of women.

We construct a panel database consisting of eighteen MENA countries from 1980 to 2008. The panel includes 522 observations for each sex and age group. However, the data on GDP growth is not available for all the years in every country. Therefore, by controlling for GDP growth, we lose some observations.

RESULTS: THE EFFECT OF KHUL ON LABOR FORCE PARTICIPATION

Divorce rates and labor force participation

Figure 2 shows average divorce rates for countries that did and did not implement Khul.[15] The theoretical prediction for the effect of Khul on

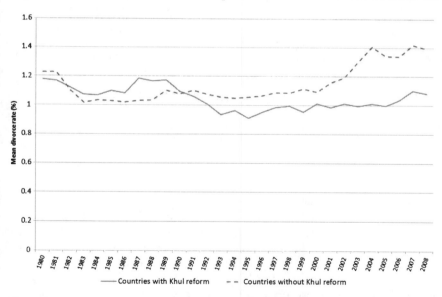

Figure 2 Divorce rate trends comparisons in countries with and without Khul reform
Note: The divorce rate is defined as number of granted divorces divided by mid-year population estimates of a country. The selected countries with Khul reform are Egypt, Libya, Tunisia, Jordan, and Qatar, and the selected countries without Khul reform are Bahrain, Iran, Kuwait, and Syria.
Source: The graph is created by the authors using divorce rate data from United Nations Demographic Yearbooks. The missing data are imputed as the mean divorce rate of the previous and the next observed data.

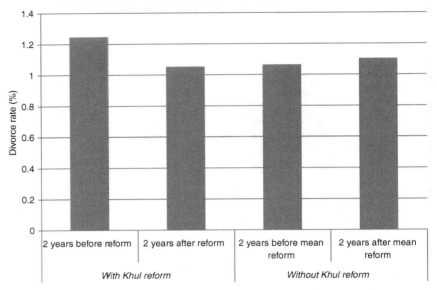

Figure 3 Mean divorce rate comparison in countries with and without Khul reform
Notes: The divorce rate is defined as number of granted divorces divided by midyear population estimates of a country. The selected countries with Khul reform are Egypt, Libya, Tunisia, Jordan, Qatar, and Palestine (West Bank and Gaza), and those without the reform include Bahrain, Iran, Kuwait, Syria, and Saudi Arabia. Mean Khul year is year 2000. Therefore, for the countries without the Khul reform, the divorce rate is the average of two years before 2000 and 2 years after 2000. The figure shows the divorce rates only in the countries for which data two years before and after are available.
Source: The graph is created by the authors using divorce rate data from United Nations Demographic Yearbooks.

divorce rates is ambiguous because there could be an immediate increase in divorce rates in existing marriages, but also a negative equilibrium effect if new unions formed are more stable. The presented figure suggests that Khul countries have experienced declines in divorce and non-Khul countries have experienced an increase in the recent decade.

In an attempt to investigate whether the trends in divorce can be linked to Khul, in Figure 3, we present mean divorce rates two years before the reform and two years after for the set of Khul countries for which divorce data are available, next to the corresponding figures for countries that did not implement Khul. For the latter group of countries, we have set a fictitious reform year to be the mean reform year for the countries that have implemented Khul. The comparison suggests, if anything, that countries that implemented Khul saw reductions in divorce rates, although differences are small. It is, however, not possible to conclude if there is an effect of Khul

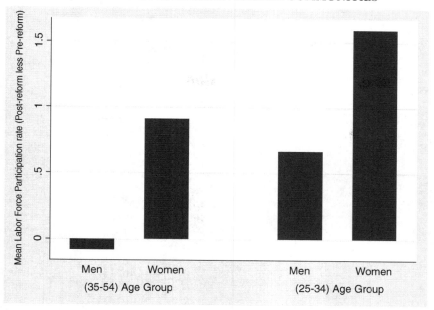

Figure 4 Comparison between changes in mean of labor force participation before and after the reform
Notes: Pre-reform is defined as year of the reform and one year before. Post-reform is defined as two years following the reform.

reform on divorce since the number of countries is too limited. Also, we are unable to control for country-specific differences in divorce trends prior to reform.

Next, we consider labor force participation. Figure 4 illustrates the differences in labor force participation after and before the reform for both women and men ages 25–34 and 35–54 using the raw country means two years before and after the reform. The mean difference in labor force participation of women is larger for women compared to men and also more important for women ages 25–34 than for women ages 35–54. In what follows, we investigate whether this pattern holds when we include controls for years of schooling, country fixed effects, year fixed effects and country-specific time trends.

Estimation results

We present the results of estimating Equation 1 in Table 2.[16] Bootstrapped-improved critical values for the Wald statistics testing the coefficient on Women*Khul are presented in Supplemental Online Table A1.[17] The first two columns report results with controls for country and year fixed effects,

GENDER AND ECONOMICS IN MUSLIM COMMUNITIES

Table 2 Impact of Khul on labor force participation of women and men

	Labor force participation			
	(1)	*(2)*	*(3)*	*(4)*
Khul	−0.799	−0.643	−1.256	−1.314
	(1.316)	(1.631)	(1.447)	(1.744)
Women*Khul	3.536+	4.834*	4.458*	4.981+
	(2.043)	(2.643)	(2.180)	(2.984)
Women*Old*Khul		−2.597		−1.051
		(1.762)		(2.219)
Old*Khul		−0.311		0.117
		(1.282)		(1.474)
Women	−62.97***	−63.15***	−59.69***	−59.77***
	(2.090)	(2.166)	(2.181)	(2.279)
Old	0.230	0.273	4.293***	4.256***
	(0.732)	(0.755)	(1.065)	(1.102)
Women*Old	−9.435***	−9.076***	−8.283***	−8.153***
	(1.021)	(1.144)	(0.898)	(0.987)
One-year lag	0.00747	0.00747	0.00721	0.00723
GDP growth	(0.00569)	(0.00569)	(0.00612)	(0.00613)
Years of schooling			2.028***	2.017***
			(0.638)	(0.650)
Observations	1,618	1,618	1,386	1,386
R-squared	0.980	0.980	0.981	0.981

Notes: Robust standard errors are reported in parentheses. Standard errors are clustered at the country level. *, **, *** denote significance at the 10, 5, and 1 percent levels, respectively. + denotes significance at 15 percent level. The regressions control for country fixed effects, year fixed effects, country-specific time trends, and one-year lag GDP growth. Columns 3 and 4 add the control for years of schooling.

as well as a control for GDP. Columns 3–4 also include a control for years of education.[18]

Column 1 reports how labor force participation of women is affected by Khul reform allowing the effect of Khul to be different for women and men. There is a marginally statistically significant coefficient on Women*Khul showing that the differential impact of Khul reform on labor force participation of women is 3.5 percentage points larger compared to men.[19] The negative coefficient on Khul suggests that men are actually affected negatively, although the effect is small and insignificant.

Other coefficients confirm that women on average have lower labor force participation compared to men and labor force participation is similar for older and younger men, but that younger women on average have higher labor force participation compared to older women.

GENDER AND ECONOMICS IN MUSLIM COMMUNITIES

In column 2, we allow the effect of the reform to vary by both age and gender. We examine the hypothesis that Khul is associated with higher increase in labor force participation of younger women compared to older women. The estimate on Women*Khul is now larger and the estimate on Women*Old*Khul is negative. This suggests that the effect of Khul on women's labor force participation is largely accounted for by the younger women. The significance level of the Women*Khul interaction is at the 15 percent level using the Wild bootstrap-t critical values in Supplemental Online Table A1. The coefficient on Women*Old*Khul is, however, imprecise; and the effect on older women is not statistically different from the effect on younger women.

In columns 3 and 4, we also control for years of schooling. The coefficient on Women*Khul becomes larger and is now statistically significantly different from zero at the 10 percent level using the students-t distribution (10 percent level using bootstrapped critical values). Considering that the average rate of women's labor force participation is approximately 27 percent, 31 for younger women (Supplemental Online Table A2), the estimated effect of Khul reform of 4.458 corresponds to an almost 17 percent increase in Women's labor supply. In column 4, when we allow the effect of Khul to differ between young and old, we find that the positive coefficient on Women*Khul is still positive, but now only marginally significant at the 15 percent level ($p = 0.117$). The negative coefficient on Women*Old*Khul suggests, as before, that younger women are responsive to the legal change, while older women are less affected or not affected. The coefficient 4.981 suggests that the implementation of Khul led to a 16 percent increase in the labor force participation of younger women.

Note also that the coefficient on years of schooling is positive and statistically significantly different from zero, showing that a one-year increase in years of schooling is associated with increase in the labor force participation of about 2 percentage points. We have also, as an alternative specification, included controls for the fraction of the relevant population group that has primary, secondary, or tertiary education. We obtained similar results. As a further robustness check, we also estimated the same equations dropping one-year lag GDP growth from the regressions, which gives qualitatively similar results to the previous estimates. The results are also robust to the exclusion of the country-specific time trends.

Although statistical power is rather weak, the results in Table 2 do suggest that the implementation of Khul reform leads to an increase in the labor force participation of women relative to men, and that the effects are similar or stronger for younger women. In Table 2, country fixed effects, year fixed effects and country-specific time trends are assumed to be common for all the groups (men and women, young and old). In Table 3, we relax this assumption and instead estimate the model separately for men and women, hence allowing fixed effects and time trends to be gender specific. This

GENDER AND ECONOMICS IN MUSLIM COMMUNITIES

Table 3 The impact of Khul on labor force participation of women and men, separate specifications.

	Women		Men	
	(1)	*(2)*	*(3)*	*(4)*
Khul	1.077+	1.741**	0.765	0.606
	(0.660)	(0.706)	(0.829)	(1.146)
Old*Khul		−1.340		0.318
		(1.651)		(1.424)
Old	−5.588	−5.587	−0.309	−0.353
	(4.083)	(4.092)	(1.180)	(1.246)
One-year lag	0.0157	0.0159	0.00190	0.00190
GDP growth	(0.0107)	(0.0109)	(0.00482)	(0.00482)
Years of schooling	1.385	1.314	−0.389	−0.391
	(1.263)	(1.249)	(0.386)	(0.385)
Observations	693	693	693	693
R-squared	0.922	0.923	0.659	0.660

Notes: Robust standard errors are reported in parentheses. Standard errors are clustered at the country level. *, **, *** denote statistical significance at the 10, 5, and 1 percent levels, respectively. + denotes significance at 15 percent level. The regressions control for country fixed effects, year fixed effects, country-specific time trends, one-year lag GDP growth, and years of schooling.

implies that we allow for the possibility that countries that implemented Khul had already had a trend in labor force participation of women that was different from that of men, for instance, as a result of other policy changes that we are not able to directly account for.

Columns 1 and 2 present the results for women, and columns 3 and 4 for men. All the estimations in Table 3 control for years of schooling. We can regard the effect of Khul on labor force participation of men as a placebo experiment, since we expect there to be no effect on men.

The coefficient on Khul in the first column suggests that labor force participation of women increased by 1.077 percentage points or 4 percent. This coefficient is only marginally statistically significant at the 15 percent level ($p = 0.125$). The same significance level is obtained using bootstrap and improves critical values. When we allow the effect of Khul to differ for younger and older women, in column 2, the main effect (on the young) becomes larger and is, in fact, significant at 5 percent level, which is also the statistical significance level if bootstrap-improved critical values are imposed. The coefficient of 1.74 percentage points implies that the labor force participation of younger women increased by almost 6 percent if we compare to the mean participation rate for the sample (Table A2 in the online appendix). The coefficient on Old*Khul is negative and almost of the same magnitude, which suggests that the reform did not affect labor

GENDER AND ECONOMICS IN MUSLIM COMMUNITIES

force participation of older women. However, the estimate is very imprecise and not statistically different from the coefficient on younger women. The estimates in columns 3 and 4 suggest, as expected, that Khul did not have any effect on the labor force participation of men.

Robustness and causality

We investigate the robustness of the specific nature of the labor markets in oil-producing countries and to the quality of the labor force participation data using the model estimated in column 2 of Table 3 as our baseline. As we discussed above, data on labor force participation are estimated for some years and derived from micro data other years. We introduce a time-varying dummy taking the value 1 if data is derived from micro data and zero otherwise. Results are available in Supplemental Online Table A6, and show that our main results are not sensitive to the data imputation.

We also explore whether Khul reform has different effects in OPEC countries. The results suggest that effects in OPEC countries may be different. However, none of the OPEC interactions are statistically significant, and importantly, the main effect of Khul is still qualitatively the same as in the main analysis (see Supplemental Online Table A6).

We also test for reverse causality by exploring if a change in labor force participation of women between 1980 and 1995 can predict the effect of the implementation of Khul reform. We find no evidence that such is the case. However, considering that the sample consists of a small number of countries, we do not get precise estimates (see Supplemental Online Table A7).

CONCLUSION

We examine how changes in divorce laws affect labor market decisions of women in the MENA. We find that Khul reform has a positive effect on the labor supply of women relative to that of men, and that the impact appears to be stronger for younger women. In the most restrictive estimations, we find that Khul reform increased the labor force participation rate of younger women by some 1.7 percentage points. This corresponds to a 6 percent increase, compared to the average participation rate of younger women in this sample of countries, and accounts for 10 percent of the overall increase in labor force participation for younger women during the studied time period, which is 17.2 percentage points. Although statistical power is weak, the results suggest that older women were less affected.

Economic theory suggests a number of reasons on how women's labor force participation could be affected by divorce reforms. First, Khul reform makes divorce less costly for women and may therefore result in higher divorce rates. Divorcées are likely to have higher labor force participation,

GENDER AND ECONOMICS IN MUSLIM COMMUNITIES

because they need to support themselves. However, anticipating a higher likelihood of divorce, women may increase their labor force participation already in marriage as a means to self-insure by making investments in an outside option. Second, Khul reform may also increase bargaining power of women and increase their influence over decision making in the household – for instance, whether she should work outside the home or not by giving her the right to exit, or threaten to exit, from the marriage if she does not get her way. This may eventually increase labor force participation of women as decisions in the household more closely reflect the wife's preferences. Both these theoretical arguments are, however, weaker for older women because their time horizon is shorter, they are more tied to their marriage, and because they may lose custody of children.

The evidence presented suggests that Khul increased the labor force participation of women, but available evidence on divorce rates does not suggest that divorce rates have increased. A possible interpretation is thus that Khul reform has improved the bargaining power of women in marriage such that more women who want to work are empowered to do so.

While the focus of this paper has been on the MENA, future studies can extend the analysis to other Muslim communities where asymmetric divorce laws cause imbalanced bargaining power within the household. More research is also needed to determine if and how Khul reform has improved the overall situation for women. Yet, Khul reform seems to be one step forward to more equal rights governing household decisions.

GENDER AND ECONOMICS IN MUSLIM COMMUNITIES

ACKNOWLEDGMENTS

The authors are grateful to the participants in the "Gender and Economics in Muslim Communities" workshop for useful comments. We specifically thank Eva Mörk for sharing the Wild bootstrap Stata code, and Steven Kapsos for providing us with the data on when the labor force participation in KILM database are imputed. Lena Hassani-Nezhad acknowledges financial support by the Austrian National Science Research Network "Labor and Welfare State" of the Austrian FWF and the National Institute on Aging (R21AG037891).

NOTES

[1] Dower (*Mahr*): "the gift the bridegroom gives the bride, which becomes her personal property" (Abdullahi A. An-Na'im 2002: 308). In Islam, *mahr* is mandatory for all bridegrooms. The gift is intended to support the bride if she becomes a widow or in the case of a unilateral divorce initiated by the husband.

[2] It is not necessarily the case that Khul increases divorce rates – at least not in the long run, since this change is also likely to encourage the formation of more stable marriages.

[3] Custody laws typically give legal custody of older children to the father in case of divorce. We lack information on how frequently such laws are enforced.

[4] For the summary of these theories of the family, see Theodore C. Bergstrom (1997).

[5] Parkman (1992) and Peters (1986) argue that unilateral divorce reform in the US increased the value of divorce for the husband. Even though Khul reform increases the value of divorce for wives, women still have the incentives to increase their labor force participation because they prefer to reduce their marriage-specific investment to self-insure against their reduced human capital, in the case that they want to file for divorce.

[6] Francine D. Blau and Lawrence M. Kahn (2007) also show that labor supply elasticities in response to change in nonlabor income are higher for mothers with young children than mothers with older children.

[7] Women in Algeria, Egypt, Iran, Jordan, Libya, Palestine, Qatar, Syria, and United Arab Emirates can stipulate the right to work in their marriage contract. Women in Tunisia and Oman have the right to work (Kelly and Breslin 2010).

[8] For more information regarding the difficulties that women might confront upon petitioning for divorce, see Farida Deif (2005).

[9] Women might be unwilling to take steps toward gender equality if, following their decision, the well-being of their children might be endangered (Nancy Folbre 2006).

[10] It is also possible that the employment of women leads to a double burden and higher overall work for women (Jennifer C. Olmsted 2005).

[11] The Supplemental Online Appendix can be accessed via the supplemental content tab at http://dx.doi.org/10.1080/13545701.2014.932421.

GENDER AND ECONOMICS IN MUSLIM COMMUNITIES

[12] Nadia Sonneveld (2012) and Azam Kamguian (2004) analyze the impact of the reform on easing the process of divorce for women in Egypt.

[13] We have made some modifications to our data to better capture the dates of ratifications for two countries: Jordan and the UAE, which adopted the reform December 31, 2001 and November 19, 2005, respectively. Since the reform in these countries was implemented at the end of the year, we will in fact use 2002 for the former and 2006 for the latter in the database.

[14] We used Welchman (2007), Kelly and Breslin (2010), and country reports of Convention on Elimination of All Forms of Discrimination against Women (United Nations 2007) jointly to provide the legal profiles for custody of children at the time of reform. Unfortunately, we do not have full information on possible changes in custody laws or their enforcement.

[15] Unfortunately, data on divorce is only available for nine countries and not for all years. We have therefore extrapolated data to fill in missing years.

[16] Throughout, the significance levels are reported at 15, 10, 5, and 1 percent levels. The reason for departing from reporting only conventional levels of significance is that the examined sample consists of a small number of countries and by controlling for country- and time-fixed effects and country-specific time trends, we cannot expect too precise estimates.

[17] See Cameron, Gelbach, and Miller (2008) for details regarding the computation of these critical values.

[18] Note that the Barro–Lee dataset has no data on years of schooling for three of our countries: Lebanon, Oman, and Palestine (West Bank and Gaza). Therefore, by controlling for years of schooling, we lose the observations for these countries.

[19] The p-value of the coefficient is 0.102 using the standard students-t distribution. However, the Wald statistic suggests that the coefficient is statistically significant at the 15 percent level when compared to the Wild bootstrap-t critical values presented in Table A1 in the Supplemental Online Appendix.

REFERENCES

Agarwal, Bina. 1997. "Bargaining and Gender Relations: Within and Beyond the Household." *Feminist Economics* 3(1): 1–51.

An-Na'im, Abdullahi A. 2002. *Islamic Family Law in a Changing World: A Global Resource Book.* London: Zed Books.

Barro, Robert, and Jong-Wha Lee. 2013. "A New Data Set of Educational Attainment in the World, 1950–2010." *Journal of Development Economics* 104: 184–98.

Becker, Gary S. 1973. "A Theory of Marriage: Part I." *Journal of Political Economy* 81(4): 813–46.

Benería, Lourdes. 1999. "The Enduring Debate over Unpaid Labor." *International Labour Review* 138(3): 287–309.

Bergmann, Barbara. 1995. "Becker's Theory of the Family: Preposterous Conclusions." *Feminist Economics* 1(1): 141–50.

Bergstrom, Theodore C. 1997. "A Survey of Theories of the Family." In *Handbook of Population and Family Economics*, vol. 1A, edited by Mark R. Rozenzwieg and Oded Stark, 21–74. Amsterdam: Elsevier.

Bertrand, Marianne, Esther Duflo, and Sendhil Mullainathan. 2004. "How Much Should We Trust Differences-in-Differences Estimates?" *Quarterly Journal of Economics* 119(1): 249–75.

Bibi, Sami and Mustapha K. Nabli. 2010. *Equity and Inequality in the Arab Region.* ERF Policy Research Report, Economic Research Forum, Cairo.

GENDER AND ECONOMICS IN MUSLIM COMMUNITIES

Blau, Francine D. and Lawrence M. Kahn. 2007. "Changes in the Labor Supply Behavior of Married Women: 1980–2000." *Journal of Labor Economics* 25(3): 393–438.

Cameron, Colin A., Jonah B. Gelbach, and Douglas L. Miller. 2008. "Bootstrap-Based Improvements for Inference with Clustered Errors." *Review of Economic and Statistics* 90(3): 414–27.

Chiappori, Pierre-Andre, Bernard Fortin, and Guy Lacroix. 2002. "Marriage Market, Divorce Legislation and Household Labor Supply." *Journal of Political Economy* 110(1): 37–72.

Deif, Farida. 2005. "Divorced from Justice." *Journal of Middle East Women's Studies* 1(3): 108–15.

Doss, Cheryl. 2005. "The Effects of Intrahousehold Property Ownership on Expenditure Patterns in Ghana." *Journal of African Economies* 15(1): 149–80.

Duflo, Esther. 2003. "Grandmothers and Granddaughters: Old Age Pension and Intra-Household Allocation in South Africa." *World Bank Economic Review* 17(1): 1–25.

———. 2012. "Women Empowerment and Economic Development." *Journal of Economic Literature* 50(4): 1051–79.

Duflo, Esther and Christopher Udry. 2004. "Intrahousehold Resource Allocation in Côte d'Ivoire: Social Norms, Separate Accounts and Consumption Choices." Working Paper w10498, National Bureau of Economic Research.

El-Masri, Samar. 2012. "Challenges facing CEDAW in the Middle East and North Africa." *International Journal of Human Rights* 16(7): 931–46.

Ferber, Marianne A. and Julie A. Nelson, eds. 2003. *Feminist Economics Today: Beyond Economic Man*. Chicago: University of Chicago Press.

Fernández, Raquel and Alessandra Fogli. 2009. "Culture: An Empirical Investigation of Beliefs, Work and Fertility." *American Economic Journal: Macroeconomics* 1(1): 146–77.

Folbre, Nancy. 1994. *Who Pays for the Kids? Gender and the Structures of Constraint*. New York: Routledge.

———. 2006. "Measuring Care: Gender, Empowerment, and the Care Economy." *Journal of Human Development* 7(2): 183–99.

Friedberg, Leora. 1998. "Did Unilateral Divorce Raise Divorce Rates? Evidence from Panel Data." Working Paper w6398, National Bureau of Economic Research.

Genadek, Katie R., Wendy A. Stock, and Christiana Stoddard. 2007. "No-Fault Divorce Laws and the Labor Supply of Women with and without Children." *Journal of Human Resources* 42(1): 247–74.

Gray, Jeffery S. 1998. "Divorce-Law Changes, Household Bargaining, and Married Women's Labor Supply." *American Economic Review* 88(3): 628–42.

Hartmann, Heidi I. 1981. "The Family as the Locus of Gender, Class, and Political Struggle: The Example of Housework." *Signs* 6(3): 366–94.

International Labour Office Global Employment Trends Unit. 2010. *Trends Econometrics Models: A Review of the Methodology*. Geneva: ILO.

Johnson, William R. and Jonathan Skinner. 1986. "Labor Supply and Marital Separation." *American Economic Review* 76(3): 455–69.

Kamguian, Azam, ed. 2004. "Women in the Middle East." Committee to Defend Women's Rights in the Middle East Bulletin 30, Center for Inquiry, December. http://www.centerforinquiry.net/isis/islamic_viewpoints/cdwrme_bulletin_30/.

Katz, Elizabeth. 1997. "The Intra-Household Economics of Voice and Exit." *Feminist Economics* 3(3): 25–46.

Kelly, Sanja and Julia Breslin. 2010. *Women's Rights in the Middle East and North Africa: Progress Amid Resistance*. Lanham, MD: Rowman and Littlefield.

Lundberg, Shelly and Robert A. Pollak. 1993. "Separate Spheres Bargaining and the Marriage Market." *Journal of Political Economy* 101(6): 988–1010.

GENDER AND ECONOMICS IN MUSLIM COMMUNITIES

Manser, Marilyn and Murray Brown. 1980. "Marriage and Household Decision-Making: A Bargaining Analysis." *International Economic Review* 21(1): 31–44.

Matouschek, Niko and Imran Rasul. 2008. "The Economics of the Marriage Contract: Theories and Evidence." *Journal of Law and Economics* 51(1): 59–110.

McElroy, Marjorie B. and Mary Jean Horney. 1981. "Nash-Bargained Household Decisions: Toward a Generalization of the Theory of Demand." *International Economic Review* 22(2): 333–49.

Moghadam, Fatemeh Etemad. 2011. "Iran's Missing Working Women." In *Veiled Employment: Islamism and the Political Economy of Women's Employment in Iran,* edited by Roksana Bahramitash and Hadi Salehi Esfahani, 256–72. New York: Syracuse University Press.

Moghadam, Valentine M. 2008. "Feminism, Legal Reform and Women's Empowerment in the Middle East and North Africa." *International Social Science Journal* 59(191): 9–16.

Nazir, Sameena. 2005. "Challenging Inequality: Obstacles and Opportunities Towards Women's Rights in the Middle East and North Africa." In *Women's Rights in the Middle East and North Africa: Citizenship and Justice,* edited by Sameena Nazir and Leigh Tomppert, 1–14. Lanham, MD: Rowman and Littlefield.

Olmsted, Jennifer C. 2005. "Is Paid Work the (Only) Answer? Neoliberalism, Arab Women's Well-Being, and the Social Contract." *Journal of Middle East Women's Studies* 1(2): 112–39.

———. 2011. "Gender and Globalization: The Iranian Experience." In *Veiled Employment: Islamism and the Political Economy of Women's Employment in Iran,* edited by Roksana Bahramitash and Hadi Salehi Esfahani, 25–52. New York: Syracuse University Press.

Parkman, Allen M. 1992. "Unilateral Divorce and the Labor-Force Participation Rate of Married Women, Revisited." *American Economic Review* 82(3): 671–78.

Peters, H. Elizabeth. 1986. "Marriage and Divorce: Informational Constraints and Private Contracting." *American Economic Review* 76(3): 437–54.

Rasul, Imran. 2006. "Marriage Market and Divorce Laws." *Journal of Law, Economics and Organization* 22(1): 30–69.

Ruwanpura, Kanchana N. 2007. "Shifting Theories: Partial Perspectives on the Household." *Cambridge Journal of Economics* 31(4): 525–38.

Seguino, Stephanie. 2011. "Help or Hindrance? Religion's Impact on Gender Inequality in Attitudes and Outcomes." *World Development* 39(8): 1308–21.

Sen, Amartya K. 1990. "Gender and Cooperative Conflicts." In *Persistent Inequalities: Women and World Development,* edited by Irene Tinker, 123–49. New York: Oxford University Press.

Shah, Nasra M. and Sulayman S. Al-Qudsi. 1990. "Female Work Roles in Traditional Oil Economy: Kuwait." In *Research in Human Capital and Development,* edited by Ismail Serageldin, 157–83. Baltimore, MD: Johns Hopkins University Press.

Sonbol, Amira El-Azhari. 2003. *Women of Jordan: Islam, Labor, and the Law.* New York: Syracuse University Press.

Sonneveld, Nadia. 2012. *Khul Divorce in Egypt.* Cairo: American University in Cairo Press.

Stevenson, Betsey. 2008. "Divorce Law and Women's Labor Supply." *Journal of Empirical Legal Studies* 5(4): 853–73.

Stevenson, Betsey and Justin Wolfers. 2006. "Bargaining in the Shadow of the Law: Divorce Laws and Family Distress." *Quarterly Journal of Economics* 121(1): 267–88.

———. 2007. "Marriage and Divorce: Changes and their Driving Forces." *Journal of Economic Perspectives* 21(2): 27–52.

Thomas, Duncan. 1990. "Intra-Household Resource Allocation: An Inferential Approach." *Journal of Human Resources* 25: 635–64.

United Nations. 2007. "Country Reports on Convention on the Elimination of All Forms of Discrimination against Women." United Nations Entity for Gender Equality and the Empowerment of Women. http://www.un.org/womenwatch/daw/cedaw/reports.htm.

GENDER AND ECONOMICS IN MUSLIM COMMUNITIES

Welchman, Lynn. 2007. *Women and Muslim Family Laws in Arab States: Comparative Overview of Textual Development and Advocacy.* Amsterdam: Amsterdam University Press.

Wolfers, Justin. 2006. "Did Unilateral Divorce Laws Raise Divorce Rates? A Reconciliation and New Results." *American Economic Review* 96(5): 1802–20.

World Bank. 2004. *Gender and Development in the Middle East and North Africa: Women in the Public Sphere.* Washington, DC: International Bank for Reconstruction and Development/World Bank.

DIVERGING STORIES OF "MISSING WOMEN" IN SOUTH ASIA: IS SON PREFERENCE WEAKENING IN BANGLADESH?

Naila Kabeer, Lopita Huq, and Simeen Mahmud

ABSTRACT

South Asia is a region characterized by a culture of son preference, severe discrimination against daughters, and excess levels of female mortality, leading to what Amartya Sen called the phenomenon of "missing women." However, the onset of fertility decline across the region has been accompanied by considerable divergence in this phenomenon. In India, improvements in overall life expectancy have closed the gender gap in mortality rates among adults, but persisting gender discrimination among children and increasing resort to female-selective abortion has led to growing imbalance in child sex ratios and sex ratios at birth. In Bangladesh, by contrast, fertility decline has been accompanied by a closing of the gender gap in mortality in all age groups. Using quantitative and qualitative data, this study explores changing attitudes toward sons and daughters in Bangladesh to explain why the phenomenon of "missing women" has played out so differently in these two neighboring countries.

INTRODUCTION: "WATERING THE NEIGHBOUR'S TREE"?

Variations in patriarchal structures across the world have given rise to marked regional patterns in both form and severity of gender inequalities. Regional variations in sex ratios, typically defined as the ratio of men to women in the population, are one manifestation of this. Sex ratios at birth (SRBs) generally converge to a norm of around 105 boys to every 100 girls (Christophe Z. Guilmoto 2012). However, the greater biological vulnerability of male infants means that, with equal care and feeding, more girls tend to survive than boys, leading to a lowering of the ratio in overall populations in much of the world. Thus, there are 100 men to every

GENDER AND ECONOMICS IN MUSLIM COMMUNITIES

100 women in Ghana, while there are 97 men to every 100 women in the United Kingdom and United States (Index Mundi 2013).

The pattern was very different in societies belonging to what has been characterized as the "belt of classic patriarchy," stretching from North Africa and the Middle East across the northern plains of South Asia, but also including countries in the East Asia region (John C. Caldwell 1982; Deniz Kandiyoti 1988). Gender discrimination in these societies was often so severe that it led to excess levels of mortality for women in most age groups, giving rise to the "masculinization" of sex ratios in their overall populations, averaging around 105 men to 100 women and resulting in the phenomenon of "missing women" – namely, the additional number of women there might have been in the population of these countries had mortality rates been less skewed (Amartya Sen 1992).

While countries characterized by adverse sex ratios vary considerably in terms of ethnicity, culture, and religious affiliation, they share certain common features in the organization of family and kinship systems: a patriarchal authority structure; patrilineal descent and inheritance; strict controls over women's mobility in the public domain, resulting in extremely low rates of women's labor force participation; and patrilocal residence patterns, so that a daughter is required to live with her husband and his kin after marriage. The loss that this represents to the parents who brought them up has been referred to as "watering the neighbour's tree" (Naila Kabeer 1985: 98). These practices interlock to produce a strong culture of son preference in the region.

These older norms and practices have, of course, been considerably altered by the recent histories and development trajectories of countries within this region – with varying implications for their sex ratios. Population sex ratios have generally declined, reflecting an improvement in women's overall life expectancy relative to that of men. The 1990s saw the share of "missing women" drop by 3–5 percentage points in Bangladesh, Pakistan, and much of the Middle East, and by a more modest 1–2 points in India and Egypt; but also saw an actual rise of 0.4 points in China (Stephan Klasen and Claudia Wink 2003).

However, the decline in overall sex ratios has been accompanied in some countries by a worrying new trend: an increase in SRBs attributed to the growing prevalence of female-selective abortions. The availability of amniocentesis and ultrasound scanning has made prenatal sex determination possible, allowing parents to use abortion to manipulate the sex composition of live births. The use of this technology has led to highly masculine SRBs in China, India, and South Korea but also, more recently, in countries conventionally not included within the patriarchal belt: Vietnam, Azerbaijan, Georgia, and Armenia. Compared to "normal" ratios of around 105 male to 100 female births in much of the world, 2010 estimates of ratios in these countries ranged from 108.5 (India) to 121.2

(China). In all cases, these figures represent a rise from 1990 estimates – with the exception of those for South Korea, where SRBs have been declining since the mid 1990s (United Nations Development Programme [UNDP] 2010). The phenomenon of "missing women" is being replaced in these countries by the phenomenon of "missing daughters."

It has been suggested that the resort to female-selective abortion in these countries represents efforts on the part of parents to reconcile their desire for smaller families with their continued preference for sons (Monica Das Gupta and P.N. Mari Bhat 1997; Alaka M. Basu 1999). Yet the transition to smaller families in societies characterized by son preference has not everywhere been accompanied by rising SRBs. Bangladesh, for instance, appears to have undergone fertility decline without resorting to such means.

It is unlikely that any single set of factors can explain the diverging trends in sex ratios in countries that share a common history of son preference. Nor can it explain the rise of adverse SRBs in countries outside the belt of classic patriarchy. Instead, this contribution explores a more localized version of this puzzle: the deterioration in child sex ratios (CSRs) in India and their improvement in neighboring Bangladesh. The study's main focus is on Bangladesh, and it draws on primary data collected as part of a larger International Development Research Centre (IDRC)-funded research project on this topic in India and Bangladesh. The comparison with India is useful because it allows us to disentangle what differentiates the experience of fertility transition in the two countries, focusing our attention on possible explanations for the diverging trends in their sex ratios. Inclusion of Pakistan, whose current SRB puts it in an intermediate position between Bangladesh and India,[1] would have enriched the analysis; but unfortunately there is very little research into this issue (Guilmoto 2012).

FERTILITY DECLINE AND CHANGING SEX RATIOS: THE INDIAN STORY

Much of the literature on adverse sex ratios in India has focused on the marked North–South divide in their distribution, with states to the south of the Vindhya–Narmada divide generally reporting more egalitarian sex ratios than those to the north (Barbara Miller 1981; Tim Dyson and Mick Moore 1983; Satish B. Agnihotri 2000). Variations in kinship and family relations between the so-called "Sanskritic north" and "Dravidian south" have featured prominently in explanations for this regional divide (Irawati K. Karve 1968). Family and kinship systems in the Sanskritic north share many of the key features of classic patriarchy described earlier, but with variations reflecting the prevalence of a caste system dominated by "Brahmanical patriarchy" (Uma Chakravarti 2003: 34). Marriage is characterized by caste endogamy and lineage and village exogamy: daughters must marry men

GENDER AND ECONOMICS IN MUSLIM COMMUNITIES

from within their own caste but outside their lineage and natal village, so that they arrive as strangers in their husbands' homes. The practice of hypergamy, most common among the dominant castes, requires that the bride's family be socially and ritually inferior to that of the groom. The giving of dowry, the transfer of wealth from the bride's family to the groom's, reflects the social and ritual inferiority of "wife-givers" to "wife-takers" within this system and again is most widely practiced by the dominant castes.

By contrast, the kinship system of the Dravidian south is characterized by lineage endogamy, with cross-kin marriage fairly common so that women often marry known persons from households near their natal homes (Rajni Palriwala 1994). There is greater social and ritual equality between families related through marriage, and marriage payments often take the form of bride-wealth rather than dowry. Women are also allowed greater public mobility, and women's labor force participation rates are higher than the rest of the country.

However, a single-minded focus on the North–South divide obscures the influence of other factors that contribute to variations in sex ratios.[2] The eastern states of India, for instance, do not fit easily into this divide, having a far more attenuated adherence to the north Indian kinship ethos and reporting sex ratios intermediate between the North and the South (Dyson and Moore 1983; Agnihotri 2000). Within the north as well, the worst sex ratios appeared to be concentrated within a number of northwestern states – namely, Punjab, Haryana, Uttar Pradesh, Rajasthan, and Gujarat. There are also class-caste dimensions to sex ratios, with more adverse sex ratios found among wealthier landowning households and households with higher per-capita monthly expenditure: a counterintuitive negative prosperity effect (Agnihotri 2000).

Recent years have seen worrying trends in the distribution of adverse sex ratios. While improvements in the life expectancy at birth of women relative to men – the product of improvements in overall health, the decline in fertility rates, and concomitant decline in maternal mortality – has resulted in a decline in overall population sex ratios, it has been accompanied by a rise in CSRs (0–6 age group) since the 1980s: latest census figures suggest that the CSR at the national level has gone from 106 in 1991 to 109 in 2011 (Mary E. John 2011). This appears to reflect the growing resort to female-selective abortion, evident from the steady rise in SRBs from already high levels of 111 in 1998 to 114 by 2005 (Mary E. John, Ravinder Kaur, Rajni Palriwala, Sarawati Raju, and Alpana Sagar 2008). At the same time, under-5 mortality rates continue to show considerable female disadvantage (Das Gupta and Bhat 1997; Yoko Niimi 2009). This suggests that the growing resort to prenatal selection has been added to older forms of postnatal gender discrimination.

There is also evidence that adverse CSRs are spreading beyond the northwestern states to "fresh regions, communities and classes where it was

GENDER AND ECONOMICS IN MUSLIM COMMUNITIES

not a big problem before" (John et al. 2008: 1). While the 2011 census shows that the worst CSRs continue to be found in the northwestern states, deterioration in CSRs are now to be found in many central, southern and eastern states as well – including West Bengal, which has considerable cultural affinity with Bangladesh (John 2011). Adverse sex ratios have also spread beyond the landed upper castes to other caste groups (Basu 1999; John et al. 2008).

Religion is another factor associated with variations in sex ratios. Here, a countertrend is worth noting. Population sex ratios were worse among Muslims than Hindus in earlier decades, but this pattern has been reversed since the 1970s (Government of India 2006). The 2001 census suggests that Muslims now also report more favorable CSRs: 950 girls to 1000 boys in the 0–6 age group, compared to 927 for the overall population (see also Sucharita Sinha Mukherjee 2013). CSRs are more favorable among Muslims in almost every state in India, although differences from the rest of the population vary across states. In fact, the worst CSRs among Muslims are to be found in same northwestern states that report the worst sex ratios for the rest of the population – (P.N. Mari Bhat and A.J. Francis Zavier 2003). The impact of religion is clearly mediated by context.

The IDRC study in India focused on selected districts in the five states (Madhya Pradesh, Rajasthan, Himachal Pradesh, Haryana, and Punjab) that reported the worst CSRs in the 2001 census (John et al. 2008). It found that many of the previous explanations for son preference continued to be relevant in explaining its persistence in these states: the centrality of sons in inheritance and descent; their importance in looking after parents in old age and performing important rituals when they died; and the loss of daughters to their parents after marriage.

At the same time, the study argued that the current trends in adverse sex ratios could not be explained simply in terms of continuity with the past. Indeed, there were many reasons to expect son preference to weaken. Questions were being raised by parents as to whether sons could indeed be relied on to look after their parents and perform other filial obligations. Many had failed to find jobs or fallen into bad habits, and there were loud criticisms of "worthless sons" in a number of study sites.

Instead, the study suggested that the explanation lay in the strengthening of the emotion and practice of "daughter aversion" (a term coined by Vani Borooah and Sriya Iyer 2004: 2). In a context where marriage was a social compulsion, especially for women, daughter aversion reflected the increasing investment of time and money that parents had to make to ensure the best possible marriage for daughters within what can be characterized as a highly "class-caste differentiated marriage market" (John et al. 2008: 72). This investment had increased across the board with the spread of the upper-caste practice of dowry and expensive weddings to other castes and social groups seeking to signal improvements in their social status. It has also

GENDER AND ECONOMICS IN MUSLIM COMMUNITIES

increased because of the need to invest in daughters' education to increase their chances in the marriage market (also argued by Mukherjee 2013).

Other factors reinforcing daughter aversion were linked to changes in the structure of the economy. The growing scarcity of land put pressure on families to diversify their occupations and find work outside the agricultural sector, particular in coveted but scarce white-collar service and public sector jobs. Parents' future expectations from sons in terms of the continued economic viability of the family unit and support in their old age led to increasing concentration of resources, including education, in sons (Ravinder Kaur 2007; John et al. 2008). This may have been reinforced by the greater instability of women's employment. While Kaur refers to the "increased demand for female labor" (2007: 238), Indrani Mazumdar and N. Neetha (2011) point out that women's economic activity rates have been declining since the late 1990s, and much of it remains concentrated in self-employment and unpaid family work.

To sum up, therefore, while the story of sex ratios in India reflects the conjuncture of diverse social, cultural, and economic forces, central to it are persisting ideologies of the male breadwinner and men's privileged access to existing job opportunities, combined with the universal necessity of marriage, particularly for women; strict caste norms restricting the choice of husbands; marital practices that lead to the loss of daughters to their parents after marriage; and escalating dowry expenses as "the most visible face of the burden associated with daughters" (Kaur 2007: 240). The strength of the growing preference for sons – or aversion to daughters – is illustrated by the fact that, in the context of a transition to smaller family size, most of the families in the locations studied by John et al. (2008) expressed a preference for either just one son, two sons, or, in some locations, two sons and a daughter. Hardly anyone expressed a preference for, *or had*, only daughters.

FERTILITY DECLINE AND CHANGING SEX RATIOS: THE BANGLADESH STORY

Bangladesh was considered in the early literature to have a great deal of affinity with the North Indian family and kinship system (Miller 1981; Dyson and Moore 1983). Its high rates of fertility were explained by a pronatalist, patriarchal culture in which parents were driven to have more children than they might want because of the strength of son preference (Mead Cain, Syeda Rokeya Khanam, and Shamsun Nahar 1979; Clarence Maloney, K.M. Ashraful Aziz, and Profulla C. Sarker 1981).

Women's dependence on men for protection and provision at different stages of their lives gave them a particularly strong stake in producing sons – both to ensure their own place within their husband's kinship group and as a form of security for their old age. Cain et al. (1979) coined the concept of "patriarchal risk" to capture the abrupt decline in women's socioeconomic status that was likely to accompany the loss of the male breadwinner and guardian through widowhood, divorce, or desertion. Although engagement in paid work might have served to mitigate patriarchal risk, the strict controls exercised over women's mobility in the public domain ensured that they remained confined to largely unpaid work in the domestic domain. As men became increasingly integrated into the cash economy, a reversal took place in the direction of wealth transfers at marriage, sometime in the 1960s–70s, with escalating dowry demands by the groom's family replacing the previous practice of bride-wealth (Tone Bleie 1990).

Given the strength of its patriarchal norms, it is not surprising that Bangladesh was characterized by excess levels of female mortality in almost every age group (Lincoln C. Chen 1982). Early studies into the attitudes of parents confirmed the existence of strong son preference. The 1975 Bangladesh Fertility Survey found that among ever-married women wanting another child, 62 percent wanted a boy, 8 percent wanted a girl, and the rest were undecided (Government of Bangladesh 1978). Two smaller-scale studies carried out in the 1970s in the districts of Comilla (Nilufer Ahmed 1981) and Faridpur (Kabeer 1985) also found high levels of son preference, higher in Comilla than Faridpur and higher among less educated women.

Fertility rates began to decline in the late 1970s, gathering momentum in subsequent years so that they had fallen below those of India by 1990 (David E. Bloom, David Canning, and Larry Rosenberg 2011). As the Indian experience suggests, one way that parents have reconciled their strong desire for sons with their desire for smaller families has been to intensify discrimination against girls, to ensure that more sons survived than daughters. Evidence from national statistics – as well as from the exceptionally good demographic surveillance system that has been in place in the Matlab area since 1966 – suggest that this has not happened in Bangladesh.

National-level data from the Bangladesh Bureau of Statistics since 1981 and successive Demographic and Health Surveys (DHS) show that, along with declines in population and child mortality rates, gender differentials have also been declining since the 1990s. This is supported by analysis of Matlab data, which found that gender disparities in under-5 mortality rates had all but disappeared after 1990 (Nurul Alam, Jeroen Van Ginneken, and Alinda Bosch 2007). Recent national data compiled by the United Nations Children's Fund (UNICEF) suggest that by 2000, female mortality rates in the under-5 age group had fallen below those of boys (2011). According to its 2009 Multiple Indicator Cluster Survey (MICS) data, they are now lower by 24 percent at the national level, but with some variation across the country.[3]

These improvements appear to be linked to declining gender discrimination in the treatment of children. 2007 DHS data confirm the

GENDER AND ECONOMICS IN MUSLIM COMMUNITIES

near-absence of gender discrimination in nutritional outcomes at the national level: 40 percent of boys and 42 percent of girls were reported as suffering from malnutrition. Data from the DHS 2007 and MICS 2006 also document the absence of gender discrimination in various forms of health-seeking behavior, including the use of oral rehydration therapy, full immunization, and exclusive breastfeeding in the first five months of a child's life (UNICEF 2011). Maternal education, household wealth, and women's economic contributions appear to be among the factors leading to this decline in discrimination (Erin M. Trapp, Jill Williams, Jane Menken, and Shannon Fisher 2004).

Nor is there any evidence of female-selective abortion: SRBs remain within the biological norm. Abortion is illegal in Bangladesh, but menstrual regulation is widely available and could be used to manipulate the sex composition of surviving children by resorting to it once parents had one or more sons. Analysis of Matlab data from the 1980s suggested that son preference increased the likelihood of abortion (Radheshyam Bairagi 2001). However, an econometric study using more recent longitudinal data for the period 1998–2003 found no evidence that the sex composition of surviving children affected the likelihood of abortion (Jessica D. Gipson and Michelle J. Hindin 2008).

An examination of the history of Bangladesh in the decades since its independence in 1971 suggests certain changes that might be expected to have improved the position of women and, by extension, the value given to daughters. With the decline in fertility, economic growth rates began to outstrip population growth by the 1990s; and there has been a gradual but steady decline in poverty rates, from 60 percent at the start of the 1990s to 40 percent by the mid 2000s (Wahid Mahmud, Sadiq Ahmed, and Sandeep Mahajan 2008). Along with the improvements in overall mortality noted earlier, maternal mortality has declined from 800 deaths per 100,000 live births in 1990 to 194 in 2011. There has been a steady rise in women's education, first closing and then reversing the gender gap at primary and secondary levels.

There has also been a slow but steady rise in women's labor force participation from 4 percent recorded by the 1974 Bangladesh census to 36 percent according to the 2010 Labour Force Survey. While some of this rise is poverty driven, it also reflects the expansion of economic opportunities for women from a number of different sources: government and nongovernmental organization (NGO) service provision; the growth of microfinance services targeted to women; and the expansion of female labor-intensive, export-oriented industries (World Bank 2008). However, as in India, the overwhelming majority of working women continue to be in self-employment (25 percent) or unpaid family labor (56 percent).

Reviewing these changes in the late 1990s, Shapan Adnan (1998) concluded that not only were these improvements in women's status likely to have been a major driving force in bringing about fertility decline, but they might also lead to a reassessment of the value of daughters:

> Changes in women's position still remain far from universal in Bangladesh, but the emergent trends were sufficiently recognizable by the 1980s. Insofar as these have had an impact on prevalent social norms and cultural perceptions, it is possible that a reassessment of the value of female children might well have begun, even if it is not always consciously articulated. Since many of the factors which made girls less preferable than boys are ceasing to hold, it is likely that parents have also begun to find female children less undesirable than before. [...] It... seems reasonable to postulate the hypothesis that the preference for sons is on the decline, given increasing value of female children to parents. (1344)

ANALYZING SON PREFERENCE IN BANGLADESH: QUANTITATIVE INSIGHTS

We use Adnan's speculative comments as the point of departure for our own investigation into this question. Our analysis relies on two sets of data collected as part of the IDRC-funded research project. The first is a survey of 5,199 women carried out in 2008.[4] The women were randomly selected from villages in eight different districts in Bangladesh, including the Faridpur village in which Kabeer had carried out the study cited earlier. The districts were selected to represent differing socioeconomic conditions. The second dataset was collected through qualitative interviews carried out in four of the eight study villages. While 15 interviews were carried out in three of the villages, a more detailed qualitative study was carried out in the Faridpur village. These interviews allowed us to explore the views expressed about sex preference in greater detail.

One of the questions included in the survey related to sex preference: "If you had only one child, what would you like to have: a son, a daughter, or you do not have any preference?" Altogether, 40 percent of the overall sample expressed a preference for sons and 7 percent expressed daughter preference, while the rest expressed indifference to the sex of the child. However, there was considerable variation by location: clearly, the factors driving changes in attitudes toward sons and daughters have not been uniform across the country.

Table 1 allows us to examine some of the district-level variations in individual and household characteristics that might contribute to variations in strength of son preference. No clear-cut patterns emerge, but the two extremes are worth noting. Women from Comilla district were most likely to express son preference – and least likely to express a preference for daughters. Comilla is one of the more socially conservative districts in our

Table 1 District-level variations in individual and household characteristics across study sample districts

Variables	Faridpur	Comilla	Tangail	C.ganj	Maulovibazar	Bagerhaat	Kurigram	Narayanganj
Son preference (%)	47	64	51	36	27	47	22	37
No preference (%)	47	34	43	57	65	48	72	54
Daughter preference (%)	7	2	6	7	8	5	6	7
Age (mean)	35.37	35.77	34.26	36.36	35.80	36.79	36.15	35.1
No formal education (%)	34	46	54	52	43	30	49	30
Education: primary (%)	23	27	29	24	29	30	23	26
Education: secondary and above (%)	42	28	18	25	28	40	28	33
Outside paid work (%)	16	5	15	5	10	9	20	20
Home-based paid work (%)	45	81	71	78	66	64	74	42
Economically inactive (%)	39	13	15	17	25	26	6	38
NGO membership (%)	53	32	49	36	31	34	31	32
Never married (%)	15	10	5	8	19	11	7	11
Currently married (%)	72	76	84	77	64	72	78	76
Widowed (%)	11	12	9	12	14	15	13	10
Divorced/separated (%)	2	2	2	3	3	3	2	2
Household size (mean)	5.1	6.2	4.3	5.3	6.0	4.8	4.4	5.3
Wealth status: low (%)	20	41	37	28	25	38	59	18
Muslim (%)	89	82	98	97	79	90	90	97
Watches TV regularly (%)	47	19	28	23	36	23	17	78
Routinely wears burkah/hijab outside (%)	41	77	65	31	57	70	22	74
Number of children (mean)	2.43	3.08	2.51	2.99	2.64	2.42	2.60	2.65
Female household head (%)	9	17	10	16	14	9	13	18
Family values her work (%)	51	35	57	53	46	57	41	55
Total numbers	635	627	653	633	643	626	690	692

sample. It had the highest percentage of women conforming to purdah norms, wearing burkah/hijab outside the home, reporting higher average numbers of children and least likely to work outside the home. Women from Kurigram district, one of the poorest in Bangladesh, were least likely to express son preference and most likely to express indifference. These women were also least likely to wear burkah/hijab outside the home and the highest rates of economic activity, including outside the home. Household wealth, forms of economic activity, and social norms thus appear to be among the factors that explain variations in son preference across our sample.

We used multivariate analysis in order to isolate the independent effects of these and other possible influences on the likelihood of son preference among women. Since our dependent variable was formulated in dichotomous terms (son preference = 1; daughter preference/neutral preference = 0), we used logistic regression techniques to carry out the analysis. Furthermore, in order to allow for the possibility that the factors shaping son preference have shifted over time, we carried out the analysis separately for two cohorts of women: ages 15–29, and ages 30+.

We drew on the secondary literature to identify likely influences on women's preferences. Given the geographical variations in expressions of son preference, we introduced dummy variables to capture the influence of location. In terms of demographic variables, age is likely to be important since the literature suggests that younger women are more open to change than older women. We included number of children since fertility has been linked to son preference in the early literature. Given the importance of patriarchal risk identified in the early literature and the likelihood of descent into poverty in the absence of a male breadwinner, we would expect divorced, separated, and widowed women to express stronger son preference than married or single women.

We also included women's education and labor force participation, both of which have emerged in the secondary literature as important influences on attitudes toward children. We distinguish between economic activity within and outside the home, since it is the latter that represents a break with tradition. In addition, given long-standing social norms curtailing women's capacity to undertake paid work, we included a variable measuring family support for their work: this was based on women who said that their families valued their work, whether paid or unpaid. While there is a close correlation between the value that women received for their work and its paid status, the additional variable allowed us to identify women whose families placed a positive value on their work. We also included the education and occupations of the household head (most often husband, followed by father) to ascertain whether the characteristics of the primary decision maker influenced women's attitudes.

While conventional economic analysis would suggest that household scarcity exercises greater pressure to discriminate against less productive members, the Indian literature suggests a negative "prosperity effect." We explore whether the same effect occurs in Bangladesh by including a measure of household wealth. Along with religion (Muslims make up 91 percent of our sample, while Hindus make up the rest), we have also sought to control for religiosity, or active adherence to religious norms, which we proxy by veiling practices in the public domain. Finally, we included a measure for routine TV watching to capture women's exposure to new ideas along with membership of NGOs, which gives women access to new ideas as well as to credit.[5]

We conducted our regression analysis in two stages for each of the age cohorts. The first stage included only the district dummy variables, while the second stage included the other explanatory variables. Given space limitations, we report only on the second stage for each cohort (Table 2). The value of the percent correctly predicted – which provide an overall indicator of the fit of the model, much in line with the R-squared in ordinary least squares – indicates that the models predicting son preference among older and younger cohorts fit the observed data fairly well. However, it is worth reporting that the unobserved community-level variables, as captured by the district dummy variables, appear to be predicting most of the variance in son preference: the addition of the other explanatory variables does not increase the value of the percentage correctly predicted by a great deal for either age cohort, although some of these variables did make a significant difference to the likelihood of son preference.

Age appears to have little influence on expressed sex preference for either cohort, once differences in education and other characteristics have been controlled for. But the fact that the significance of some of the other explanatory variables varies for the two age groups suggests that the factors influencing the preference for sons vary by cohort or have changed over time. Starting with the older cohort, our hypothesis regarding the relevance of patriarchal risk in shaping son preference is supported by the finding that widowhood significantly increases the likelihood of son preference. The very low incidence of divorce/separation – no higher than 2–3 percent across in any district – may explain why this variable is not significant.

As far as women's economic activity is concerned, Table 2 suggests that it is not the kind of work that women do that influences their preferences, but the value given to it by their family. Given that outside paid work was most likely to be valued by the family, this is an interesting result. It suggests that the impact of women's paid work on sex preferences is mediated less by its objective characteristics than by how such work is perceived by the rest of the family. Women who feel economically valued are less likely to express son preference.

The greater likelihood of women from poorer households expressing son preference conforms to conventional economic expectations, suggesting that affluence eases the pressure to have sons. Education emerges as an

GENDER AND ECONOMICS IN MUSLIM COMMUNITIES

Table 2 Determinants of son preference by age cohort

	Women ages ≥ 30		Women ages < 30	
	Odds ratio	(SE)	Odds ratio	(SE)
Faridpur (base = Comilla)	0.722*	(0.172)	0.643**	(0.201)
Tangail	0.664**	(0.166)	0.748	(0.190)
Chapainawabganj	0.299***	(0.175)	0.643**	(0.204)
Maulabhibazar	0.201***	(0.170)	0.365***	(0.199)
Bagerhat	0.575***	(0.162)	0.698*	(0.191)
Kurigram	0.137***	(0.181)	0.335***	(0.210)
Narayanganj	0.414***	(0.173)	0.524***	(0.208)
Age (years)	0.990	(0.023)	1.013	(0.150)
Age square ('00)	0.997	(0.022)	0.927	(0.335)
Never married (base = married)	1.437	(0.510)	0.778	(0.163)
Widow	1.323**	(0.135)	0.868	(0.835)
Divorced/separated	0.888	(0.246)	1.356	(0.399)
Number of children of respondent	1.029	(0.024)	1.121	(0.071)
Respondent is household head	0.891	(0.139)	1.484	(0.286)
Formal paid work	0.903	(0.265)	0.892	(0.260)
Informal paid work (outside)	0.885	(0.197)	0.785	(0.280)
Informal self-employment (outside)	0.939	(0.211)	0.900	(0.312)
Informal paid work (inside)	0.933	(0.119)	0.935	(0.124)
Subsistence production	0.892	(0.138)	0.874	(0.147)
NGO member	1.083	(0.088)	1.220*	(0.111)
Wealth score	0.786***	(0.072)	0.849**	(0.079)
Household size	1.001	(0.022)	1.048**	(0.022)
Primary education (base = none)	0.803**	(0.109)	0.846	(0.145)
Secondary education	0.786	(0.162)	0.710**	(0.158)
Secondary education and above	0.685	(0.302)	0.624**	(0.234)
Watch TV regularly	0.974	(0.111)	0.968	(0.110)
Muslim	0.696**	(0.151)	0.541***	(0.184)
Wear hijab	1.112	(0.098)	1.469***	(0.114)
Work valued by family	0.793***	(0.084)	0.742***	(0.101)
Head has primary education	0.990	(0.110)	0.860	(0.121)
Head has secondary education	1.015	(0.137)	0.740**	(0.145)
Head has secondary education and above	1.105	(0.179)	0.786	(0.186)
Head is day laborer (base = farming)	1.083	(0.118)	0.971	(0.138)
Head is business/skilled/salaried employee	1.040	(0.109)	1.043	(0.128)
Head is unemployed	1.094	(0.140)	1.153	(0.191)
Constant	3.898**	(0.620)	2.106	(1.682)
Observations	3074		2124	
Correctly predicted	66.27%		64.83%	
Pseudo R-square	0.0849		0.06	
Log likelihood	−1906.81		−1344.24	
Wald Chi-square	299.64	(35)	159.51	(35)

Note: ***, **, * denote statistical significance at the 1, 5, and 10 percent levels, respectively.

GENDER AND ECONOMICS IN MUSLIM COMMUNITIES

important factor in shaping attitudes. We find that women with primary education are significantly less likely to express son preference than those with no education. The effect of higher levels of education is also negative, but not statistically significant, perhaps because only 14 percent of the older cohort had attained higher education.

The Hindu women in our sample are significantly more likely than Muslim women to express son preference. While the more conservative Muslims, those who adhered more closely to purdah norms, were more likely to express son preference than those who did not, the difference was not statistically significant. Neither the education nor the occupation of the household head had any significant impact on the attitudes expressed by the women in our survey.

Turning to the younger cohort of women, we find that "patriarchal risk" is less of a factor, perhaps because so few had experienced widowhood or divorce. Household size is associated among the younger age group with increased likelihood of son preference. Since we have controlled for women's fertility behavior, it is likely that these are extended family households that – particularly among the younger generation of women – are likely to be more conservative than the rest.

Once again, women's economic activity has very little direct influence on whether they expressed son preference, but those whose work is valued by their families are less likely to do so. Once again, household wealth is associated with significantly less likelihood of expressing son preference. As younger women are more likely than older women to be members of NGOs, the significance of the NGO variable is not surprising. But given that NGOs generally subscribe to a discourse of gender equality, what is unexpected – and difficult to explain – is the fact that women who are members of NGOs are much more likely to express son preference than those who are not.

The rapid spread of primary education in Bangladesh means that it no longer serves to differentiate attitudes among the younger cohort of women, but secondary and higher education are now both significantly associated with the likelihood of expressing indifference to the sex of the child. Interestingly, secondary level of education among household heads, generally women's husbands, is also associated with the likelihood that women will express indifference to the sex of the child.

The impact of religion among younger age groups is worth comment. As with the older cohort, Muslim women continue to be significantly less likely to express son preference than Hindu women. However, Muslim women who adhere to purdah norms are now significantly more likely to express son preference than those who do not. Given that similar percentages of women adhere to these norms in both age groups (around 50 percent), this suggests that new forms of religious conservatism noted among some of the younger generation (Santi Rozario 2006) may be reinforcing son preference – or slowing down its decline.

GENDER AND ECONOMICS IN MUSLIM COMMUNITIES

To sum up, the results of our analysis suggest that improvements in the survival chances of girls relative to boys documented in Bangladesh's national statistics is consistent with, and may be driven by, the weakening of son preference evident in our survey, more strongly in some districts than others but nevertheless widespread. Our results also point to some of the forces of change that may have been particularly influential in weakening son preference: rising levels of education among women and, among the younger cohort, the education of men, along with household prosperity. While women's access to paid work per se does not appear to influence their preferences, women in both age cohorts are less likely to express a preference for sons if they feel supported in their work by their families. The effect of "patriarchal risk," as captured by widowhood, is largely confined to older women. The lower levels of son preference expressed by Muslim compared to Hindu women echoes the Indian findings and suggests that religious factors may be influencing differentials in sex ratios via their influence on son preference.

Perhaps the most important finding from our analysis is the continued significance of location, after controlling for other possible influences on son preference. It suggests that unobserved community-level variables exercise a greater influence on attitudes than individual and household characteristics. It would thus appear that the weakening of son preference in Bangladesh is occurring at the level of community norms, rather than individual preferences, and that these norms are changing to a greater extent in some communities than others.

ANALYZING SON PREFERENCES IN BANGLADESH: QUALITATIVE INSIGHTS

We turn next to our qualitative interviews to explore what they can tell us about the apparent decline in son preference reported by our quantitative data.[6] We have noted that there were sizable percentages of women in our survey who continued to express son preference. Some, such as Minara Begum, a 50-year-old woman from Comilla, believed that son preference remained the norm – as it may well have done in her locality:

> Most people want sons even in this day. People in the past also preferred sons. [. . .] There have been no changes in people's preferences, they are still the same.

While a few of these women pointed to the role of sons in perpetuating the family line, for most, economic considerations predominated. They took it

GENDER AND ECONOMICS IN MUSLIM COMMUNITIES

for granted that sons would take up employment, would remain with their parents after marriage, and look after them in their old age:

> Most people prefer sons. This is because girls get married and go to someone else's house. Sons always remain by your side. When I get my son married, his wife and children will stay with me. If he lives in Comilla town or Dhaka, he will come every month. [...] My daughter can get my news from her husband's house, but she cannot come and stay and take care of me. (Nasreen Akhter, 38 years, Comilla)

The costs associated with daughters were the other side of the coin to the value given to sons. Not only were they considered lost to their parents once they got married, but the expenses incurred in marrying them off had risen dramatically with the emergence and escalation of dowry demands. It had become a constant source of anxiety for parents of daughters, threatening to impoverish them if the demands were too large:

> If you have a daughter, you have to educate her and then give a dowry when she gets married. One has to give one lakh, two lakhs, whatever one can afford. [...] Is this not difficult for parents? Take our situation... If we have to give fifty thousand for our daughter, is that not a problem? If this one was also a son, then I wouldn't have had to give dowry. How will I save so much money, where will I get it from? Is this not a cause for tension? (Rahela, 43 years, Faridpur)

It will be seen that explanations given by those respondents for preferring sons displayed many continuities with the past, although dowry has emerged as an additional factor in reinforcing son preference. We therefore turn to the other women in the qualitative sample to find out what their accounts can tell us about the changing attitudes documented by our survey. The majority of these women appeared to value both sons and daughters, and wanted at least one of each.

This has sometimes given rise to forms of behavior that would be considered extremely unusual in the contexts studied by John et al. (2008). For instance, Keya (39 years, Faridpur) had wanted her first born to be a son; her husband was indifferent. But she also wanted a daughter, and continued to try for one without success until she ended up with four sons. For most other parents, however, the overriding concern was to limit family size, irrespective of the sex of their children, in order to give their children a proper upbringing. This was the view expressed, for instance, by Fawzia, a 28-year-old woman from Faridpur:

> No, I don't want any more children. With the little income that my husband earns, if I cannot bring up my one daughter properly, then

153

GENDER AND ECONOMICS IN MUSLIM COMMUNITIES

there is no point in having more children. It's not simply a question of deciding to have more children, it is also a question of bringing them up.

For a number of women, the weakening of son preference reflected the perception that sons had become less responsible toward their parents. They pointed out that sons were moving out of the parental sphere of influence after marriage, often setting up their own households with their wives and children, and becoming more oriented to their nuclear family. As Mahfuza (38 years, Narayanganj) observed:

> People still want sons, but in the past they wanted them more... They used to think of boys as the torch of the lineage; that they continue the line of descent. They did not like girls so much because they leave once they get married. [...] The change has occurred because now once married, sons and daughters are the same. Sons do not do that much for their parents any more. They are busy with their households. They do not feel that their parents have become old and they need to feed and look after them.

She herself had three daughters, and had decided not to try for a son:

> We will get by on our own in our old age. Even if girls can't look after their parents, I don't see boys looking after them. I don't see them doing much for their parents. They are busy with their own households, just like girls.

The increasing disaffection with sons also reflected the view that boys were mixing with the "wrong" crowd, taking drugs, and escaping parental discipline – factors that were leading to problems within the community. In some cases, this decline in son preference had been accompanied by a greater appreciation of what daughters had to offer. This was certainly the view expressed by Farah (48 years, Faridpur):

> I hear from a lot of people now that they prefer daughters. Earlier, their faces would fall if they had a daughter... [...] My aunt had a daughter – she tried to smother her with her hand, but if Allah decides to make her breathe, who can stop Him? They were happy with sons, because they would be able to bring their earnings home. People don't feel like that anymore ... now, they think girls are better.

There was an emotional dimension to this revaluation, the belief that daughters would continue to show care and concern for their parents, even after they left the parental home. As Farah put it:

> If I had one child, I would want a daughter. Daughters have more affinity with their mothers... As soon as boys grow up, all they are interested in

154

GENDER AND ECONOMICS IN MUSLIM COMMUNITIES

is finding a beautiful girl and if they find one, then they take no notice of either their mother or their father. Nowadays, I think girls are better. They are pulled by the feelings for their mother... Daughters want to know whether you have eaten, how you are doing, what you are doing. Yes, they can keep a look out for you even after marriage, if they want to.

But there was also a material dimension, reflecting the perception that many more young women could now earn their own way. Rahela, a 43-year-old woman from Faridpur, hoped that by educating her daughter, she would enable her to get a reasonably paid job and sufficient bargaining power within marriage to persuade her husband to let her provide financial support to her parents:

If I can bring up my daughter properly, if she can get a job and earn five thousand taka, then she can give some to her parents. But if I can't help her along to that level, then how will she give anything? If she can stand on her own feet, if she can work independently, then she can tell her husband, "Look, my parents have given me an education, they have spent money to educate me and now they are suffering so much. I want to give them something now."

One other finding from our qualitative research worth noting was that, despite frequent references to abortion as a family-limitation measure, the practice of sex-selective abortion appeared extremely rare. Women reported having had ultrasound scanning to establish the health of the fetus and late in the pregnancy, making voluntary termination difficult. Only one woman reported using ultrasound scanning for sex determination. Others had heard of the possibility (often from public-service announcements on Indian TV), but did not know of anyone who had taken advantage of it. There was also a widespread belief among our respondents, which was not verified by health experts that we consulted, that the government forbade doctors from using ultrasound for sex determination. If doctors are reluctant to use the technology for this purpose, then this difference in attitude on the part of Bangladeshi health providers to those in India needs explanation.

CONCLUSION: SPECULATING ON DIVERGING SEX RATIOS IN INDIA AND BANGLADESH

There is no immediately obvious explanation for the diverging trends in son preference and sex ratios reported in India and Bangladesh. Many of the factors put forward for the deterioration in CSRs in India also apply to Bangladesh, but do not appear to have had the same outcomes. Both countries have experienced declining fertility rates – a major factor contributing to the rise of female-selective abortions in the Indian context.

GENDER AND ECONOMICS IN MUSLIM COMMUNITIES

Many of the costs associated with daughters in India are also relevant in Bangladesh, particularly with the emergence and spread of dowry. While women's labor force participation rates have risen more steadily in Bangladesh than India, women in both countries are largely confined to self-employment and unpaid family labor. What we need to know, therefore, is what differentiates the two contexts sufficiently to explain the divergence in their attitudes and behavior. In what follows, we explore a number of possible explanations. These relate to differences in the timing and spread of ultrasound technology; in state–society relations and the ease of social change; and in religious and cultural norms, values, and practices.

First of all, it is possible that the divergence in sex ratios reflects differences in ease of access to the relevant technologies. Abortion was legalized in India in 1971, while technologies for prenatal sex determination were introduced in the mid 1970s. They gradually spread to rural areas, although the rate of expansion is believed to have escalated exponentially with liberalization in the early 1990s (Sabu M. George 2002). Ultrasound technology was introduced in government health hospitals somewhat later in Bangladesh, sometime in the early 1980s. In a context where abortion was not legal, it was initially used for general health purposes and later extended to screening pregnant women. The private sector has been importing the technology since 1985. By the early 1990s, the technology was available in district hospitals and clinics at the sub-district level. However, mobile services are still not common, and most people must go to district or sub-district headquarters for an ultrasound scan.

There are a number of reasons why this is not a very satisfactory explanation for the divergence in sex ratios. One is that Bangladesh embarked on liberalization much earlier than India, so it is difficult to understand why it did not report a more rapid expansion in the use of ultrasound technology for sex-selection purposes. The other is that, along with adverse SRBs, Indian data show continued evidence of postnatal gender discrimination, giving rise to excess levels of female mortality in the under-5 age group. By contrast, we noted that the evidence from Bangladesh suggests that postnatal discrimination against daughters has been declining. According to United Nations Population Fund estimates (Guilmoto 2012), the ratio of male to female mortality rates in the under-5 age group was 103 for Bangladesh and 88 for India. Divergences in sex ratios thus appear to reflect real divergences in sex preferences in the two countries.

Another possible explanation relates to differences in the role of the state and civil society in the two contexts. India is, of course, the world's largest democracy, with near-uninterrupted democratic rule since independence in 1947; while Bangladesh has spent a great deal of this period under military rule. While both countries have legal and policy provisions to address gender

GENDER AND ECONOMICS IN MUSLIM COMMUNITIES

inequality, it is hardly likely that the increased value given to daughters in Bangladesh relative to India reflects the higher quality of its governance or the greater progressiveness of its state. The difference may lie instead in the ease with which such policies and laws are translated into intended outcomes.

As Rehman Sobhan (2000) has noted, while class inequalities have widened in Bangladesh in the course of economic growth, they are not as closely bound up with the deep-rooted and durable inequalities based on the ascribed identities that characterize the semifeudal or caste-based social structures in India and Pakistan. Bangladesh society remains more fluid, with considerable scope for upward mobility. Its hierarchies are more exposed to challenges from below because their legitimacy is not as rooted in the deep structures of society. Progressive discourses about women's rights and gender equality may be easier to disseminate in the more socially homogenous context of Bangladesh than within the more caste-stratified context of India, or the semifeudal and ethnically divided context of Pakistan.

It is this fluidity in social relations and the ease with which new norms, values, and ideas travel across society that may distinguish Bangladesh from the contexts featured in the Indian component of the IDRC study. Indirect evidence for this hypothesis relates to the remarkable progress that Bangladesh has made on a number of human development and gender equality indicators, out-achieving both India and Pakistan, despite its far lower levels of per capita Gross National Product (Mahmud, Ahmed, and Mahajan 2008; see also *Economist* 2012). These improvements have relied not only on purposive policy interventions on the part of government and NGOs, but also on behavioral responses on the part of ordinary people. Bangladesh was ranked 112 out of 186 countries according to the UN's Gender Inequality Index for 2013, while India was ranked 132, and Pakistan was ranked 123 (UNDP 2013). Bangladesh was ranked 69 out of 135 countries according to the Global Gender Gap Index 2011, compared to 113 for India and 133 for Pakistan. Progress on gender equality in Bangladesh has thus been part of a larger story of progress on human development.

The NGO sector in Bangladesh has played an important role in this process of change. NGOs are present in more than 70 percent of its villages. Not only are they important providers of social and financial services, but they also act as important conduits for new norms and values at grassroots level, particularly as a substantial percentage of them are funded by Western donors and subscribe to discourses of gender equality. While NGO membership appears in this study to be associated with an unexpected reinforcement of son preference, analysis of the same survey data in a study of women's empowerment found that NGO membership had a positive impact on a number of indicators of women's empowerment, both behavioral and cognitive (Naila Kabeer, Simeen Mahmud, and Sakiba

Tasneem 2011). This suggests that NGOs may be facilitating changes in attitudes and practices within the wider society – including, of course, access to paid work and greater mobility in the public domain.

The third possible explanation relates to differences in religious norms and values. Religion has certainly begun to emerge as an explanation within the Indian literature because of evidence of religious differentials in son preference, CSRs, SRBs, and likelihood of sex-selective abortion (P.N. Mari Bhat and A.J. Francis Zavier 2003, 2007; Vani Borooah, Quy-Toan Do, Sriya Iyer, and Shareen Joshi 2009; Sonia Bhalotra and Tom Cochrane 2010). One version of the explanation relies on the "pure religion" effect (Borooah et al.: 3), focusing on religious differences in the value given to women in injunctions regarding abortion.

However, it is difficult to believe that differences in religious beliefs and values alone constitute an adequate explanation for variations in sex ratios, given the considerable diversity in the sex ratios reported by Hindus in India by state, caste, and class, the considerable state-level variation in CSRs noted among Muslims in India, and the geographical diversity among Muslims within our Bangladesh study. A more relevant explanation may relate to the way in which religion intersects with the organization of social life within different ethnic or cultural communities in different economic contexts. The rules and norms governing marriage and kinship are of particular relevance here because of their importance for how different communities seek to preserve, reproduce, or transform their identity and place within the larger society. Such an explanation would draw attention to religion as one, perhaps relatively enduring, aspect of social organization.

Particularly striking in the Indian literature on this topic is the complexity of the rules, norms, and values that govern its caste-class differentiated marriage market (John et al. 2008: 72; Sharada Srinivasan 2012). While the most restrictive norms and practices are associated with the dominant Brahmin castes, they have gradually spread to other sections of the population. M. Narasimhachar Srinivas (1962) used the term "Sanskritization" to describe the process by which lower-caste groups adopt the values and practices of higher, often more affluent, caste groups to signal their upward mobility. As Basu (1999) points out, while role models in most societies are shaped by dominant groups, in the Indian context, role models have been shaped by caste groups who are most conservative with regard to women: "Sanskritization results in harshness towards women" (Srinivas 1962: 61).

Thus while the marriage market may be highly differentiated by class status in both India and Bangladesh, caste and the way it defines the acceptable boundaries of kinship adds an additional layer of complexity in the Indian context. Bangladeshis share many of the marriage practices that prevail in northern Indian states, including village exogamy, patrilocal residence, and, in recent decades, dowry; but these practices generally express "preference"

GENDER AND ECONOMICS IN MUSLIM COMMUNITIES

rather than "prescription." There is no evidence of strict religious norms either dictating or prohibiting these practices. Indeed, cross-kin marriage may be more prevalent in Bangladesh than widely believed, and certainly appears to have been so in the recent past (Bleie 1990). Women may marry "up" or "down" as well as into families of similar status. Caste endogamy is largely irrelevant among its Muslim population.[7] Provision for maintenance in case of divorce is built into Muslim marriages and, provided they are young enough, both widows and divorced women often remarry. Such an "exit" clause does not feature among many Hindu communities, although clearly divorce is much easier than it used to be. In short, while parents in both countries may face particular challenges when it comes to ensuring "good" marriages for their daughters, parents in the Indian context must deal with the additional considerations of caste and kinship over and above concerns with occupation and social status that are likely to preoccupy parents in Bangladesh.

What we are suggesting, therefore, is that while individual and household characteristics contribute to some of the variations in attitudes to sons and daughters found in the South Asia region, the main explanation must be sought at the level of community norms and practices, with religion appearing as an important aspect of community identity. It is only by appreciating the different ways in which religious values and cultural norms mediate the larger forces of socioeconomic change in the South Asian context that we can make sense of the finding that, despite the growing belief in both contexts that sons are less likely to fulfill their filial duties than they used to, along with some evidence that daughters are valued for providing emotional support to parents, daughter aversion appears to have deepened and spread in India while son preference appears to have weakened in Bangladesh.

To conclude, religious beliefs and values can play a part in explaining variations in attitudes and behavior, but religions operate in specific social and cultural contexts that serve to mediate both their interpretation and impact. Thus, despite sharing Islam as the majority religion, sex ratios at birth are much higher in Pakistan than in Bangladesh – and, indeed, in the "abnormal" range, according to some estimates (Christophe Z. Guilmoto 2009). Of the four countries in Asia that have recently reported a sharp deterioration in SRBs, Azerbaijan is a majority Muslim country, Georgia and Armenia are largely Christian, and Vietnam is officially Buddhist. We need a far more complex explanation for changing trends in sex ratios than a focus on religious norms and values alone can provide.

ACKNOWLEDGMENTS

We are grateful to the International Development Research Centre (IDRC) for providing the funding for this research project, and to Navsharan Singh for her support during the process. We also thank Deepita Chatterjee, Mary John, Ashwini Deshpande, Rajni Palriwala, and Ratna Sudarshan for comments on an earlier draft of the paper, as well as the anonymous reviewers for *Feminist Economics*.

GENDER AND ECONOMICS IN MUSLIM COMMUNITIES

NOTES

[1] UNDP (2010) suggests SRBs of 108.5 for India, 105.8 for Pakistan, and 103.6 for Bangladesh.

[2] For a variety of reasons, including the impact of sex-specific migration patterns, the literature on sex ratios often focuses on younger age groups to ascertain the presence of gender discrimination. CSRs can vary from 0 to 4, 5, or 6 years.

[3] A 20 percent difference is considered normal.

[4] The survey was carried out as part of a larger program of research on Pathways of Women's Empowerment, a five-year research program (2006–11) funded by the Department for International Development (DFID).

[5] Most frequently, microfinance NGOs.

[6] All personal information that would allow the identification of any persons described in this contribution has been removed.

[7] By contrast, the consequences of intercaste marriage can be severe, particularly among the upper castes: a man who marries outside his caste may face sanctions, but a woman who does so "is considered dead" (Srinivas 1962: 92).

REFERENCES

Adnan, Shapan. 1998. "Fertility Decline under Absolute Poverty: Paradoxical Aspects of Demographic Change in Bangladesh." *Economic and Political Weekly* 33(22): 1337–49.

Agnihotri, Satish B. 2000. *Sex Ratio Patterns in the Indian Population: A Fresh Exploration.* New Delhi: SAGE.

Ahmed, Nilufer. 1981. "Family Size and Sex Preferences Among Women in Rural Bangladesh." *Studies in Family Planning* 12(3): 100–9.

Alam, Nurul, Jeroen Van Ginneken, and Alinda Bosch. 2007. "Decreases in Male and Female Mortality and Missing Women in Bangladesh." In *Watering the Neighbour's Garden: The Growing Demographic Female Deficit in Asia*, edited by Isabelle Attane and Christophe Guilmoto, 161–82. Paris: CICRED.

Bairagi, Radheshyam. 2001. "Effects of Sex Preference on Contraceptive Use, Abortion and Fertility in Matlab, Bangladesh." *International Family Planning Perspectives* 27(3): 137–43.

Basu, Alaka M. 1999. "Fertility Decline and Increasing Gender Imbalance in India, including a Possible South Indian Turnaround." *Development and Change* 30(2): 237–63.

Bhalotra, Sonia and Tom Cochrane. 2010. "Where Have All the Young Girls Gone? Identification of Sex Selection in India." IZA Discussion Paper 5381, Institute of Labor Studies.

Bhat, P.N. Mari and A.J. Francis Zavier. 2003. "Fertility Decline and Gender Bias in Northern India." *Demography* 40(4): 637–57.

———. 2007. "Factors Influencing the Use of Prenatal Diagnostic Techniques and Sex Ratio at Birth in India." In *Watering the Neighbour's Garden: The Growing Demographic Female Deficit in Asia*, edited by Isabelle Attane and Christophe Guilmoto, 131–60. Paris: CICRED.

Bleie, Tone. 1990. "Dowry and Bridewealth Presentations in Rural Bangladesh: Commodities, Gifts and Hybrid Forms?" DERAP Working Paper 10, Chr. Michelsen Institute.

Bloom, David E., David Canning, and Larry Rosenberg. 2011. "Demographic Change and Economic Growth in South Asia." Program on the Global Demography of Aging, Working Paper Series 67, Harvard School of Public Health, Harvard University.

GENDER AND ECONOMICS IN MUSLIM COMMUNITIES

Borooah, Vani and Sriya Iyer. 2004. "Religion and Fertility in India: The Role of Son Preference and Daughter Aversion." Cambridge Working Papers in Economics 436, University of Cambridge.

Borooah, Vani, Quy-Toan Do, Sriya Iyer, and Shareen Joshi. 2009. "Missing Women and India's Religious Demography." Policy Research Working Paper 5096, Development Research Group, Poverty and Inequality Team, World Bank.

Cain, Mead, Syeda Rokeya Khanam, and Shamsun Nahar. 1979. "Class, Patriarchy, and Women's Work in Bangladesh." *Population and Development Review* 5(3): 405–38.

Caldwell, John C. 1982. *Theory of Fertility Decline.* London: Academic Press.

Chakravarti, Uma. 2003. *Gendering Caste: Through a Feminist Lens* Calcutta: Stree.

Chen, Lincoln C. 1982. "Where Have the Women Gone? Insights from Bangladesh on Low Sex Ratio of India's Population." *Economic and Political Weekly* 17(10): 364–72.

Das Gupta, Monica and P.N. Mari Bhat. 1997. "Fertility Decline and Increased Manifestation of Sex Bias in India." *Population Studies* 51(3): 307–15.

Dyson, Tim and Mick Moore. 1983. "On Kinship Structure, Female Autonomy and Demographic Behaviour in India." *Population and Development Review* 9(1): 35–60.

Economist. 2012. "Bangladesh and Development: The Path through the Fields." November 23. http://www.economist.com/news/briefing/21565617-bangladesh-has-dysfunctional-politics-and-stunted-private-sector-yet-it-has-been-surprisingly.

George, Sabu M. 2002. "Sex Selection/Determination in India: Contemporary Developments." *Reproductive Health Matters* 10(19): 190–2.

Gipson, Jessica D. and Michelle J. Hindin. 2008. "'Having Another Child Would Be a Life or Death Situation for Her': Understanding Pregnancy Termination Among Couples in Rural Bangladesh." *American Journal of Public Health* 98(10): 1827–32.

Government of Bangladesh. 1978. *Report on Bangladesh Fertility Survey 1975–76.* Ministry of Health and Population Control, Population Control and Family Planning Division, Dhaka.

Government of India. 2006. *Social, Economic and Educational Status of the Muslim Community in India.* Report to the Prime Minister's High Level Committee, New Delhi.

Guilmoto, Christophe Z. 2009. "The Sex Ratio Transition in Asia." *Population and Development Review* 35(3): 519–49.

———. 2012. *Sex Imbalances at Birth: Current Trends, Consequences and Policy Implications.* Bangkok: UNFPA Asia and Pacific Regional Office.

Index Mundi. 2013. http://www.indexmundi.com.

John, Mary E. 2011. "Census 2011: Governing Populations and the Girl Child." *Economic and Political Weekly* 46(16): 10–2.

John, Mary E., Ravinder Kaur, Rajni Palriwala, Sarawati Raju, and Alpana Sagar. 2008. *Planning Families, Planning Gender: The Adverse Child Sex Ratio in Selected Districts of Madhya Pradesh, Rajasthan, Himachal Pradesh, Haryana, and Punjab.* New Delhi: Action Aid/IDRC.

Kabeer, Naila. 1985. "Do Women Gain from High Fertility?" In *Women, Work and Ideology in the Third World.* edited by Haleh Afshar, 83–96. London: Tavistock Press.

Kabeer, Naila, Simeen Mahmud, and Sakiba Tasneem. 2011. *Does Paid Work Provide a Pathway to Women's Empowerment? Empirical Findings from Bangladesh.* IDS Working Paper 375, Institute of Development Studies, Brighton.

Kandiyoti, Deniz. 1988. "Bargaining with Patriarchy." *Gender and Society* 2(3): 274–90.

Karve, Irawati K. 1968. *Kinship Organization in India.* Bombay: Asia Publishing House.

Kaur, Ravinder. 2007. "Declining Juvenile Sex Ratios: Economy, Society and Technology Explanations from Field Evidence." *Margin: The Journal of Applied Economic Research* 1(2): 231–45.

Klasen, Stephan and Claudia Wink. 2003. "Missing Women: Revisiting the Debate." *Feminist Economics* 9(2–3): 263–99.

GENDER AND ECONOMICS IN MUSLIM COMMUNITIES

Mahmud, Wahid, Sadiq Ahmed, and Sandeep Mahajan. 2008. "Economic Reforms, Growth, and Governance: The Political Economy Aspects of Bangladesh's Development Surprise." Working Paper 22, Commission on Growth and Development, World Bank.

Maloney, Clarence, K.M. Ashraful Aziz, and Profulla C. Sarker. 1981. *Beliefs and Fertility in Bangladesh*. Dhaka: ICDDR, Bangladesh.

Mazumdar, Indrani and N. Neetha. 2011. "Gender Dimensions: Employment Trends in India, 1993–94 to 2009–10." *Economic and Political Weekly* 46(43): 118–26.

Miller, Barbara D. 1981. *The Endangered Sex: Neglect of Female Children in Rural North India*. Ithaca, NY: Cornell University Press.

Mukherjee, Sucharita Sinha. 2013. "Women's Empowerment and Gender Bias in the Birth and Survival of Girls in Urban India." *Feminist Economics* 19(1): 1–28.

Niimi, Yoko. 2009. *Gender Equality and Inclusive Growth in Developing Asia*. Economic Working Paper Series 186, Asian Development Bank, Manila.

Palriwala, Rajni. 1994. *Changing Kinship, Family, and Gender Relations in South Asia: Processes, Trends, and Issues*. Leiden: Women and Autonomy Centre, Leiden University.

Rozario, Santi. 2006. "The New Burqa in Bangladesh: Empowerment or Violation of Women's Rights?" *Women's Studies International Forum* 29(4): 368–80.

Sen, Amartya. 1992. "Missing Women." *British Medical Journal* 304: 586–7.

Sobhan, Rehman. 2000. "The State of Governance in Bangladesh." In *Changes and Challenges: A Review of Bangladesh's Development, 2000*, edited by the Centre for Policy Dialogue, 77–114. Dhaka: Centre for Policy Dialogue.

Srinivas, M. Narasimhachar. 1962. *Caste in Modern India: And Other Essays*. Bombay: Asia Publishing House.

Srinivasan, Sharada. 2012. *Daughter Deficit: Sex Selection in Tamil Nadu*. New Delhi: Women Unlimited.

Trapp, Erin M., Jill Williams, Jane Menken, and Shannon Fisher. 2004. "Disappearing Sex-Bias in Child Health in Bangladesh." Population Aging Centre, Working Paper PAC 2004-0003, Institute of Behavioral Science, University of Colorado at Boulder.

United Nations Children's Fund (UNICEF). 2011. *A Perspective on Gender Equality in Bangladesh*. Dhaka: UNICEF.

United Nations Development Programme (UNDP). 2010. *The Real Wealth of Nations: Pathways to Human Development*. Human Development Report 2010. New York: UNDP.

———. 2013. *The Rise of the South: Human Progress in a Diverse World*. Human Development Report 2013. New York: UNDP.

World Bank. 2008. *Whispers to Voices: Gender and Social Transformation in Bangladesh*. Dhaka: World Bank.

FUNDING PAIN: BEDOUIN WOMEN AND POLITICAL ECONOMY IN THE NAQAB/NEGEV

Nadera Shalhoub-Kevorkian, Antonina Griecci Woodsum, Himmat Zu'bi, and Rachel Busbridge

ABSTRACT

This contribution focuses on the experiences and voices of Palestinian Bedouin women surviving and challenging Israeli colonial policies while residing in their own land and, in particular, the Bedouin women of the Naqab living in unrecognized villages. Through interviews and focus groups, this study learns from and engages with the voices of Palestinian Bedouin women because colonized women's criticisms of the political economic apparatus are seldom invoked to influence policy. Exploring these women's voices offers an opportunity to examine the political economy of their unrecognized, officially nonexistent villages and homes and to rectify the gap in bottom-up knowledge of political economy by investigating the institutional structures that define and circumscribe women's lives. Privileging Bedouin women's production of knowledge carries the analytical value of studying political economy based on women's own experiences and struggles against hegemony.

INTRODUCTION

Colonized women's perceptions and criticisms of the political economic apparatus are seldom invoked to influence policy. Learning from and engaging with the voices of Palestinian Bedouin women from the Naqab/Negev region in southern Israel (hereafter the Naqab), this study seeks to remedy this absence of bottom-up knowledge of political economy by investigating the institutional structures that define and circumscribe the women's lives. Privileging Bedouin women's production of knowledge carries the analytical value of studying political economy through women's

GENDER AND ECONOMICS IN MUSLIM COMMUNITIES

own experiences to centralize their struggle for a more contextualized practice and politics.

Women's participation in the contemporary political economy is complex, especially for those designated as cultural/religious/ethnic/racial Others. More often than not, the role of Othered women in the political economy is embedded in a wider discourse of culturalization, where, supposedly, their culture is the hindrance to their full participation and is directly or indirectly responsible for the socioeconomic disadvantages they face (Gamze Çavdar and Yavuz Yaşar 2014). In Jennifer C. Olmsted's (2002) response to Shoshana Grossbard-Shechtman's and Shoshana Neuman's article (1998) on the impact of religion on the value of married women's time, Olmsted points to ways in which analyses of Arab women, in particular, promote and endorse a fundamental culturalization of their problems and often lapse into Orientalist images of cultural and patriarchal oppression. Olmsted's call to thoughtfully disentangle religious, political, cultural, social, historical, and economic factors is of particular importance when engaging with women's words and descriptions of their socioeconomic disadvantages.

This study focuses, generally, on the experiences and voices of Palestinian Bedouin women surviving, resisting, and challenging Israeli colonial policies while residing in their own land and, in particular, the Bedouin women of the Naqab living in what the Israeli state has officially defined as "unrecognized" villages. As many scholars have argued, Bedouin women in the Naqab are frequently portrayed as typical Third World women whose lives are culturally restrained and bound by patriarchy, whose oppression is ahistorical and rooted in their culture and is therefore beyond the scope of contemporary political economy (Tovi Fenster 2002; Henriette Dahan-Kalev, Niza Yanay, and Niza Berkovitch 2005; Ismael Abu-Saad 2008; Çavdar and Yaşar 2014). Exploring these women's voices offers an opportunity to examine the political economy of their unrecognized, officially nonexistent villages and homes (Haya Noach 2009). Some 35 percent (or 70,000) of the 200,000 Naqab Bedouin population lives in approximately thirty-five or forty unrecognized villages that, due to their status, are accorded no state services and exist under the constant threat of demolition (Farah Mihlar 2011: 3). Even the remaining population living in recognized villages or government-planned townships may endure an unrecognized status of sorts, with Bedouin society, culture, and politics typically misrepresented and unacknowledged in the wider Israeli setting. Not only do dominant Israeli/Zionist narratives create an image of the Bedouin as an ahistorical, apolitical, and nomadic people (Ronen Shamir 1996; Oren Yiftachel 2008), but the designation of state land as Jewish has also meant that Palestinian Bedouin people have no rights to the land on religious grounds – despite their formal status as Israeli citizens (Haneen Zoabi 2009). As Abu-Saad suggests, "After more than half a century as citizens of Israel, the [Bedouin] remain illegal invaders, and a threat to the vision of Zionism," and are as

165

GENDER AND ECONOMICS IN MUSLIM COMMUNITIES

such "reduced to the illegitimate and dehumanized status of 'the non-Jewish threat' " in the Naqab (2008: 1745). This categorization renders invisible the Bedouin's legitimate claims and rights to the land as an indigenous people (Shamir 1996; Amal Jamal 2007), while also justifying the Israeli settler colonial policies and practices that maintain the Bedouin's unrecognized status and define the uncertainty of daily life in the Naqab (Yiftachel 2008).

As both indigenous and non-Jewish, the Bedouin in the Naqab occupy a space of "unrecognizability" sustained by a state structure unwilling to acknowledge their historic, social, economic, and cultural relationship to the land ([Sandy] Alexander Kedar 2004; Noach 2009). The women's voices central to this study suggest that such unrecognizability is supplemented by an international perception of Bedouin society as one in need of modernization and Western-style "development" – a positioning that is also highly racialized and gendered. This Orientalist representation of Bedouin society is replicated and repeated in numerous Western and Zionist discourses and forums (Nadera Shalhoub-Kevorkian 2012). Bedouin women's voices suggest that the notion of the "average third world woman's oppression" these Orientalist representations indicate is embedded in and guides hegemonic discourses of development in the Naqab, as well as the funding agendas of donors (Chandra Talpade Mohanty 1988). According to some Bedouin women, donor funding agendas are regularly experienced as endeavors that aim to "save" the Bedouin from their cultural "backwardness" (Abu-Saad 2008), and, in the context of women, are often akin to the colonial notion of "saving the brown woman from the brown man" (Lila Abu-Lughod 2002: 784). In this context, unrecognizability is a cycle maintained by the Israeli state as well as by the funding agendas of many donors, through both culturalized and mythologized conceptions of Bedouin disadvantage.

This study argues that a political economy of "funding pain" – an economy of international donors offering funding through the lens of Arab/Muslim/Bedouin women's individualized and violent oppression – emerges from this paradigm, where the overall context of undermining development (or "de-development") facing Bedouin people in the Naqab is bound to and propelled by two colonial logics (Sara Roy 1999). One such logic is that of the colonial state toward an indigenous Palestinian minority, which creates and maintains poverty through colonial practices of denying land and resources and by limiting avenues of integration into the state's dominant economy. The other logic is that of donors who interpret the oppression of Bedouin women through colonial mythologies of culture, thereby individualizing the collective struggle of the unrecognized communities and focusing on (mis)perceptions and (mis)interpretations of gender dynamics and individual empowerment (of women). Together, these logics echo a colonial understanding and ordering of the world into racial hierarchies which become entrenched in political economy. Furthermore, and most significantly in the context of donors who proclaim to improve the

166

GENDER AND ECONOMICS IN MUSLIM COMMUNITIES

lives of the Bedouin, both logics fail to acknowledge Bedouin struggles in the Naqab as battles for collective indigenous rights, and in doing so work to stifle anti-colonial rhetoric and practice.

METHODOLOGY

The voices of the Bedouin women that drive this study were gathered between 2009 and 2011 through extensive interviews, focus groups, and participatory observations with women living in unrecognized villages in the Naqab.[1] The interviews and focus groups centered on Bedouin women's experiences of human rights activism. The individual interviews with twenty Bedouin women took place in the women's own houses, following their approval and consent. Each interview lasted over two hours to allow women to share their stories of life in the Naqab and to reflect on the effect of donor policies, politics, and modes of intervention on their lives. The interviewed women ranged from 19 to 60 years old: nine were 30–49 years old, three were over 50 years old, and the remaining eight women were between 19 and 30 years old. Analyses of the individual interviews were shared, examined, and validated through two workshops. The first workshop comprised a small group that met in May 2011 to study the insights gained from the women interviewed. The second workshop was a public forum in June 2012 aimed at sharing the study results more widely with women activists and Bedouin women and men.

The first workshop was organized by Dr. Shalhoub-Kevorkian and coordinated with Ma'an – The Coalition of Bedouin Women in May of 2011. The workshop took place at Mada al-Carmel – Arab Center for Applied Social Research in Haifa, a location chosen by the nine women in attendance from Ma'an. Dr. Shalhoub-Kevorkian and two research assistants also participated in the workshop. The three-hour meeting was opened with an explanation of the purpose of the study, which was to juxtapose ordinary women's critiques of the politics of funding with the experiences of non-governmental organizations (NGOs) working in the Naqab. The participants were asked to speak on three major issues: (1) their experience with funding organizations; (2) the influence of funding on women's lives in the Naqab; and (3) to tell a story that might be an example of their experience. After the introduction, the group was separated into three smaller groups, each one nominating a moderator and a representative to share the discussion with the other two groups. After discussions in the small groups, the participants met again, and representatives shared what had been discussed in their small groups, which was followed by a dialogue on the raised topics. Following the workshop, the lead researcher and the research assistants met to reflect on the meeting. This process was meant to enhance understanding of the insights shared by the women, and the

GENDER AND ECONOMICS IN MUSLIM COMMUNITIES

research assistants who joined the workshop helped the researchers confirm and endorse the findings gathered from the individual interviews.

The second workshop was organized in the Naqab area, and took place at Ma'an – The Coalition of Bedouin Women. The invitation was open to the public, and aimed at sharing the results of the study, gathering the locals' reactions and criticism, and verifying the study's results. The twenty-eight participants of the workshop included social and political activists from various feminist, women's, and other local and national NGOs. The three-hour meeting took place in June 2012.

UNRECOGNIZED CITIZENS IN THE NAQAB

The Bedouin occupy a unique space in the Israeli context. Despite their forced expulsion along with other Palestinians in 1948 and transfer *en masse* to their current location in the Naqab/Negev area, the Bedouin are nevertheless one of the few Arab groups to have a sizeable (albeit increasingly under threat) hold on the land (Sholmo Swirski and Yael Hasson 2006: 2). In spite of this, or perhaps because of it, the Bedouin are accorded a unique, yet inferior, citizenship status in Israel and perceived as almost entirely superfluous to the Israeli economy and society (Yiftachel 2008).

In terms of socioeconomic status, Palestinian Bedouin people in the Naqab are among the worst-off groups in a society where Jewish–Arab discrepancies are already significant (Shlomo Swirski 2007; Suleiman Abu Bader and Daniel Gottlieb 2009; Association for Civil Rights in Israel [ACRI] 2011) and where there are acknowledged poverty gaps between the Jewish majority and Palestinian minority. According to the Israeli National Insurance Institute, 49.4 percent of Arab families in Israel are considered poor, compared to 19.9 percent of all families (Miri Endeweld, Alex Fruman, Netanela Barkali, and Daniel Gottlieb 2008: 16, 22). This is a statistically significant overrepresentation of Arabs among the poor when one considers that Arab citizens account for approximately 20 percent of the overall population. As the National Insurance Institute acknowledges, "there is a large, almost threefold gap between Arab families' share of the entire population and their share of the poor population" (Endeweld et al. 2008: 80). Palestinians consistently rank below Jewish citizens across a wide range of socioeconomic indicators, leading the Organisation for Economic Co-operation and Development (OECD) to conclude that "in terms of economic well-being, the Arab Israeli population is at a net disadvantage compared to the Jewish population" (Jack Habib, Judith King, Assaf Ben Shoham, Abraham Wolde-Tsadick, and Karen Lasky 2010: 34).

The level of disadvantages experienced by Palestinian citizens of Israel is widely recognized to be a result of official and unofficial discrimination. As Katie Hesketh, working with Adalah – The Legal Center for Arab Minority

GENDER AND ECONOMICS IN MUSLIM COMMUNITIES

Rights in Israel, has documented, Arabs encounter discrimination in employment opportunities, pay, and working conditions due to inadequate implementation of the law as well as structural barriers (2011). This discrimination is compounded over multiple levels, with Arab women in particular faring worse than Arab men. For instance, the number of Arab women aged 15 years and older in the civilian workforce is 21.1 percent, compared to 57 percent of Jewish women. These are among the lowest figures in the world concerning women's workforce participation and are well below other OECD countries where 58 percent of women participate in paid work (OECD 2010: 8).

While the economic situation of the Palestinian Bedouin in unrecognized villages has not been fully or adequately documented by the state (Abu Bader and Gottlieb 2009; Adalah 2010), the statistics available attest to conditions of extreme discrimination. Statistical reports of poverty are far higher among the Bedouin population, where some 67.2 percent of families are considered poor (OECD 2008: 31) – figures that are likely higher in reality when one considers that the unrecognized villages are not included in formal statistics. Even so, Palestinian Bedouin people are reported among the lowest in terms of socioeconomic indicators; indeed, out of the eight local councils and municipalities ranked within "cluster one" (the poorest of the Israeli 10-point scale), seven are Bedouin villages in the Naqab (Ahmad Sheikh Muhammad and Mohammad Khatib 2011). These Bedouin villages are afforded no official status and referred to as "illegal clusters" unrecognized by the state, and although levels of poverty and social deprivation are significantly higher in these areas, accurate representations of the poverty and deprivation are not included in state statistical calculations and publications (Abu Bader and Gottlieb 2009; Hesketh 2011). Lack of official statistics documenting socioeconomic conditions in the unrecognized villages is a significant matter of concern for many, including the women in our study. As we hear from the various narratives shared in the individual and focus group meetings and as Samia, a Bedouin woman in her late twenties from an unrecognized village, notes, "[the] statistics don't reflect my situation as a woman ... And that means I will never get any support." Furthermore, when statistics do exist, they are often inaccurate or partial. As Samia suggests: "In my tribe, the statistics show that we have eighty kids. But actually we have over 180 kids. So if they have eighty kids formally registered instead of 180, they're not opening health centers, schools or nurseries, and definitely not transportation."

While direct state policy measures to reduce poverty disproportionately target Jewish Israelis over Arabs (with the result of Arab poverty declining by just 13.5 percent in 2008 due to such measures, compared to 46.2 percent for Jewish citizens [Endeweld et al. 2008: 15]), poverty is actually exacerbated by these policy measures in the unrecognized villages of the Naqab. Officially, these villages do not exist. They are excluded from state planning and government maps; they have no local representative councils or are inadequately represented as part of other local governing bodies; and they receive little to no basic services, including health and educational facilities, telephone lines, or even electricity and running water (Adalah 2010: 21). The particular consequences of this state-driven system of unrecognizability on Bedouin women in the Naqab has been of concern for some time, and in 2005 the United Nations Committee on the Elimination of Discrimination Against Women noted:

> Bedouin women living in the Negev desert remain in a vulnerable and marginalized situation, especially in regard to education, employment and health. The committee is especially concerned about the situation of Bedouin women who live in unrecognized villages with poor housing conditions and limited or no access to water, electricity and sanitation. (UN CEDAW 2005: 7)

The situation in the unrecognized villages is rendered worse by a persistent state policy of house demolition. While official figures are hard to come by, between 2000 and 2007 at least 3,084 Palestinian homes were estimated to have been destroyed in Israel, of which a vast majority were in the Naqab (Adalah 2010: 20). While housing demolitions are legally supported under the pretext of Bedouin violations of land and planning laws (Human Rights Watch 2008), it is apparent that the policy is one of dispossession: designed to get rid of the unrecognized villages as a means to force villagers into overcrowded and impoverished government-planned townships grouped in just 0.8 percent of the entire Naqab area (Adalah 2010: 21). Sari Hanafi terms this "spacio-cide," whereby the state's intention is to "appropriate land while ignoring the people on it" (2009: 106). Spacio-cide describes the destruction of Palestinian space, the transfer and relocation of Palestinians away from their land and the view of Jewish Israeli citizens, and the intensification of borders and boundaries between indigenous people and the colonizing society (Hanafi 2009: 106–7).

Through the state policy of house demolition, a number of unrecognized Bedouin villages have been wholly or partially demolished in recent years – including Al-Araqib, which, at the time of writing, has been demolished over forty times since July 2010. With the approval of the Prawer Plan in September 2011, which will forcibly displace some 40,000 Bedouin people to townships, the situation in the unrecognized villages will undoubtedly become worse despite the plan's supposedly "enlightened" intentions which arguably support a culturalized and Orientalized settler colonial agenda. Prime Minister Binyamin Netanyahu claims that the Prawer Plan will "allow for home construction according to the law and for the development of enterprises and employment [for the Bedouin community]. This will jump the population forward and provide it with economic independence"

GENDER AND ECONOMICS IN MUSLIM COMMUNITIES

(2011). The Prawer Plan thus operates under a guise of "modernizing" the Bedouin community by according them socioeconomic independence and a lawful status. Despite claims to the contrary, however, there is little question that state-sponsored housing demolition and the forced relocation of Bedouins are discriminatory policies enacted within a Zionist settler colonial framework: the "Judaization" of the Naqab (Abu-Saad 2008; Yiftachel 2008). Unlike Bedouin villages, Jewish inhabitants of the Naqab are both supported and promoted, with individual settlements generally occupied by a single Jewish family provided with hundreds and sometimes thousands of dunams of land for their exclusive use.[2] In 2005, there were approximately sixty such settlements, stretching over 81,000 dunams of land (Hana Hamdan 2005). Policies that support the allocation of significant amounts of land to one group in the Naqab while demolishing the homes and attempting to forcibly relocate another strongly testify (at the very least) to a lack of government commitment to ensure equal access to the land for the entire population of the Naqab.

THE POLITICAL ECONOMY OF UNRECOGNIZABILITY IN THE NAQAB

Since I was born, I knew that as Bedouin living in this area, we are not noticed at all, we are not counted, even when dead, we are not wanted, for they want to settle Jews in our land, and not Palestinians; we are not respected, for all they do is step on our dignity every time they mention us… Just look at the way my late father was treated by Israeli officials… they used to come, eat at our place, but talk to him from a distance; they are disgusted by us. This is how I was also treated when searching for a job… As if the land is not ours, the place is not ours, and even the right to live… the mere living, is not ours. (Nuha, feminist activist, 32 years old)

Nuha's voice and analysis is indicative of her profound sense of disempowerment and anger, which cuts to the core of her existence and raises questions about the possibilities of genuine social and economic development in the Naqab. For Nuha, the issue of development is almost spurious in the context of her unrecognized status; as she puts it simply, "so you don't have water and you don't have electricity, how do you expect us to transform economically?" It is possible to argue that the fundamental issue at stake is not one of expecting Bedouins to "transform economically" despite the daily challenges they face, but rather – as Nuha's words clearly suggest – of locking them into an overall and explicit situation of de-development and slow erasure. Sara Roy defines de-development as not only "distort[ing] the development process, but undermining it entirely… A de-developed economy is deprived of its capacity for production, rational structural transformation and meaningful reform, making it incapable even of distorted development" (1999: 65). Therefore, practices of de-development include:

> Dispossession of key economic resources, preventing formation of productive capacity; integration and externalization, whereby Palestinian economic growth is conditioned on employment opportunities in the Israeli market and on externally generated sources of income, away from indigenous agriculture and industry, local economy and infrastructure is left with no resources. (Roy 1999: 65)

While de-development is a concept that emerged from the Palestinian context of the Gaza Strip, it is apparent that the situation of the Naqab – and especially the unrecognized villages – is exceptionally well captured in de-development's purview.

For Bedouin women in the Naqab, disadvantage in the areas of paid employment, education, and health coalesce to produce a spiral effect of de-development, where each reinforces the other. In terms of paid employment, only a mere 16.8 percent of Arab women in the Naqab are part of the labor force, which is due in large part to the isolation of Bedouin villages (recognized and unrecognized) from larger cities, and hence there is limited access to paid labor opportunities and state-funded vocational trainings (Muhammad and Khatib 2011). There is an "almost total absence" of public transportation from and between Arab towns and villages, which, since the major public-transport system is majority owned by the government, is the responsibility of the state. Yet the lack of public transport services is not seriously acknowledged by the state as a structural barrier to paid employment, where "traditional values and cultural stigmas among the Arab population" are argued to be the decisive reasons in "defin[ing] the acceptable limits to traveling alone to school and work" (Adalah 2010: 9). However, as Raieda, a focus group participant (29 years old), asserts, "if we cannot reach anywhere and there are no buses and no streets and it's very expensive, how do you want us to work?" Furthermore, the argument based on traditional values and cultural stigmas the state suggests ignores that very little attention has been paid to genuine cultural differences that must be taken into consideration with regard to the opportunities for paid employment of Bedouin women. Bedouin activists participating in one of the focus groups, for instance, spoke of refusing specific paid employment offered through government agencies because of low and potentially jeopardizing safety measures and "dress codes that do not fit their society." Furthermore, during the focus group Bedouin women shared with the researchers the oppressive nature of the limited labor opportunities available to them. For example, private employment agencies provided them with jobs as cleaners in hotels, meaning the women

GENDER AND ECONOMICS IN MUSLIM COMMUNITIES

had to use transportation very early in the morning, returning back to their villages very late at night. The dress code for paid employment as cleaning women in such hotels was uncomfortable for the women because they were required to wear see-through shirts inappropriate to the Bedouin mode of dressing. Many women lost their chance to earn income due to such circumstances.

Moreover, low levels of employment for Bedouin women are to be expected considering the lack of schools and educational institutions for Palestinians in the Naqab (Sarab Abu Rabia-Queder 2006). No high schools exist in any of the unrecognized villages, and existing schools for the Bedouin suffer from serious underinvestment and underfunding. Some schools, for instance, lack basic services and facilities like toilets, electricity, telephone and internet connections, and sometimes even connecting roads (Adalah 2010: 39; ACRI 2011). This lack of basic facilities translates to a lack of professional staff. Rabha, a 30-year-old Bedouin social worker in a women's organization, stated:

> I want my kids to have modern development supported by professionals and not the old way of my mother. But the problem is the lack of professionalism of teachers and kindergarten teachers, [and] mainly [the need for teachers] who speak our language, and who do not look at us as dirt.

Rabha's voice betrays her sensitivity to the lack of resources accessible to schools in the Naqab and raises an important issue: the lack of native Arabic-speaking teachers in schools.

For those living in unrecognized villages, the nearest schools are often kilometers away and difficult to access, both because of the lack of public transportation for students and many parents' unwillingness to send their children (especially girls) outside the village. These circumstances contribute to high drop-out rates. In the region of Abu Tulul–ElShihabi, for example, around 750 students are of high school age, yet only 170 attend, with a dropout rate of 77 percent (Adalah 2010: 39). Such conditions compel us to revisit the individualizing concept of "dropping out," to focus instead on the structural factors that shape students' experiences at school. Illiteracy rates are high among Bedouin women in the Naqab, but especially among older women: in 2007, 13.5 percent of 35- to 29-year-olds were illiterate, compared to 92.3 percent among women 60 years and older (Hesketh 2011). The high levels of illiteracy among older Bedouin women mean that they have to depend on children or men to accompany them when they go out – not only because of tradition, but also because many of them cannot communicate in Hebrew or read road signs (Mihlar 2011: 5). This is particularly a problem when accessing basic health services.

GENDER AND ECONOMICS IN MUSLIM COMMUNITIES

While Bedouin in Israel have the highest rate of certain diseases such as diabetes, heart disease, and asthma (Mihlar 2011: 4), the health situation is most critical in the unrecognized villages of the Naqab where the provision of health services is limited or nonexistent. There are only twelve clinics in the unrecognized villages, and these lack medical specialists, pharmacies, and Arabic-speaking staff; they are only capable of providing healthcare for 20 percent of all inhabitants in the Naqab (Adalah 2010: 33). Furthermore, the lack of clean drinking water causes significant health problems. Most residents in unrecognized villages obtain water via plastic hose hook-ups or unhygienic metal containers from single water points located on main roads far from their homes, a practice which contributes to higher rates of infant mortality among the Bedouin due to unclean water. For Palestinian Bedouin, the infant mortality rate in 2005 was 15 per 1,000 live births, an increase from 13.3 deaths per 1,000 live births in 2003 (Adalah 2010: 32). In 2008, infant mortality rates within the Jewish majority in Israel stood at 2.9 per 1,000 live births; for the Palestinian minority, it was double that at 6.5 per 1,000 live births (Central Bureau of Statistics 2009: 11). The persistently high rate of infant mortality is arguably compounded further by the lack of specialized healthcare for women and children; none of the clinics in the unrecognized villages employ pediatricians or gynecologists (Adalah 2010: 33).

The process of de-development in the Naqab, we argue, is embedded in a wider colonial fantasy and discourse of culturalization, where imagined ideas of culture are used to erase critical examination of socioeconomic inequities in a settler colonial context, and *actual* cultural differences are overlooked and left unexamined in relation to their effects on disadvantage. This is certainly a tactic adopted by the state – and one that is evidenced in the narrative of modernization embedded in government discourse surrounding the Prawer Plan. By arguing that the forced relocation of Bedouin will "jump the population forward," Netanyahu speaks to the supposed "backwardness" of the Bedouin. His discourse suggests that Bedouin culture, which is bound to the land like indigenous peoples everywhere, is not "modern" enough and may, indeed, even be "pre-modern." The socioeconomic difficulties and disadvantages facing the Bedouin people face are the result of their "backward" culture and are most certainly unrelated to government policies and (intentional) oversights. This external culturalization of oppression and disadvantage is something well understood by Bedouin women themselves. As Zakeyi, a 26-year-old woman from a village that was officially recognized but still suffers a lack of regular services, explains:

> I am from a recognized village when it comes to building, but unrecognized when it comes to collecting trash... if they give water it's only specific hours... and they give electricity when they activate the generator... At night we have to use gas, so if the statistics that there

GENDER AND ECONOMICS IN MUSLIM COMMUNITIES

are so many burns [she means people suffering from physical burns] among Bedouin it is not because we are backward, it is because we don't have electricity and have to use gasoline lanterns.

Zakeyi's argument is simple but powerful, and it is fundamentally grounded in the everyday lives of and conditions facing Bedouin women in the Naqab. As she alludes, the lack of services and social support for Bedouin communities in the Naqab ultimately has little to do with culture, if anything at all; rather, it is embedded in Israeli colonial, bureaucratic, legal, and political systems and is institutionalized as official state policy.

Considering official government policies of de-development and "pseudo-development" projects like the Prawer Plan, which are fundamentally settler colonial initiatives dressed up in the seemingly reasonable language of liberal modernization, the question herein is how the situation of the Bedouin of the Naqab can truly be improved; how can Bedouin women receive the basic services and social support accorded to Jewish Israeli citizens? Here, we shift to the other side of the issues raised by Bedouin women: the donors who fund the various NGOs that attempt to fill the enormous gaps left behind by Israeli government policies of neglect. As Elora Shehabuddin (2008) argues in relation to Bangladesh, poor Muslim women are often the focus of international and national humanitarian concern, although very little attention is ever paid to their own experiences and perspectives. This dynamic, we argue, is similarly present in the Naqab, where Bedouin women (especially from unrecognized villages) become the focus of a humanitarian concern that limits itself to individualizing and culturalizing discourses at the expense of actual engagement with state policies of Judaization. In such a context, Bedouin women's patriarchal oppression is supposedly the central impediment to their socioeconomic disadvantage. The following description of one of the young Bedouin women participating in a SHATIL study tour of the Knesset (Israeli parliament) provided by the New Israel Fund illuminates this problematic dynamic:

Nida is the first Bedouin woman to study film and had to struggle long and hard to convince her father and eight brothers to let her do so. Despite their access to the internet, most of these women still dress modestly and go home to fathers and brothers who make the major decision in their lives – including whom and when they will marry. It's one of the things they want to see changed.[3]

For the Bedouin women in the workshop, this translation of public issues of structural disadvantage into personal matters of patriarchal family dynamics as a central issue shaping their lives gives them a sense they are "on display"

GENDER AND ECONOMICS IN MUSLIM COMMUNITIES

and compelled to satisfy donors' curiosity about their private lives. This sense, they suggested, structured their encounters with and experiences of various funding organizations.

FUNDING PAIN AS COLONIAL EXHIBIT: WOMEN'S VOICES

We became an exhibit... They [the donors] asked me to speak to an international conference, there were over 5,000 Jews; I was there and another Bedouin woman like me, and a head of an NGO, the three of us were the only Arab women. There were *zacham sahyuni* [many Zionists]; I needed to talk about myself as a Bedouin woman for the sake of funding. I told the audience about our needs, and they started asking me about my family, my husband, my feelings, about my fears... I told them about the problem of language and they asked me about my feelings toward mingling with people who are not from the family and they turned the problems in the Naqab into personal problems and they asked me to leave the Naqab alone and tell them my personal story. They started digging and digging. I felt uneasy. They were enthusiastically curious. I was in a dilemma. Should I say more to get more funding, or should I tell them that I can't talk more about myself, and it's not about me, it was about the Naqab. (Rab'aa, project coordinator in a small women's NGO in the Naqab, 35 years old)

Commenting upon time spent in France in the eighteenth century, an Egyptian scholar noted, "one of the beliefs of the Europeans is that the gaze has no effect" (Timothy Mitchell 1988: 2). Mitchell explores this theme of imperialist curiosity and voyeurism and remarks, "Spectacles like the world exhibition and the Orientalist Congress set up the world as a picture. They ordered it up before an audience as an object on display, to be viewed, experienced and investigated" (6). For the Bedouin women, the location of this "exhibit" has now shifted to the colonized landscape of the Naqab and the indigenous Bedouin communities living there. Donors funding many of the NGOs that seek to engage with these communities have in fact brought this European "gaze" to Southern Israel, to the Bedouin villages unrecognized by the Israeli state. As we see in the quotation above, curiosity about Rab'aa's private life was privileged over her own priority to fight for the recognition and survival of Bedouin communities. Just as curiosity mediated the relationship between Europe and the Middle East in the nineteenth century, so non-Europeans are again finding themselves on display – this time in order to create relationships with donors. And the gaze does have an effect. Edward W. Said famously articulates this effect in *Orientalism* (1978), whereby the West's economy of knowledge about the East helped solidify and maintain the unequal power dynamic between Europeans and their colonial subjects. As Lila

GENDER AND ECONOMICS IN MUSLIM COMMUNITIES

Abu-Lughod reminds us, "it must be recalled that *Orientalism* was not just about representations or stereotypes of the Orient, but about how these were linked and integral to projects of domination that were ongoing" (2001: 105).

Representations of Arab and Muslim women perpetuated by Orientalist discourse reinforce perceptions of the supposed inferiority or backwardness of non-European peoples, and these perceptions help to justify Western military and economic hegemony across the postcolonial world (Abu-Lughod 2002). Writing about the War on Terror and American discourse concerning women in Afghanistan, Abu-Lughod asks, "Do Muslim women really need saving?" in order to show us how the language of "liberating" the "Other" dangerously locates oppression within religion and culture, rather than questioning historical and political forces responsible for contemporary circumstances of suffering (2002: 784). As the Western gaze insists on locating oppression within Islamic culture, the superiority of the West and the legitimacy of its imperial endeavors are once again justified. Thus:

> When you save someone, you imply you are saving her from something. You are also saving her *to* something... What violences are entailed in this transformation and what presumptions are being made about the superiority of that to which you are saving her...? (Abu-Lughod 2002: 788–9)

According to the Bedouin women, the nature of funding agendas in the Naqab parallels the American relationship with women in Afghanistan. Both narratives are those of a superior culture (whose values are assumed to be universal): Saving women from an inferior culture; refusing to situate oppression within political, historical, or economic spheres; and instead locating it within a caricatured image of "Muslim culture."

The Bedouin women quoted in this study highlight the "violences entailed in saving to." One of the most ambiguous of these is the ways in which "women's empowerment" programs can dislocate women from their communities. As Ula, an activist in her late twenties who lives in Rahat, reflects, "they empower women, educate them, teach them how to speak up, and her situation becomes much better; but her family, her community does not understand her, and she no longer knows where she stands." For Ula, donor agendas in the Naqab are saving women to their *own* perceptions of womanhood, freedom, and justice by promoting an individualized notion of empowerment at the expense of collective struggles. As Ula suggests, the notion of individual empowerment – if done with uncritical conceptions of cultural oppression – misreads the politics of colonized women and works to decontextualize their struggles. Indeed, as Abu-Lughod (2002) suggests, the emphasis on individual empowerment of the "oppressed Third World

GENDER AND ECONOMICS IN MUSLIM COMMUNITIES

woman" is quite often a fundamental element of colonialism's contemporary logic and practice.

Mohanty (1988) and Cynthia Wood (2001) argue that Third World development discourse has created an "average third world woman," a passive victim and object of development, a designation similar to the sense that the Bedouin women often garnered from their interactions with donors. Women as objects of development therefore serve as justifications to perpetuate Western colonial logics, and this justification "recodes imperialism's 'civilizing mission'" (Wood 2001: 441). This continuity of colonial practice maintains the position of the Western world "as the primary referent in theory and praxis" (Mohanty 1988: 62). In the context of the Naqab, it serves to centralize Jewish Israeli society as the model of modernity to which Bedouin people ought to conform. The oppression of the "average third world woman" represented in gender and development discourse is also presented as "outside of history" (Mohanty 1988), which decontextualizes the function and role of colonization in the oppression of Palestinian Bedouin women.

Salma, the director of a women's organization that aims to empower Bedouin women in Laqiye village, describes her experience of decontextualization:

> A year ago, one of the foreign groups – a potential funder – that we usually host, visited our organization; usually I meet the groups from overseas to describe and explain the life of Bedouin in the Naqab, sometimes the group was joined by a Jewish guide. During one of these visits, the guide asked me in front of them all, to tell my personal story, and share details from my life; and I did. Following this meeting, the guide recommended to our director [that we] stop talking about the Naqab and the difficulties facing Bedouin communities and Bedouin women, and concentrate [instead] on personal stories. It was very hard and I felt very bad, because I am not asking for their sympathy. I want them to believe in my cause.

Salma alludes to the colonizing nature of such personalizing interventions, where questioning and invading women's private lives has become normalized and is even seen as a means to "help" these women. From Salma, we hear that donors "asked [her] to leave the Naqab alone and tell them [her] personal story." The focus on culturalizing and personalizing the suffering of the Bedouin women and the desire to know more about and invade their private lives often conflicts with what the women themselves want to prioritize. In this way, the women's position as Palestinian Bedouin is what compels intervention, but only insofar as the women maintain the donors' place as "primary referent," referring back to using the Jewish Israeli society as the model to which Bedouin people should conform (Abu-Lughod

GENDER AND ECONOMICS IN MUSLIM COMMUNITIES

2002). As colonized women are made into objects of benevolence, donors' voyeuristic curiosity regarding the private lives of these women becomes an inherent part of the funding economy in the Naqab. The exhibit has always been part of colonialism's scope.

The women reported that funding in the Naqab is mediated through local NGOs whose agendas are increasingly controlled by donors. The disconnect and disparity between donors' agendas and the local lived experience of women is articulated by Islah Jad, who writes that NGOs are increasingly seen as "donor-driven" and "reflecting a Western agenda" (2007: 623). In the type of voyeuristic, decontextualized interaction experienced by Salma, Bedouin women become objects who suffer rather than subjects with agency to create change. As Manal, a 35-year-old Bedouin woman working for a Bedouin women's organization, comments, "The funders are suffocating the organizations. The question is, do we have the power to face them, can we survive if we don't please them?" This relationship, between donors and women living in unrecognized villages, is marked by distance, a lack of trust, and a severe power disparity. Fatmeh, a young feminist activist working for the same organization, made clear the limits of activism and resistance because of donor power over NGOs: "They want you to become better and develop to a certain limit, till you start becoming a threat to them, then you are not allowed to speak up." What, or whom, could this "speaking up" threaten?

Requiring Bedouin women to share their private pains in the public sphere of funding works to re-center the role of donors and thus reinforces the starkly disparate relations of power that characterize the Naqab. Bedouin culture is more often than not portrayed as inferior and backwards. Donor relationships can become a transaction in which they "steal the pains of others," which, as Sherene H. Razack suggests (2007), institutionalizes conceptions of Western superiority. Razack takes the example of the Rwandan genocide and the ways in which it was presented to the Canadian public. She contends, traumatic stories of Canadian peacekeepers, served pervasive narratives of white superiority and heroism "through images of black suffering" (2007: 379). Tracing this narrative's historical circumstance, where the white narrative is positioned above all others, Razack shows how the suffering of nonwhite bodies is consumed by a white audience in order to tell a story of white compassion and objectivity. Here, "whiteness" is normalized and black and brown bodies are Othered. This is how the "universalist standpoint" – a perspective wherein one can view and know, but where one is "not himself of the landscape" and therefore not responsible for the circumstances of suffering – comes into being (380). It is not surprising, then, that in the Naqab donor consumption of Bedouin women's private lives hinders these donors' capacity to engage with the wider political, social, and economic conditions that shape the women's lives.

Manal's comment – "can we survive if we don't please them?" – raises an interesting point: how does the pain of the Bedouin women have the potential to become "pleasure" for donors? The other side of consuming others' pain, Razack says, is "the good feeling we get from contemplating our humanity" (382). The value of pain, for those who witness it, is the authority it gives them to judge but not be responsible for the suffering itself: "From our position as witness, we help to mark out the terrain of what is good and what is evil" (381). Engaging in this witnessing may allow us to demarcate good and bad, but most problematically, it does not necessarily compel us to act. Bedouin women like Manal suggest that donors may (re)produce an economy of oppression and suffering where pain is a valued commodity. Apart from the obvious implications of such a commodification, the Bedouin women raised important questions concerning the possibilities of such a framework to empower women in their struggles.

As much as consuming the private pain of Bedouin women may facilitate a certain humanitarian image, it problematically locates their struggle in the sphere of Islamic and Arab culture represented through Orientalist sexualized and intimate spaces (Meyda Yegenoglu 1998). Emphasizing the individual pain and private spaces of Arab Bedouin women allows donors to feel as though they are intervening in "indigenous patriarchal domination" without ever having to confront its entanglement with Orientalism's legacy; it allows for "saving the Third World woman" without the need to question one's own participation in the systems and ideologies of oppression Bedouin women face. The women described how the donors' desires to gaze into the homes of the Bedouin women, to inquire about their personal, individual stories of suffering, transform their private lives into public, transparent ones, while at the same time turn their public struggle into a private one. Zahra, a 23-year-old woman participating in a public forum, calls us to challenge the privatization and culturalization of women's status and rights, demanding that power holders

> stop suffocating us, build schools, proper roads, open new work opportunities, and give us some space so as to be able to work on our internal issues... Israel keeps us busy in preventing our houses from being demolished, and families from being displaced. We will never develop, and we will be always frustrated.

She continues,

> How do you turn the issue from a public issue to a private and individual issue? The issue of the Bedouin is not an issue of women and culture; it's the issue of the Palestinians and the state, Bedouins as a community versus the state. [It is an issue of] the unrecognizability of the Bedouins and the state's interest not to recognize them.

GENDER AND ECONOMICS IN MUSLIM COMMUNITIES

For unrecognized communities in the Naqab, the women's voices point toward two complementary, and potentially paralyzing, logics. On the one side, the Bedouin must negotiate aggressive settler colonial policies of de-development, which are used as a method to hinder their sovereignty as an indigenous community. On the other side, the donors proclaim to challenge these structures by personalizing and culturalizing the context, hearing the private pains of the Bedouin and "empowering" individual women. These donors are, at the very least, missing the point and, at worst, willing contributors to an overall context of deliberate state neglect and dispossession. As Rina Sen Gupta argues (2003), part of development and the assertion of citizens' rights is developing effective accountability of the state. By culturalizing rather than politicizing and individualizing rather than collectivizing, donors ignore the structural and state-led oppression directed toward Bedouin citizens. They shy away from dealing directly with historical injustice. The cultural replaces the political, and liberation replaces revolution. When funders focus on culture and "liberating" women from the cultural contexts that supposedly bind them, donors overlook what is clearly a far more complex structure of the state, using the claims of culture for their own gains and exploiting actual cultural differences (such as dress codes) by not paying them serious heed. Paradoxically, such a context may actually empower patriarchy in Bedouin communities, for women are positioned as passive objects and victims of their culture. "Our revolution," argues Najat, a 23-year-old Bedouin feminist activist, is "against patriarchy. [Our] men sit at home and 'allow you' to work, but they still give orders. And the state gives them the card in their hands." As Zahra puts it, "this is how they empower patriarchy... [by] leaving [us] no space to develop."

CLOSING REMARKS

What goes on with us is beyond criminal. All the funding is geared toward Al-Araqib; and here I am, from Al-Araqib, we all became the center of attention to funders and activists, but our houses are still under attack, our lives are under the cameras, and funding or no funding... employment or no employment... we remain *persona non grata*. (Suhad, a young feminist activist from Al Araqib)

Suhad speaks directly to the Bedouin women's critique of funding pain, whose voices demand that we take a closer look at the dual contexts of their oppression and resistance. As Suhad, Nuha, and the other women suggest, the failure to analyze political economy from the perspective of those who have been racialized, who have been made into "others" in a framework of culturalization and Orientalism, can work to entrench domination and oppression (Andrea Smith 2010; 2008). The women quoted throughout this study argue that the agendas of many funding organizations – namely the emphasis on the patriarchal/cultural oppression that Bedouin women face – ignore the colonial realities shaping and policing their lives that maintain their status as unrecognized entities (see also Shalhoub-Kevorkian [2012]). Sourcing funding to better the lives of discriminated and oppressed Bedouin people by state settler colonial politics was an experience that resulted in pain for many of the women who were expected to hold their private lives up to the scrutiny of donors. Funding pain, they suggest, fails to look beyond donor desires and the state's ideological underpinning and neglects Bedouin women's own analyses of the political economy in which they live.

We have argued that colonial logics, along with culturalizing interpretations of oppression, have erased the political, legal, and historical modes of oppression that propel Bedouin women's struggle against their unrecognized and colonized status inside the Israeli state. Bedouin women's battles to challenge ahistoricity and apoliticization are constrained by Israeli policies and practices, on the one hand, and the funding agendas of many donor organizations on the other. Particularly for women living in unrecognized villages, the state's refusal to recognize them as citizens with rights buttresses the enduring historical and continuing injustices of settler colonialism, spacio-cide, and racial and gendered Otherization. Donor desires to view the Bedouin women's private pain as an exhibit and their concurrent inability to comprehend the interlocking effect of Bedouin women's racial categorization feed into and preserve women's unrecognized status. Women must "play the game" of funding, where they must navigate and make use of the culturalizing stereotypes that reduce them to the nameless and faceless "Third World women." As Sana explained, "it is very hard to be in need of others… knocking on the doors of funders, sharing with them our stories… even my divorce story, to get some support for my village."

Bedouin women seeking to develop their communities must negotiate these twin dynamics of state ideology and funding agenda politics. The question remains: what space is there for development in the Naqab when unrecognizability and oppression are culturalized and Orientalized, when Bedouin women are discursively transformed into singular "Third World women" positioned as objects of funding but rarely as subjects of change? Bedouin women's political economic analyses suggest that without confronting the myth of "saving the (Muslim) Bedouin woman" and without resisting the politics of unrecognizability that perpetuate funding pain and (re)insert Bedouin women into colonial agendas and politics, endeavors to develop these communities will only be partial.

GENDER AND ECONOMICS IN MUSLIM COMMUNITIES

ACKNOWLEDGMENTS

We thank all the Bedouin women and local Nagab organizations that supported this research by sharing their stories with us and discussing their

GENDER AND ECONOMICS IN MUSLIM COMMUNITIES

NOTES

[1] All personal information that would allow the identification of any person or person(s) described in the study has been removed.

[2] A dunam equals 1,000 square meters.

[3] See http://www.nif.org/index.php?option=com_content&view=article&id=1409:young -negev-bedouin-women-gain-advocacy-tips-in-tour-of-knesset&catid=13:stories.

REFERENCES

Abu-Bader, Suleiman and Daniel Gottlieb. 2009. *Poverty, Education and Employment in the Arab–Bedouin Society: A Comparative View.* Jerusalem: Van Leer Institute.

Abu-Lughod, Lila. 2001. "Orientalism and Middle East Feminist Studies." *Feminist Studies* 27(1): 101–13.

———. 2002. "Do Muslim Women Really Need Saving? Anthropological Reflections on Cultural Relativism and its Others." *American Anthropologist* 104(3): 783–90.

Abu Rabia-Queder, Sarab. 2006. "Between Tradition and Modernization: Understanding the Problem of Bedouin Female Dropout." *British Journal of Sociology of Education* 27(1): 3–17.

Abu-Saad, Ismael. 2008. "Spatial Transformation and Indigenous Resistance: The Urbanization of the Palestinian Bedouin in Southern Israel." *American Behavioral Scientist* 51(12): 1713–54.

Adalah. 2010. "Adalah's NGO Report to the UN Committee on Economic, Social and Cultural Rights Regarding Israel's Implementation of the International Convenant on Economic, Social and Cultural Rights (ICESCR)." http://adalah.org/newsletter/ara/ oct10/Adalah%20CESCR%20Report%20October%202010.pdf

Association for Civil Rights in Israel (ACRI). 2011. "Shadow Report to the UN Committee on Economic and Social Rights." http://www.acri.org.il/en/2011/11/02/acris-shadow-report-to-un-committee-on-economic-and-social-rights/

Çavdar, Gamze and Yavuz Yaşar. 2014. "Moving Beyond Culturalism and Formalism: Islam, Women, and Political Unrest in the Middle East." *Feminist Economics.* doi:10.1080/1354 5701.2014.933858

Central Bureau of Statistics. 2009. "Israel in Figures." http://www.cbs.gov.il/publications/ isr_in_n09e.pdf

Dahan-Kalev, Henriette, Niza Yanay, and Niza Berkovitch. 2005. *Women of the South: Space, Periphery, Gender.* Tel Aviv: Xargol Books (in Hebrew).

Endeweld, Miri, Alex Fruman, Netanela Barkali, and Daniel Gottlieb. 2008. "2008 Poverty and Social Gaps: Annual Report." National Insurance Institute: Research and Planning Administration. http://www.btl.gov.il/Pages/default.aspx

Fenster, Tovi. 2002. "Planning as Control – Cultural and Gendered Manipulation and Mis-use of Knowledge." *HAGAR – International Social Science Review* 3(1): 67–86.

Grossbard-Shechtman, Shoshana and Shoshana Neuman. 1998. "The Extra Burden of Moslem Wives: Clues from Israeli Women's Labor Supply." *Economic Development and Cultural Change* 46(3): 491–517.

Habib, Jack, Judith King, Assaf Ben Shoham, Abraham Wolde-Tsadick, and Karen Lasky. 2010. *Labour Market and Socio–Economic Outcomes of the Arab–Israeli Population.* OECD.

184

GENDER AND ECONOMICS IN MUSLIM COMMUNITIES

http://www.oecd.org/officialdocuments/displaydocumentpdf?cote=DELSA/ELSA/WD/SEM%282010%292&doclanguage=en

Hamdan, Hana. 2005. "The Policy of Settlement and 'Spatial Judaization' in the Naqab." *Adalah's Newsletter* 11. http://adalah.org/newsletter/eng/mar05/ar2.pdf

Hanafi, Sari. 2009. "Spacio-cide: Colonial Politics, Invisibility and Rezoning in Palestinian Territory." *Contemporary Arab Affairs* 2(1): 106–21.

Hesketh, Katie. 2011. "The Inequality Report: The Palestinian Minority in Israel." http://www.adalah.org/upfiles/2011/Adalah_The_Inequality_Report_March_2011.pdf

Human Rights Watch. 2008. "Off the Map: Land and Housing Rights Violations in Israel's Unrecognized Bedouin Villages." http://www.hrw.org/sites/default/files/reports/iopt0308webwcover.pdf

Jad, Islah. 2007. "NGOs: Between Buzzwords and Social Movements." *Development in Practice* 17(4–5): 622–9.

Jamal, Amal. 2007. "Nationalizing States and the Constitution of 'Hollow Citizenship': Israel and its Palestinian Citizens." *Ethnopolitics* 6(4): 471–93.

Kedar, (Sandy) Alexander. 2004. "From Arab Land to Israel Lands: The Legal Dispossession of the Palestinians Displace by Israel in the Wake of 1948." *Society and Space* 22: 809–30.

Mihlar, Farah. 2011. "Israel's Denial of the Bedouin." Minority Rights Group International. http://www.minorityrights.org/download.php?id=1074

Mitchell, Timothy. 1988. *Colonising Egypt.* New York: Cambridge University Press.

Mohanty, Chandra Talpade. 1988. "Under Western Eyes: Feminist Scholarship and Colonial Discourse." *Feminist Review* 30: 61–88.

Muhammed, Ahmad Seikh and Mohammad Khatib. 2011. "The Palestinians in Israel: Third Socio-Economic Survey, 2010." The Galilee Society and Rikaz Databank. http://www.gal-soc.org/?LanguageId=1&System=Item&MenuId=103&PMenuId=8&MenuTemplateId=1&ItemId=146&ItemTemplateId=1

Netanyahu, Benjamin. 2011. "PM Netanyahu Meets with Negev Bedouin Mayors." Press Release, Israeli Ministry of Foreign Affairs, November 3. http://mfa.gov.il/MFA/PressRoom/2011/Pages/PM_Netanyahu_meets_Negev_Bedouin_3-Nov-2011.aspx

Noach, Haya. 2009. *The Unrecognized Villages that Do Not Exist: The Unrecognized Villages in the Naqab.* Haifa, Israel: Pardes (in Hebrew).

Olmsted, Jennifer C. 2002. "Assessing the Impact of Religion on Gender Status." *Feminist Economics* 8(3): 99–111.

Organisation for Economic Co-operation and Development (OECD). 2008. "Social Policy Division: Directorate of Employment, Labour and Social Affairs Country Chapter – Benefits and Wages." http://www.oecd.org/israel/47346847.pdf

———. 2010. "Gender Brief." http://www.oecd.org/els/family/44720649.pdf

Razack, Sherene H. 2007. "Stealing the Pain of Others: Reflections on Canadian Humanitarian Responses." *Review of Education, Pedagogy and Cultural Studies* 29(4): 375–94.

Roy, Sara. 1999. "De-Development Revisited: Palestinian Economy and Society Since Oslo." *Journal of Palestine Studies* 28(3): 64–82.

Said, Edward W. 1978. *Orientalism: Western Conceptions of the Orient.* London: Penguin.

Sen Gupta, Rina. 2003. "Ensuring Accountability of the Local Health Authorities and Health Services Providers to People, Specially Women in Bangladesh." In *On M'appelle a Regner: Mondialisation, Pouvoirs et Rapports de Genre,* edited by Fenneke Reysoo and Christine Verschuur, 117–135. Geneva: DDC/Unesco/IUED. http://graduateinstitute.ch/home/research/centresandprogrammes/genre/publications/actes_colloques/actes-2003.html

GENDER AND ECONOMICS IN MUSLIM COMMUNITIES

Shalhoub-Kevorkian, Nadera. 2012. "The Grammar of Rights in Colonial Contexts: The Case of Palestinian Women in Israel." *Middle East Law and Governance* 4(1): 106–51.

Shamir, Ronen. 1996. "Suspended in Space: Bedouins Under the Law of Israel." *Law and Society Review* 30(2): 231–58.

Shehabuddin, Elora. 2008. *Reshaping the Holy: Democracy, Development and Muslim Women in Bangladesh.* New York: Columbia University Press.

Smith, Andrea. 2010. "Indigeneity, Settler Colonialism, White Supremacy." *Global Dialogue* 12(2): 1–12.

Smooha, Sammy and Zohar Lechtman. 2010. "Civic Service for Arabs in Israel: 2009 Research Findings." University of Haifa. http://soc.haifa.ac.il/~s.smooha/uploads/editor_uploads/files/CivicServiceForArabs2009.pdf

Swirski, Shlomo. 2007. "Current Plans for Developing the Negev: A Critical Perspective." http://www.adva.org/default.asp?pageid=1002&itmid=486 (accessed June 2014).

Swirski, Sholmo and Yael Hasson. 2006. "Invisible Citizens: Israeli Government Policy Toward the Negev Bedouin." http://www.adva.org/uploaded/NegevEnglishSummary.pdf

UN CEDAW. 2005. "The Concluding Observations of the UN Committee for the Elimination of Discrimination Against Women." http://www.un.org/womenwatch/daw/cedaw/cedaw33/conclude/israel/0545042E.pdf

Wood, Cynthia. 2001. "Authorizing Gender and Development: 'Third World Women,' Native Informants, and Speaking Nearby." *Nepantla: Views from the South* 2(3): 429–47.

Yegenoglu, Meyda. 1998. *Colonial Fantasies: Towards a Feminist Reading of Orientalism.* Cambridge: Cambridge University Press.

Yiftachel, Oren. 2008. "Epilogue: Studying Naqab/Negev Bedouins – Toward a Colonial Paradigm?" *HAGAR Studies in Culture, Policy and Identities* 8(2): 83–108.

Zoabi, Haneen. 2009. "The Concept of the Jewish State." *Jadal* 5. http://mada-research.org/en/2009/12/04/jadal-issue-5-december-2009

PEACE IN THE HOUSEHOLD: GENDER, AGENCY, AND VILLAGERS' MEASURES OF MARITAL QUALITY IN BANGLADESH

Fauzia Erfan Ahmed

ABSTRACT

Although development studies have emphasized quality of life, the quality of marriage remains uninvestigated. This study challenges the bargaining model by arguing that theories of marital quality, derived from women's voices and subaltern knowledge, should be integral to feminist economic theories of marriage and intrahousehold gender relations. Findings from a longitudinal (1999–2009) ethnographic study of microcredit loanee families in rural Bangladesh reveal that Muslim women believe high marital quality or togetherness leads to peace in the household. This local model of marriage is central to the moral economy of social life. The study identifies eight local measures of marital quality that define what low-income women think a good Muslim husband should be like. The study concludes that the peace-in-the-household model emphasizes the transformation of masculinity as a program strategy that should be implemented in microcredit households in various parts of the world.

INTRODUCTION

I do not need my husband's permission to leave the house ... I try to understand him; he tries to understand me. That is why we have *shangshare shanti* [peace in the household] whether we have money or not; happiness is something that is separate.

Shefali (wife, Muslim, Kunjpukhi village)

GENDER AND ECONOMICS IN MUSLIM COMMUNITIES

If there is no peace in the household, then what will happen to my children?

Shafiqul (husband, Muslim, Kunjpukhi village)

If there is no peace in the household, how will society survive?

Amin (mother-in-law, Muslim, Kunjpukhi village)

Although quality of life is highlighted as central to development studies, it is curious that the quality of marriage remains unexamined (Martha Nussbaum and Amartya Sen 1993). Amartya K. Sen notes that unlike employers and employees, husbands and wives live together; therefore, theories of intrahousehold gender relations must include what this "togetherness" means (1990: 147).[1] Little, in fact, is known about what togetherness means to low-income men and women in Muslim communities. Based on a continuing longitudinal (1999–2009) ethnographic study of gendered identity, poverty alleviation, and agency of ninety-two women and men belonging to microcredit loanee households in rural Bangladesh, I investigate local meanings and measures of togetherness in Muslim households. As the above quotations illustrate, villagers in Bangladesh believe that marital quality is foundational to a good society. Low-income women argue that this togetherness, or everyday shared space with their husbands, is important because it leads to peace at home (*shangshare shanti*) – a key syncretic Islamic concept that is understood by both Muslims and Hindus in rural Bangladesh.

Peace in the household has always been a gendered concept in Bangladesh: a "good" Muslim woman is responsible for maintaining this peace, and it is she who is blamed if there is "trouble" in the household (*shangshare oshanti*). Against the current backdrop of the country's changing social landscape, this concept is hotly debated. Nongovernmental organizations (NGOs) argue that women's microcredit activities do not cause trouble in the household, but patriarchal Islamicists contend that in Islam, peace in the household is contingent upon women staying at home. Both sides of the debate focus on the definition of a good Muslim woman. But, as my findings reveal, village women ingeniously shift the locus of the debate to ask an equally important question: What should a good Muslim husband be like?

This contribution presents sharecropper women's answers to this question. My study reveals eight local measures of marital quality, ranging from a husband understanding a wife's need to rest to his willingness to put property in his wife's name. Together, these measures define low-income women's expectations of a good Muslim husband. Sharecropper women want their husbands to change their attitudes and practices to

GENDER AND ECONOMICS IN MUSLIM COMMUNITIES

improve the quality of the marriage; they told me in no uncertain terms that development organizations need to also "put men right" (Fauzia E. Ahmed 2003). As the opening quotations reveal, love means mutuality in work and life (*mile mishe kaj kora, mile mishe ak shathe thaka*). The measures of togetherness (*ak shathe mile mishe thaka*), therefore, constitute low-income women's theories of intrahousehold gender relations; peace in the household, as the outcome of these measures, is their model of marriage.

Challenging Gary Becker's (1991) altruistic head of the household model, feminist economists have posited a model of intrahousehold relations based on bargaining power (Amartya K. Sen 1987, 1990; Nancy Folbre 1986a, 1986b; Bina Agarwal 1997). John Nash's game theory, in which two individuals have clear and specific interests represented by two cardinal utility functions, is the theoretical foundation of this model. This theory is the basis of Folbre's (1986a) initial critique of neoclassical and Marxist theories of the household, and of Sen's (1987) cooperative conflict model. Adding various levels of complexity to the original Nash model, the cooperative conflict model introduces well-being levels and perceived interests and contributions. Agarwal (1997) provides even more sophistication by investigating the impact of qualitative variables, such as social norms, on bargaining power.

The models, however, do not emphasize the quality of the marriage. Rather, they reflect the assumptions of an employer–employee relationship: if a woman strengthens her breakdown position through increased resources, then she will secure a more favorable bargaining outcome. Implicit in this schema is the assumption that a strong breakdown position means strong exit options. In other words, as in negotiations over a job contract, the employee can withdraw or leave if he or she has other resources or opportunities to fall back upon. But is marriage, in essence, just a job?

The village women with whom I lived in Bangladesh do not think so. These women do not view bargaining power as the essence of happiness in a marriage, and they do not see exit or divorce as freedom. They want marriage to be a lifelong commitment and believe that peace in the household also depends on a loving husband. As the opening quotations indicate, sharecropper women feel that making a commitment "to understand each other" creates happiness and leads to peace in the household, which is important for the general care and well-being of children and for the larger community. Furthermore, a poor woman knows only too well that if she divorces her husband, or even threatens to do so, he will likely be able to find another, younger woman to marry, whereas it is unlikely that she would find anyone to marry her. The bargaining model ignores the patriarchal structure of marriage in a patrilocal and patrilineal gender order. More importantly, it ignores what women think about intrahousehold gender relations. To them, togetherness is more than just a solution to asymmetric remarriage possibilities. My study finds that women do not want the marriage to end because they value the companionship and intimacy of a long union.

This investigation is significant in three ways. First, by presenting empirically derived local measures of marital quality, this study argues that theories of marriage, based on women's voices and subaltern knowledge, need to be a feminist economics project. Folbre (1986a) mentions the moral economy of the household but neither describes nor analyzes it. I argue, here, that the quality of the spousal relationship is an essential part of the moral economy of the household, which is based on values of sharing and caring. This contribution presents peace in the household as a local theory of the moral economy of Bangladeshi society, which has, in fact, explicit components.[2]

Second, local theories of marital quality may resolve some of the problems microcredit has created in loanee households. Evaluations of microcredit programs are mixed, at best (Naila Kabeer 2001). Investigations of marital quality may resolve puzzles, such as, limited decision-making power of the loanees (Anne Marie Goetz and Rina Sen Gupta 1996) and why gender trumps women's employment income (Michael Bittman, Paula England, Liana Sayer, Nancy Folbre, and George Matheson 2003). Katherine N. Rankin (2002) and Ruth Pearson (2004, 2007) have not only critiqued microenterprise and women's wage employment as too simplistic, but they also argue that, in the absence of other interventions, these may actually exacerbate gender inequalities within the household. Women loanees feel husbands need to be equally committed to peace in the household, so including men in the gender and development endeavor should be a priority.

Third, this study responds to a call by leading feminist economists to emphasize qualitative frameworks of inquiry to reflect women's experiences (Diana Strassmann 1997) and the processes that undergird economic outcomes (Günseli Berik 1997).[3] Leading scholars have highlighted the need for qualitative studies, specifically in the study of women's agency in the household (Sen 1990; Agarwal 1997; Kabeer 2001) and local meanings of empowerment (Naila Kabeer 1998). Drawing on Antoni Gramsci (1971), who states that each class produces organic intellectuals who represent the interests of their own group, I argue that the sharecropper women with whom I lived should be considered intellectuals, and their analyses of their own lives should be the fundamentals of theory. This perspective challenges the epistemological paradigm of feminist economics bargaining models; it also challenges the "intellectual hierarchy of economics" (Strassmann 1997: viii). I want to emphasize that I do think structural analyses of the household are critical; undeniably, the much-needed critique of the Becker household model was timely and courageous. Clearly, feminist economists value qualitative methods and are committed to low-income

GENDER AND ECONOMICS IN MUSLIM COMMUNITIES

women. Rather, my argument here, in essence, is we cannot build valid models about togetherness, that intimate space fraught with expressed and unexpressed desire, expectation, disappointment, and fulfillment, without basing these models, at least in part, on what poor women believe, think, and feel about the concept.

SOCIAL TRANSFORMATION IN BANGLADESH: PEACE IN THE HOUSEHOLD AND SYNCRETIC ISLAM

The Bangladeshi rural household and gender relations within it are best understood as embedded within a landscape of dramatic social transformation (Elora Shehabuddin 2008). Since Bangladesh gained independence in 1972, the gender and development indicators have shown remarkable progress. The fertility rate decreased from 6.9 in 1970 to 2.2, near replacement rate, in 2013 (World Bank 2014a).[4] The net enrollment percentage of girls to boys for primary and secondary school was 106 in 2011 and 114 in 2012, respectively (World Bank 2014b, 2014c);[5] maternal mortality decreased from 574 in 1990 per 100,000 births to 170 in 2013 (World Bank 2014d); and women's entrepreneurial activities have increased household income (Katushi S. Imai and Md. Shafiqul Azam 2012). Women now have more control over their bodies; they are defying or adapting purdah norms to work outside the home; they are joining the hitherto all-male *shalish* (traditional justice system) as jurors (Fauzia E. Ahmed 2013); and they are running for public office at the village level. Clearly, concerted efforts to challenge the patriarchal structure of the gender order have been made at the national level.

A strong and visionary women's movement continues to voice women's concerns and has achieved legislative success, such as the 2010 Family Violence Act, a parliamentary bill declaring domestic violence a criminal offense punishable by law (*Daily Star* 2010). Moreover, NGO activities not only provide microcredit to women but also organize them into collectives. These changes impact the household, challenging the order of the patriarchal family. Daughters-in-law, traditionally at the bottom of the household hierarchy, are now members of women's collectives and no longer content to be silent. There has been a patriarchal backlash to this development, which utilizes a rigid interpretation of Islam as its ideology.[6] However, village women have developed their own feminist interpretations of Islam based on syncretic rural traditions as a collective ideology of resistance (Fauzia E. Ahmed 2008a).

Peace in the household as a tenet of syncretic Islam

Defined by Willem van Schendel (2009) as a spiritual unity between Hinduism, Islam, and rural folklore, the syncretic Islamic tradition has a long history in Bengal. When the first Muslims came to South Asia in the eighth century, they found a land rich with diverse religious traditions. Rather than being extinguished, these preexisting cultures prevailed and were assimilated into Islam, the religion of the conquerors. This syncretic process was particularly strong in Bengal, where Hinduism, Buddhism, and Islam all mingled with animistic customs at the village level. Sufi Islam, which emphasized love of God, was particularly syncretic in approach and nature, allowing new converts to retain some of their previous beliefs and customs. Salma Sobhan (1994) has likened syncretic Islam to the two-hued silverware in Bengal, one side of which is gold washed. Just as the convergence of the contrasting gold and silver colors adds depth and richness to the silverware, so, too, the fusion of Hinduism with Islam in this region creates richness and flexibility in spiritual traditions. The syncretic tradition of early Islam in Bengal survives to this day in rural Bangladesh (Santi Rozario 2004). Indeed, peace in the household is one such tradition I discovered in my study.

"Household" is at best an inadequate translation for the Bengali word, *shangshar*. This word derives from the Sanskrit word *samsara*, which is a composite of *sam*, or "together with" and *sr*, "to flow or move." Within ancient Hindu philosophical tradition, *shangshar* means the world and all of the cycles of births and deaths that humans and other living beings go through together (Sarah Lamb 2000). In Hinduism, all life stages have implications for men and women, and the householder (*shangshari*) stage, with prescribed duties for both husband and wife, is central to the Hindu cosmic cycle.[7] Though Hindu in origin, I found that this stage was also an intrinsic belief among the Muslim sharecropper families with whom I lived.

Vested with the most responsibility, including caring for children and elders, the householder stage sustains all of the other stages. The married couple occupies a position of centrality, functioning as the "warm, reproductive, redistributive center" of the family and community, and they gradually make all the decisions for the extended family (Lamb 2000: 38). The household is the backbone of the community and sustains social life. It is, therefore, a karmic duty to complete the householder stage before moving on to the next stage, and peace in the household (*shangshare shanti*) is an imperative part of this stage. Trouble in the household (*shangshare oshanti*), therefore, disturbs both family and community life. Divorce (*shangshar bhenge jawa*), which literally means breaking the household, breaks the cosmic cycle. As the opening quotations illustrate, Muslim villagers also believe that society will not survive if there is trouble in the household.

But different ideas of what constitutes peace in the household and who is responsible for trouble in the household exist – often in stark contrast to the backdrop of national societal transformation. In common patriarchal rural narratives, a good woman is *noromponthi*, a subordinate woman who

GENDER AND ECONOMICS IN MUSLIM COMMUNITIES

obeys her husband, as opposed to an *ugroponthi*, an aggressive woman who talks back to her husband (*mukher upor kotha bole*), and both Hindu and Muslim orthodoxy condemn "aggressive" women on religious grounds (Fauzia E. Ahmed 2008b). Many men feel microcredit and women's rights NGOs have created trouble in the household by creating an "aggressive" femininity (Ahmed 2003). In focus groups, a village elder stated such women should be hit like "snakes on the head" (Ahmed 2008b). It is, therefore, hardly surprising that 47 percent of reproductive-age women in Bangladesh report having been beaten by their husbands (Michael A. Koenig, Saifuddin Ahmed, Mian B. Hossain, A. B. M. Khorshed, and Alam Mozumder 2003). But village women refuse to be cowed. Many of the women I spoke with stated that it is, in fact, violent husbands who disturb the peace of the household and who should be punished by the *shalish* (Ahmed 2013). These different definitions of peace in the household are also a contrast between the Islam of the mosque orthodoxy and syncretic Islam of rural culture.

THE LIMITS OF BARGAINING MODELS: SUBALTERN KNOWLEDGE AND MARITAL QUALITY IN THE HOUSEHOLD

The bargaining model silences the subaltern, however unwittingly. Although clearly an improvement over "altruistic head of the household" and "harmonious optimal division" models of the household, the basis, direction, and vision of the game-theoretic bargaining model need to be challenged in order for marital quality to become a feminist economics project. Even the critics of this model do not derive theories directly from women and their answers. The non-cooperative intrahousehold models question the symmetric treatment of different family members, introducing gender- and age-based power asymmetries (Elizabeth Katz 1997). Although they correctly criticize the cooperative model by arguing that marriage is an institutional structure with a gendered history that impacts decision making, they do not question its basic assumptions. Non-cooperative models do not focus on marital quality and what it means to the village women themselves. Bargaining power, which is the pillar of the cooperative model, still defines the boundary within which their argument is framed. Clearly, the very locus of the debate needs to shift. My ensuing critique, therefore, focuses on influential feminist economists' works on the bargaining model, including Sen (1987, 1990), Agarwal (1997), and Folbre (1986a, 1986b).

The need to build theory based on subaltern knowledge

What is subaltern knowledge? My findings reveal that this knowledge is encapsulated in proverbs, songs, and sayings that women have developed to

GENDER AND ECONOMICS IN MUSLIM COMMUNITIES

resist patriarchal norms. Passed down through generations by poor women, these traditions provide a sense of agency and solidarity. Although rooted in rich oral traditions of rural Bangladeshi society, such knowledge is invisible to the middle class. An epistemology based on this knowledge validates subaltern experiences: it centers the subaltern as an intellectual qualified to produce theory, especially about her own life. Accumulated over time, this knowledge is not static; my findings reveal that as the social landscape changed, women created new proverbs to reflect this transformation. Similar to the subjugated knowledge Patricia Hill Collins (2000) analyzes in her now classic *Black Feminist Thought,* subaltern knowledge needs to be included as a basis of theory and vision in models of intrahousehold relations.[8]

Feminist economists have criticized unitary household models, which assume that household members seek to maximize utility on the basis of a set of common preferences represented by an aggregate utility function. They have turned to Nash and Marx as the theoretical counterpoints to Becker, but lost in the interstices of this debate are women's own voices and subaltern knowledge. Neither the neoclassical nor Marxian paradigms examine inequality within the home, and Folbre (1986a) analyzes this ironic convergence extensively. She, however, does not mention another irony: neither neoclassical *nor* feminist Marxist revisionist perspectives utilize women's voices as the basis of theory.

A curious vein of ambivalence runs through Sen's (1987, 1990) pioneering writings on cooperative conflict, which, as he states, is a more complex form of the Nash game-theoretic scenario. Sen critiques the informational base of the bargaining model as weak because it does not take into account the gendered structures of inequality within and outside the family *not* because it excludes village women's analyses. For a theoretical foundation, he returns to the "neat" format of the bargaining model (Sen 1987: 17), and not to the nuanced traditions of subaltern knowledge. But is togetherness simply a matter of relative power in intrahousehold gender relations?

Another theme that underlies Sen's work is the need to distinguish between "subjective" perceptions of interest and "objective" determinants of well-being. True, it is essential to measure objective indicators such as longevity, maternal mortality, morbidity, nutrition, health, and educational achievement through positivistic methods. There is an implicit assumption, however, that subjective utility, such as pleasure and fulfillment, cannot be a basis of intrahousehold theories because of perception problems. In his schema, these utilities are subjective and run the risk of false consciousness. Villagers' perceptions about their own lives, therefore, are seen as a problem. I do not deny that false consciousness or internalized oppression both exist. Nevertheless, what is missing from Sen's theoretical *Weltanschauung* is the possibility that resistance can exist

GENDER AND ECONOMICS IN MUSLIM COMMUNITIES

simultaneously with oppression, and a consciousness of injustice can exist simultaneously with false consciousness, even in the most marginalized of communities, as Agarwal (1997) also argues and as Collins (2000) reveals.[9]

In her ethnographic study of aging in rural West Bengal, India, Lamb (2000) notes that social groups resisted conformation to socially assigned and expected roles; contrary to upper-caste beliefs, the scheduled castes felt their treatment was unjust, and widows did not always want to renounce their attachments to material things.[10] In a similar study in North India, Gloria Goodwin Raheja and Ann Grodzins Gold (1994) found that women rejected patriarchal sayings with sarcasm and irony and sang their own songs of rebellion. My own research in rural Bangladesh reveals that such songs of resistance have always existed and are part of the invisible, neglected oral tradition. This Gramscian concept of the organic intellectual who does not accept the status quo and, therefore, is herself a reservoir of knowledge, is absent from Sen's perspective.

Unlike Sen (1987, 1990) and Folbre (1986a, 1986b), Agarwal (1997) does include quotes from women, albeit from secondary sources. Bargaining theory, nevertheless, remains the backbone of her argument, with a focus on how qualitative factors such as social norms and perceptions impact bargaining power. Although Agarwal correctly states that the "full complexity of gender interactions within the household and the simultaneity of various processes and forms of decision making" need to be taken into account (1997: 2), she does not describe these other processes. In fact, anthropologists have described reciprocity, centrality, and hierarchy, along with mutuality, as important aspects of family relations (Raheja and Gold 1994; Lamb 2000). Naila Kabeer (1999) argues that in addition to bargaining and negotiation, other processes, such as manipulation and resistance as well as reflection and analysis, exist in the marital relationship. Agarwal also seems to utilize women's quotes to validate her theories about the bargaining model rather than as potential rival hypotheses for an entirely different paradigm of intrahousehold gender relations. Clearly, she values discussions with low-income women, as do other feminist economists; but I posit that including quotations is not quite the same as building theory based on women's perspectives. Agarwal does not ask a basic question: do women themselves equate bargaining power with togetherness?

What do poor women really expect from marriage? Feminist economists need to pose this question directly to village women and include their answers as the building-blocks of a theory of household relations. Instead, influential studies of the household contain assumptions about poor women and what they want. Arguing that the structure of patriarchy is duplicated in the household, Folbre (1986a) presents bargaining power as the solution; for her, the most important questions pertain to defining the nature of bargaining power and identifying the determinants of its levels (Folbre 1986b). She clarifies that women's potential utility positions outside the household are critical because they will exit if they gain from leaving. Is exit indeed the subaltern vision? The women, with whom I lived, believe that peace at home should be the goal, and they argued that this outcome could be achieved if husbands were more altruistic. This subaltern vision is not reflected in the bargaining model of intrahousehold relations.

The underlying assumption of the bargaining model is that the problem of gender inequality resides in women; therefore, gender justice has meant empowering women with resources in order to transform subordinate notions of femininity. Sen (1990) unequivocally states that women's gainful employment outside the home will result in a change in their perceptions. Microcredit for poor women, the envisaged NGO programmatic solution for women's economic disempowerment, continues to be the focus of gender and development scholarship in Bangladesh and other countries. Pearson, however, characterizes microcredit and women's employment outside the home as an "Engelian myth" (2007: 201). Evaluations of microcredit programs do not indicate a clear empowerment trajectory (Kabeer 2001). Some find that microcredit increases women's agency (Syed M. Hashemi, Sidney Ruth Schuler, and Ann P. Riley 1996). Others indicate that violence increased in loanee families despite the wife's increased income (Aminur Rahman 1999; Lisa M. Bates, Sidney Ruth Schuler, Farzana Islam, and Mohammed Khairul Islam 2004), and the majority of women do not have control over their loans (Goetz and Sen Gupta 1996). Sidney Ruth Schuler, Lisa M. Bates, and Farzana Islam (2008) contend that microcredit can put women loanees at risk because women whose material resources have increased are more vulnerable. My research reveals that women become borrowers in order to increase household material standards, so they want microcredit programs to continue even though it has increased the double burden (Ahmed 2003, 2008a, 2008b). But women recognize that microcredit alone is not enough for empowerment because the gender inequality problem also resides in men; in other words, the attitudes and practices of their husbands, with whom their lives are intertwined, also need to change.

RESEARCH METHODS: UNLEARNING AND THE QUEST FOR SUBALTERN KNOWLEDGE

The quest for subaltern knowledge, which framed the basis of my research philosophy and methods, was not easy. It required unlearning. In fact, I did not really know the extent and depth of this accumulated knowledge until after the first few weeks of living in the village. I realized my findings have no meaning unless they were based on how the villagers themselves viewed intrahousehold relations. So after much reflection, and not a little trepidation, I abandoned the ten-page questionnaire I had so carefully prepared in the United States with the intent of "administering" it to the villagers.

It is not true that villagers cannot analyze things because they are illiterate, as is often assumed; they just do not analyze things in the way that middle-class educated people do. The proverb is the unit of analysis in the rich oral tradition of rural Bangladesh. Replete with hyperbole, metaphor, song, and allegory, this tradition enables villagers to make sense of their world. So my first task was to learn these gender-related proverbs and other components and to include them in my research design rather than apply a predetermined questionnaire.

I chose to understand the world of the villager by living in it. Participant observation, the pillar of the anthropological method, was central to this study not only as research method but also as research philosophy. It enabled a comprehensive understanding of the context and helped me to make the essential distinction between "life as lived, life as experienced, and life as told" (Edward M. Bruner 1984: 267).

The larger investigation began with a pilot study in 1999 in rural Bangladesh. This study is based on ninety-two individual interviews and five videotaped focus groups of men and women villagers. My most recent visit took place in 2009. I interviewed about twelve men and women villagers in 1999, seventy-three villagers in 2001, and nineteen in 2009. The bulk of the interviews took place in 2001, when I also conducted five videotaped focus groups, consisting of around twenty villagers each in four different neighborhoods. This subset of men and women interviewees was chosen from three Hindu, Muslim, and Rishi villages that were within a five-mile radius of each other.[11] In this article, I focus on Muslim households from the same village to highlight how variations exist, even in micro contexts. I also hired a male interviewer for the full study in 2001. All of these households had Grameen Bank borrowers who had left Oporajito, a women's NGO, because of its management problems.[12] In 2009, I conducted a follow-up study of Hindu and female-headed households since I considered them to be the most vulnerable.[13]

Purposive rather than random sampling defined the sample population (Matthew B. Miles and A. Michael Huberman 1994). Grounded theory and theoretical sampling helped me integrate anthropological and sociological methods (Anselm Strauss and Juliet Corbin 1998). The sample was chosen through snowballing and theoretical sampling, the basis of grounded theory in qualitative sociological research methods. I developed, challenged, and redeveloped hypotheses as I collected data. I used triangulation and various types of validity in the search for coherent explanations (Miles and Huberman 1994) in the discovery of the

GENDER AND ECONOMICS IN MUSLIM COMMUNITIES

underlying logic of the patterns of marital quality and indicators. Rural proverbs and songs were part of the grounded theory technique and were used as *nvivo* (local) codes for data analysis to explore local indicators of marital quality.

In qualitative research, the researcher is the data instrument, so reflexivity is ever present (Rosanna Hertz 1997). In fact, it is used to construct knowledge. I kept a separate journal that include villagers' reactions to me as well as my changing reactions to them. These perceptions were not monolithic, and I utilized the diverse reactions in my research design. I analyzed these entries concurrently with interview and field note data.

We bring our different selves and past experiences to our research projects. For example, in 2001, I saw myself as an impecunious graduate student struggling to finish my dissertation. But the villagers' reaction to me illuminated another truth. They perceived me as an upper-class Bangladeshi who lived in America, the "land of plenty." I acknowledged this self and, therefore, did not make the false claim that participant observation would somehow transform me into one of the villagers. In fact, I was more of an outsider than an insider in rural Bangladeshi culture. My respect for villagers' perceptions of my identity increased trust, enabling me to attempt to reduce the degree of "outsiderness." However, given the class divide and other differences between me and the sharecropper women, I focused on continued trust building as my goal.

CREATING PEACE IN THE HOUSEHOLD: LOCAL MEASURES OF MARITAL QUALITY

Although different cultures shape different meanings of togetherness, love is a universal need, as a study of 150 countries reveals (Shaifali Sandhya 2009). To the village women, with whom I lived, love means mutuality in work and life (*mile mishe kaj kora, mile mishe thaka*). Trust, respect, and affection are the bases of everyday empathy. The willingness of husbands to make an effort to listen (*shonar chesta*) to the wife and understand (*bojhar chesta*) her viewpoint is the basis of this mutuality. A high degree of marital quality results in a *moner mil* (mutuality of minds) marriage; low marital quality leads to a *moneeb chakor* (master–servant) marriage. Though an extensive discussion of low-income masculinities (Ahmed 2008a) is beyond the scope of this paper, as Kabeer's (1998) findings also reveal, a village woman's relationship with her husband is important to her.[14] Village women refer to an ideal husband as *udaar*, or high-minded, and an abusive husband as *nisthur*, or cruel. In fact, the attitudes of the husband shape the quality of the marriage to a large extent (Ahmed 2008a). The eight local measures of marital quality, therefore, are based on expectations of the husband, his beliefs, and practices: respect for women's reproductive labor,

GENDER AND ECONOMICS IN MUSLIM COMMUNITIES

understanding a wife's need for rest, joint decision making, willingness to put property in the wife's name, investment in fatherhood, entrusting the wife with physical mobility, termination of domestic violence, and using the Prophet as role model. Together, these measures define a good Muslim husband.

Respect for women's reproductive labor

I have six people in my family ... cows, goats, ducks, chickens ... I am doing everything, cooking etc. But you will hear my husband saying: "What work do you do? What do you do the whole day?" His work is measured by the hands of the clock. There is no value for the time I spend doing household chores.

Qulsum (young mother, Muslim, Kunjpukhi village)

Qulsum feels upset when her husband dismisses her unpaid reproductive labor. In stark contrast to men's agricultural labor, which is remunerated in a direct relationship to the time they invest in these activities, women's care work remains unrecognized, as Paula England and Nancy Folbre (2002) also point out in their US-based study. Village women feel this negation of their contribution to the household is a slap in the face. This common indignity can result in a smoldering resentment that adversely impacts marital quality.

On the other hand, husbands value women's paid work. My findings revealed that most men are well aware that women's income has increased the material standards of the entire household; so not surprisingly, most men want their wives to continue their entrepreneurial activities. Microcredit has reduced the male breadwinner burden. Kabeer's (1998) study indicates that village women receive more love from their husbands, when, as microcredit loanees, they bring money into the household. But I discovered that village women do not consider this to be love. What if a woman is too sick to work? A loving husband will care for them even if they are too ill to earn money. Local meanings of marital quality are more profound: women want to be valued for themselves – not just for the money they can earn:

Women need extra attention and care from their husbands at special times. For example, when a woman has just had a baby and she is breastfeeding, she needs more food. Husbands need to understand what agony it is to have a hungry baby crying at your breast when you have no milk because you yourself have an empty stomach.

Mariama (Muslim woman, young mother, Kunjpukhi)

GENDER AND ECONOMICS IN MUSLIM COMMUNITIES

Women want husbands to be especially loving when they are pregnant, after childbirth, and when they are breastfeeding. In a poor household with limited resources, an expression of this caring is simple: the husband should give his wife more food, even if it means sacrificing part of his own portion.

Understanding a wife's need for rest

Q. A man complained to me that he had come home after a long day's work, and that his wife had not finished cooking dinner. Instead, she had gone somewhere else and was chatting. What do you think?

A. As far as dinner is concerned ... we have a small farm to manage ... Women don't have just one kind of work to do. They have to do many things to keep the household going. Many times, I return home very late at night. I see that dinner has been left right here for me. But I don't wake her. I know that she has worked so hard. I just eat and go to sleep. In the morning, I have to go work; I just eat the leftovers and go out.

Shafiqul (husband, Muslim, Kunjpukhi village)

I really look forward to going to my *baper bari* [natal home]. My maternal uncles [*mamas*] are very affectionate. There, I do not have to do household chores. I am fussed over. My hair is oiled and combed, and my feet are massaged.

Rabia (young mother, Muslim, Kunjpukhi village)

In a landscape of social change, proverbs, such as ones that describe a good daughter-in-law as someone "who eats little and works much," are being replaced by a wish for a daughter-in-law with a salaried job (*chakriwallah bou*). Nevertheless, words like "rest" (*bisram*) or "vacation" (*chhooti*) are still not part of women's vocabulary. Many village women's days consisted of a packed schedule of unremitting work inside and outside the home.[15] Women's paid work has increased as a result of their entrepreneurial activities, but their reproductive labor has not decreased and, as Shelley Phipps, Peter Burton, and Lars Osberg (2001) note, most housework cannot be postponed. For many women, a caring husband should know when she is tired and should be willing to mind the children so that she can rest for a few hours.

As the quotation above shows, Shafiqul understands that sometimes his wife is tired, so he does not insist that she wait for him to return to have dinner. He does not mind her eating before him, and he eats the cold plate of rice that she has left for him. Most husbands would insist that their wives eat after them. Although patriarchal village norms may dictate that cold rice warrants a beating, Shafiqul understands his wife's need for rest.

As Rabia's quote shows, visits to the natal home are precious. Perhaps the only time when women are free of household responsibilities, these visits mean that they are cared for by others. Some men, however, see visits to the *baper bari* as a threat and often use it as a source of control over their wives since the latter cannot go without their husband's explicit permission. They feel that once a woman has her own income, "it goes to her head," and she can go off to her father's home at a moment's notice! Husbands who understand the need for these visits help to create positive marital quality.

Willingness to put property in wife's name

I'll never forget the day my husband agreed to put the land in my name. My in-laws didn't want this and threatened never to speak to him again. But he stood up to his parents, and for my sake! He understood how important it was to me.

Mehrun (young Muslim woman, Kunjpukhi village)

Property, as the most valued asset, means prestige and security for women (Agarwal 2004). Yet few village women ever have the opportunity to own land. Even though Islam gives women property rights, women in South Asia often give up their property inheritance in favor of their brothers in order to be able to visit natal kin (*naior*). Since the Grameen Bank provides housing loans for mature borrowers, women see the profits from their entrepreneurial activities as one of the few opportunities to own property in a patrilocal and patrilineal gender system.[16]

Most husbands, however, do not want their wives to own property; even those who have no objection to wives' participation in Grameen Bank loans are reluctant. Stories are circulated about how wives who owned property immediately took the opportunity to throw their husbands out of their homes to live with their lovers instead – a common male nightmare in rural Bangladesh. As the above quotation reveals, what is important here, in terms of marital quality, is the willingness of the husband to stand up for women's property rights in defiance of the wishes of village elders.

Joint decision making

I want my son to be educated at least to the intermediate level. But we are poor, and I need my husband to sit down with me and to make a financial plan together. He doesn't share his earnings with me. Raising our child is all up to me. I feel as if I am a single mother.

Nasima (young Muslim woman, Kunjpukhi village)

GENDER AND ECONOMICS IN MUSLIM COMMUNITIES

My daughter was a good student. She wanted to continue her studies. I received a good marriage proposal. But my mind was divided. My husband left the decision entirely up to me. Pressured by village elders, I married her off, a decision that I will regret forever. But if my husband had been together with me on this, things would have been different.

Sakina (middle-aged Muslim woman, Kunjpukhi village)

Eager to pool income, women loanees share information about their microcredit earnings with their husbands. But some men are unwilling to even disclose their income to their wives, let alone share it. As Nasima's words reveal, such asymmetries of information are not beneficial for peace at home; joint decision making, especially in financial matters, is imperative for a stable household economy.

Women do not think it is fair for them to make decisions, especially controversial ones, alone. When I first met Nasreen, Sakina's daughter, in 1999 she was a feisty young woman who told me that she wanted "to study, and study, and study." I was disturbed when, on my return in 2001, I discovered that Nasreen was married and already pregnant with her first child. Sakina told me that a refusal of the marriage proposal, which would have enabled Nasreen to continue her studies, would have violated village norms. Completely on her own in the face of mounting social pressure, she made an unwise decision. Sakina blamed her husband for keeping quiet; she thought he did not support her because he was too cowardly to confront the village elders. Women want to make important decisions together with their husbands because such a team process increases intimacy and sharing. It also provides a bulwark of solidarity for the woman, so, if the decision goes against rural conventions, she does not have to face the onslaught of societal recrimination by herself. As Kabeer's (1998) findings also confirmed, joint decision making does not necessarily indicate male dominance.

Investment in fatherhood

My two girls mean everything to me. Dolly, the elder one, comes first in her class. The younger one, my baby, is good in sports. I want them to study all the way up to a Master's. I will do whatever it takes for them to achieve that.

Shafiqul (husband, Muslim, Kunjpukhi village)

Shafiqul exemplified investment in fatherhood, a key indicator of marital quality. And this is true of high-minded men, fathers who invest in fatherhood. The first time I met him, Shafiqul told me all about how well

GENDER AND ECONOMICS IN MUSLIM COMMUNITIES

his oldest daughter was doing in school. He kept track of her academic prowess. He wanted his girls to study as much as they wanted to, even if this meant all the way to a Master's degree. Women want husbands to show this degree of investment in the family because it unites the couple toward a common purpose, thereby sustaining mutuality.

In contrast, Nasima's husband, Nurul, showed little interest in how his son was doing at school. Apart from an abstract statement that he would like his son to pass matric,[17] he did not share details of his son's current classroom activities nor how he plans for his further education. For him, fatherhood was burdensome, not joyous.

Entrusting the wife with physical mobility

We know that the Grameen Bank is against Islam. Women are going there to show their legs. But we are forced to allow them to stay on as loanees because we are poor. As soon as my household is financially stable, I will ask my wife to quit the bank.

Rezwan (father-in-law, Muslim, Kunjpukhi village)

I don't have to get his [my husband's] permission before I leave the house. But other husbands want reasons, and if their wives leave, they will not take them back. Some husbands are not open to reason.

Shefali (wife, Muslim, Kunjpukhi village)

Women's increased social and physical mobility as a result of their microcredit activities is a major source of marital conflict. In a show of temper, Rezwan made a crude gesture as he talked, in the focus group, lifting up his *lungi* (sarong worn by male villagers) to show how women were violating purdah, and therefore Islam, by exhibiting their bodies (legs are considered sexy) in the Grameen Bank office. He felt that his wife's entrepreneurial activities were making her (and women, in general) *ugroponthi* and therefore not a good Muslim wife. Rezwan looked forward to the day when he would force his wife to quit the Grameen Bank and revert to the "Islamic way of life."

But, as Shefali's quotation reveals, women feel this is unreasonable and shows a lack of trust in them. Women argue that they leave the *bari* (household) to work because of *peter jala* (fire in the belly or hunger), not to have affairs with Grameen Bank staff, which is a common accusation. They know that it is through their efforts that the material standards of the entire household have improved, and they want to be respected for this. Women make a distinction between informing their husbands of their whereabouts and having to obtain prior permission. Requiring prior

GENDER AND ECONOMICS IN MUSLIM COMMUNITIES

permission to work is seen as an expression of lack of trust between the couple and, therefore, an indication of poor marital quality.

Commitment to termination of domestic violence

When the children did not want to study, he used to get angry. He would say, "I work hard to earn money; why don't children study?" Then he would take it out on me. He would say, "Your sons, your daughters, they don't listen to me." He could not get at them, so he beat me.

Aleya (mother-in-law, Muslim, Kunjpukhi village)

I always ask myself , "Allah, what happened? What has happened to my life? Why did my father get me married? Why did I have to suffer this fire?" My heart was always sobbing. I was beaten by everybody. But now I have no tears left. I know that I have to stick it out and maybe one day, my parents-in-law will value me.

Samina (daughter-in-law, Muslim, Kunjpukhi village)

Aleya describes a household of extreme violence. Abused by her husband, Rezwan, she in turn, beat Samina, her daughter-in-law, and often incited her husband and son to do so, generating a continuous cycle of violence. But women know that a battle-torn household will ultimately spiral downward into poverty, and children will not do well in their studies. Given her husband's violent nature, Aleya worried about her children's future.

Despite microcredit, daughters-in-law like Samina, who came from a poorer family that did not live close by, remain vulnerable. Natal ties were weak: Samina's mother had died, and she was able to visit her father only infrequently. Rural women in such marriages feel they have nowhere else to go. "We have a *baper bari* and a *shoshur bari* (father-in-law's home), but no *bari* of our own," said one woman interviewee.[18] Yet, when further questioned, women responded that they did not want to leave because it would be breaking the karmic cycle. They want the violence to stop; they want a happy marriage and peace at home.

Using the Prophet as role model

Sultana (middle-aged Muslim woman, Kunjpukhi village):

In our *shariat* [Islam], women went out – the Prophet's daughter, Fatima, went to war [beside him], on a horse. How did they do it [get out of the home]? If they can do it, we have the right to do it, too.

GENDER AND ECONOMICS IN MUSLIM COMMUNITIES

Kareem (male village elder, Kunjpukhi village):

> You don't have the right to say one word, not one word! You have talked about the Prophet's daughter, Fatima. Who are you? Are you Fatima? Can you do what she has done? You answer my question.

Sultana:

> Can you do what the Prophet has done? It's really you men who are giving us problems. But our Prophet was so different. Can you be like him? The Prophet gave his wife equal rights, in public! Why can't we get equal rights? Now you answer my question.

Sharecropper women love and revere the Prophet. This spirited exchange, which took place in a focus group about equal pay for equal work, illustrates that they see his relationships with his women relatives as exemplary, especially as a model for husbands. Women recount stories about his life and the Hadith (sayings of the Prophet), such as, "heaven lies at the feet of the mother (*mayer paye behest*)" to counter those men who state that it lies at the feet of the husband. The Prophet is central to the feminist grassroots spirituality that serves as the collective ideology of Muslim sharecropper women's struggle for gender justice (Ahmed 2008a).[19] The use of the Prophet as a role model also illustrates that sharecropper grassroots women activists, who are involved in entrepreneurial activities, envision their practices as completely aligned with the Quran and the Hadith. It is as good Muslim wives that they ask their husbands to be as compassionate as the Prophet.

CONCLUSION

Peace in the household is central to the moral economy of rural society in Bangladesh. Low-income village women believe high marital quality leads to peace in the household. Based on my long-term ethnographic study in rural Bangladesh, I have identified the following eight local measures of marital quality: respect for women's reproductive labor; understanding a wife's need to rest; willingness to put property in wife's name; joint decision making; investment in fatherhood; entrusting a wife with physical mobility; commitment to termination of domestic violence; and using the Prophet as role model. These measures, in fact, describe the processes of everyday love and intimacy that underlie household well-being outcomes, as a whole and without which, I argue, our understanding of intrahousehold gender relations would be incomplete.

GENDER AND ECONOMICS IN MUSLIM COMMUNITIES

Feminist economists have long argued that the moral economy of the household should be included within the realm of economic theory (Folbre 1986b). Marriage as structure and marriage as togetherness need to be investigated as two interlinked, yet discrete, areas of inquiry. Marital quality needs to be conceptualized as central to a theory of the moral economy of the household, and the above-mentioned measures, explicit and specific as they are, illustrate how marital quality can be a feminist economics project. Together, they lead to peace in the household, a local vision that connects the moral with the rational, the material with the spiritual, and marital quality with women's agency in the household and in the community. Wives who work outside the home have more responsibility for the household than their husbands, and divorce, the exit option, has serious socioeconomic implications for women.[20] Clearly, theories of togetherness impact women's agency, the household economy, and the quality of community life all over the world.

Poor women's visions of intrahousehold relations are based on the axis of peace, not on the calculus of bargaining. To them, marriage is neither a zero sum game wherein one individual has to lose in order for the other to win, nor a nonzero sum game in which winnings are equally divided through cooperation with their husbands. Sharecropper women do not want power as much as love, and they do not view good exit options as the desired outcome. Instead, they want gender relations in the household to be framed by mutual altruism with peace in the household as the ultimate goal. Do the assumptions of the bargaining model accurately illuminate the path to peace and love? The causal arrow from increased resources to better threat points to good exit options for women is far too simple for an analysis of marital quality, which, as the village women with whom I lived unequivocally state, also depends on the husband's behavior and practices.

The peace-in-the-household model emphasizes the transformation of oppressive masculinity. Women insist that the problem of gender inequality also resides in men and therefore, they must also change. As I argue elsewhere (Ahmed 2003, 2008a, 2008b), if oppressive notions of masculinity are also defined as a major obstacle to gender empowerment, then ways in which they can be transformed will become an investigative arena for gender and development scholars. Furthermore, ways in which high-minded men, like Shafiqul, can be supported will become a program strategy for development organizations. Such an impetus would respond to sharecropper women's wishes. They do not want to be less altruistic, as implied by Folbre (1996a)[21]; instead they want their husbands to become more altruistic. To summarize, the local peace-in-the household model indicates that what poor women want is not quite the same thing as what we, gender and development "experts," think they should want.

GENDER AND ECONOMICS IN MUSLIM COMMUNITIES

Clearly, a major paradigm shift is required to construct marital quality as a feminist economics project. It is not simply a matter of asking different questions, nor even of gathering primary data. More profoundly, the underlying framework that guides inquiry itself needs to shift: we need to change our assumptions of what knowledge is and where its locus lies. Feminist economists have presented the game-theoretic bargaining model as an alternative to Becker's altruistic head-of-the-household theory. It can legitimately be asked whether we have replaced one quantitative framework, which has incorrect qualitative assumptions as its basis, with yet another, which does not place women's narratives at its core. In this contribution, I have argued that we need to listen to local voices in order to learn from them. The subaltern, not Nash, is the counterpoint to Becker, and she needs to speak in feminist economic theories of the household.

ACKNOWLEDGMENTS

I shall always be indebted to the sharecropper men and women who shared their lives with me and from whom I learned so much. I am grateful to Dr. Farida Khan for her inspiration, encouragement, and support. This study was made possible by the financial support of the American Institute of Bangladesh Studies.

GENDER AND ECONOMICS IN MUSLIM COMMUNITIES

NOTES

1. I use the terms "togetherness" and "marital quality" interchangeably throughout the study. I do the same with marriage and household. Also, in this study intrahousehold relations refer exclusively to the marital relationship.

2. Although village women make profits from their entrepreneurial activities and have their own bank accounts, they do not see this income as exclusively their own. To them, the very purpose of earning money is to share it within the household, and both the husband and the wife must be willing to do so. The moral economy of rural society is based on ways in which social status is derived from the communal sharing of income, not the individual accumulation of wealth. Village women link the moral economy of the household to that of society, at large, in specific ways (for further details, see Ahmed [2003]).

3. For an excellent expose of what economists term as "quantitative" data, and how it, invariably, has an underlying qualitative narrative, see Strassmann (1997).

4. See Naila Kabeer, Lopita Huq, and Simeen Mahmud (2014) for a contrasting analysis of different countries within South Asia.

5. The enrollment of girls in secondary schools has increased over sevenfold since 1980 (United Nations Educational, Scientific and Cultural Organization [UNESCO] 2012).

6. Although the religious right utilizes patriarchal Islam as a convenient tool to oppress women, patriarchal ideology also exists independently of religious interpretations.

7. Hinduism prescribes four stages of life necessary to maintain this cosmic order: *brahmacarya* (celibate studenthood); *shongshari* (householder); *sannyasin* (ascetic); and *vanaprasth* (forest dweller).

8. Collins (2000) makes it clear that this is not the same thing as Michel Foucault's naive knowledge (1980), which owes its existence to harsh opposing forces and is incapable of unanimity.

9. Collins (2000) analyzes Black women's voices and experiences as both reflecting oppression and resistance.

10. Scheduled castes are the lowest castes in India.

11. Rishi are known as Dalit in India.

12. The names of the interviewees and NGO have been changed to ensure confidentiality.

13. I did notice changes, but since this article focuses on Muslim families, such an analysis will be the subject of another publication. I have applied for a grant that will enable me to conduct follow-up interviews of the Muslim families, including those analyzed in this contribution. (For an excellent analysis of insider/outsider identities of researchers in a Muslim society, see Altorki and Solh [1988]).

14. The nature of the relationship with the in-laws and the proximity of the natal home, *inter alia*, impact marital quality, but here I focus on the relationship with the husband.

15. For example, Aleya interrupted a NGO meeting that ran over time, stating that she had to leave to prepare lunch, otherwise she would be beaten by her husband (*mar khabo*).

16. My findings revealed that few husbands allowed their wives to reach the mature borrower stage, which makes them eligible for housing loans. Forced to drop out by her husband, one such loanee quit the Grameen Bank in tears (Ahmed 2008b).

17. Matric is a national exam taken after Class 10.

18. With the support of collectives, such women take their husbands to NGO-mediated *shalish*, which also has women jurors (Ahmed 2013).

19. For a detailed analysis of this spirituality known as *buddhi* (wisdom), see Ahmed (2008a).

20. In her US-based study, Susan Moller Okin found that husbands of predominantly wage-working wives, on average, did about two minutes more work than those with

GENDER AND ECONOMICS IN MUSLIM COMMUNITIES

stay-at-home wives – "hardly enough time to prepare a soft-boiled egg!" (2008: 609). She argues that husbands of working wives simply did not want to do their share of household work, and wives could not use their earning power to convince them to do so for complex socioeconomic reasons.

[21] Subsequently, Folbre does write about the involvement of fathers (England and Folbre 2002). But the US-based study focuses on the impact of bargaining power and father involvement, not on martial quality and processes of everyday reciprocity. As they emphatically state, their analytic framework is based on the bargaining model; it is not derived from the men and women for whom they prescribe policy recommendations.

REFERENCES

Agarwal, Bina. 1997. "Bargaining and Gender Relations Within and Beyond the Household." *Feminist Economics* 3(1): 1–51.

————. 1994. *A Field of One's Own: Gender and Land Rights in South Asia.* Cambridge: Cambridge University Press.

Ahmed, Fauzia E. 2003. "Low-Income Progressive Men: Microcredit, Gender Empowerment, and the Redefinition of Manhood in Rural Bangladesh." PhD diss., Brandeis University.

————. 2008a. "Hidden Opportunities: Islam, Masculinity and Poverty Alleviation." *International Journal of Feminist Politics* 10(4): 542–62.

————. 2008b. "Microcredit, Men, and Masculinity." *National Women's Studies Association (NWSA) Journal* 20(2): 122–55.

————. 2013. "The Compassionate Courtroom: Feminist Governance, Discourse, and Islam in a Shalish." *Feminist Formations* 25(1): 157–83.

Altorki, Soraya and Camillia Fawzi El-Solh, eds. 1998. *Arab Women in the Field: Studying Your Own Society.* Syracuse, NY: Syracuse University Press.

Bates, Lisa M., Sidney Ruth Schuler, Farzana Islam, and Mohammed Khairul Islam. 2004. "Socioeconomic Factors and Processes Associated with Domestic Violence in Rural Bangladesh." *International Family Planning Perspectives* 30(4): 190–9.

Becker, Gary. 1991. *A Treatise on the Family,* 2nd ed. Cambridge: Harvard University Press.

Berik, Günseli. 1997. "The Need for Crossing the Method Boundaries in Economics Research." *Feminist Economics* 3(2): 121–5.

Bittman, Michael, Paula England, Liana Sayer, Nancy Folbre, and George Matheson. 2003. "When Does Gender Trump Money? Bargaining and Time in Housework." *American Journal of Sociology* 109(1): 186–214.

Bruner, Edward M. 1984. "Introduction: The Opening Up of Anthropology." In *Text Play and Story: The Construction and Reconstruction of Self and Society,* edited by Stuart Plattner and Edward M. Bruner, 1–18. Washington, DC: American Ethnological Society.

Collins, Patricia Hill. 2000. *Black Feminist Thought.* New York: Routledge.

Daily Star. 2010. "Family Violence Law: Six Month Jail for Offenders." October 6.

England, Paula and Nancy Folbre. 2002. "Involving Dads: Parental Bargaining and Family Well-Being." In *Handbook of Father Involvement: Multidisciplinary Perspectives,* edited by Catherine S. Tamis Le-Monda and Natasha Cabrera, 387–409. Mahwah, NJ: Lawrence Erlbaum Associates.

Folbre, Nancy. 1986a. "Hearts and Spades: Paradigms of Household Economics." *World Development* 14(2): 245–55.

————. 1986b. "Cleaning House: New Perspectives on Households and Economic Development." *Journal of Development Economics* 22(1): 5–40.

GENDER AND ECONOMICS IN MUSLIM COMMUNITIES

Foucault, Michel. 1980. *Power–Knowledge: Selected Interviews and Other Writings*, 1972–1977. Edited by Colin Gordon. Great Britain: Haweater Press Ltd.

Goetz, Anne Marie and Rina Sen Gupta. 1996. "Who Takes Credit? Gender, Power, and Control over Loan Use in Rural Credit Programmes in Bangladesh." *World Development* 24(1): 45–63.

Gramsci, Antoni. 1971. *Selections from the Prison Notebooks*. Edited and translated by Quintin Hoare and Geoffrey Nowell Smith. New York: International Publishers Co.

Hashemi, Syed M., Sidney Ruth Schuler, and Ann P. Riley. 1996. "Rural Credit Programmes and Women's Empowerment in Bangladesh." *World Development* 24(4): 635–53.

Hertz, Rosanna, ed. 1997. *Reflexivity and Voice*. Thousand Oaks, CA: SAGE.

Imai, Katushi S. and Md. Shafiqul Azam. 2012. "Does Microfinance Reduce Poverty in Bangladesh? New Evidence from Household Data." *Journal of Development Studies* 48(5): 633–53.

Kabeer, Naila. 1998. "Money Can't Buy Me Love? Re-evaluating Gender, Credit, and Empowerment in Rural Bangladesh." Discussion Paper 363, Institute of Development Studies University of Sussex. http://www.ids.ac.uk/idspublication/money-can-t-buy-me-love-re-evaluating-gender-credit-and-empowerment-in-rural-bangladesh.

———. 1999. "Resources, Agency, Achievement; Reflections on the Measurements of Women's Empowerment." *Development and Change* 30(3): 435–64.

———. 2001. "Conflict over Credit: Re-Evaluating the Empowerment Potential of Loans to Women in Rural Bangladesh." *World Development* 29(1): 63–84.

Kabeer, Naila, Lopita Huq, and Simeen Mahmud. 2014. "Diverging Stories of 'Missing Women' in South Asia: Is Son Preference Weakening in Bangladesh?" *Feminist Economics* 20(4). doi:10.1080/13545701.2013.857423

Katz, Elizabeth. 1997. "The Intra-Household Economics of Voice and Exit." *Feminist Economics* 3(3): 25–46.

Koenig, Michael A., Saifuddin Ahmed, Mian Bazle Hossain, A. B. M. Khorshed, and Alam Mozumder. 2003. "Women's Status and Domestic Violence in Rural Bangladesh: Individual- and Community-Level Effects." *Demography* 40(2): 269–88.

Lamb, Sarah. 2000. *White Saris and Sweet Mangoes: Aging, Gender, and Body in North India*. Berkeley: University of California Press.

Miles, Matthew B. and A. Michael Huberman. 1994. *Qualitative Data Analysis: An Expanded Sourcebook*, 2nd ed. Thousand Oaks, CA: SAGE.

Nussbaum, Martha and Amartya Sen, eds. 1993. *The Quality of Life*. Oxford: Clarendon Press.

Okin, Susan Moller. 2008. "Vulnerability by Marriage." In *The Feminist Philosophy Reader*, edited by Alison Bailey and Chris Cuomo, 600–22. Boston: McGraw-Hill.

———. 2004. "Women, Work and Empowerment in a Global Era." *IDS Bulletin – Institute of Development Studies* 35(4): 117–20.

Pearson, Ruth. 2007. "Reassessing Paid Work and Women's Employment: Lessons from the Global Economy." In *Feminisms in Development: Contradictions, Contestations and Challenges*, edited by Andrea Cornwall, Elisabeth Harrison, and Ann Whitehead, 201–13. London: Zed Books.

Phipps, Shelley, Peter Burton, and Lars Osberg. 2001. "Time as a Source of Inequality Within Marriage: Are Husbands More Satisfied with Time for Themselves than Their Wives?" *Feminist Economics* 7(2): 1–21.

Raheja, Gloria Goodwin and Ann Grodzins Gold. 1994. *Listen to the Heron's Words: Reimagining Gender and Kinship in North India*. Berkeley: University of California Press.

Rahman, Aminur. 1999. *Women and Microcredit in Rural Bangladesh: An Anthropological Study of the Realities and Rhetoric of the Grameen Bank*. Boulder, CO: Westview Press.

GENDER AND ECONOMICS IN MUSLIM COMMUNITIES

Rankin, Katherine N. 2002. "Social Capital, Microfinance, and the Politics of Development." *Feminist Economics* 8(1): 1–24.

Rozario, Santi. 2004. *Purity and Communal Boundaries: Women and Social Change in a Bangladeshi Village.* Dhaka: The University Press Limited.

Sandhya, Shaifali. 2009. "The Social Context of Marital Happiness in Urban Indian Couples: Interplay of Intimacy and Conflict." *Journal of Marital and Family Therapy* 35(1): 74–96.

van Schendel, Willem. 2009. *A History of Bangladesh.* Cambridge: Cambridge University Press.

Schuler, Sidney Ruth, Lisa M. Bates, and Farzana Islam. 2008. "Women's Rights, Domestic Violence and Recourse Seeking in Rural Bangladesh." *Violence Against Women* 14(3): 326–45.

Sen, Amartya K. 1987. "Gender and Cooperative Conflicts." Working Paper 18, World Institute for Development Economics Research, Helsinki.

———. 1990. "Gender and Cooperative Conflicts." In *Persistent Inequalities: Women and World Development*, edited by Irene Tinker, 123–49. New York: Oxford University Press.

Shehabuddin, Elora. 1999. "Contesting the Illicit: The Politics of Fatwas in Bangladesh." *Signs: Journal of Women in Culture and Society* 24(4): 1011–44.

———. 2008. *Reshaping the Holy: Democracy, Development, and Muslim Women in Bangladesh.* New York: Columbia University Press.

Sobhan, Salma. 1994. "National Identity, Fundamentalism and the Women's Movement in Bangladesh." In *Gender and National Identity: Women and Politics in Muslim Societies*, edited by Valentine Moghadam, 63–80. Helsinki: United Nations University World Institute for Development Economics Research (WIDER).

Strassmann, Diana. 1997. "Editorial: Expanding the Methodological Boundaries of Economics." *Feminist Economics* 3(2): vii–ix.

Strauss, Anselm and Juliet Corbin. 1998. *Basics of Qualitative Research: Techniques and Procedures for Developing Grounded Theory*, 2nd ed. London: SAGE.

United Nations Educational, Scientific and Cultural Organization (UNESCO). 2012. *Country Programming Report for Bangladesh 2012–2016.* Dhaka, Bangladesh: UNESCO Office.

World Bank. 2014a. "Fertility Rate, Total (Births per Woman)." http://data.worldbank.org/indicator/SP.DYN.TFRT.IN.

———. 2014b. "Ratio of female to male primary enrollment (percent)." http://data.worldbank.org/indicator/SE.ENR.PRIM.FM.ZS.

———. 2014c. "Ratio of female to male secondary enrollment (percent)." http://data.worldbank.org/indicator/SE.ENR.SECO.FM.ZS.

———. 2014d. "Maternal Mortality Ratio (Modeled Estimate, per 100,000 live births)." http://data.worldbank.org/indicator/SH.STA.MMRT.

"JUST LIKE PROPHET MOHAMMAD PREACHED": LABOR, PIETY, AND CHARITY IN CONTEMPORARY TURKEY

Damla Isik

ABSTRACT

Based on research conducted in Konya, Istanbul, Afyon, Izmir, Manisa, and Denizli, Turkey, in 2004–9, this contribution documents how gendered individual religious practices are conjoined to transnational business competition, changing labor conditions, and broader projects of economic transformation. The study focuses on the carpet-weaving and textile industries and civil society organizations in Turkey, investigating the ways in which charitable giving, pious practice, and local labor conditions create uniquely complex ways in which socioeconomic policies, processes, and commitments affect gendered lives. What is witnessed in weaving neighborhoods, civil society organizations, and the transnational linkages of production–consumption is neither a wholesale translation of Weberian capitalism nor a strict implementation of Islamic texts and practices. It is a unique Turkish assemblage of faith, religious practice, charitable giving, and flexibility of labor. This contribution calls for feminist researchers to empirically examine "pious economies" – that is, the linkages between pious practice and economic behavior.

During my second visit to her home in Konya, which, as she told me, was always "under construction," Meloş took me to her small kitchen, one of the four rooms attached to the main rectangular entertaining/dining area, via a wooden door.[1] The kitchen had an opening to an undersized balcony with a larger backyard. On one side was the small counter space, which itself was not fully finished – half of it in white tile, the rest in gray concrete waiting to be tiled. The kitchen had a sink and a portable gas burner that Meloş occasionally carried to the entertainment/dining area to cook. Several

GENDER AND ECONOMICS IN MUSLIM COMMUNITIES

empty and full plastic containers were stored under a small table with two chairs. I noticed the lack of a refrigerator immediately, which resulted in the grand tour of the garden and the balcony where she was storing her vegetables. She told me that they had to consume everything quickly before things went bad. "I buy only so much because we do not still have a fridge. Yet, God willing, we will get one soon I hope."

Meloş had written to the Deniz Feneri Aid and Solidarity Association (DF), a charitable nongovernmental organization (NGO), requesting a refrigerator and was waiting for their reply; she was also thinking of filing for some monetary help through the organization during the winter. Meloş's husband was a construction worker who was employed during summers but had a hard time finding employment during winter. Meloş herself wove carpets, but, unknown to the carpet manufacturer who employed her, she also occasionally worked as a cleaning lady to make some extra money to support her husband and her two daughters, ages 10 and 6. The family received help from the municipality during winter; the neighborhood *muhtar* had designated them as suitable for receiving coal for heating.[2] Additionally, she would receive various kinds of help from neighbors throughout the year, such as food and clothing, especially during Ramadan. She also frequented the *sohbets* (religious gatherings) at her neighborhood regularly with other weavers from the neighborhood.[3]

The mixed economy of charity, semiformal,[4] and informal work that Meloş participated in points to the relevance of civil society organizations, especially charitable associations and *vakfs* (foundations), in the everyday lives of those who struggle with poverty and precariousness of jobs. Meloş was anything but a victim to her circumstances. She was flexible as a worker and adept at searching for additional options for her family; she saw her religious beliefs, duties, and obligations as closely intertwined with the kinds of work she preferred to do. This was not solely the case with Meloş; many women I met and talked to in Istanbul, Izmir, and Denizli also did not see economic choices and pious conduct as separate from each other. In many ways, each was a reflection of the other.

What is witnessed in weaving neighborhoods, in civil society organizations, and in transnational linkages of production–consumption in Turkey is neither a wholesale translation of Weberian capitalism nor a strict implementation of Islamic texts and practices. It is an assemblage of pious conduct, charitable giving, and flexibility of labor in which both men and women devise their own strategies to improve their conditions through forming affective relationships that are always local and never stable, rather than relying on globalized Islamist or secularist explanations of their situations.[5]

Recent research has pointed out how, challenged by ongoing neoliberalization and globalization, Muslim women and men throughout

GENDER AND ECONOMICS IN MUSLIM COMMUNITIES

the world are refashioning their labor in various public, institutional, and work spaces, including developmental NGOs in Africa and in Bangladesh (Erica Bornstein 2005; Elora Shehabuddin 2008), mosque participation in Cairo (Saba Mahmood 2005), political parties in Turkey (Jenny White 2002), urban spaces in Beirut (Lara Deeb 2006), steel factories in Indonesia (Daromir Rudnyckyj 2009, 2010), as acts of piety. Importantly, Rudnyckyj (2010) reminds us that this dual emphasis on both material and spiritual progress in performance of piety and everyday life is not uniquely Islamic. Weber's discussion of the recursiveness of Protestant ideas of predestination and everyday practice of work is a working example of how, regardless of belief system, what was most relevant was the way that the "moral conduct of the average man was thus deprived of its planless and unsystematic character and subjected to a consistent method for conduct as a whole" (Max Weber 1905/1990: 117).

Read closely, Weber's emphasis is not solely on the beliefs of devotees inspiring a specific mode of capitalist conduct; he focuses on the formation of disciplinary individuals as the most important strategic shift that enabled capitalist transfiguration of economic life. This emphasis on everyday conduct as a form of cultivating individual discipline frames my research – globalization and neoliberalization are not abstract concepts imported or exported wholesale; they are ubiquitous, daily, quotidian assemblages of organization and governance of proper conduct. My goal is to explore the nexus of proper conduct framed by charitable giving, daily work, and economic uncertainties. In doing so, I underscore the inseparability of pious conduct and economic globalization and neoliberalization that shape conservative women's and men's lives in contemporary Turkey.

A BRIEF NOTE ON METHODS

Based on ethnographic fieldwork, interviews, and archival research conducted in Konya, Denizli, Afyon, Izmir, and Istanbul, Turkey in the years of 2004–5 and the summers of 2007–9, this contribution specifically focuses on the carpet-weaving and textile industries and charitable civil society organizations in Turkey. I discuss the methodology for this ongoing research in detail elsewhere (Damla Isik 2008, 2010); the multi-sited ethnography consisted of several visits to weavers' homes in Konya, Afyon, and Izmir. I talked to countless women and girls in the process; I specifically revisited the homes of forty-one weavers in Konya, Turkey in 2004–5 as part of my dissertation fieldwork. I spent time at these women's homes, wove with them, helped in chores, and our conversations largely happened during the process of weaving and during breaks throughout the day. I also interviewed eight of the then eleven carpet exporters who had transnational ties to

214

GENDER AND ECONOMICS IN MUSLIM COMMUNITIES

various stores, collectors, and individual clients in the United States, Europe, and Saudi Arabia. The nature of the weaving industry was such that the weavers were exclusively women, while the exporters and manufacturers were men. I only met one exporter in Istanbul who was a woman. Since women weavers in Konya worked from home, and since men were largely absent during the day, most of my conversations with women happened exclusively in women's company.

This research relies on qualitative research; hence, I rarely, if ever, used structured interviews, most of my interviews taking place while the women and I were talking casually or while the women were weaving. I shadowed a carpet manufacturer as he visited the homes of women, which allowed me to meet weavers whom I later visited at their homes. They were not chosen as a representative sample, or for some other specific reason, other than the fact that they worked as weavers on a regular basis. No other sampling strategies were used. My research relied on participant observation and unstructured interviews. Feminist economists have noted how typical conceptions of economics as a positive science do not hold, hence no researcher can avoid being influenced by the belief system she or he occupies (Julie A. Nelson 1995; Diana L. Strassmann 1997); hence, economic research "cannot escape being inherently qualitative, regardless of how it is labeled" (Strassmann 1997: viii). Qualitative research highlights the social context of economic transactions as crucial to understanding the transaction itself. Knowledge is "inextricably linked to the lives of its producers and the circumstances of its production" (Diana L. Strassmann 1994: 155), and economic knowledge – and, I would note, practice – is no exception. Feminist economists have proven, time and time again, that econometric methods are insufficient to answer some context-based questions that inevitably play a large role in economic transactions (Günseli Berik 1997; Michele C. Pujol 1997; Jennifer C. Olmsted 1997; Simel Esim 1997). As Berik (1997) details, qualitative research is helpful in allowing more creative conceptualizing and measurement of economic processes, and a bias against qualitative research within the context of feminist economics may lead "economists to impugn alternative or qualitative methods as 'unscientific' and impose disciplinary pressures to conform to the standard empirical practice ... which isolates economics from other social sciences" (122). In my case, understanding the contours of pious and economic practice necessitated long-term fieldwork and a more qualitative lens.

Due to the conservative nature of Konya, I was especially careful not to stay at the homes of weavers, to avoid any potential gossip. I met most of the male young adults and children as they came home from school or came by to have lunch or a snack; however, I did not get to meet all of the women's husbands. Almost all of the men of the households I visited did not have a permanent job or were jobless; yet, despite this fact, they chose to frequent coffee houses instead of staying at home. As several women told me, home was a "woman's place"; besides, this gave the women the opportunity to be free of the controlling gaze of men – they felt more comfortable in their own space, which enabled me to have longer conversations and observe the daily routine of the weavers uninterrupted.

Initially, I was concentrating on labor politics and working conditions; however, during this research I encountered several women who were also receiving aid from various charitable institutions. I was not able to delve deeper into the meanings and practices of charity during my dissertation project, but my observations in the field prompted me to start a related research project concentrating on conservative civil society organizations and charitable work. This research is ongoing. During this second phase, I frequented meetings, gatherings, and various poverty alleviation and charitable projects of three well-known conservative charitable civil society organizations: the Deniz Feneri Aid and Solidarity Association (DF), the Foundation for Human Rights and Freedom and Humanitarian Relief (IHH), and Istanbul International Brotherhood and Solidarity Association (IBS) in Izmir and Istanbul, Turkey.

I participated as a volunteer, conducted structured and unstructured interviews, and had frequent casual conversations with several volunteers and employees; I also met and talked with several aid recipients. Once again, most of my interviews, talks, and conversations were unstructured and resulted from concerns that arose during informal conversations and volunteer work. Some of the conversations and interviews took place at the charitable organizations, others at the homes of volunteers, and others during focus group interviews arranged by the organizations themselves. These focus group interviews allowed me to obtain volunteers' contact information and revisit them later in their own homes, or meet them in coffee shops, to continue our conversation. Most of these exchanges were casual and unofficial in nature, and several interesting conversations took place while all of us were working as volunteers preparing aid packages, visiting aid recipients and applicants, entering data into computers, and reading and cataloging aid applications. I have continued to revisit these organizations regularly during subsequent summer fieldwork.

My research evolved largely as a result of what I encountered in the field and what the women I talked to considered as relevant in their lives. What started out as a research project on labor politics and rights turned into more detailed research on the interconnected nature of pious conduct, economic circumstances, and charitable giving/receiving. Work becomes a vehicle through which women's piety is most clearly brought into the public realm. Pious conduct, in turn, induces neither blind acceptance nor spontaneous resistance to the effects of ongoing globalization and neoliberalism. Rather, it creates shifting assemblages through and within which women advance their own interests in emerging pious economies.

GENDER AND ECONOMICS IN MUSLIM COMMUNITIES

RETHINKING ECONOMY AND RELIGION:
PIOUS ECONOMIES

The idea that public and private boundaries are insufficient to understand human relationships is by no means novel. Both economy and religion, as particular spheres of existence and "problems" of social science research, are rooted in the distinction of the public and the private spheres, which is crucial to the functioning of the secular liberal understanding of economic and political culture (Hannah Arendt 1958/1998; Talal Asad 2003; Brian Silverstein 2008). This gendered distinction, relegating women to the private sphere as keepers of tradition while men occupy the public sphere of economics as breadwinners, has been effectively foregrounded and criticized by several feminist researchers. This contribution is grounded in the formative work of feminist researchers who investigated women's agency and turned a critical eye on liberal economic theory. These researchers demystified the political distinction of the public and the private through empirically grounded studies of local labor politics and working conditions that pointed to the existence of stark power inequalities within the context of global capitalism (Maria Mies 1982; Annette Fuentes and Barbara Ehrenreich 1983; Daisy Dwyer and Judith Bruce 1988; Lourdes Benería and Shelley Feldman 1992).[6]

Furthermore, more recent research on globalization has pointed out that the economic realm was not an autonomous and removed space of production, exchange, and consumption, but needed to be analyzed as historically and contextually specific assemblages that produced specific types of subjects while at the same time giving meaning to their practices (Michel Callon 1998; Timothy Mitchell 2002, 2005; Aihwa Ong and Stephen Collier 2005). The experiences of women weavers described here remind us of the fact that no economic transactions and relations can be conceptualized apart from the moral makeup and constraints of society, regardless of whether such transactions and relations are profitable. The ideal of a self-regulating economy for economy's sake is indeed a "stark utopia" (Karl Polanyi 1944: 3–4). Polanyi's (1944) description of societies existing before the advance of a self-regulating market, which relied heavily on reciprocity and non-maximizing behavior, can be applied to contemporary societies as well (Lourdes Benería 2000: 12). In fact, feminist research has been central in going against the rational economic man and highlighting the complexities of economic behavior; agents may pursue their self-interest in ways that are not so neatly defined by economic rationality, leading to complex assemblages of behavior from competition to solidarity or selfishness to altruism (Jane Guyer 1980; Nancy Folbre 1994, 2000; Lourdes Benería 2003). Once again, feminist research has pointed out that traditional self-interested models and static economic models cannot adequately explain economic practice as a social interaction in which

217

GENDER AND ECONOMICS IN MUSLIM COMMUNITIES

"collective action and empathetic, connected economic decision-making are observed" (Stephanie Seguino, Thomas Stevens, and Mark Lutz 1996: 200).

Despite the fact that feminist theories of the economy were crucially important in situating the economic sphere within the context of relations and communities, the danger still remained of overemphasizing economic relations and practices as somehow separate, categorically exploitative, and less genuine than familial, kin, and religious affiliations and practices (Isik 2008). As Patricia Fernandez-Kelly and Diane Wolf (2001) have pointed out, the relentless concentration on exploitation in feminist theory and research without bringing in what workers experienced faces the danger of providing one-dimensional views of women as victims of global capital. Indeed, some feminist research emphasized how working conditions and labor relationships had contradictory results and meanings for women, who might benefit or lose out to economic liberalization and globalization (Diane Wolf 1992; Carla Freeman 2000; Johanna Lessinger 2002). However, despite this concern over specificity, feminist research on global capitalism and neoliberalism has been mostly silent when it comes to the relevance of local understandings of piety and pious conduct for economic transactions and relationships and vice versa.

The contemporary revival of religion and the rise in religious sentiment across the world has been studied in social science literature.[7] Feminist research also analyzed religious practices by women as varied forms of resistance to patriarchy, globalization, and capitalist discipline within the factory space (Aihwa Ong 1987; Janice Boddy 1990). Additionally, such practices are seen to help fashion subjects who give value to the communal and the familial sentiments and dependencies that center on "relational selves" (Suad Joseph 1999) rather than the neoliberal, individualistic self (White 2002; Mahmood 2005). In pious economies, such as the one in which Meloş participated, the ethos of reciprocity and patron–client relationships of a "moral economy" is wedded to the ethos of individual accountability to God. Neoliberalization is not something to be resisted, or "the other" of the communal and the relational; nor can it be understood as a direct importation of Western ideals of individualism. It is the ongoing inculcation of dispositions conducive to both pious practice and productive labor within institutional and private spaces; Meloş's example thus prompts us to look critically at how such inculcation is realized.

Relatively few feminist studies examine the ways in which economic and pious conduct simultaneously give meaning and constitute each other in specific locales, which may mean that both communal and individualistic sentiments could be present in how subjects react to specific circumstances (Nickola Pazderic 2004; Bornstein 2005; Peter Cahn 2008; Rudnyckyj 2009, 2010). This is also the case with studies on Turkey (White 2002; Kimberly Hart 2007). Similarly, longer volumes that specifically focus on globalization have very few or no discussions of women's understanding of piety and pious

GENDER AND ECONOMICS IN MUSLIM COMMUNITIES

conduct, and they do not specifically analyze the interconnected nature of pious conduct and economic behavior (Marianne H. Marchand and Anne Sisson Runyan 2000; Jonathan Xavier Inda and Renato Rosaldo 2002; Ong and Collier 2005; Tine Davids and Francien van Driel 2005; Ann Kingsolver and Nandini Gunewardena 2007). Yet for women like Meloş, any economic transaction needs to be firmly situated in the pious conduct of the individual. Meloş's example prompts us to go beyond the dichotomies of communal–familial/individual to think seriously about the interconnections between piety, economy, charity, family life, and the individual as they give meaning to each other within the context of neoliberalization and globalization.

New research shows how such interconnections take shape in institutional spaces such as NGOs (Shehabuddin 2008) and factories (Rudnyckyj 2010). This work portrays how globalization is not an imported given, but rather constitutes individually and communally developed and nurtured ethical conduct, allowing globalization to be seen as a reflexive continual process. In a similar vein, while investigating public piety in Shi'i Lebanon, Deeb notes how piety and modernity reshape each other and observes "pious modern" as "an ethos, a way of being in the world, and a self-presentation" (2006: 228). I would add to this that the distinction between economic practices determined by autonomous structures versus ideologies determined by spiritual belief systems that are disconnected from disciplinary practices is difficult to sustain when one encounters women such as Meloş. This observation is also not novel,[8] but it can be easily forgotten when we try to make sense of pious conduct and economic choices as separate from each other (Katherine E. Browne 2008).

As Meloş juggled various different ways of keeping her family afloat, she also invested in her self-development as a pious Muslim. In Turkey's neoliberalizing economy and social life, conservative women like Meloş increasingly faced the conundrums of working to make a living and performing piety. Opportunities such as working from home, taking part in religious gatherings, and being charitable with time and money created what I term "pious economies" – spaces of belonging that merge economic and pious conduct, simultaneously giving meaning to piety and economy. Muslim pious practice and religious comportment may not be in conflict with modernity and globalization, as some have claimed (Samuel Huntington 1996); however, this emphasis on the compatibility of communal and individual actions and preferences of pious selves within the context of a globalizing capitalist world does not mean instant equality and harmony. In fact, these linkages may end up facilitating capitalist exploitation. Meloş's circumstances caution us to be critical of such celebratory representations. I want to inspire reflection on how economic calculations and uncertainties that are a result of ongoing neoliberalization and globalization penetrate into diverse domains of human life and the complex results of such penetrations.

GENDER AND ECONOMICS IN MUSLIM COMMUNITIES

SITUATING PIOUS WOMEN: NEOLIBERALISM AND GLOBALIZATION IN TURKEY

The choices Meloş made when it came to being part of the informal economy were closely intertwined with one of the problems that is a result of ongoing neoliberalization since the 1980s. During my fieldwork in Turkey, regardless of place and working conditions, women's number one demand of the Turkish government and their desire for their families was availability of job opportunities for the men in the family, and their number one complaint was the lack of initiative and drive that some men showed in seeking jobs. The choices Meloş made and her engagement with both semiformal and informal labor were directly linked to her husband's temporary job opportunities as a construction worker. Meloş noted several times how her husband would always be looking for job opportunities but could only find temporary positions. It did not help that he was not even a high school graduate, but even high school and university graduates continue to have difficulty securing permanent jobs.[9]

Additionally, neoliberalization processes since the 1980s necessitated workers to at times juggle multiple jobs to make ends meet. For example, the husband of Kerime, a carpet weaver I met in Konya, had a government job as a street cleaner; however, he could not make ends meet, so to make some extra money he sold the vegetables and fruits grown by his wife in their backyard and by their relatives in a nearby village. He also occasionally worked at various odd jobs for an electrician nearby. This example is not unique, as both men and women navigate formal (regulated) and informal/semiformal (unregulated) economies. The head of the Social Security Institution stated that unregulated economy is a threat to the functioning of social security in Turkey (Emin Zararsız 2010). Yet, despite this fact, the flexibility and continuing instability of the global economy makes it harder to have an overarching plan to counter unregulated labor. The 2010–4 strategic plan of the Social Security Institution remarks on the need to raise the auditing measures against establishments to ensure that they do not employ unregulated, uninsured laborers, yet the success of such planning remains to be seen. In the meantime, people such as Kerime and her husband have no option but to participate in the informal economy due to low-paying government jobs or the increasing lack of job security and flexibility of the labor force (Çağlar Keyder and Ayşe Buğra 2005; Ayşe Buğra 2008).

What does this suggest about poor households such as Meloş's? Despite continuous and impressive economic growth, there has been a rather small reduction in social risks and income inequality in Turkey; informalization of the labor market has exacerbated this effect. The government has not taken effective steps to reverse these damaging developments and indeed contributed to the flexibility and insecurity. It is no surprise,

GENDER AND ECONOMICS IN MUSLIM COMMUNITIES

then, that most conservative women situated in Konya and other places in Turkey prefer being homemakers to being workers in the labor force. Interviews conducted by the author show that women do not like the idea of working outside the home because of the instability of the labor, the lack of insurance, and the lack of stable pay. Another reason for the preference of working from home or not working is due to moral and religious reasons. For most conservative women and their families, work is something demanded and needed, yet the type of work and its conditions largely determine whether women enter both the formal and informal economies.

Unlike the assumptions made by some feminist researchers who saw women's employment outside the home as a way of gaining freedom and equality, Meloş and others I have talked to had a very different perspective on their options. Very few women expressed the desire for employment outside the home; they saw weaving and other informal work as a way to support their families and not as a path to individual freedom. These women's views corroborate recent feminist research that questions the equation made between women's employment and empowerment: women's employment does not guarantee that they have control over decision making, their working conditions are secure and free of conflict, and they gain individual autonomy through their work (Christine Koggel 2005; Jennifer C. Olmsted 2005; Samia Huq 2010; Naila Kabeer 2011; Naila Kabeer, Simeen Mahmud, and Sakiba Tasneem 2011). Studying Bangladeshi women workers, Kabeer (2011) notes, for example, how factors such as women's ability to save, their marital and educational status, and mobility interact with their employment status in complex ways making it harder to draw direct causal relationships between employment and empowerment. As a woman raised by a single mother who continuously emphasized the importance of having one's own job, I was challenged by women such as Meloş to encounter my own ethnocentrisms about what I termed as liberating: working outside the home. As Meloş noted:

> I would not consider working outside, because I think women can be taken advantage of when they work outside the home. It is also hard – I like my neighborhood and what I do here. I visit people when I can and I help out when I can. I wish I did not have to work so hard. I don't mind work so much, because work keeps you away from idle gossip. Our Prophet said that we should never be idle. Idle women gossip and sin. I do this (weave) to pass my time and to bring income. It is honest, good work. I like it, but at the same time I wish I did not have to do it all the time as I do now. It takes away from worship, prayer, and I miss visiting friends and family. If I had the option, I would not work.

GENDER AND ECONOMICS IN MUSLIM COMMUNITIES

Meloş's quote above is a perfect example of the way individual and communal moral dispositions, Islamic edict, pious conduct, and production for a neoliberal, global marketplace reaffirm each other. It also is a testament to the complex and at times contradictory nature of such assemblages. On the one hand, Meloş was purporting that the self-discipline provided by weaving was a way to avoid gossip and sin; on the other hand, she remained dubious since "hard work" took her away from visiting neighbors and going to religious gatherings, which are all places for potential gossip as well as learning. Meloş was not alone in complaining about the changing nature of weaving from home.

As I have discussed extensively elsewhere (Isik 2008), the ongoing competition in the hand-woven carpet sector from cheaper producers such as China and the decline of backpacking tourism, largely superseded by travel packages to five-star hotels, has changed the nature of business in Turkey. This does not entail a switch from low-end to high-end tourism; in fact, it is just the opposite. Tourists are able to buy cheap package deals in Europe and travel to Turkey quite inexpensively. In turn, they are shuttled around within Turkey by travel agencies and guides to stores and shops that have exclusive deals with the agents and the guides. This means that tourists are less inclined to have the initiative and the drive to wander around and discover stores on their own, which was a common complaint by the store owners in Konya. This, in turn, has replaced producing carpets for tourists with producing custom-ordered and custom-made carpets for specific clientele, pushing the male entrepreneurs and exporters to demand faster production and lower production costs. Increasing pressure for flawless carpets adhering to strict measurements, colors, and timelines has affected women weavers, who have had to produce faultless carpets faster. Although neoliberalization and globalization were not discussed much by the weavers themselves, the male entrepreneurs constantly debated the various effects of ongoing market liberalization and producing for a global rather than a local market.

Similar to many developing countries, government policies for neoliberalization in Turkey have a history that stretches to the 1980s. When the Justice and Development Party (AKP) came to power in 2002, it inherited a long legacy of continuous neoliberalization. Researchers have documented the distinctive effects of neoliberalization and globalization on Turkey's party politics (White 2002); governmental organizations and patron–client relationships (Catherine Alexander 2002); informal economy (Jenny White 2004); and popular culture (Yael Navaro-Yashin 2002). Yet, Meloş's example also points to the need to examine such assemblages from the perspective of self-governance and nurturing of pious conduct. Two of the main reasons for the AKP's continued success in the polls and the government has been its ability to claim free market and human rights discourses as central to its mission. This choice is also in line with the main

GENDER AND ECONOMICS IN MUSLIM COMMUNITIES

supporters of the AKP. Throughout the 1980s and 1990s, Turkey witnessed the growing political and economic power of conservative, Anatolia-based male entrepreneurs who have come to constitute the major voter base of the conservative AKP government. It is also the case that calling these entrepreneurs "Anatolian" has become a misnomer, since they have become transnationalized in their connections; most have either moved themselves to major cities, such as Istanbul and Izmir, or have representatives or interests in these global cities (Yıldız Atasoy 2009).

With the rise of a new conservative, moneyed entrepreneur class was the concomitant decline of the welfare state. As government shrank, most government-sector jobs that were considered a safety net were gradually replaced by unstable service-sector jobs.[10] In this sense, Turkey's so-called economic growth took a similar path to that of many other developing countries which saw the shrinking of government as international business competition became the mantra. In his recent work, Cihan Tuğal sees this process as a "passive revolution" where "Islamism had mobilized activists and workers, and the AKP appropriated this mobilization to reinforce neoliberalization in Turkey" (2009: 7). This "passive revolution" wed civil society (especially business associations formed by conservative industrialists and businessmen and charitable associations that work to curb poverty) with political society (AKP and municipal governance), creating a fusion between the state, economic globalization and neoliberalization, and civil society. As Tuğal rightfully states, this hegemonic and molecular perspective is much more effective in understanding Turkish social and economic transformation than the "secular state"/"conservative civil society" dichotomy found in some current literature on Turkish civil and political society, as the state can at times act conservatively while civil society can employ neoliberal, secular practices – dichotomies are never effective in explaining actual practices (White 2002; M. Hakan Yavuz 2006). Yet, Tuğal (2009) himself largely focuses on male, bureaucratic, and organized governmental, civil, and political authority in a local district in Istanbul. Women such as Meloş are not present in his analysis. In the *sohbets* she attended, Meloş not only learned how to pray properly, avoid gossip, and act as a better mother, but she also found ways to rationalize the "hard work" she did as a weaver, viewing it as a way of cultivating proper pious conduct through the example of the Prophet.

"JUST LIKE PROPHET MOHAMMAD PREACHED": THE VALUE OF PIOUS LABOR

Sitting in the IHH offices in Istanbul, a female employee, Çiğdem, and I started conversing about women's employment opportunities in Turkey. IHH is an Islamic charitable association that has effective and focused projects to curb poverty – projects situated mostly outside of Turkey,

223

GENDER AND ECONOMICS IN MUSLIM COMMUNITIES

although there are also some within Turkey – such as in-kind and monetary aid to needy families, monetary and educational support to orphans, and crisis aid. I asked Çiğdem if she thought women should be more proactive in seeking employment and being active as donors and volunteers. As Çiğdem noted, this depended on a lot of factors:

> We need to think about the kind of work women should and should not be doing. The work I do here, I consider *helal* work.[11] I can work freely without worrying about my honor and my family's honor. Not all women work like that. If you are to unveil and work within the company of other men, then that is not *helal*. So, no, not all work is good for women.

IHH offices were gender segregated, and Çiğdem and several other workers and volunteers felt content and worry free when working. Çiğdem herself was a very well-read and active woman; she was proud of working and contributing to her family's income, and, furthermore, she was also proud to work for a charitable association. Many conservative women I met echoed Çiğdem's thoughts and concerns regardless of where they were located. It did not matter whether they were carpet weavers in Konya or volunteers and employees in Istanbul; for conservative women, the meaning and relevance of work varied with its conditions. Meloş, for example, complained about weaving at times, despite the fact that she was also very much proud to be a wage earner. I asked her where she used her income and what she thought about her work:

> You see most money goes to household expenses – basic stuff like eating and drinking and water and all of that. I also have a daughter who is 10 and needs money for school. Our younger one will start school soon. I buy myself things, too, that I needed, if I get a chance, but that happens only when my husband has work so there is more money coming in. We make do otherwise. I like weaving; it takes my mind off of things, and when I weave fast it is like I am on a roll and time flies by. At times, though, I don't like weaving so much because if you need to complete it at some specific time, let's say, then you need to work, work, work. You don't have time to visit neighbors; you don't have time to pray or go to *sohbet*. Then I get mad and quarrel with the carpet manufacturer.

Elsewhere, I have discussed the importance of weekly *sohbet* sessions for women weavers in Konya, both as a way to socialize with others and a way to share important information regarding work (Isik 2008). Here, it is important to note that as women like Meloş made time to attend *sohbet*, they were aware that they were losing precious working time; however, they

GENDER AND ECONOMICS IN MUSLIM COMMUNITIES

saw pious conduct not as separate from their understanding of work, but *sohbet* gave meaning to the work that they did. Meloş's next door neighbor, Hatçe, who also wove regularly for the same carpet manufacturer as Meloş, described it best in a conversation we had about how she used her leisure time:

> I don't know if I would call it leisure time or not. I don't like to just sit around and do nothing – for me, I do some kind of something all the time. I talk to friends, I visit neighbors, I listen to the radio. I keep busy. We talked about this in a *sohbet* recently. Our Prophet praises those who work. We women need to also work, just like Prophet Mohammad preached; but we must pay attention to how we work – the conditions of our work, so we meet our religious obligations. This kind of work, weaving, yes it is hard, but it keeps me busy; I avoid gossiping all the time. I have time to think to myself when I weave. I think a lot when I work or I listen to the radio. I like listening to *Gözyaşı FM*, where they give advice about how to behave, and also they talk about the Koran.[12] Weaving is good, honorable work for women. I can do this from home and I don't need to be out and about. That is not something I want to do. I work from my home and, yes, not everything is perfect, and I could be making more money; but I like this all the same.

Meloş "argued" with the carpet manufacturer about her workload, and Hatçe certainly did not see weaving as an easy job; however, for both, weaving gave them the opportunity to be pious and professional workers. The value and meaning they gave to their work was directly related to proper pious conduct and family honor. What was even more interesting was that both Hatçe and Meloş, despite their financial problems and needs, made an effort to be active within their neighborhoods. Meloş admitted that she never had any money or anything to donate to charitable organizations and associations to return the favor, yet she felt that she was indebted all the same:

> My belief demands that I think of others, not only of myself. I do what I can. If a neighbor is in need, I share what I can from my garden, and I may cheer her up by showing up at her doorstep. I am ashamed to be asking for help for myself, but I could really use a fridge. If I get a fridge, I promised myself that I would do something in return. What, I don't know yet, but I want to. I would want to reciprocate. As the Koran says, one day you may be rich, the next day you may be poor. It is God's will. I have to remind myself that often.

Yeşim was a close friend of another woman whom I met at an Istanbul focus group meeting organized by a DF employee at their Marmara storage

GENDER AND ECONOMICS IN MUSLIM COMMUNITIES

facility in Istanbul. DF had similar projects to IHH; however, most of DF's projects were geared towards relieving poverty within Turkey. Unlike Meloş and Hatçe, who had to struggle to make ends meet, Yeşim had a husband who owned his own business; she considered herself middle class. They had grown children, and one of them was thinking of going to the United States to pursue university education. Although they could not support him financially, they were doing what they could so that he might get a scholarship. Yeşim was a housewife and had been one since her marriage, yet she was one of the most socially active women I met during my research. She volunteered for DF; she organized and attended *sohbet* sessions within her neighborhood; she regularly followed up on and helped the poor and needy she knew, by directly giving money or visiting them to see what they might need; and she volunteered at the local branch of the AKP and attended various functions. She had also participated in several *kermes* (bazaars) organized by various charitable foundations and organizations. She was a vibrant woman who always carried an air of fresh energy wherever she went. After a focus group meeting at DF, she and her husband drove me to the bus stop. I asked her if she felt bored or found something missing in her life as a housewife. Did she ever think about working? What would she want to do if she had the opportunity?

> I am working. I am doing what I love. I am always active. That is thanks to the fact that we have a good income from the store, and I am blessed that way. I know others who aren't, but I think for a woman, this is the best work she can do. Would I have worked if we needed money and were poor? I guess I would have, there is no shame in that; but I would have preferred to work in my neighborhood with people I know and trust. Here, I love what I do. As Muslims, it is our duty to help the needy and the poor. I feel blessed that I have the opportunity to do this. This is also work, and I take great pride in it. I don't see myself as a volunteer as such – volunteers at times may not be that dedicated. I put my heart and my labor on this path [*ben kalbimi ve emeğimi koydum bu yola*]. If there is something little I am doing to make things better for people, that means one prayer for me from a poor person.

Yeşim conceptualized what she did as a volunteer as work; it took serious organizing skills and dedication on her part to put together successful bazaars and to push people to be active in their neighborhoods. A lot of the women volunteers in organizations such as DF and IHH took the initiative to contribute to projects through raising money, organizing dinners, lunches and bazaars, and approaching possible donors.

Yeşim and Meloş's daily work sustains their communities, which also gives them the ability to perform their religious duties as Muslims both in work and

226

GENDER AND ECONOMICS IN MUSLIM COMMUNITIES

in service. In this sense, the practice of working is never too far removed from the practice of piety. The question always remains, though, whether such pious conduct actually aids neoliberalization efforts by curbing discontent without actively combating the structural problems that are a result of globalization. Similar questions have been asked in places other than Turkey, where populations are witnessing the aftermath of neoliberalization policies such as the increasing gap between the rich and the poor, the dismantling of social safety nets, the rise of the informal sector, and the decline of working conditions. As Shehabuddin (2008) effectively argues, the role of women often becomes something of a battleground in defining the parameters of reform within the context of both state and society. This battle goes beyond Islam understood as contextually complex and varied forms of religious ideology and discourse to encompass usage of work to mold and sustain moral subjects and citizens of a conservative, neoliberal state – be that Turkish Islamist, Hindu nationalist, or Christian (Gul Marshall Aldikacti 2005; William E. Connolly 2008; Gul Marshall Aldikacti and Anu Sabhlok 2009). What this varied research shows is that there is no automatic logic to how such formations take shape. A collectivity of individuals, institutions, and economic dynamics work in conjunction with each other within a specific historical context, and this collectivity comes to being through such work. Morally purposive agents such as Meloş and Yeşim come into being within a system based on inequality; their shared practices as pious Muslims and morally upright citizens sustain consent in times of intensifying inequalities in a neoliberalizing Turkey.

CONCLUSIONS: EFFECTIVE AND AFFECTIVE PIOUS ECONOMIES

What I experienced in neighborhoods, cities, and villages in Turkey were strategic maneuvers on the part of all parties – women weavers, employers, and charitable associations and foundations – that constantly challenged economic boundaries. Although the distinction between paid/unpaid and formal/informal work may be useful as basic ways of categorizing for the researcher what s/he saw in the field, these terms were not used by the women themselves in how they defined what they did. This is not unique to Turkey. In his research on urban employment in Ghana, Keith Hart (1973) deconstructs the understanding of informal economy as inherently exploitative and marginal by focusing on the rich networks developed in Ghana to support the informal economy and the personal freedom these networks present to the participants. For Hart (1973) and many other feminist researchers, terms like "wage employment" and "unemployment" are merely abstractions that do not really explain the diversity witnessed in the field. Additionally, market relations that developed between employees and employed also included ties of "nurturing, love, and altruism" and

227

GENDER AND ECONOMICS IN MUSLIM COMMUNITIES

these economic relations were only part of a bigger web of relations that included charitable associations, neighborhood religious gatherings, and volunteerism activities. This shows the importance of communal, affective ties in the inculcation of proper pious conduct and ethical practice that are both central to neoliberal and religious practices. What my research points to is the fact that neoliberalization is not about the fashioning of detached, individuated subjects; on the contrary, it is about the mobilization and nurturing of affective ties that bind various types of work together (in this case, semiformal work of weaving and civil societal work of charitable giving).

None of this erases the fact that women face inequalities within the global economy (June C. Nash and Maria P. Fernandez-Kelly, 1983; Benería and Feldman 1992; Mary Beth Mills 2003; Marcia Segal and Vasilikie Demos 2005), and in some places women's work can be construed as cheap and expandable within the context of global production (Diane Elson 1992; Jane Collins 2003). However, women's work – whether carried out in the context of household labor, of subcontracted labor performed in the home, or, in this specific case, of charitable work – means more than exploitation. In the neighborhoods and cities of Turkey, conservative, Muslim women gave meaning to their work within the context of pious practices such as going to *sohbet*, working from home, keeping away from gossip, being charitable, and accruing *sevap* (good deeds) through what they did and through other people's prayers. As they navigated various types of work, whether they were construed as "formal," "informal," or "semiformal," their concerns remained with their own pious conduct and affective relationships developed within the neighborhoods and charitable institutions they worked.

The ideal pious woman and man were committed to God, faith, family, and community; neoliberalization in Turkey worked with and not against such sentiments, linking daily pious conduct to productive citizenship and flexible labor. As documented, pious conduct is seen not as a refuge from, but conducive to increasing transnational competition, free markets, and privatization; it remains to be seen whether pious economies foster greater awareness of structural problems inherent to globalization and neoliberalization. This research documents that such consciousness is far from developed in Turkey, as governance and cultivation of pious conduct at homes, *sohbets*, and charitable institutions indirectly end up supporting current economic policies that promote privatization of welfare and flexibilization of labor.

GENDER AND ECONOMICS IN MUSLIM COMMUNITIES

NOTES

[1] All names and at times other distinctive qualifications of interviewees and participants has been altered to ensure full anonymity. At times, to ensure anonymity certain information on the participants has been altered or knowingly not included. The research took place in Konya, Istanbul, Afyon, Izmir, Manisa, and Denizli, Turkey.

[2] *Muhtar* is the elected head of government of a village or of a neighborhood within a town.

[3] *Sohbets* are weekly religious gatherings that can be initiated by men or women. While men's *sohbets* takes place mostly in the mosque and are more organized and are led by a religious authority figure (Brian Silverstein 2008), women's *sohbet* gatherings are much more loosely organized; they take place in neighborhoods and are attended by neighborhood women on a weekly basis (Damla Isik 2008).

[4] Unregulated work without insurance benefits or job security and with low pay is called "casual," "informal," and "undocumented" labor in the literature. For example, as a cleaning lady, Meloş is an undocumented, informal laborer. However, I see the weaving industry that Meloş also participated in as semiformal labor. Mehran Kamrava defines the semiformal sector as those industries that "appear to be governed by formal rules and procedures, but are, in fact, largely unregulated and unrecorded by the state" (2004: 63). The carpet exporters in Konya had legitimate stores in the Konya bazaar and were listed as exporters; however, their production procedures were not regulated by the state. They subcontracted production and kept secret the number of weavers they employed. In this sense, Meloş at times worked as a laborer in the informal economy and at other times she worked in the semiformal economy. Due to the fact that workers in Turkey usually navigate several different jobs in both formal and informal economies, it is difficult and generally unhelpful to draw a strict line between formal and informal labor, which usually feed of off each other.

[5] The idea of assemblage springs from the discussions of Gilles Deleuze and Félix Guattari (1987) and can be defined as "a heterogeneous collection of elements – scientific practices, social groups, material structures, administrative routines, value systems, legal regimes, technologies of the self, and so on – that are grouped together for the purposes of inquiry" (Stephen Collier and Aihwa Ong 2003: 423). Aihwa Ong and Stephen Collier (2005) apply this term to the study of globalization. They underline the importance of reflexive practices, the lived experiences within the context of globalization that stays focused on "'trajectories of change' . . . what Deleuze has called 'little lines of mutation,' minor histories that address themselves to the 'big' questions of globalization in a careful and limited manner" (Ong and Collier 2005: 15). What makes the concept of assemblage useful is its emphasis on the moments where agents, institutions, practices, and theories meet; and these meeting places are never fully finalized. An assemblage is

229

GENDER AND ECONOMICS IN MUSLIM COMMUNITIES

never stable, immutable, and unchanging; just the opposite, it formulates itself through instability and potentiality of conflict, stasis, and turbulence. Actors participate in, call into question, and reflect on the assemblages they are engaged in, and global forms "interact with other elements occupying a common field in contingent, uneasy, unstable interrelationships" (Ong and Collier 2005: 6).

[6] The works noted here were part of foundational volumes that appeared in the 1980s and early 1990s, many of which focused on women's work in the household and in factories. These works critically examined the effects of neoliberalization policies on women's lives.

[7] Some researchers see this rise in religiosity as a direct and largely negative response to globalization and neoliberalization (Jean Comaroff and John Comaroff 2000), while others trace the genealogies of religion and power (Talal Asad 1993). Another trend is to detail how this resurgence of religion affects cultural and economic practices – such as Islamic banking (Bill Mauer 2005; Charles Hirschkind 2006; Talal Asad 2007).

[8] In his study of governmentality, Michel Foucault (1994) has continuously noted the inherent flexibility of modernity in his work and shown that disciplinary and ethical practices were central to the formation of the modern self. Long before him, Weber (1905/1990) also noted the interconnected nature of capitalist development and Protestant ideals and practices. Ong and Collier (2005) have done similar work in noting how globalization should be understood as a flexible orientation of various assemblages of structures, ideals, and, most importantly, disciplinary practices.

[9] Although the overall unemployment rate has declined continuously, as of June 2011, it remains quite high at 9.2 percent (TurkStat 2011). According to the International Labour Organization's (ILO) report in 2007, youth unemployment is one of the most crucial issues facing in Turkey, hovering around 18 to 19 percent (Hakan Ercan 2007). More recent reports show that unofficial youth unemployment rate in Turkey has reached around 21 percent (Asım Erdilek 2010).

[10] With the reduction of public expenditure and public-sector jobs as they transitioned to market economies, many countries witnessed a transformation in public employment; however, comparative data are almost nonexistent (Messaoud Hammouya 1999). Recent comparative data for Turkey are equally hard to come by: 1998 data shows that public-sector employment made up about 14 percent of overall employment in Turkey (Hammouya 1999: 13), while another report shows that public-sector employees represent about 3.4 percent of total employment (Organisation for Economic Co-operation and Development [OECD] 1996). The privatization of state-owned enterprises (SOEs) since the 1990s has also resulted in the dismissal of a number of workers (Aysit Tansel 1998). Regardless of statistical information, almost all the women I talked to saw government jobs as more stable and secure than employment in either the private or the informal sector and lamented the fact that their relatives could not find jobs within the government sector.

[11] The direct translation of *helal* is canonically lawful and legitimate. It also relates to the kind of work that is considered good and acquires the favor and approval of God.

[12] *Gözyaşı FM* is a conservative radio station that broadcasts nationally and internationally from Konya, Turkey.

REFERENCES

Aldikacti, Gul Marshall. 2005. "Ideology, Progress, and Dialogue: A Comparison of Feminist and Islamist Women's Approaches to the Issues of Head Covering and Work in Turkey." *Gender and Society* 19(1): 104–20.

GENDER AND ECONOMICS IN MUSLIM COMMUNITIES

Aldikacti, Gul Marshall and Anu Sabhlok. 2009. "'Not for the Sake of Work': Politico-Religious Women's Spatial Negotiations in Turkey and India." *Women's Studies International Forum* 32(6): 406–13.

Alexander, Catherine. 2002. *Personal States: Making Connections Between People and Bureaucracy in Turkey*. New York: Oxford University Press.

Arendt, Hannah. 1958/1998. *The Human Condition*. Chicago: University of Chicago Press.

Asad, Talal. 1993. *Genealogies of Religion: Discipline and Reasons of Power in Christianity and Islam*. Baltimore: Johns Hopkins University Press.

———. 2003. *Formations of the Secular: Christianity, Islam, Modernity*. Stanford, CA: Stanford University Press.

———. 2007. "Explaining the Global Religious Revival: The Egyptian Case." In *Religion and Society: An Agenda for the Twenty-First Century*, edited by Gerrie ter Haar and Yoshio Tsuruoka, 83–104. Leiden: Brill Press.

Atasoy, Yıldız. 2009. *Islam's Marriage with Neoliberalism: State Transformation in Turkey*. New York: Palgrave Macmillan.

Benería, Lourdes. 2000. "The Construction of Global Markets: Engendering Polanyi's *The Great Transformation*." In *Gender and Identity Construction: Women of Central Asia, the Caucasus, and Turkey*, edited by F. Acar and A. Güneş-Ayata, 1–22. Boston: Brill.

———. 2003. *Gender, Development, and Globalization: Economics as if All People Mattered*. New York: Routledge.

Benería, Lourdes and Shelley Feldman, eds. 1992. *Unequal Burden: Economic Crises, Persistent Poverty, and Women's Work*. Boulder, CO: Westview Press.

Berik, Günseli. 1997. "The Need for Crossing the Method: Boundaries in Economics Research." *Feminist Economics* 3(2): 121–5.

Boddy, Janice. 1990. *Wombs and Alien Spirits: Women, Men, and the Zar Cult in Northern Sudan*. Madison: University of Wisconsin Press.

Buğra, Ayşe. 2008. *Kapitalizm, Yoksulluk ve Turkiye'de Sosyal Politika*. İstanbul: İletişim Yayınları.

Bornstein, Erica. 2005. *The Spirit of Development: Protestant NGOs, Morality, and Economics in Zimbabwe*. Stanford, CA: Stanford University Press.

Browne, Katherine E. 2008. "Economics and Morality: Introduction." In *Economics and Morality: Anthropological Approaches*, edited by Katherine E. Browne and B. Lynne Milgram, 1–41. New York: Alta Mira Press.

Cahn, Peter. 2008. "Consuming Class: Multilevel Marketers in Neoliberal Mexico." *Cultural Anthropology* 23(3): 429–52.

Callon, Michel. 1998. *The Laws of the Markets*. Oxford: Blackwell.

Collier, Stephen and Aihwa Ong. 2003. "Oikos/Anthropos: Rationality, Technology, Infrastructure." *Current Anthropology* 44(3): 421–6.

Collins, Jane. 2003. *Threads: Gender, Labor, and Power in the Global Apparel Industry*. Chicago: University of Chicago Press.

Comaroff, Jean and John Comaroff. 2000. "Millennial Capitalism: First Thoughts on a Second Coming." *Public Culture* 12(2): 291–343.

Connolly, William E. 2008. *Capitalism and Christianity, American Style*. Durham, NC: Duke University Press.

Davids, Tine and Francien van Driel. 2005. *The Gender Question in Globalization: Changing Perspectives and Practices*. Burlington, VT: Ashgate.

Deeb, Lara. 2006. *An Enchanted Modern: Gender and Public Piety in Shi'i Lebanon*. New York: Princeton University Press.

Deleuze, Gilles and Félix Guattari. 1987. *A Thousand Plateaus: Capitalism and Schizophrenia*. Translated by Brian Massumi. Minneapolis: University of Minnesota Press.

Dwyer, Daisy and Judith Bruce. 1988. *A Home Divided: Women and Income in the Third World*. Stanford, CA: Stanford University Press.

GENDER AND ECONOMICS IN MUSLIM COMMUNITIES

Elson, Diane 1992. "From Survival Strategies to Transformation Strategies: Women's Needs and Structural Adjustment." In *Unequal Burden: Economic Crises, Persistent Poverty, and Women's Work*, edited by L. Beneria and S. Feldman, 26–49. Boulder, CO: Westview Press.

Ercan, Hakan. 2007. "Youth Employment in Turkey." International Labour Organization. http://www.ilo.org/public/english/region/eurpro/ankara/areas/youth/1_04_youth_employment_in_turkey_hakan%20ercan.pdf.

Erdilek, Asım. 2010. "The Scourge of Youth Unemployment Around the World and in Turkey." *Today's Zaman*, August 30. http://www.todayszaman.com/columnist-220438-the-scourge-of-youth-unemployment-around-the-world-and-in-turkey.html.

Esim, Simel. 1997. "Can Feminist Methodology Reduce Power Hierarchies in Research Settings?" *Feminist Economics* 3(2): 137–9.

Fernandez-Kelly, Patricia and Diane Wolf. 2001. "A Dialogue on Globalization." *Signs* 26(4): 1243–9.

Folbre, Nancy. 1994. *Who Pays for the Kids? Gender and the Structures of Constraint*. New York: Routledge.

———. 2000. *The Invisible Heart: Economics and Family Values*. New York: The New Press.

Foucault, Michel. 1994. "Governmentality." In *The Essential Foucault: Selections from the Essential Works of Foucault 1954–1984*, edited by N. Rose and P. Rabinow, 229–45. New York: The New Press.

Freeman, Carla. 2000. *High Tech and High Heels in the Global Economy: Women, Work, and Pink-Collar Identities in the Caribbean*. Durham, NC: Duke University Press.

Fuentes, Annette and Barbara Ehrenreich. 1983. *Women in the Global Factory*. Boston, MA: South End Press.

Guyer, Jane. 1980. "Households, Budgets and Women's Incomes." Africana Studies Center Working Paper, Boston University.

Hammouya, Messaoud. 1999. "Statistics on Public Sector Employment: Methodology, Structures, and Trends." International Labour Office. http://www.ilo.org/public/english/bureau/stat/download/wp_pse_e.pdf.

Hart, Keith. 1973. "Informal Income Opportunities and Urban Employment in Ghana." *Journal of Modern African Studies* 11(1): 61–89.

Hart, Kimberly. 2007. "Performing Piety and Islamic Modernity in a Turkish Village." *Ethology* 46(4): 289–304.

Hirschkind, Charles. 2006. *The Ethical Soundscape: Cassette Sermons and Islamic Counterpublics*. New York: Columbia University Press.

Huntington, Samuel. 1996. *The Clash of Civilizations and the Remaking of World Order*. New York: Simon & Schuster.

Huq, Samia. 2010. "Negotiating Islam: Conservatism, Splintered Authority and Empowerment in Urban Bangladesh." *IDS Bulletin* 41(2): 97–105.

Inda, Jonathan Xavier and Renato Rosaldo. 2002. *The Anthropology of Globalization: A Reader*. Malden, MA: Blackwell.

Isik, Damla. 2008. "On Sabir and Agency: The Politics of Pious Practice in Konya's Weaving Industry." *International Feminist Journal of Politics* 10(4): 518–41.

———. 2010. "Personal and Global Economies: Male Carpet Manufacturers as Entrepreneurs in the Weaving Neighborhoods of Konya, Turkey." *American Ethnologist* 37(1): 52–67.

Joseph, Suad, ed. 1999. *Intimate Selving in Arab Families: Gender, Self, and Identity*. Syracuse: Syracuse University Press.

Kabeer, Naila. 2011. "Between Affiliation and Autonomy: Navigating Pathways of Women's Empowerment and Gender Justice in Bangladesh." *Development and Change* 42(2): 499–528.

GENDER AND ECONOMICS IN MUSLIM COMMUNITIES

Kabeer, Naila, Simeen Mahmud, and Sakiba Tasneem. 2011. *Does Paid Work Provide a Pathway to Women's Empowerment? Empirical Findings from Bangladesh.* IDS Working Paper 2011(375). London: Institute of Development Studies.

Kamrava, Mehran. 2004 "The Semi-Formal Sector and the Turkish Political Economy." *British Journal of Middle Eastern Studies* 31(1): 63–87.

Keyder, Çağlar and Ayşe Buğra. 2005. "Poverty and Social Policy in Contemporary Turkey." http://www.spf.boun.edu.tr/docs/WP-Bugra-Keyder.pdf.

Kingsolver, Ann and Nandini Gunewardena, eds. 2007. *The Gender of Globalization: Women Navigating Cultural and Economic Marginalities.* Santa Fe, NM: School for Advanced Research Press.

Koggel, Christine. 2005. "Globalization and Women's Paid Work: Expanding Freedom?" In *Amartya Sen's Work and Ideas: A Gender Perspective*, edited by Bina Agarwal, Jane Humphries, and Ingrid Robeyns, 165–85. New York: Routledge.

Lessinger, Johanna. 2002. "Work and Love: The Limits of Autonomy for Female Garment Workers in India." *Anthropology of Work Review* 23(2): 13–18.

Mahmood, Saba. 2005. *Politics of Piety: The Islamic Revival and the Feminist Subject.* New York: Princeton University Press.

Marchand, Marianne H. and Anne Sisson Runyan, eds. 2000. *Gender and Global Restructuring: Sightings, Sites and Resistances.* London: Routledge.

Mauer, Bill. 2005. *Mutual Life, Limited: Islamic Banking, Alternative Currencies, Lateral Reason.* Princeton, NJ: Princeton University Press.

Mies, Maria. 1982. *The Lace Makers of Narsapur: Indian Housewives Produce for the World Market.* London: Zed Press.

Mills, Mary Beth. 2003. "Gender and Inequality in the Global Labor Force." *Annual Review of Anthropology* 32: 41–62.

Mitchell, Timothy. 2002. *Rule of Experts: Egypt, Techno-Politics, Modernity.* Berkeley: University of California Press.

———. 2005. "The Work of Economics: How a Discipline Makes Its World." *European Journal of Sociology* 46(2): 297–320.

Nash, June C. and Maria P. Fernandez-Kelly, eds. 1983. *Women, Men, and the International Division of Labor.* Albany: State University of New York Press.

Navaro-Yashin, Yael. 2002. *Faces of the State: Secularism and Public Life in Turkey.* Princeton, NJ: Princeton University Press.

Nelson, Julie. 1995. "Feminism and Economics." *Journal of Economic Perspectives* 9(2): 131–48.

Olmsted, Jennifer C. 1997. "Telling Palestinian Women's Economic Stories." *Feminist Economics* 3(2): 141–51.

———. 2005. "Is Paid Work the (Only) Answer? Women's Well-Being, Neoliberalism, and the Social Contract in Southwest Asia and North Africa." *Journal of Middle East Women's Studies* 2(1): 112–39.

Ong, Aihwa. 1987. *Spirits of Resistance and Capitalist Discipline: Factory Women in Malaysia.* New York: State University of New York Press.

Ong, Aihwa and Stephen Collier, eds. 2005. *Global Assemblages: Technology, Politics, and Ethics as Anthropological Problems.* Malden, MA: Blackwell.

Organisation for Economic Co-operation and Development (OECD). 1996. *Economic Surveys: Turkey.* Paris: OECD.

Pazderic, Nickola. 2004. "Recovering True Selves in the Electro-Spiritual Field of Universal Love." *Cultural Anthropology* 19(2): 196–225.

Polanyi, Karl. 1944. *The Great Transformation.* New York: Farrar & Rinehart.

Pujol, Michele. 1997. "Explorations – Introduction: Broadening Economic Methods." *Feminist Economics* 3(2): 119–20.

GENDER AND ECONOMICS IN MUSLIM COMMUNITIES

Rudnyckyj, Daromir. 2009. "Spiritual Economies: Islam and Neoliberalism in Contemporary Indonesia." *Cultural Anthropology* 24: 104–41.

———. 2010. *Spiritual Economies: Islam, Globalization, and the Afterlife of Development*. New York: Cornell University Press.

Segal, Marcia and Vasilikie Demos, eds. 2005. *Gender Realities: Local and Global*. Amsterdam: Elsevier.

Seguino, Stephanie, Thomas Stevens, and Mark Lutz. 1996. "Gender and Cooperative Behavior: Economic Man Rides Alone." *Feminist Economics* 2(1): 195–223.

Shehabuddin, Elora. 2008. *Reshaping the Holy: Democracy, Development, and Muslim Women in Bangladesh*. New York: Columbia University Press.

Silverstein, Brian. 2008. "Disciplines of Presence in Modern Turkey: Discourse, Companionship, and the Mass Mediation of Islamic Practice." *Cultural Anthropology* 23(1): 118–53.

Strassmann, Diana L. 1994. "Feminist Thought and Economics; Or, What Do the Visigoths Know?" *American Economic Review* 84(2): 153–8.

———. 1997 "Editorial: Expanding the Methodological Boundaries of Economics." *Feminist Economics* 3(2): vii–ix.

Tansel, Aysit. 1998. "Workers Displaced Due to Privatization in Turkey: Before Versus After Displacement." *METU Studies in Development* 25(4): 625–47.

Tuğal, Cihan. 2009. *Passive Revolution: Absorbing the Islamic Challenge to Capitalism*. Stanford. CA: Stanford University Press.

TurkStat (Turkish Statistical Institute). 2011. "January 17 Household Labour Force Survey for the Period of October 2010 (September, October, November 2010)." http://www.turkstat.gov.tr/PreTablo.do?tb_id=25&ust_id=8.

Weber, Max. 1905/1990. *The Protestant Ethic and the Spirit of Capitalism*. Translated by Talcott Parsons. London: Unwin Hyman.

White, Jenny. 2002. *Islamist Mobilization in Turkey: A Study in Vernacular Politics*. Seattle: University of Washington Press.

———. 2004. *Money Makes us Relatives: Women's Labor in Urban Turkey*, 2nd edition. New York: Routledge.

Wolf, Diane. 1992. *Factory Daughters: Gender, Household Dynamics, and Rural Industrialization in Java*. Berkeley: University of California Press.

Yavuz, M. Hakan. 2006. "Introduction: The Role of the New Bourgeoisie in the Transformation of the Turkish Islamic Movement." In *The Emergence of a New Turkey: Islam, Democracy and the AK Party*, edited by Hakan Yavuz, 1–19. Salt Lake City: University of Utah Press.

Zararsız, Emin. 2010. "Sosyal güvenliğin en büyük sorunu kayıtdışı istihdam" [The biggest problem of social security is unregistered labor]. *Hurriyet Daily News*, November 5. http://hurarsiv.hurriyet.com.tr/goster/ShowNew.aspx?id=14684706.

ENTREPRENEURIAL SUBJECTIVITIES AND GENDERED COMPLEXITIES: NEOLIBERAL CITIZENSHIP IN TURKEY

Özlem Altan-Olcay

ABSTRACT

This contribution explores the promotion of women's entrepreneurial activities in Turkey. Using participant observation and semi-structured interviews conducted during 2011–12 in two civil-society organizations that run programs fostering women's entrepreneurship, this study shows how neoliberal ideologies interact with ideas of labor, responsibility, and gender. Emphasizing individual rationalities and entrepreneurial attitudes, these civil-society programs contribute to the construction of model subjects of neoliberal citizenship, who are expected to be self-governing and self-sufficient. Yet problems embedded in the neoliberal paradigm and these particular organizations' commitment to women's rights produce contradictions in implementation. The goal of entrepreneurial women is predicated on the assumption that women contribute more to their families' well-being than men. The programs' attempts to construct potential entrepreneurs out of women for this purpose reveal problems with discourses of individual self-sufficiency and responsibility.

INTRODUCTION

In recent decades, there has been a surge in attention paid to encouraging entrepreneurship among disadvantaged populations in less-developed countries to generate employment and reduce household poverty. Such discussions have also linked women's entrepreneurial activities and gainful work to gender equality. The argument has been that there is a need to cultivate and respond to the existing potential of entrepreneurship among the poor (and especially poor women) as a means to reduce poverty. This contribution investigates the circulation of the idea of entrepreneurship among these actors, together with its gendered effects on understandings of responsibility and citizenship.

Based on fieldwork in two Turkish civil-society organizations, which promote women's entrepreneurship, I argue that there is a connection between the emergence of gendered meanings of responsibility and citizenship, on the one hand, and broader contradictions in the formation of neoliberal subjectivities, on the other. These initiatives not only find and encourage entrepreneurial women but also contribute to the construction of entrepreneurial gendered subjectivities, creating the conditions through which women come to define their labor in terms of individual responsibility, effort, and market capacity. The goal of women's gainful labor comes with the assumption that they contribute more to their families' well-being than men. This assumption reproduces neoliberal discourses of individual rationality and self-sufficiency at the level of women's subjectivities. However, the same processes also reveal how the discourse of giving mothers emerges; this is because the idea of individual self-sufficiency does not actually work. These processes have gendered implications for how citizenship is perceived and practiced. By citizenship, I denote the discourses and practices that govern citizens' conduct. Neoliberal citizenship promotes individual responsibility, but it also encourages communitarian support in familial networks and assumes "natural" divisions of labor, responsibility, and affect between men and women.

These arguments are rooted in data collected by qualitative methods of participant observation and semi-structured interviews in two civil-society organizations (CSOs) promoting women's empowerment through labor force participation. The Women Entrepreneurs Association of Turkey (Kadın Girişimcileri Destekleme Derneği [KAGİDER]) and the Association for the Support of Women's Labor (Kadın Emeğini Değerlendirme Vakfı [KEDV]) are part of the terrain of civil-society and government initiatives encouraging women's entrepreneurship.[1] The founding members of KAGİDER are businesswomen who aimed to create a network of women entrepreneurs in Turkey. Eventually, they also began tackling issues of gender equality. KAGİDER had a powerful membership roster and significant economic resources. KEDV was established for the purpose of catering to the economic well-being of women from lower classes. Both had office personnel, but KEDV relied more on volunteers. At the time of the fieldwork, KEDV housed various activities including advocacy, training, consultancy, cooperative meetings, and a microcredit program, while KAGİDER organized training sessions, consultancy, and entrepreneurship meetings for women. These two organizations are different from most others because they define their primary focus as women's empowerment through labor force participation;[2] moreover, in both, women occupy

GENDER AND ECONOMICS IN MUSLIM COMMUNITIES

all decision-making and field positions.[3] They also walk the uneasy terrain between feminist advocacy and exigencies of competition for funding, making contradictions in their work more readily visible.[4] These two organizations were chosen because they promoted women's gainful economic activity with gender awareness, reached diverse socioeconomic backgrounds, and had a plethora of programs, some of which required outside funding.

Capturing the complexity of actual experiences and everyday realities necessitated in-depth interviews and participant observation of program officers and beneficiaries' interactions (Günseli Berik 1997; Jennifer Olmsted 1997). Thus the fieldwork involved periodic office visits as well as involvement in projects, meetings, and field trips over the course of twelve months during 2011–12. I conducted semi-structured, in-depth interviews with the women who benefited from the programs and had numerous conversations with the officers. Fieldtrips and some of the interviews took me outside of Istanbul, but most of my work was concentrated in various districts of the city. In the trips, the officers and I visited local bazaars, the local branches of the organizations and the businesses of women who benefited from the programs. The research looked at the processes that unfolded in the construction of women's subjectivities through activities promoting entrepreneurship. My goal was to see how neoclassical assumptions regarding *homo economicus* materialized in these programs and to explore the conflicts and contradictions that emerged in everyday implementation.

THE GLOBAL SOUTH, DEVELOPMENT, AND WOMEN'S ENTREPRENEURIALISM

The scholarship on development programs targeting women in the Global South is part of a larger critical literature on the connection between neoliberalism and development paradigms. Even though the post-Washington consensus has broadened the concept of economic welfare with its attention to human development, critical scholars have pointed to the resilience of market logics and lack of attention to inequalities within global and local structures of power (Ben Fine 2003; Ashwani Saith 2006). Aneel Karnani (2009) has argued that these initiatives are unable to provide a meaningful alternative to government-funded welfare programs, which, due to structural adjustment programs, are shrinking. Heloise Weber (2002, 2004) and Ananya Roy (2010) have added that the rise of such development initiatives function as a safety net, without challenging financial liberalization and structural adjustment. This contribution speaks to the critical literature, which argues that because these development initiatives abstain from such challenges, they enable the normalization of neoliberal norms about rational economic individuals.

237

GENDER AND ECONOMICS IN MUSLIM COMMUNITIES

Feminist scholars have questioned the gendered assumptions of this so-called rational economic man. They have argued that flexible boundaries for selfhood (Nancy Folbre 2009), practices of care (Victoria Lawson 2007), provisioning (Julie Nelson 1996), reciprocity, and redistribution can better capture economic life. Paula England (1993) has shown the inconsistencies in assuming a clear-cut boundary between altruistic decision making in the family and self-interested behavior in the marketplace. Nancy Folbre and Julie A. Nelson (2000) have proposed there is a need for a more complex understanding of subjectivity, one that will ease the tension between hypothetical constructs of market behavior and what actually transpires in real life. In light of the complexity of behavioral motivations as well as sources and processes of identity construction, they have called for a complete restructuring of the conceptualization of economic behavior.

Feminist critiques have also shown that neoliberal economic policymaking based on assumptions of rational, utility-maximizing self of neoclassical economics is deeply gendered. Lourdes Benería (1999) has argued that neoliberal globalization involves the construction of a market society, in the way Karl Polanyi (1944) had envisaged, adding that it is a thoroughly gendered process because it makes women's home-based care work invisible and thrives because of the "feminization" of the labor force. The dismantling of welfare states has resulted in the intensification of home-based care work because it has become less available as part of state social services (Isabella Bakker 2007). While the availability of jobs in the market has meant more power for some women, for many it has not changed their experience of gender-based hierarchies and divisions of labor (Lourdes Benería, Maria Floro, Caren Grown, and Martha MacDonald 2000; Roksana Bahramitash and Jennifer C. Olmsted 2014). As a result, by deploying the model of the rational, individualist, economic actor and ignoring the work of social reproduction, neoliberalization has contributed to gendered vulnerabilities among large numbers of people.

And yet, strong connections have persisted between the assumptions of neoclassical economics and neoliberal economic restructuring in the Global South. Postcolonial economists have shown that the realization of the model is a historical effect of colonial domination and postcolonial development (Eiman Zein-Elabdin 2001). The image of the "modern" self has been a part of colonial discourses, posing Western modernity as superior to its Eastern others (Antonio Callari 2004; Robert W. Dimand 2004). Current development discourses use a similar logic, in so far as they approach the "underdeveloped" in terms of the need to cultivate rational and responsible human beings (Joseph Medley and Lorrayne Carroll 2004). These definitions of responsibility and self-governance frequently mean individual capacity to participate in market relations. The observation also applies to deployment of the figure of "the Muslim woman" or "women in Muslim communities," as someone to be saved from herself and from her

GENDER AND ECONOMICS IN MUSLIM COMMUNITIES

culture so she has the chance to choose actions more or less couched in the neoliberal paradigm (Jennifer Olmsted 2004; Lila Abu-Lughod 2009; Fida Adely 2009). This effect is not only discursive; these institutions have created the material conditions under which the subaltern actor finds herself making choices and forming resistance strategies (Eiman Zein-Elabdin and S. Charusheela 2004). Tania Murray Li (2005, 2007) has argued that the plans, programs, and implementation strategies of various development programs create the conditions for altering the incentives and, therefore, behaviors of their beneficiaries. As such, institutions' concepts of competition, accountability, and self-governance can become part of the experience of their beneficiaries. Yet, these are always embattled processes, neither stabilized nor final (Murray Li 2007).

Initiatives that fall under the purview of this study devise programs, including advocacy, microcredit, and cooperatives, to encourage women's labor force participation through entrepreneurship. Feminist sociologists and economists have argued that such programs reduce women's empowerment to participation in the paid labor market without questioning broader power inequalities (Benería 1999). These programs can also further consolidate hierarchical gender roles when predicated on existing gender norms (Katherine Rankin 2002; Rachel Silvey and Rebecca Elmhirst 2003; Lamia Karim 2008). Scholars have also warned that the new development programs can deploy discourses of gender equality and women's empowerment in reductive ways while becoming more persuasive by association with demands for feminist mobilization (Hester Eisenstein 2005).

This contribution is concerned with practices that add to the spread of discourses of responsibility and self-governance. These discourses signal a shift from citizenship narratives of egalitarianism and universal rights to those of individualism and market freedom. They deploy governmental strategies that constitute women's citizenship in terms of self-help and normalize reliance on market relations (Katherine Rankin 2001, 2002). Accordingly, such practices can contribute to expanding the universe in which market rationalities are consolidated (Margaret Somers 2008). As a result, "desirable" citizens end up being those who have individual market capacity to thrive in contemporary capitalism and who honor market-based contractual obligations.

The growing popularity of discourses of entrepreneurship can be considered a part of the rise of neoliberal citizenship. I make use of governmentality studies, which trace how social actors are constructed with respect to a set of "desirable" qualities and, at the same time, how the actors themselves participate in these processes (Michel Foucault 1991; Nikolas Rose and Peter Miller 1992; Mitchell Dean 1999). In line with studies arguing that citizenship norms in modern liberal societies emphasize qualities such as responsibility, self-governance, and rationality (Graham Burchell 1996; Barry Hindess 2002), I propose that the promotion of entrepreneurship, women's productivity, and assertiveness is part of the processes that construct ideals of market-savvy, hard-working, and productive female citizens. These programs involve everyday practices that make women knowledgeable of market logics, train them to conceive of their labor in marketized ways, and discipline their everyday actions through the conditions attached to their participation. Even though the local organizations genuinely advocate policies that will lead to improving women's chances of labor force participation, the conditions under which they run the programs also enable the naturalization of ideas about individual responsibility and worth, both defined in relation to one's market capacity.

Nevertheless, the same processes also reveal the contingent nature of these subjectivities and their reliance on the "traditional" logics that they appear to disavow (Damla Isik 2013). Critics argue that such initiatives are the response of mainstream development institutions to the growing social exclusion resulting from the neoliberal restructuring of economies. I add to this argument that these programs lay bare the problems in neoliberalism's foundational logic. On the one hand, programs targeting women's entrepreneurship encourage women to think of themselves as individualized, rational agents with entrepreneurial capacities to earn a living. On the other hand, there is an embedded gender dynamic: women are expected to utilize their entrepreneurship for the benefit of their families, because this is coded as part of their caregiving responsibility. Ironically, this can end up being the case even for explicitly feminist initiatives. The organizations' struggles to show the enormous labor that women undertake in the household can be hijacked by narratives about the "naturally" caring tendencies of women toward their families. Thus, there is a danger that existing gender hierarchies are deployed and reproduced (Rankin 2002; Silvey and Elmhirst 2003; Karim 2008). This coupling of caregiving and women's entrepreneurship points to contradictions in the discourse of a rational, self-sufficient individual.

Critical studies on economic-development programs targeting women focus especially on microcredit (Rankin 2002; Murray Li 2007; Karim 2008). Ethnographic work shows how such programs integrate local actors into market mechanisms, create subjectivities, and rearticulate gender relations, but not necessarily for the better. With this case study from Turkey, I want to contribute to this scholarship in the following ways: First, in the Turkish case, the running of these programs are coeval with a thorough neoliberal transformation at the state level, to the degree that mainstream economic indices have identified the country as a case of successful economic transformation. Thus, I am able to look at how women's subjectivities are articulated not only in response to their relations with the organizations, but also in the larger economic context. Second,

GENDER AND ECONOMICS IN MUSLIM COMMUNITIES

I explore the construction of the neoliberal citizen at the juncture of a more diverse set of programs, which include microcredit but are not limited to it. So this contribution is not about microcredit programs in Turkey, which are much less pervasive than in other locations in the Global South. Instead, it is about discourses of women's entrepreneurship emerging out of civil-society activism. Finally, I aim to draw attention to the complex and sometimes contradictory processes that unfold in implementation by focusing not on programs, whose sole purpose is poverty alleviation, but on non-governmental organizations (NGOs) which run programs to promote women's empowerment through labor force participation.

THE TURKISH CONTEXT

Following the 1980 coup and gaining speed in the 1990s, the Turkish state, in collaboration with business classes, has pushed for market liberalization, deregulation of finance, privatization of state enterprises, and shrinking of the welfare state.[5] The post-coup government was able to undertake this massive restructuring due to the repression of resistance (Çağlar Keyder 2004). Over the course of the 1990s and 2000s, when the government became too strapped for capital and economic crises ensued, the International Monetary Fund (IMF) agreements also facilitated further privatization and public expenditure cutbacks (Mathieu Dufour and Özgür Orhangazi 2009). The consequences were manifold for citizens. First, there was the general ascendancy of a neoliberal paradigm, promoting ideas of self-governing citizens (Özlem Altan-Olcay 2011) who are able to bear individually the costs of restructuring. The state's capacity for offsetting marginalization and inequality was reduced and delegitimized. Second, trade union activism was severely repressed, lowering the share of labor income over time (Korkut Boratav 1995). The power of waged labor was also curbed by a dramatic increase in outsourcing and subcontracting (Ümit Cizre Sakallıoğlu and Erinç Yeldan 2000). Finally, scholars have pointed to a growing trend of social exclusion, exacerbated by deruralization and urban transformations (Çağlar Keyder 2005; Fikret Adaman and Çağlar Keyder 2006; Çağlar Keyder and Zafer Yenal 2011).

In this context, unlike other settings undergoing similar transitions, women's labor force participation and employment declined. The percentage of women with gainful employment dropped from 33 percent in 1988 to 23.5 percent in 2009 (World Bank 2009), with a rise to 30.2 percent at the beginning of 2014 (Turkish Statistics Institute 2014). The decline is explained by the fact that industry and services have not been able to absorb women workers released from agriculture due to deruralization, migration to the cities, and internal displacement (Deniz Yükseker 2006). State action has not fared well in terms of policymaking

GENDER AND ECONOMICS IN MUSLIM COMMUNITIES

that promotes women's participation in the labor force (Ayşe Buğra and Burcu Yakut-Çakar 2010). Like many other contexts, much of the work available for women is concentrated in the informal market (Buğra and Yakut-Çakar 2010), which is more likely to exploit women's labor, render it invisible and less important, and reproduce existing gender inequalities in society (Jenny White 1994; Saniye Dedeoğlu 2010). Furthermore, studies of the social-security system show its growing reliance on disproportionate care work done by women at home (Ayşe Buğra and Çağlar Keyder 2006; Berna Yazıcı 2008).

In this context, civil-society programs began focusing on women's entrepreneurship as an answer to the decline in women's gainful labor participation, feminist concerns of unequal power relations in the family, and growing social exclusion and poverty. These programs did not necessarily start with microcredit, but ended up also including it given the availability of funds. Ironically, the same programs have found room in government policies, which see women-owned small businesses as an answer to the precarious living conditions of a growing number of families, without challenging the existing gendered divisions of labor (Buğra and Yakut-Çakar 2010), or the neoliberal economic restructuring (Damla Gürses 2009).

In the last decade we have witnessed the proliferation of programs that encourage entrepreneurship in different ways. There have been collaborations between the state, the United Nations Development Programme (UNDP), commercial banks, business associations, civil-society organizations, and the Grameen Bank.[6] Grameen has also provided partial funding to the first microcredit program in Turkey, Maya Enterprise, which was established by KEDV. KEDV runs programs that support business development by low-income women, with finance, cooperatives, and childcare (Gürses 2009). KAGİDER targets entrepreneurship and empowerment through technical support and training to foster small and medium-sized businesses operated by women. Alongside and in cooperation with these organizations are several government offices and intergovernmental organizations aiming to support small businesses and individual entrepreneurial activities (Yıldız Ecevit 2007).[7]

There is little critical research on programs about women's entrepreneurship in Turkey (Fikret Adaman and Tuğçe Bulut 2007; Ecevit 2007; Buğra and Yakut-Çakar 2010). This case study contributes to this scholarship by tracing the circulation of ideas and practices of women's entrepreneurship in such initiatives. The literature on development programs, particularly studies of microcredit, is remarkable in its critique of the alliance between development goals and neoliberal restructuring of economies. The Turkish case shows that neoliberal citizenship emerges at the constellation of various programs – not just microcredit – and actors, who do not all share the ideals of neoliberalism.

242

GENDER AND ECONOMICS IN MUSLIM COMMUNITIES
INDIVIDUAL RESPONSIBILITY

The construction of a neoliberal subjectivity starts from the naturalization of discourses about the ability to improve existing circumstances through hard work and individual responsibility. Such discourses are crystallized in the assumptions and requirements of these programs. These contribute to the cultivation of women, who take their individual circumstances as given, do not question them, and use their individual resources to improve them. The moment of recognition of *ceteris paribus* is important for entrepreneurial activities, because this is how women are expected to assess opportunities and obstacles and calculate costs and benefits for themselves. Then, given these conditions, they work hard to improve their lives. This construction also has the effect of ruling out a questioning of broader structures of inequality and precariousness.

Finding women seeking credit is not easy for field officers. Officers approach women in low-income neighborhoods and bazaars, explain the project, and hand them brochures and contact numbers. This initial interaction varies in response to subtle cues from the woman addressed. Those with whom the field officers spend more time are the ones with questions. In the next stage, some of these women initiate contact with the field officer, with a plan of their own for how to utilize the money disbursed.[8] If the proposal is seen as valid, the field officers arrange a committee meeting with senior field managers. In these meetings, the rules are discussed once again; the field managers evaluate the proposal and, if they approve of the candidates, sign off on the credit. These committee meetings are another place where applicants learn about proper conduct; that is, learning to think of themselves as clients and not targets of charity organizations, and learning to talk about themselves and their work aspirations with emphasis on individual empowerment, group solidarity, and business curiosity and confidence.

One such meeting took place in one of the local offices in a shopping mall in a working-class neighborhood. I had traveled there with the field manager from Istanbul, and the local field officer joined us. The field officer, the field manager, and I sat across a table from a group of women who were seeking credit. Two of the three were sisters; a third was a friend. The older sister had learned about the program from a neighbor. She was planning to open a hair salon and to give a room to the younger sister for a waxing business. This was the first instance of rearrangement: what seemed more like a family business was described as two separate businesses. They learned the lesson that each had to have their own business proposal to qualify for the credit. The third woman was planning to utilize the cash to diversify her home-based tailoring. After the introductions, the field manager emphasized that this was not a charity organization, but they provided credit for women who wanted to be entrepreneurs. Accordingly,

243

it was absolutely essential that the women were committed to making payments on time, because their payments allowed other women to receive credit. The field manager then linked this explanation to mutual support and women's empowerment, reminding them that they were responsible for each other and that they should be willing to support each other. She emphasized that they took on this loan together. This meant that it would be very important that they trusted and watched out for each other. This narrative, which I repeatedly saw in all the meetings I attended, affected how the applicants responded to questions and how they talked about their businesses.

In this particular case, however, one of the group members turned out to be a bit more questioning. She inquired about the compulsory savings account and why they had to set aside money. The manager and the officer explained that this was in case there was a default on their repayments due to an emergency. The prospective client did not look happy about this imposition. Then she asked about the interest rates. The field manager explained that they needed to charge something to cover the cost of making loans. She went on to say that they had given credit to numerous women and, if they did not charge interest, by now the money would have been eaten up by inflation and the costs of implementation. At this point, exasperated about having to give these explanations to someone who seemed not very pleased with the conditions, the field manager suggested that maybe they should take another week and reconsider whether they really wanted this loan or not. The other two women, now worried that they might not get the loan, jumped in and began talking about how excited they were about their businesses. In response to the cue of mutual support, they gushed examples of how they always prioritized helping women around them. The older sister repeatedly said that they had no doubt in their minds about taking on the loan and opening their businesses. Nevertheless, the committee meeting came to an end with the conclusion that they would convene again the following week. Later, I learned that they received the credit and that, in the second meeting, this sort of questioning did not take place.[9]

During the process of receiving the loan, women learned how to act; what kinds of questions represented them as enthusiastic participants (those about technical legal advice, future loan prospects, experiences of other clients); and what responses were undesirable (for example, questioning the logic of the operation, acting too hapless, criticizing the macro situation instead of focusing on what the individual can do). This was not because officers were indifferent to women's predicaments. On the contrary, many were anxious to help them as much as possible. Occasionally, they expressed ambivalence about the methods the programs allowed them to use, reflecting on what they saw as the difference between international assumptions; central-office visions; and the local, everyday

GENDER AND ECONOMICS IN MUSLIM COMMUNITIES

circumstances. One privately questioned the logic of the loan; another argued against the myriad forms the women filled out and signed; and yet another saw the worth of her work in the larger advocacy programs, not loan disbursal. Despite the ambivalence officers occasionally displayed, the program designs and interactions ended up disciplining the ways in which the women talked about their circumstances as challenges to be overcome.

One woman who had worked in the informal textile industry since age 12 proudly explained to me how she was finally able to start her own small tailoring shop:

> I have survived many obstacles ... [Every time] I said to myself, I will fight back. I opened this shop and I won't close it... How did I do it? I worked day and night. Where people worked eight hours, I worked twelve. Sometimes I did not even go home. I worked; I always fought. I wanted more. I wanted more for myself.

During the rest of the interview, she told me how, throughout her childhood, she drifted from one city to another as her father looked for work; how she ended up not finishing primary school as a result; how she escaped home to work and then came back to find herself the primary breadwinner; and how she still loses money to relatives, bad loans, and clients who do not pay for their merchandise because, in her interpretation, they think they can get away with it because she is a single woman. What she called obstacles actually demonstrated a life of precariousness. Yet, she chose to narrate all of this as a story of progress.

This discourse of hard work, dedication, and perseverance was not necessarily a stance learned only in their experience with these organizations. Similar to what Murray Li has shown in her work on development practices in Indonesia (Murray Li 2007), conditions under which the loans were disbursed solidify these narratives. Yet, these microbusinesses do not necessarily perform as expected. Even if one took charge and worked extremely hard, still nothing could change, or things could even go for the worse. As indicated also by Ecevit (2007), these women usually established very precarious businesses, given the limitations of their resources and care responsibilities. Periodic economic fluctuations often resulted in bankruptcies and accumulating debts, showing the problem with the assumption that microenterprises will bring sustained poverty alleviation. In other words, the idea that people can fend for themselves through hard work in the market and that markets will provide jobs through economic growth is, at best, too optimistic. One woman, going through such a period as I was speaking to her, could not reconcile her years of arduous efforts of walking door-to-door, selling women's merchandise with the fact she was burdened with debt today. She suggested that maybe the problem was something else: "I continue trying to buy and

GENDER AND ECONOMICS IN MUSLIM COMMUNITIES

sell small things. But nothing is as it was before. I just can't get things to work. I don't believe that the evil eye is a superstition. These are true things that affect one tremendously." Thus, the rationality of individual responsibility could work only insofar as she found ways of attributing her precariousness to the "evil eye."

CALCULATING SELF-INTEREST

In an opening ceremony of a local branch of the microcredit program run by the Turkish Foundation for Waste Reduction (Türkiye İsrafı Önleme Vakfı [TİSVA]) in collaboration with the Grameen Bank, the Deputy Prime Minister Cemil Çiçek said:

> Coal is for free; medicine is for free; the doctor is for free; food is for free; everything is for free. When this is the case, we become a freebie society. But a human being is a human being to the extent that they are working. If a person has a disability making it impossible for them to work, then yes, the state should help them. But 20-year-old, 30-year-old people who can squeeze their bread from stone are expecting state aid. (*Zaman* 2009)

In this and many other similar examples, public officers code poverty in terms of individual irresponsibility, lack of will, and lack of rationality. They associate welfare provisioning with perverse incentives. Such discourses are integral to discursive and structural assemblages that make truth productions (Andrew Barry 2006) around neoliberal citizenship possible. Thus people are constantly encouraged to think of themselves as responsible for their fates; and not in terms of multiple inequalities, lack of meaningful job opportunities, and decreased willingness on the part of public institutions to ameliorate these situations.

The entrepreneurial woman is also expected to develop the ability to calculate costs and benefits and approach decision making in these terms. In two separate training sessions for women who sought technical advice (not credit), these calculations were evident, especially during discussions of social security. In one meeting, women mostly came from lower middle-class backgrounds and were interested in starting limited companies for businesses such as small restaurants, hair salons, and organic agriculture. For most, employing people did not appear to be in their foreseeable future. However, when the presenter started to talk about payments for the social-security benefits of potential employees, she was bombarded with questions about how to evade these payments. The participants assumed the position of being a victim of unfair legal requirements. They protested that if they employed people legally, their costs would rise because of minimum wage requirements and social-security payments. One woman

GENDER AND ECONOMICS IN MUSLIM COMMUNITIES

who was trying to initiate a cooperative among low-income women said they did not want to pay social-security benefits because it was an additional start-up cost. Another said in her line of work, there was a frequent circulation of workers. She wondered why she had to go through the trouble of arranging social-security payments for someone who might work for her for as little as one month.

Learning to become entrepreneurs requires familiarity with law and calculations of cost and revenue. This is a process in which market logics and commodification of employment relations are internalized. Various general mechanisms of socialization promote a particular understanding of self-interest, where the self comes closer to the neoliberal model of the isolated individual. These sessions in themselves do not necessarily make this shift possible; yet, they provide a venue for the crystallization of discourses supporting individualistic calculations of cost and benefit. As a result, social security is registered as a cost, which can be abused by the employee or the state, rather than a right. In this sense, discourses of entrepreneurship disciplined the participants to perform as savvy businesswomen, no matter how small-scale their operations might have been. They also began to talk in a language that actually put them at a disadvantage in terms of social rights.

On the other hand, later in the same meeting, when the discussion switched to their own experiences as workers at risk of being cheated out of social-security benefits, the tone changed dramatically. Turkish business law stipulates there has to be a minimum of two partners to establish a limited company. Many of the participants intended to turn to family members to become partners on paper, but they were worried about jeopardizing the latter's pension. This concern was justified, given the very complex Turkish social-security system, which until recently offered unequal pension programs to different segments of the working population.[10] One woman said she lost her rights to a retirement pension after paying 5,000 days of premium because, once she had legalized her business, her social-security benefits had been transferred to a different program which obliged her to make payments for 7,000 days. Another remarked that, if the partner was retired, 10 percent of their pension could be cut. People angrily remarked: "So they are saying to the retired, die."

In another meeting between the representatives of the women's cooperatives and state officers, the women insistently asked the officers why the board members of cooperatives could receive salaries but not be registered with the state social-security benefits. Someone said that the members were not rich people, did not have access to any social-security program, and having such benefits through the board of the cooperative was essential for them. The public officer explained, in what women sitting around me saw as a patronizing manner, that they had banned the provision of social-security benefits to cooperative board members because

GENDER AND ECONOMICS IN MUSLIM COMMUNITIES

they did not want the system to be "abused." The language of "abuse" was similar to previous remarks that had located social security in the sphere of unnecessary costs. In response to challenges from the floor, he resorted to phrases such as "preventing people from getting something that their work did not justify," and he argued that the law aimed to make sure that self-serving acts on the part of individuals did not implode the system from within. He appeared surprised when women demanded more of a rights-based explanation and implied that "the system" was a natural order not to be disturbed and an order that seemed to select the "deserving" ones for social-security benefits. In his words, it was not only that the system was built on individual responsibility for self and on workfare instead of welfare (Bob Jessop 1999); there also seemed to be a hierarchy among different types of labor, only some of which qualified a working person for social security. These exchanges allowed me to see how women recognized the problems with the discourse and the implications of the idea of individuals fending for themselves.

It was not necessarily that the women in these situations were hypocritical. On the contrary, meanings attached to social security could shift in this dramatic manner because of the crucial characteristics in the language that accompanies becoming "rational" entrepreneurs. Once again, these exchanges were not the sole cause of dizzying switches in the way in which social security was evaluated. Together with the general discourses and everyday practices, they extended the ideal of the self-sufficient individual to the lives of these women. As a result, they became accustomed to narrating stories of opportunities and challenges as they attempted to make sense of their circumstances. This neoliberal citizenship assumes capacity for calculations based on self-interest and responsibility. However, the contradictions in the same women's narratives, their resistances, as well as the broader economic circumstances – which themselves do not validate the lexicon of the calculating, rational, and hard-working women – show that these processes are neither stable nor free of challenges.

GENDERING RESPONSIBILITY

The same women who are expected to conduct entrepreneurial activity based on individual resources in a market economy are also supposed to be responsible familial subjects, using their income for their loved ones. Suad Joseph (1996, 2000) argues that in the Middle East, family plays a significant role in the construction of women (and men's) selfhoods, citizenships, and rights. Accordingly, contradictions between gendered norms of familial responsibility and individualist understandings of market performance especially discourage women's entry into the labor force. I propose that this is not a contradiction bound to this specific region. The coexistence of these seemingly contradictory logics should be understood in terms

GENDER AND ECONOMICS IN MUSLIM COMMUNITIES

of the hidden gender transcripts of neoliberal subjectivity. During the fieldwork, the paradoxes of assuming a demarcation between home and work and individual aspirations and familial responsibilities became clear when women talked about experiences of motherhood and family.

On a trip to a bazaar with a field officer, we met with a woman who sold women's and men's undergarments. When the field officer had first met her, she had been abandoned by her husband and was living with her two children in a makeshift hut. For a month, the field officer took her to a bazaar every week so that she would get used to becoming a seller. She told me how she cried the entire time, but said that she was a mother, and that there was really no other option to take care of her children. At the end of the month, she went to a wholesale merchant who was known for his good prices. The first time she visited him, he yelled at her that he sold merchandise in tons and that he was not interested in small business. She left the shop desolate, but other places were so expensive that she had to go back. When she called again, she talked with his assistant and explained that she was a single mother with two children. The next time she visited the man, who in the meantime had learned her story, apologized and broke his practice of selling only in tons. In this case, she was able to obtain merchandise because the merchant sympathized with her obligation to take care of her children. On the one hand, the woman was able to strike a patriarchal bargain and form a strategy that would help her. On the other hand, the fact that this exchange took place within the limitations of a series of assumptions about women's labor contributed to the reproduction of these assumptions. It was not entrepreneurial potential, but rather entrepreneurial obligation tied to gendered responsibility for family care that framed her economic activity.

In relation to a different program where women are given technical advice for their entrepreneurial activities, several officers told me another story that is of interest here. The wife of a shop owner had been preparing dowry sets (of linens, towels, and other embroidered household textiles) for her friends and extended family for a while when people began asking her to turn this "pastime" into a business. She received assistance from the organization and started a successful business. Yet, she was part of a patriarchal household, and there was always the danger, if her husband became jealous, she would have to terminate the work. Therefore, she continued to downplay her success so that the delicate balance at home would not be upset. The first person who told me this story said she did not necessarily agree with the household setup in which the woman operated. Still, she praised the woman for her ability to juggle familial circumstances with her business savvy. In this particular example, the woman was not obliged to make money, but she wanted to work. She could do so by continuing to highlight her gendered role within the family. Once again, economic activity was constructed around and, therefore, reproduced existing gender norms.

These examples, in which women strategically juggle income-generating activity and homemaking, reveal how the neoliberal assumption of an isolated and self-sufficient individual is actually one that is predicated on an unequal division of labor between sexes, because it ignores them. In the case of development programs, Lamia Karim's (2011) work in Bangladesh has documented how those programs targeting women's businesses can rely on existing gender norms in communities. In the case of Turkey, government officers have also emphasized how women generating income were more likely to spend it on their children and families and how microcredit offered them the chance to do so without disrupting their household responsibilities.[11] Different from Karim's study, the officers in these two organizations voiced awareness of the problems with claims about women contributing more from their earnings to the well-being of their families. They made sure I understood they used the language selectively and strategically in their interactions with funding agencies or government officials when they were seeking support for policies that would improve women's conditions. Notwithstanding this subtlety in their use of the language of sacrificial mothers and the gratitude many women felt to the CSO officers who reached out to them when no one else did, they still elucidated gendered paradoxes. The construction of women as potential entrepreneurs and sacrificial mothers and wives emerges precisely because discourses of individual responsibility do not work in real life. Despite the intentions of the officers and women themselves, when state institutions of redistribution are being ideologically challenged and physically dismantled, citizenship becomes gendered in a way that asks women to be innovative in taking care of themselves and their families because this is what they are "naturally" inclined to do.

These examples show a paradoxical overlap between existing gender norms, individual entrepreneurial activity, and the structural and discursive changes in the economy that bring these two together. Yet, women also inserted their own stories into narratives of success; they recognized the limits in the discourses of self-made women and the costs of staying afloat. Even when they were actively participating in the construction of their own neoliberal subjectivities, their narratives revealed the contingency of the process.

During a visit to one of the organizations, I helped make phone calls to candidates for a national entrepreneurship prize. We asked the candidates how their small businesses had changed their lives. The expectation was to elicit stories from the women about how they had become confident and improved their self-respect. I must have sounded too sympathetic when I made the calls, because initially all I heard were complaints of exhaustion

GENDER AND ECONOMICS IN MUSLIM COMMUNITIES

and decreased time for family and friends. After the first few phone conversations, I decided to speak in a more distant tone and asked about positive and negative changes in their lives so that I could maximize their chances of getting the award. The stories of innovation and empowerment belonged on the form, while other, more negative experiences did not, even though they came embroiled with one another.

In the interviews I conducted for my own research, women also questioned this demarcation in different ways, ranging from elaborate descriptions of social isolation to exhaustion. They also talked of the help they received from other family members. In one case, I interviewed two sisters, who proudly recounted their success story of starting a small beauty salon. We were conversing in the shop, frequently interrupted by their young children. The older sister explained that the children usually stayed with their grandmother, but that they had not been able to make this arrangement for that day. Later, when the conversation turned to their family's story, the younger sister said: "One person's success equals another's slavery." She explained how they could not have worked, had it not been for their own mother who cooked for them, cleaned their houses, and looked after their children. She acknowledged that nobody recognized this cost. Even they had forgotten to include this detail in their own business story.

These instances reveal how the assumption of sacrificial motherhood is an integral, yet invisible part of the entrepreneurial neoliberal citizen. These women are expected to continue their familial obligations alongside their income-generating activities. Frequently their ability to do the second depends on guaranteeing that they can continue performing the first. If they could not perform their familial obligations, then it was an arrangement with another woman that lifted the burden off their shoulders. But, this did not change the gendered division of labor at home.[12] Focusing only on women's income-generating activity would have rendered this complementarity invisible.

As indicated above, these microenterprises also suffer from the same invisible complementarity. Many women start similar small businesses, such as sewing, cooking, jewelry making, and the sale of beauty and cleaning products (Ecevit 2007). Although some programs attempt to diversify these business preferences through training, choices remain limited given the gendered division of household reproductive work. Similarities in the microenterprises can also create a crowding-out effect, driving prices down and restricting further growth potential, which becomes worse as a result of periodic economic fluctuations. In fact, performance analysis of micro and small enterprises reveals their higher precariousness in times of economic crises, rendering misguided the hopes placed on them for poverty alleviation (Şemsa Özar, Gökhan Özerten, and Zeynep Burcu İrfanoğlu 2008). Thus, the ideal neoliberal subjectivity is not only

GENDER AND ECONOMICS IN MUSLIM COMMUNITIES

gendered, but this internal contradiction also makes it less likely that women will achieve its promises of improved private and public status.

These vignettes reveal two fundamental aspects of neoliberal subjectivity, rendered invisible if the discussion is limited to the cultivation of entrepreneurial, market-capable individuals. First, women's narratives show that they are not really expected to be isolated individual decision makers. They are to be market savvy in service of their families. Thus neoliberal subjectivity is a gendered, familial one, even if it does not appear to be so. Second, this dual expectation from women also points to a crisis of the discourse of individual success through hard work. These women work extremely hard, but given their limited choices and the general economic circumstances, very few can actually make it.

CONCLUDING REMARKS

Over the last few decades, neoliberal logic has vigorously promoted the value of individual rationality, responsibility, and entrepreneurial skills. The dismantling of social protection is justified on the basis that individuals should have the capacity to fend for themselves. The expectation that women become self-governing citizens fits within this logic. Civil-society initiatives that cater to this expectation, albeit with different motivations, provide a fruitful venue for discussing the logical limits and practical implications of the model of the economic, hard-working, and self-governing citizen.

This contribution has drawn on literature critiquing the neoliberal paradigm and the development programs couched in their logic, particularly those focusing on microcredit programs. This study differs from and adds to the body of knowledge emerging from them in two interrelated ways. First, it takes up the case of Turkey, where the consolidation of the neoliberal state has already happened. This context provides for a coherent articulation of neoliberal citizenship ideals that are the discourses and practices that formulate expectations of citizens' conduct. It makes sense to talk in terms of neoliberal citizenship, generalized discourses of individual responsibility as well as familial support only in the context of an economic environment which espouse it as much as these programs, if not more.

Second, in this study, I am not interested in poverty-alleviation programs in general, nor specifically in microcredit. Most ethnographic work available explores the relations between domestic actors and international NGOs, as they interact in the provisioning of microcredit to the poor. My focus has been on the idea of entrepreneurship and entrepreneurial women emerging out of local programs of women's empowerment through market-related activities. So, the focus was both narrower and wider: narrower in the sense of working with actors who put their gender

GENDER AND ECONOMICS IN MUSLIM COMMUNITIES

sensitivities before poverty alleviation; wider in the sense that I have looked at a terrain that includes microcredit but is not limited to it.

There are two advantages of this particular focus. It reveals the hidden gender transcripts of the market-based understanding of neoliberal citizenship. And it does so in the context of program officers who would not wholeheartedly buy into its logic. The procedures and requirements of these initiatives, their narratives about entrepreneurship, individual self-sufficiency, and rationality reveal tense gendered impossibilities of the neoliberal citizen. The expectation from women to become entrepreneurs, whose rationality is defined by self-sufficiency and market savvy, reproduces neoliberal norms for citizens. Yet, the same women are also expected to take care of their families. It is because of the practical failure of a market-based notion of individual self-sufficiency that we see the hidden gendered transcripts of neoclassical economic assumptions. Both the officers and the beneficiaries participate in the construction of these subjectivities, even when their intentions may vary greatly. Yet, organization members' and beneficiaries' own narratives and everyday implementations reveal sharply the inconsistencies of models of neoliberal citizenship and the contingency of these subjectivities.

In sum, the analysis of everyday practice provides us with a new space for rethinking theoretical and practical bottlenecks in existing neoliberal discourses. Taking into account real experiences can open up novel paths to think about relations between gendered assumptions and expectations from individuals in the market space.

ACKNOWLEDGMENTS

This research has been made possible by a grant from Middle East Research Competition. I would like to thank the officers of KEDV and KAGİDER,

GENDER AND ECONOMICS IN MUSLIM COMMUNITIES

who allowed me to conduct participant observation of their activities. I am especially grateful for the generous support by Berrin Yenice, Aylin Tuncel, Doğa Tamer, and Nuray Özbay, without whom the work would have been impossible. I would like to thank Nina Ergin, whose editorial suggestions were invaluable, and Şebnem Keniş, who transcribed most of the interviews. Additionally, I would like to express gratitude for the insightful suggestions provided by the anonymous referees as well as the guest editors of the special issue at *Feminist Economics*. Finally, I would like to thank all the women who shared their stories with me. All personal information that would allow the identification of interviewees has been removed.

NOTES

[1] The main offices of the organizations are located in Istanbul. KEDV had local branches in the greater Marmara region, while KAGİDER also ran an office in Brussels for European Union relations. Both are connected to various networks spanning the rest of Turkey that organize outreach programs.

[2] Even though the concept was not clearly defined, the organizations' activities revealed a definition that included control of money and ability to make decisions (Anne Marie Goetz and Rina Sen Gupta 1995) as well as broader goals such as economic security, evading family domination, and legal awareness (Syed M. Hashemi, Sidney Ruth Schuler, and Ann P. Riley 1996).

[3] Class positions and educational backgrounds showed variation. Because KEDV ran a microcredit program, they catered more to poorer women with less formal schooling, while KAGİDER's training programs reached women with more financial means and higher-level diplomas. These differences also influenced women's businesses. While most opened bazaar stands or neighborhood beauty salons, the smaller number with professional experience and higher education chose consultancy and hospitality. The women who worked in the organizations came from various backgrounds. In the central offices, they were mostly college graduates and, on average, younger. In KEDV, there were also a number of field officers – mostly retired, middle-age women – with established connections to the districts where they worked. For the implications of the class positions of the officers, consult Özlem Altan-Olcay (forthcoming).

[4] Consult Altan-Olcay and İçduygu (2012) for the civil society scene in the region at large and what outside funding means for advocacy networks.

[5] Studies of the last decade show a shift: AKP, the governing political party, has introduced new informal and formal redistribution mechanisms and increased public expenditure on health and education (Ziya Öniş 2012), but these have been formulated in terms of social aid, creating political dependency (Erdem Yörük 2012).

[6] For instance, in 2007 the Turkish Economy Bank (Türk Ekonomi Bankası [TEB]), the Association of Young Executives and Businessmen (Genç Yönetici ve İşsadamları Derneği [GYİAD]), and the UNDP together started a microcredit program targeting young potential entrepreneurs and investors. HSBC has made agreements with the Turkish Foundation for Waste Reduction (Türkiye İsrafı Önleme Vakfı [TİSVA]) as well as with the Community Volunteers Association (Toplum Gönülüleri Vakfı [TOG]). The collaboration of TİSVA with the Turkish Grameen Bank resulted in fifty-six microcredit branches by the end of 2009 and close to 30,000 loan recipients since 2003. This is a modest number compared with programs elsewhere.

GENDER AND ECONOMICS IN MUSLIM COMMUNITIES

[7] These include the Ministry of Industry and Commerce's Küçük ve Orta İşletmeleri Geliştirmeve Destekleme İdari Başkanlığı (Office of Support for Small and Medium Enterprises [KOSGEB]), which train and fund individual initiatives for small enterprises; the Social Assistance and Solidarity Fund, which administers conditional cash-transfer programs and training for women's individual and collective entrepreneurial activities; and various collaborations with the UNDP and World Bank that release funds for microfinance.

[8] This happens either individually or the candidates form a group.

[9] I did not attend committee meetings where women were denied the credit because those refusals, if they happened, took place before this stage.

[10] Until recently, for those in the formal sector, a fragmented and hierarchical pension system prevailed, differentiating between public- and private-sector workers as well as business owners. Switching between these sectors also meant dramatic changes in individual premiums, the number of years of contribution, as well as the value of the pension. Employers are expected to contribute to the system from employees' gross salaries. See Mehmet Cansoy (2012) for further details on the Turkish case as well as comparison with European models.

[11] Consult Hürriyet (2008) and Zaman (2008) for two of examples where women's entrepreneurial work is articulated in connection with "support for the family budget."

[12] This story crosscuts cultures. Studies show that women in the Global North and South undertake a heavier share of household labor, despite having a paid job. In fact, this factor also explains job choices outside of the home. For studies of labor participation and unequal division of household labor, consult Josephine E. Olson, Irene Hanson Frieze, and Ellen G. Detlefsen (1990); Joni Hersch and Leslie S. Stratton (1994); also for gendered time poverty, see Elena Bardasi and Quentin Wodon (2010).

REFERENCES

Abu-Lughod, Lila. 2009. "Dialects of Women's Empowerment: The International Circuitry of the *Arab Human Development Report 2005*." *International Journal of Middle East Studies* 41: 83–103.

Adaman, Fikret and Tuğçe Bulut. 2007. *500 Milyonluk umut hikayeleri: Mikrokredi-maceraları* [Stories of hope for 500 million: Adventures in microcredit]. Istanbul: İletişim.

Adaman, Fikret and Çağlar Keyder. 2006. *Poverty and Social Exclusion in the Slum Areas of Large Cities in Turkey.* Brussels: European Commission Employment, Social Affairs and Equal Opportunities.

Adely, Fida. 2009. "Educating Women for Development: *The Arab Human Development Report 2005* and the Problem with Women's Choices." *International Journal of Middle East Studies* 41: 105–22.

Altan-Olcay, Özlem. 2011. "Reframing the Ideal Citizen in Turkey: National Belonging and Economic Success in the Era of Neo-Liberalism."*New Perspectives on Turkey* 44(1): 41–72.

———. forthcoming. "The Figure of the Entrepreneurial Woman in Development Programs: Thinking through Class Differences." *Social Politics.*

Altan-Olcay, Özlem and Ahmet İçduygu. 2012. "Mapping Civil Society in the Middle East: The Cases of Egypt, Lebanon, and Turkey." *British Journal of Middle Eastern Studies* 39(2): 157–79.

GENDER AND ECONOMICS IN MUSLIM COMMUNITIES

Bahramitash, Roksana and Jennifer C. Olmsted. 2014. "Choice and Constraint in Paid Work: Women from Low-Income Households in Tehran." *Feminist Economics.* doi:10.1080/13545701.2014.957710.

Bakker, Isabella. 2007. "Social Reproduction and the Constitution of a Gendered Political Economy.' *New Political Economy* 12(4): 541–56.

Bardasi, Elena and Quentin Wodon. 2010. "Working Long Hours and Having No Choice: Time Poverty in Guinea." *Feminist Economics* 16(3): 45–78.

Barry, Andrew. 2006. "Ethical Capitalism." In *Global Governmentality: Governing International Spaces,* edited by Wendy Larner and William Walters, 195–211. London: Routledge.

Benería, Lourdes. 1999. "Globalization, Gender and the Davos Man." *Feminist Economics* 5(3): 61–83.

Benería, Lourdes, Maria Floro, Caren Grown, and Martha MacDonald. 2000. "Introduction: Globalization and Gender." *Feminist Economics* 6(3): vii–xviii.

Berik, Günseli. 1997. "The Need for Crossing the Method Boundaries in Economics Research." *Feminist Economics* 3(2): 121–5.

Boratav, Korkut. 1995. *İstanbul ve Anadolu'dan sınıf profilleri* [Profiles of class from Istanbul and Anatolia]. Istanbul: Tarih Vakfı Yurt Yayınları.

Buğra, Ayşe and Çağlar Keyder. 2006. "The Turkish Welfare Regime in Transformation." *Journal of European Social Policy* 16(3): 211–28.

Buğra, Ayşe and Burcu Yakut-Çakar. 2010. "Structural Change, the Social Policy Environment and Female Employment in Turkey." *Development and Change* 41: 517–38.

Burchell, Graham. 1996. "Liberal Government and Techniques of the Self." In *Foucault and Political Reason: Liberalism, Neo-Liberalism and Rationalities of Government,* edited by Andrew Barry, Thomas Osborne, and Nikolas Rose, 19–36. Chicago: University of Chicago Press.

Callari, Antonio. 2004. "Economics and the Postcolonial Other." In *Postcolonialism Meets Economics,* edited by Eiman Zein-Elabdin and S. Charusheela, 113–29. London: Routledge.

Cansoy, Mehmet. 2012. "Turkish Welfare State in the Neoliberal Era: Emergence of Class-Based Citizenship Regimes." MA diss., Koç University.

Dean, Mitchell. 1999. *Governmentality: Power and Rule in Modern Society.* London: SAGE.

Dedeoğlu, Saniye. 2010. "Visible Hands – Invisible Women: Garment Production in Turkey." *Feminist Economics* 16(4): 1–31.

Dimand, Robert W. 2004. "Classical Political Economy and Orientalism: Nassau Senior's Eastern Tours." In *Postcolonialism Meets Economics,* edited by Eiman Zein-Elabdin and S. Charusheela, 73–90. London: Routledge.

Dufour, Mathieu and Özgür Orhangazi. 2009. "The 2000–2001 Financial Crisis in Turkey: A Crisis for Whom?" *Review of Political Economy* 21(1): 101–22.

Ecevit, Yıldız. 2007. *A Critical Approach to Women's Entrepreneurship in Turkey.* Ankara: International Labor Office.

Eisenstein, Hester. 2005. "A Dangerous Liaison? Feminism and Corporate Globalization." *Science and Society* 69(3): 487–518.

England, Paula. 1993. "The Separative Self: Androcentric Bias in Neoclassical Assumptions." In *Beyond the Economic Man: Feminist Theory and Economics,* edited by Marianne Ferber and Julie Nelson, 37–53. Chicago: University of Chicago Press.

Fine, Ben. 2003. "Neither the Washington Consensus nor the Post-Washington Consensus." In *Development Policy in the 21st Century – Beyond the Post-Washington Consensus,* edited by Ben Fine, Costas Lapavitsas, and Jonathan Pincus, 1–27. London: Routledge.

Folbre, Nancy. 2009. *Greed, Lust and Gender: A History of Economic Ideas.* Oxford: Oxford University Press.

GENDER AND ECONOMICS IN MUSLIM COMMUNITIES

Folbre, Nancy and Julie A. Nelson. 2000. "For Love or Money – Or Both?" *Journal of Economic Perspectives* 14(4): 123–40.

Foucault, Michel. 1991. "Governmentality." In *The Foucault Effect: Studies in Governmentality*, edited by Graham Burchell, Colin Gordon, and Peter Miller, 87–104. Chicago: University of Chicago Press.

Goetz, Anne Marie and Rina Sen Gupta. 1995. "Who Takes the Credit? Gender, Power and Control Over Loan Use in Rural Credit Programs in Bangladesh." *World Development* 24(1): 45–63.

Gürses, Damla. 2009. "Microfinance and Poverty Reduction in Turkey." *Perspectives on Global Development and Technology* 8: 90–110.

Hashemi, Syed M., Sidney Ruth Schuler, and Ann P. Riley. 1996. "Rural Credit Programs and Women's Empowerment in Bangladesh." *World Development* 24(4): 635–53.

Hersch, Joni and Leslie S. Stratton. 1994. "Housework, Wages, and the Division of Housework Time for Employed Spouses." *American Economic Review* 84(2): 120–5.

Hindess, Barry. 2002. "Neo-liberal Citizenship." *Citizenship Studies* 6(2): 127–43.

Hürriyet. 2008. "Van'da 879 kadın iş sahibi oldu"[879 women in Van now have jobs]. September 2.

Isik, Damla. 2013. "'Just Like Prophet Mohammad Preached': Labor, Piety, and Chanty in Contemporary Turkey." *Feminist Economics*. doi:10.1080/13545701.2013.825376.

Jessop, Bob. 1999. "The Changing Governance of Welfare: Recent Trends in Its Primary Functions, Scale, and Modes of Coordination." *Social Policy and Administration* 33(4): 348–59.

Joseph, Suad. 1996. "Gender and Citizenship in Middle Eastern States." *Middle East Report* 198: 4–10.

———. 2000. "Gendering Citizenship in the Middle East." In *Gender and Citizenship in the Middle East*, edited by Suad Joseph, 3–30. New York: Syracuse University Press.

Karim, Lamia. 2008. "Demystifying Micro-Credit: The Grameen Bank, NGOs, and Neoliberalism in Bangladesh." *Cultural Dynamics* 20(1): 5–29.

———. 2011. *Microfinance and Its Discontents: Women in Debt in Bangladesh.* Minneapolis: University of Minnesota Press.

Karnani, Aneel. 2009. "Romanticizing the Poor Harms the Poor." *Journal of International Development* 21: 76–86.

Keyder, Çağlar. 2004. "The Turkish Bell Jar." *New Left Review* 28: 65–84.

———. 2005. "Globalization and Social Exclusion in Istanbul." *International Journal of Urban and Regional Research* 29(1): 124–34.

Keyder, Çağlar and Zafer Yenal. 2011. "Agrarian Change under Globalization: Markets and Insecurity in Turkish Agriculture." *Journal of Agrarian Change* 11(1): 60–86.

Lawson, Victoria. 2007. "Geographies of Care and Responsibility." *Annals of the Association of American Geographers* 97(1): 1–11.

Medley, Joseph and Lorrayne Carroll. 2004. "The Hungry Ghost: IMF Policy, Global Capitalist Transformation, and Laboring Bodies in Southeast Asia." In *Postcolonialism Meets Economics*, edited by Eiman Zein-Elabdin and S. Charusheela, 145–64. London: Routledge.

Murray Li, Tania. 2005. "Beyond 'the State' and Failed Schemes." *American Anthropologist* 107(3): 383–94.

———. 2007. *The Will to Improve: Governmentality, Development, and the Practice of Politics.* Durham, NC: Duke University Press.

Nelson, Julie. 1996. *Feminism, Objectivity, and Economics.* London: Routledge.

Olmsted, Jennifer. 1997. "Telling Palestinian Women's Economic Stories." *Feminist Economics* 3(2): 141–51.

GENDER AND ECONOMICS IN MUSLIM COMMUNITIES

————. 2004. "Orientalism and Economic Methods – (Re)Reading Feminist Economic Texts." In *Postcolonialism Meets Economics*, edited by Eiman Zein-Elabdin and S. Charusheela, 162–82. London: Routledge.

Olson, Josephine E., Irene Hanson Frieze, and Ellen G. Detlefsen. 1990. "Having It All? Combining Work and Family in a Male and a Female Profession." *Sex Roles* 23(9/10): 515–53.

Öniş, Ziya. 2012. "The Triumph of Conservative Globalism: The Political Economy of the AKP Era." *Turkish Studies* 13(2): 135-152.

Özar, İemsa, Gökhan Özerten, and Zeynep Burcu İrfanoğlu. 2008. "Micro and Small Enterprise Growth in Turkey: Under the Shadow of Financial Crisis." *Developing Economies* 46(4): 331–62.

Polanyi, Karl. 1944. *The Great Transformation: The Political and Economic Origins of Our Time.* Boston: Beacon Press, 2001.

Rankin, Katherine. 2001. "Governing Development: Neoliberalism, Microcredit, and Rational Economic Woman." *Economy and Society* 30(1): 18–37.

————. 2002. "Social Capital, Microfinance, and the Politics of Development." *Feminist Economics* 2(1): 1–24.

Rose, Nikolas and Peter Miller. 1992. "Political Power beyond the State: Problematics of Government." *British Journal of Sociology* 43(2): 173–205.

Roy, Ananya. 2010. *Poverty Capital: Microfinance and the Making of Development.* New York: Routledge.

Saith, Ashwani. 2006. "From Universal Values to Millennium Development Goals: Lost in Translation." *Development and Change* 37: 1167–99.

Sakallıoğlu, Ümit Cizre and Erinç Yeldan. 2000. "Politics, Society, and Financial Liberalization." *Development and Change* 31: 408–581.

Silvey, Rachel and Rebecca Elmhirst. 2003. "Engendering Social Capital: Women Workers and Rural-Urban Networks in Indonesia's Crisis." *World Development* 31(5): 865–79.

Somers, Margaret. 2008. *Genealogies of Citizenship: Markets, Statelessness, and the Right to Have Rights.* Cambridge: Cambridge University Press.

Turkish Statistics Institute. 2014. *Household Labor Force Survey Results.* http://www.tuik.gov.tr/PreTablo.do?alt_id=1007.

Weber, Heloise. 2002. "The Imposition of a Global Development Architecture: The Example of Microcredit." *Review of International Studies* 28(3): 537–55.

————. 2004. "The 'New Economy' and Social Risk: Banking on the Poor?" *Review of International Political Economy* 11(2): 356–86.

White, Jenny. 1994. *Money Makes Us Relatives: Women's Labor in Urban Turkey.* Austin: University of Texas Press.

World Bank. 2009. *Female Labour Participaton in Turkey: Trends, Determinants and Policy Framework.* Report No. 48508-TR. Washington, DC: World Bank Human Development Sector Unit.

Yazıcı, Berna. 2008. "Social Work and Social Exclusion in Turkey: An Overview." *New Perspectives on Turkey* 38: 107–34.

Yörük, Erdem. 2012. "Welfare Provision as Political Containment: The Politics of Social Assistance and the Kurdish Conflict in Turkey." *Politics and Society* 40(4): 517–47.

Yükseker, Deniz. 2006. "Severed from Their Homeland and Livelihoods: The Internal Displacement of Kurds in Turkey as a Process of Social Exclusion." In *Poverty and Social Exclusion in the Slum Areas of Large Cities in Turkey,* edited by Fikret Adaman and Çağlar Keyder, 41–54. Brussels: European Commission Employment, Social Issues and Equal Opportunity DG.

GENDER AND ECONOMICS IN MUSLIM COMMUNITIES

Zaman. 2008. "Muğlalı kadın giriþimciler sertifika aldı" [Women entrepreneurs from Muğla awarded certificates]. November 8. http://www.zaman.com.tr/haber.do?haberno=758281.

Zaman. 2009. "Elazığ'da mikro kredi uygulama merkezi açıldı" [A microcredit center has been opened in Elazığ]. October 10. http://www.zaman.com.tr/haber.do?haberno=904851&keyfield=6D696B726F6B72656469.

Zein-Elabdin, Eiman. 2001. "Contours of a Non-Modernist Discourse: The Contested Space of History and Development." *Review of Radical Political Economics* 33(3): 255–63.

Zein-Elabdin, Eiman and S. Charusheela. 2004. "Introduction: Economics and Post-Colonial Thought." In *Postcolonialism Meets Economics,* edited by Eiman Zein-Elabdin and S. Charusheela, 1–18. London: Routledge.

CHOICE AND CONSTRAINT IN PAID WORK: WOMEN FROM LOW-INCOME HOUSEHOLDS IN TEHRAN

Roksana Bahramitash and Jennifer C. Olmsted

ABSTRACT

Based on interviews and participant observation conducted in 2009–10 in Tehran among women living in low-income communities, this contribution examines the complex ways in which women experience paid work. Most low-income Iranian women interviewed had conflicted views about paid employment. Some held up the male breadwinner as ideal, occasionally invoking Islam to limit their engagement in work they viewed as socially stigmatizing, physically difficult, or low paying. Others, particularly younger and unmarried women, had more positive views of work. Class, age, type of employment, and marital status all played roles in shaping women's experiences; but among women with similar characteristics, considerable differences were also apparent. Building off previous work that rejects simplistic dualisms such as choice versus constraint or exploitation versus empowerment, this contribution argues for more nuanced categories that allow for an emphasis on the conflicted ways women experience paid work.

PROBLEMATIZING WOMEN'S EMPLOYMENT: THEORETICAL FRAMEWORK

Particularly in the context of the Middle East and North Africa, development agencies have argued that women's low labor force participation is costly to societies and a sign of low levels of women's empowerment (World Bank 2004). Feminists, however, have cautioned against "falsely homogenizing accounts of women's lives" (Kanchana N. Ruwanpura and Jane Humphries 2004: 174), pleading for more nuance when it comes to discussions of the benefits of paid work. In this contribution, we challenge a number of dualisms that have been reinforced in the literature on women's employment. The main dualisms we address

GENDER AND ECONOMICS IN MUSLIM COMMUNITIES

include the often-made juxtaposition between paid work as a choice or a constraint for women and the related argument that while for middle-class women paid work may be a choice, this is not the case for low-income women.

Economic theory, of course, allows for both choice and constraint to shape labor force participation decisions, through the notion of constrained choice; but even within such a theoretical framing, the degree to which women choose paid employment is contested and a number of authors have emphasized the importance of contextualizing constrained choice in the context of gender, class, and other factors (Diana Strassmann 1999, Jennifer Olmsted 2005). S. Charusheela (2003) and Fatma Umut Beşpınar (2010), for example, emphasize the important role that class plays in shaping women's employment experience. Middle-class and elite women, they argue, may enter paid work out of choice; but for women of lower-class backgrounds, work is generally undertaken out of economic necessity. Christine Koggel, who is also interested in interrogating the question of whether paid work "necessarily increase[s] women's agency and well-being" (2003: 167), examines a number of possible factors that she identifies as important for answering the question of how women experience paid work. These include

> whether women's paid work is located inside or outside the home; whether they have sole responsibility for domestic work in addition to their paid work; whether they work in the formal or informal sector; whether other family members have control over their income; whether the labor market permits high or low earnings; and whether jobs provide safety and leave provisions or control over conditions of work.

We find that while almost all the women in our sample were motivated primarily by financial reasons, about half indicated that even without economic need they would still work. Divorced and widowed women, no doubt due to their first-hand experience with the failure of the male-breadwinner model, were more committed to participating in paid work than their married counterparts. The double burden and social stigma (shame) were given as reasons for why women preferred not to work, with certain jobs in particular being perceived as undesirable. But even "bad jobs" were seen as enjoyable for some women. Finally, even among those who articulated a preference not to engage in paid work, forms of subversion and reinterpretation of gender norms were occurring, with Islam often being invoked to control work hours or income.

Age played an important role in shaping employment experiences. Younger women in Iran, who, interestingly, were born and raised after the 1979 revolution, are the most likely to embrace paid employment as rewarding and worth doing, even in the absence of economic need, and also more likely to prefer paid work that is not home based. We cannot entirely rule out this finding as a function of a life-cycle effect, since younger women also have fewer unpaid work responsibilities; but we also suggest that this finding provides a challenge to the assumption that since the rise to power of the Islamist government, greater adherence to traditional norms has prevailed.[1]

OVERVIEW OF IRAN'S POLITICAL ECONOMY AND WOMEN'S EMPLOYMENT

In 1979, after the Iranian revolution, Ayatollah Khomeini emerged as the first leader of the Islamist government. Compulsory veiling was imposed, and this was perceived by many as emblematic of the reintroduction of more traditional gender norms. Haideh Moghissi (2008) provided evidence that middle-class and elite women particularly suffered setbacks during this period, but Roksana Bahramitash (2004, 2013c) argues that, for women who supported the rise to power of the Islamist government, many of whom came from lower-income households and were advocates for stricter dress codes, the revolution paved the way for these women to perceive themselves differently. These women became more comfortable in the public sphere, following the revolution, as they were encouraged to become volunteers and became involved in a number of state-sponsored projects, such as the nationwide literacy campaign.

In 1997, a second political shift with gender implications occurred, with Khatami elected on a reformist platform, with support from youth and women (Mehdi Moslem 2002; Farhad Nomani and Sohrab Behdad 2006). Since Khatami and the reform movement had earned its support from women, the government in turn became more open to gender rights advocates, and women's organizations increased. The reformist government, in fact, ratified the Convention of Elimination of all Kinds of Discrimination Against Women (CEDAW), although Iran's Guardian Council ultimately blocked that decision.

Religious conservatives of course severely attacked the Reformist parliament and, in 2005, the conservatives regained power with Ahmadinejad, who campaigned on the platform of economic justice, winning the election. In 2009 Ahmadinejad won a deeply contested re-election campaign, and in the aftermath of that election, the government was increasingly at odds with the West, which tightened sanctions against Iran during this period. It is within this context that we carried out our recent fieldwork.[2]

This history points to the contested nature of gender politics in Iran, as well as raising a number of questions about the impact this contested terrain may have had on young Iranian women who were raised during the

GENDER AND ECONOMICS IN MUSLIM COMMUNITIES

period after the Islamic revolution. On the one hand, in the post-revolution period, Khomeini, and later Khamenei, in some ways pushed for a return to traditional gender norms, putting in place compulsory veiling and discouraging women from engaging in paid employment. But, on the other hand, Iran was going through a period of rapidly rising literacy, and particularly among veiled women, engagement in the public sphere, in the context of the new government, was perceived more positively. Given this, it is not clear how such mixed messages may have impacted working-class women (Azadeh Kian-Thiebaut 2002; Nayereh Tohidi 2007). Our study sheds light on the question of how differing generations of Iranian women from low-income communities view their participation in paid employment following the revolution.

Although there is some dispute about how to measure it, there is agreement that in the immediate aftermath of the revolution, Iranian women's labor force participation declined. Census data suggest that in 1976 the rate of labor force participation for women was 12.6 percent, which then fell to 8.2 percent in the post-revolutionary period (1986), and rose to 12.5 percent over the next two decades. Rates estimated using labor force surveys suggest that women's employment rates are somewhat higher than those reported in the census. And the International Labour Organization estimates even higher women's employment rates of 20.6 percent in 1986 and a rate of 38.6 percent for 2005 (Jennifer C. Olmsted 2011),[3] but no figures are available for the pre-revolution period.

A number of analysts have suggested that the drop experienced in the post-revolution period was due to the conservative regime discouraging women's employment. In particular, in the aftermath of the revolution, when compulsory veiling was put in place, women who did not wear the hijab – many of whom were middle-class or elite women – were dismissed from their jobs (Valentine Moghadam 1995, 2003; Parvin Alizadeh 2003; Nomani and Behdad 2006; Moghissi 2008). Other analysts, however, have focused on other factors that could have contributed to changes in employment patterns during that time. There is substantial evidence, for example, that just after the revolution, sanctions imposed by the United States had a severe negative impact on the carpet industry, which was a large employer of young women in the pre-revolution period (Zahra Karimi 2011; Olmsted 2011). Finally, Azadeh Kian (1995), Maryann Povey (1999), Roksana Bahramitash (2004, 2007), and Roksana Bahramitash and Hadi Salehi Esfahani (2011) propose that while a drop in women's employment occurred in the immediate aftermath of the revolution, the introduction of mandatory hijab also facilitated the entry of more conservative women into the public sphere.[4] In other words, women's employment in Iran was, and continues to be, impacted by both internal ideological shifts, and externally imposed economic factors.

GENDER AND ECONOMICS IN MUSLIM COMMUNITIES

Of the studies that have examined the determinants of women's labor force participation in the post-revolution period, one that is most relevant to this study is a recent econometric analysis of women's employment in Iran by Djavad Salehi-Isfahani, who suggests that

> [m]ost of the increase in participation [in Iran] comes from the less educated women, and there is a shift away from wage and salary work (especially at the expense of the public sector) toward self-employment and informal work (unpaid family labor). (2005: 2)

He goes on to state that that "these developments raise questions about whether this increase is an improvement in women's social and economic status in Iran" (2). Through intensive interviews with employed, working-class Iranian women of various ages, all of whom are in the informal sector and many of whom are self employed, we are able to shed additional light on this question, with our main conclusion being that for many women the need to enter paid employment is viewed with shame and unhappiness. Still, our data also suggest a rather complex story, with younger women in particular viewing paid work much more positively.

A NOTE ON HOW THE DATA WERE GATHERED

For the past three decades, West-based academics have faced major challenges in their attempts to carry out fieldwork in Iran. The situation became particularly difficult in 2009 since the political turmoil following that election led to strict security rules, making it difficult to gain permission to conduct large surveys. By maintaining ties with a number of research institutes inside Iran, Roksana Bahramitash and Fereshteh F. Farahani gathered the data for this study in 2009–10, but because of the difficult political situation, a randomized survey could not be conducted. In addition, the research was designed to target low-income working women, employed in the informal sector, so a nonrandomized snowballing technique was seen as more effective.[5] A semi-structured questionnaire, which included detailed questions about work conditions and family relationships, as well as open-ended questions about how the women felt about being in paid work, was used, after several focus group meetings were held to finalize the questionnaire.

As far as sampling was concerned, great care was taken in identifying and interviewing women working in diverse jobs, with a variety of methods used to locate them. Some were found by going to their employment locations. For example, housecleaners were identified through contacts with their middle-class employers; women who worked in more public locations – such as hairdressers, masseuses in sports clubs, and those who worked as

GENDER AND ECONOMICS IN MUSLIM COMMUNITIES

vendors, either in the metro system or on the streets – were approached directly by the fieldworkers.

Once an initial group of women had been identified, snowballing was used to find other interviewees – including those who were difficult to reach in the initial stage, especially those who worked from home. Altogether, Bahramitash and Farahani conducted ninety interviews. In addition, participant observation provided details that might not have come out during the interview process. For example, Bahramitash traveled with vendors and acquired services from hairdressers and masseuses, while engaging women in long conversations. She also attended a number of all-women religious ceremonies, which are common in low-income neighborhoods, in order to build a network and recruit research assistants from within low-income communities. Interviews with academics and Iranian policymakers also supplemented the data obtained from the semi-structured questionnaires and the participant observation.

As a result of extensive networking, interviews were conducted with women who were engaged in a range of economic activities. The four largest groups in the sample were hairdressers, vendors who worked in the metro, retail sales personnel, and seamstresses. Other service-sector jobs included masseuses in sports clubs, women who performed cleaning services, homecare providers, food processors (producing pickles or prepared herbs), as well as other home-based workers, such as those involved in catering for parties and weddings.

CHOICE, CONSTRAINT, AND THE MALE-BREADWINNER MODEL

The answers women provided to the questions of why they worked and how they viewed their work brought insight into the complex ways that women experience work. Almost all of the respondents (90 percent) stated that a primary reason for paid work was economic necessity, but identifying economic necessity as a reason for working did not necessarily lead to women concluding that they would stop working if they no longer felt economically pushed to do so. Table 1 suggests that half of the women would stop working if they did not feel economically compelled to do so, although important differences were also observed when age and marital status were taken into account.

Married women were far more likely to express a desire to drop out of the labor force, with only a third saying they would continue to work if their economic situation improved. Women who were divorced and widowed were more evenly split, with half of divorced women and 44 percent of widowed women stating that not working would have been preferable. But even among those women, between a half (divorced and widowed) and a quarter (abandoned) expressed a preference not to work, suggesting

GENDER AND ECONOMICS IN MUSLIM COMMUNITIES

Table 1 Without economic need, would you work?

	No	*Yes*	*Total*
Marital status			
Abandoned	2	5	7
	28.6%	71.4%	100.0%
Divorced	4	4	8
	50.0%	50.0%	100.0%
Married	32	17	49
	65.3%	34.7%	100.0%
Never Married	3	14	17
	17.6%	82.4%	100.0%
Widowed	4	5	9
	44.4%	55.6%	100.0%
Total	45	45	90
	50.0%	50.0%	100.0%
Age			
16–30	6	20	26
	23.1%	76.9%	100.0%
31–45	27	15	42
	64.3%	35.7%	100.0%
46–60	12	10	22
	54.5%	45.5%	100.0%
Total	45	45	90
	50.0%	50.0%	100.0%

that even after having experienced first-hand the fragility of the male-breadwinner model, many women continued to cling to this as an ideal.

Conversations with a number of the women revealed the degree to which most of the women we interviewed experienced the double burden – one of the major factors that contributed to their dissatisfaction with their work schedule. Fatimah, a married woman with four children, was in her early 50 s, had completed primary school, and worked as a domestic worker in an upper-middle-class household. She explained:

> I wake up very early in the morning, feed everyone, and four days a week I have to go to work. I leave home in the winter when it is still dark, after breakfast is prepared. Then I take two buses and to avoid traffic I am out of the house before 6 and it takes me two hours each way to get to and from my work. People are nice, but I work for eight hours four days a week, and my knees are giving up.[6]

In addition to having knee problems, she also suffered from back pain, which was another factor that led her to conclude: "I really look forward

GENDER AND ECONOMICS IN MUSLIM COMMUNITIES

to not having to work. I keep telling my husband: 'When are you going to make enough money so that I can stay home?'"

Fatimah's husband was in construction, but his work was seasonal and the family could not rely only on his income. Fatimah's income was steady, because she had worked for the same family for the past fifteen years and from time to time they gave her a break from work and paid her extra or provided her with in-kind contributions, knowing that her family needed extra assistance. In the case of Fatimah, having a steady income brought a sense of security to a household that would otherwise have had to weather constant fluctuations in income. Fatimah talked about her husband with understanding, and wished he were capable of being a "real" breadwinner.

Among those who embraced a male-breadwinner model, Islamic jurisprudence, which emphasizes that women have the right to control their own assets (cash, property, or in this case, earnings), even though it is the responsibility of the husband to provide *kharghi* (income required to support the household), was sometimes invoked.[7] Some women even went so far as to use this to their advantage and to maintain their right to control both their work efforts and their earnings. Azar, a migrant street vendor from a small town in Azerbaijan province, for example, stated that she worked to ensure that her daughter had options. "I don't give a penny of what I earn to my husband. My husband is responsible for *kharghi*. I save what I earn, and it will all go to my daughter. He doesn't ask how much I earn and I don't bother to tell him." Similarly, Fereshteh, who worked as a street vendor, stated:

I only sell as much as I need for daily food, rice or something for that day, because I don't want my husband to get used to the idea of me being responsible for *kharghi*. It is his responsibility to provide and I only make 50,000 Rial [about US$4 per day]. As soon as that is done, I pack and leave.

Fereshteh was a woman in her early forties with three children, and her husband was working as causal laborer. In the discussion, she also suggested that if a woman is capable of earning enough for the family, then the husband might not put enough effort into his work. She also talked about how much she enjoyed having free time, being a housewife and spending more time with her family, free of the hassle of working as a street vendor. She particularly disliked her job because of the fear that the city government, which from time to time clamped down on street vendors, would confiscate her merchandise.

GENDER AND ECONOMICS IN MUSLIM COMMUNITIES

GOOD, BAD, AND SHAMEFUL WORK

For a number of women, paid work was perceived as shameful, with certain jobs in particular being identified as "bad jobs." About a quarter of the women stated that their work was shameful and that they hid the fact that they were working from family or friends. For example, Zahra, a married grandmother in her mid-50 s who worked as a vendor, stated: "It's really embarrassing for someone of my age to have to work, and I have to hide it." Five days a week, early in the morning before her neighbors could see her, Zahra dragged her inventory of small kitchen items in two large plastic bags to the bus station, which took her to the closest metro station. She sold items such as oven mitts and dishwashing gloves in the women-only cars of the Tehran subway. Selling these items involved an element of physical effort, since it required her to carry two large bags first from her house to the nearest metro and then up and down the subway cars. In addition, like other vendors, she carried a large purse around her waist – which at times contained a considerable amount of cash, a further source of distress. Like other metro vendors, she avoided the rush hour, when millions of Tehran residents, including large numbers of women, traveled across the city in the packed metro, making getting in and out of the cars difficult. To avoid rush hours, she had to increase the total number of hours she worked; as a result, adding her commuting time, she generally worked more than ten hours a day, five days a week.

Zahra's work also involved convincing her customers that they were getting the best value; this was done through sales pitches made in the subway cars. "I spend my day going up and down the metro, saying how much they would appreciate these small items for their kitchen, shouting: 'Ladies, you will love the colors of this oven mitt, it will brighten up your kitchen and it is durable, and machine washable. My price is half that of the shops, if you find it cheaper, I will pay the difference."[8]

Like Fereshteh, Zahra's work also involved run-ins with law-enforcement agents. At least on one occasion, Zahra's inventory had been taken during a police raid on metro vendors. She stated: "I fought hard to get back my wares from the police station. The officer was nice and let me have them back. He was a young man; they know we would not do this, especially older women, unless we had to."[9]

Somayeh was another vendor who greatly disliked her work, but saw herself as having no choice. As she explained: "My husband and children were against me working, being a vendor is a shame to the family, but what my husband earns cannot bring food on the table. I told them, 'If you don't like my work, *you* bring money!'"

Working as a vendor involved hours spent in public spaces, where women were often exposed to public scorn. During participant observation, for example, there were occasions when other passengers

GENDER AND ECONOMICS IN MUSLIM COMMUNITIES

made condescending remarks. Vendors are often viewed as nuisances – particularly when the train cars are crowded and passengers, who are already tired from their long commute, do not wish to hear vendors pitching their products.

Another job that brought feelings of shame was working as a masseuse in a sports club. During participant observation, Sima talked about why she disliked her job and the fact that she hid her work from her family. "My family doesn't know I work as a massage lady, I tell them I work as a saleswoman at the sports center." She went on to explain how frustrating the job is for a number of reasons:

> People [clients] think I am their servant. Mind you, some women call themselves massage ladies and have no training. I paid to get trained by a physiotherapist, but many enter into these jobs with no training. So in the mind of many people, being a massage lady means having no skill. And they are very condescending; I hate my job. I have to travel long hours and then have to give massages to women who do not know what massage is about and order me around. Then some of them want hard massage, some soft massage, and if I am not always at their service they complain and I can lose my job. I have to smile and say "Yes ma'am, sorry ma'am, I will try harder." The other day, there was a really fat woman and she wanted to lose weight through massage. If you keep eating you cannot lose weight by massage, no matter how hard and deep I massage you.

Sima, who was in her late 30s, found the job physically and psychologically taxing, and complained about pain in her lower back. The table on which she was working was low for her, which put pressure on her spine; but she did not dare to complain because she was afraid she would lose her job and that, given high rates of unemployment, she would be unable to find another. Her husband had abandoned her, and she and her daughter were living with her parents. Although she did not have to pay rent, she helped her parents with the household expenses.

Massage workers in sports centers also expressed considerable anxiety concerning the income uncertainty they faced, since they are generally self-employed and so are only paid when they have clients. Some explained that because the work is seasonal, with less demand in the summer and during holidays, including the entire month of Ramadan, they faced considerable fluctuation in their earnings.

Clearly very public types of employment, and those that involved direct humiliation, were a particular source of shame, but – as is discussed in more detail in the next section – some women enjoyed these jobs that were viewed in a particularly negative fashion. It should also be noted that even jobs that took place in the private sphere, and were viewed as more typical

GENDER AND ECONOMICS IN MUSLIM COMMUNITIES

women's occupations, were seen as shameful by some. Nadine, who worked in her home as a knitter, stated: "When I'm knitting and I have a problem, I go to see friends or attend a religious function and as soon as I mention my problem, my friends know I'm working. I feel ashamed of having to work and earning so little. They start to feel sorry for me and I feel bad." Similarly, Shirin, who was married and in her 40s, with two children, and who worked both as a seamstress and in hairdressing, stated: "If I mention my work I will lose face, so I've stopped telling people."

COMPLICATING THE QUESTION OF "BAD WORK"

For many women, work, even if not entirely preferred, was a source of newfound respect and admiration. This was the case for about half the women interviewed. A number of women stated that their work gave them power over decision making within their household. At the same time, a number of the women interviewed stated that their personality, rather than their income-generating ability, was the primary reason why they had decision-making power within their homes. Among our respondents, just under a quarter (24 percent) stated that their work had brought them increased status in their communities and had turned them into people whose advice was sought concerning various matters. Zahra K., for example, said: "my family members are proud of me now because they know I can take care of myself." Being economically independent brought respect, as explained by Zeynab: "My family looks at me with more respect and thinks of me as a strong woman, someone who can organize her life." Similarly, Masomeh said: "They tell me that I am a strong woman and resourceful and respect me for what I do. They tell me, 'You are a man.' I love working hard and paying for myself."

Also important to note is that although certain jobs were in general perceived as shameful, not everyone agreed with these categorizations. Soghra, a young woman in her early 20s who lived with her parents, stated that she had always been fascinated by fashion:

> Since I was a little girl I have liked dressmaking. I learned to sew from my mother, and now I really enjoy making dresses. I like to play with design and give my touch to dresses I make for friends. I like working at home because my friends come and it is like a little party. I make dresses for the fun of it and experiment with different fashions. I love to go window shopping, then come home and try to make the same dress at a much lower cost for my friends and myself. I do not charge a lot, and they always come to me because they know I can make fashionable clothes cheaper than the shops and my touch is even better. My mother complains that I should charge more and have a

GENDER AND ECONOMICS IN MUSLIM COMMUNITIES

proper place [dedicated workshop], but I am happy to stay with my parents, make a little money on the side, and love what I do.

Soghra, another woman who worked in apparel from home, stated: "I work because I really didn't want to study. I liked sewing, knitting, and dressmaking. I enjoy doing it at home."

Even more surprising was that some vendors enjoyed the work. Nadia was a young, single woman working as a metro vendor who felt the work was fun.

I wanted to go to university, but private university is expensive and my parents cannot afford to pay for everything. I saw women selling this and that. I like hair accessories and went to someone in the Bazaar whom my aunt knew and asked him to help me start up, with my aunt becoming my guarantor. Now I am good at selling accessories. I wear them over my scarf and I like the way I arrange them so each looks nice and my customers see how beautiful they look, even when worn over the scarf. Sometimes, when it is not too busy, I show them how they can wear their pins and how to keep their scarves with accessories and they love them and buy them.

Working as a metro vendor has enabled Nadia, who still lived at home, to finance her own university education, while at the same time enjoying her work. Similarly, Razieh recounted:

My mother is sick and is asthmatic, she was hospitalized, and every day I had to go and see her. I traveled by metro and there I learnt about women who work in the metro and it seemed something I could do too. I now sell jewelry in the metro. I like it because I work when I can and it is among other women. I first started selling food in the metro, but then found out that jewelry sells better because there are a lot of young university students who travel. I am good at talking them into buying my jewelry. I earn enough money and sometimes if I don't have enough to pay for my inventory I am able to take jewelry from people from the Bazaar who trust me and know that I will always pay them back.

For Nadia and Razieh, who were not forced to work due to financial need, but instead have discovered their skills as entrepreneurs, vending in the metro is both fun and lucrative.

For a number of the younger women, the type of paid work they were engaged in was seen as a temporary plan in order to finance their education. Golarn, another young unmarried woman in her 20s, stated: "I saw how women sell in the metro, and to pay for my university [she was

GENDER AND ECONOMICS IN MUSLIM COMMUNITIES

attending a private open university], I sell makeup and I make enough to pay for my education."

Although it would be tempting to link differences in how they viewed work only to age or marital status, which in turn could be related to the fact that younger, unmarried women had less economic need and fewer household responsibilities, not all young women without children enjoyed their work. Parivash, a single woman in her late 20s, for instance, stated:

> [My work as a salesperson] is very boring and it really puts a lot of pressure on my nerves. Some of my customers are demanding and never happy and some don't pay me for a long time. I'm standing all day and my employer is a man. He's always in the shop and I don't feel comfortable with him around. We don't have a washroom here and I try, as much as possible, not to drink, so that I won't have to use the washroom.

Her statement is telling, for a number of reasons. First of all, Parivash is young and single, so her main complaint is not related to the double burden, or a fear that her family members will judge her. Instead, her complaints are related to the poor working conditions and notably the lack of a toilet, which is a major inconvenience and possible health risk. Also of interest is that Parivash disliked working in the close proximity of a man, particularly given the lack of adequate infrastructure. Despite the government's claim to have promoted stricter sex segregation in Iran after the revolution, men and women still often work together and our interviews suggest that at least some women are uncomfortable with this arrangement.

AGE DIFFERENCES: SHIFTING NORMS, LIFE-CYCLE CHANGES, OR BOTH?

While Parivash was an exception, younger women, who were also on average considerably more educated than older ones, were by far the most likely to express the desire to continue working even if they no longer faced economic need (over three-fourths), with the middle-aged group (ages 31–45) having almost opposite outcomes (two-thirds preferring not to work), and the majority of older women also preferring not to work. Although because of the small sample size the data were not broken down finely in the table, when younger women were examined by marital status, the never married were the most interested in working; but even within the other categories, positive views of work were fairly strong. Similar patterns were observed when it came to the question of whether women would prefer to work in the house or outside (Table 2). Over two-thirds of young women expressed a preference for working outside of their homes; but the older a woman was, the more likely she was to prefer working at home, out of the public gaze.

272

GENDER AND ECONOMICS IN MUSLIM COMMUNITIES

Table 2 Where do you prefer to work?

	In house	Out of house	Total
Marital status			
Abandoned	3	4	7
	42.9%	57.1%	100.0%
Divorced	1	7	8
	12.5%	87.5%	100.0%
Married	23	25	48
	46.9%	51.0%	97.9%
Never Married	1	15	16
	5.9%	88.2%	97.9%
Widowed	4	5	9
	44.4%	55.6%	100.0%
Total	32	56	88
	35.6%	62.2%	97.8%
Age			
16–30	5	21	26
	19.2%	80.8%	100.0%
31–45	16	25	41
	38.1%	59.5%	97.6%
46–60	11	11	22
	50.0%	50.0%	100.0%
Total	32	56	90
	35.6%	62.2%	100.0%

Note: Totals reflect the fact that some respondents did not answer all questions.

Because we are only observing a snapshot in time, and have a small sample, a question we are unable to fully address is whether age and women's desire to work even in the absence of economic need, as well as their preference to work outside the home, are illustrative of the different types of constraints facing women in different age cohorts, or whether this finding suggests a shift in gender norms. It does seem clear that life-cycle factors are driving some of our results. For some young, unmarried women without children, paid work may actually be a way from escaping from the drudgery of household labor.[10] Roya, a single woman in her 20s, who was also in sales, viewed her work as freeing her from having to serve her brothers:

I needed money and had too much work at home, my brothers were bullying me and I had no freedom. I could not even use the phone or listen to music. Now that I work, I have more freedom. When I was at home, my brothers would get on my nerves and we had fights. Now I am happy working.

More generally, it is notable that it is the middle, not the oldest, group who are the most negative about the issue of paid work; and this group no doubt faces the highest reproductive labor burden, lending some weight to the argument that life-cycle effects do play a role in shaping women's experience of paid work. Our data also suggest that gender norms may be age specific, given that some informants suggested that it is particularly taboo in Iran for older women to seek paid work or to be seen in the public sphere because of the implication that other family members are unable or unwilling to support them financially. For older women in particular, the need to enter paid work may be perceived as a reflection of their male kin's inability to support them.

At the same time, rapidly rising educational levels and age of first marriage rates in Iran suggest that our findings also reflect a change in gender norms, with younger cohorts rejecting narrow gender-norm constructs that limit women's contributions to the private sphere or reproductive labor. At the same time, we did identify a group of young, married women who expressed a preference to not work, or to work from home, although they were the minority among the younger cohort.

CONCLUSION

The aim of this contribution is to illustrate some of the complexities involved in understanding women's experiences of work and to articulate women's own views of their employment experiences. One important contribution of this research is to shed light on motivations and experiences of low-income women in Iran, an understudied population. Since this research was carried out, two important changes, one internal and one external, have occurred that are likely to affect low-income Iranian women's economic situation, and in turn their experiences with paid work. The first is the victory of Hassan Rouhani, who is more moderate concerning the role of women, in the 2013 presidential election. The second, externally imposed change is the tightening of sanctions.[11] Our previous research suggests that sanctions in Iran reduced the employment opportunities for low-skilled, low-wage women, since the carpet industry was among those most affected by restricted trade flows, as well as more generally causing economic hardships for women (Olmsted 2011; Roksana Bahramitash 2013b). While we argue that paid work is not a panacea for a women, we also are of the view that policies should never be imposed that limit women's economic options, which sanctions against Iran undoubtedly do. Despite the claim that the current sanctions will be "smart," there is substantial evidence that all sanctions impose an economic cost on average

GENDER AND ECONOMICS IN MUSLIM COMMUNITIES

citizens, and that the impact of sanctions is to increase economic hardship; further research is needed to understand the gender implications of the newly imposed sanctions (Daniel Drezner 2003).

Economic need was a motivating factor among almost all the women we interviewed. A significant number of them embraced a male-breadwinner model and insisted that it is the man's responsibility to provide for his family, rejecting the idea that women's engagement with paid work was a positive development. This was particularly true of married women; but a surprising number of divorced and widowed women also clung to the idea of a male breadwinner, despite the fact that this "ideal" had not served them personally very well. Still, about half the women we interviewed stated that even without economic need they would continue to engage in paid work, suggesting the difficulties of parsing out issues of choice and constraint.

Among women who did articulate a desire to maintain clear gender roles with an emphasis on men's responsibility for income generation, this did not imply that they lacked agency or power within their households. In fact, among women who invoked Islam to support their argument and articulated the strongest attachment to the notion of *kharghi*, we found strong evidence of women's agency, with women using religion to argue for their right to maintain control over their own income and to limit their overall work burden.[12]

Another important finding concerned the fact that certain types of work were perceived as particularly shameful, such as work as a vendor or a masseuse. These jobs involved women interacting with members of the public (in particular members of the elite, who were often disrespectful), shining light on the role that class interactions may play in shaping women's paid work experiences. Yet even within these professions, which were stigmatized, risky, and physically taxing, we found a minority of women who embraced this work and enjoyed it. Work that contained a considerable amount of income uncertainty was also, not surprisingly, less positively viewed by these women. And income volatility among their partners similarly was often a reason why women sought paid employment in the first place.

Age was also an important factor that explained women's work experience. Not only were young women much more likely to reject the male-breadwinner model as the ideal, but they were also much more comfortable working in the public sphere. While we cannot determine with certainty the degree to which this is due to life-cycle effects, the fact that young women were far more likely to state that they would work even in the absence of economic need, and to state that they preferred work in the public sphere rather than home-based employment, suggests that the younger generation raised after the revolution does not embrace the notion of a strict gender division of labor as much as previous generations did.

GENDER AND ECONOMICS IN MUSLIM COMMUNITIES

Our data and findings provide further insights into the diversity of working-class women's experiences and demonstrate theoretical points made by Koggel (2003), Charusheela (2003), and Beşpınar (2010) by adding evidence on how Iranian women's work experiences are shaped by the intersection of class, age, marital status, and type of employment. The women we interviewed had a complex relationship to paid employment; many did not fit neatly into the constraint binary that has been proposed by some scholars. This research therefore contributes to challenging the monolithic claim still made by a number of development agencies, that paid work is an unequivocal improvement for women, while at the same time rejecting the equally monolithic claim that low-income women never find paid employment rewarding. Questions about the type of work that is the most or least empowering are also complicated by our findings. Koggel, for example, argues that "hidden" employment was particularly disempowering to women; but among some of the women we interviewed, it was precisely the type of work that was "invisible" to the larger community, and therefore reduced the problem of shame, that was more desirable. Our data suggest that particularly among older Iranian women, who feel uncomfortable in the public sphere, working at home is preferred. By contrast, among younger women, work that got them out of their houses and into the public domain was preferred.

While we do find that an examination of the intersection of sex, age, marital status, and type of employment is important in order to be able to make some generalizations about women's experiences of paid work, there were enough outliers within our sample to suggest that it is also dangerous to overgeneralize. In fact, from a policy perspective, the findings of our research suggest some real challenges, since it is clear that a "one size fits all" approach to assuring women's empowerment is not possible. For some women the male-breadwinner model remains an ideal, while for others decent paid work is a top priority. For some women work that involves engaging with the public is preferred, while for others it is a source of extreme shame. Assuring that women can adequately balance paid and unpaid work responsibilities is of course key; but our data suggest that no easy solutions are likely to emerge, given the disagreement among women about what they prefer. Instead, carefully crafted policies will be needed to assure that women have adequate choices and are neither denied access to paid work when they desire it, nor forced into unacceptable work situations due to severe economic constraints being imposed on them.

ACKNOWLEDGMENTS

We are grateful for the feedback received during the special issue workshop, as well as from anonymous reviewers, Caitlin Killian, and guest editors Ebru Kongar and Elora Shehabuddin. Special thanks also go to former Drew University student and research assistant Michele Schuler and to Fresheh F. Farahani, our wonderful research assistant in Iran. All personal information that would allow the identification of any person or persons described in the article has been removed.

NOTES

[1] Interestingly, Naila Kabeer and Ayesha Khan (2014: 12, 13) find that some poor urban Afghan women who fled to Iran and then returned stated that "life was better in Iran," where "society ... respected and delivered on women's rights."

[2] In June 2013, Iranians elected Hassan Rouhani to replace Mahmoud Ahmedinejad.

[3] It should also be noted that in the case of Iran, the ILO uses econometric techniques to derive their estimates, since they argue that official figures underestimate women's employment and therefore need to be adjusted upward.

[4] Before the revolution, women who wore hijab were banned from certain positions, such as taking an administrative role in the education system.

[5] Note also that this research builds off a previous survey on women's employment carried out in the city of Tehran, which was a randomized sample that made use of a map of the city of Tehran obtained from the Mayor's office to identify poor neighborhoods (Roksana Bahramitash and Shahla Kazemipour 2011).

GENDER AND ECONOMICS IN MUSLIM COMMUNITIES

[6] Note that although technically she was only working 32 hours a week, because of her long commute, her effective work scheduled spanned 48 hours in the space of just four days and this calculation does not include time spent on unpaid work.

[7] As indicated also by Fauzia Ahmed (2014), assuring that analysis of gender relations, family ties, and religion is contextualized and that local beliefs (and legal frames) are fully understood is of key importance. In Iran, the term *kharghi* is the colloquial word used for the concept of *nafagheh* – the Islamic notion of the financial entitlement owed to the wife by the husband, which should allow her to live in the manner to which she is accustomed, and which in Iran is included as part of Iranian civil law. See Arzoo Osanloo (2009) for discussion of *nafagheh* in the context of Iran, and Roksana Bahramitash (2002) for discussion in the context of Indonesia.

[8] An entire analysis could be done of the ingenious marketing techniques employed by these women, but that will have to be the topic of a future study.

[9] An Iranian academic interviewed in the spring of 2011 stated that Zahra Sadat Moshiri, the wife of Mohammad Bagher Ghalibaf, who was then Mayor of Tehran, had in fact pleaded with officials not to harass Metro vendors because they were mainly single mothers who needed the work to make ends meet, although our fieldwork suggests that many are also young single women without children. Leaving aside the question of the age and marital status of the vendors, the fact that the wife of a public official had openly addressed this issue and raised concerns about official policies surrounding street vendors suggests the degree to which social awareness of the hardships faced by these workers and the negative impact of government enforcement of laws are part of public discourse in Iran.

[10] The notion that women's views of employment might vary depending on where they are in their life cycle is closely linked to the degree to which they may be expected to provide reproductive labor. On average, young women, who are more likely to be single, as well as older women who are done raising their families, may have fewer reproductive responsibilities.

[11] As this contribution was being finalized, a breakthrough was also made in that regard, with the media reporting that Iran had agreed to limit their nuclear program; this may lead to a reversal of the earlier decision to tighten sanctions.

[12] Other authors have also explored how women frame their employment experiences in the context of their spiritual beliefs. See for example Damla Isik (2013).

REFERENCES

Ahmed, Fauzia. 2014 "Peace in the Village: Gender, Agency, and Villagers' Measures of Marital Quality in Bangladesh." *Feminist Economics*. doi:10.1080/13545701.2014.963635

Alizadeh, Parvin. 2003. "Recent Economic Reforms and Structural Trap: Iranian Quandary." *Brown Journal of the World Affairs* 1(2): 267–81.

Bahramitash, Roksana. 2002. "Islamic Fundamentalism and Women's Employment in Indonesia." *International Journal of Politics, Culture, and Society* 16(2): 551–68.

———. 2004. "Market Fundamentalism versus Religious Fundamentalism: Women's Employment in Iran." *Critique: Critical Middle Eastern Studies* 13(1): 33–46.

———. 2007. "Female Employment and Globalization during Iran's Reform Era (1997–2005)." *Journal of Middle East Women's Studies* 3(2):86–109.

———. 2013a. "Women and Children Pay for Smart Sanctions on Iran: What's Next." *Turkish Review* 3(2): 148–52.

———. 2013b. *Gender and Entrepreneurship in Iran: Microenterprise and the Informal Sector.* New York: Palgrave Macmillan.

GENDER AND ECONOMICS IN MUSLIM COMMUNITIES

————. 2013c. "Iran." In *The Oxford Encyclopedia of Islam and Women*, edited by Natana J. DeLong-Bas, 497–503. Oxford: Oxford University Press.

Bahramitash, Roksana and Hadi Salehi Esfahani. 2011. *Veiled Employment: Islamism and the Political Economy of Women's Employment in Iran.* Syracuse, NY: Syracuse University Press.

Bahramitash, Roksana and Shahla Kazemipour. 2011. "Veiled Economy: Gender and the Informal Sector." In *Veiled Employment: Islamism and the Political Economy of Women's Employment in Iran*, edited by Roksana Bahramitash and Hadi Salehi Esfahani, 226–55.New York: Routledge.

Beşpınar, Fatma Umut. 2010. "Questioning Agency and Empowerment: Women's Work-Related Strategies and Social Class in Urban Turkey." *Women's Studies International Forum* 33: 523–32.

Charusheela, S. 2003. "Empowering Work? Bargaining Models Reconsidered." In *Toward a Feminist Philosophy of Economics*, edited by Drue Barker and Edith Kuiper, 287–303. London: Routledge.

Drezner, Daniel. 2003. "How Smart are Smart Sanctions?" *International Studies Review* 5: 107–10.

Isik, Damla. 2013. "'Just Like Prophet Mohammad Preached': Labor, Piety, and Charity in Contemporary Turkey." *Feminist Economics* http://dx.doi.org/10.1080/13545701. 2013.825376 .

Kabeer, Naila and Ayesha Khan. 2014. "Cultural Values or Universal Rights? Women's Narratives of Compliance and Contestation in Urban Afghanistan." *Feminist Economics* 20(3): 1–24.

Karimi, Zahra. 2011. "The Effects of International Trade on Gender Inequality in Iran: The Case of Women Carpet Weavers." In *Veiled Employment: Islamism and the Political Economy of Women's Employment in Iran*, edited by Roksana Bahramitash and Hadi Salehi Esfahani, 166–90. New York: Routledge.

Kian, Azadeh. 1995. "Gendered Occupation and Women's Status in Post-Revolutionary Iran." *Middle Eastern Studies* 31(3): 407–21.

Kian-Thiebaut, Azadeh. 2002. "Women and the Making of Civil Society in Post-Islamist Iran: Twenty Years of Islamic Revolution." In *Twenty Years of Islamic Revolution*, edited by Eric Hooglund, 56–73. Syracuse, NY: Syracuse University Press.

Koggel, Christine. 2003. "Globalization and Women's Paid Work: Expanding Freedom?" *Feminist Economics* 9(2–3): 163–83.

Moghadam, Valentine. 1995. "Women's Employment Issues in Contemporary Iran: Problems and Prospects in the 1990s." *Iranian Studies* 28(3–4): 175–202.

————. 2003. *Modernizing Women: Gender and Social Change in the Middle East.* Boulder, CO: Lynne Rienner.

Moghissi, Haideh. 2008. "Islamic Cultural Nationalism and Gender Politics in Iran." *Third World Quarterly* 29(3): 541–54.

Moslem, Mehdi. 2002. *Factional Politics in Post-Khomeini Iran.* Syracuse, NY: Syracuse University Press.

Nomani, Farhad and Sohrab Behdad. 2006. *Class and Labor in Iran: Did the Revolution Matter?* Syracuse, NY: Syracuse University Press.

Olmsted, Jennifer C. 2005. "Is Paid Work the (Only) Answer? Women's Well-Being, Neoliberalism and the Social Contract in Southwest Asia and North Africa." *Journal of Middle East Women's Studies* 2(1): 112–39.

————. 2011. "Gender and Globalization: The Iranian Experience." In *Veiled Employment: Islamism and the Political Economy of Women's Employment in Iran*, edited by Roksana Bahramitash and Hadi Salehi Esfahani, 25–52. New York: Routledge.

Osanloo, Arzoo. 2009. *The Politics of Women's Rights in Iran.* Princeton, NJ: Princeton University Press.

Povey, Maryann. 1999. *Women, Work and Islamism: Ideology and Resistance in Iran.* London: Zed Books.

GENDER AND ECONOMICS IN MUSLIM COMMUNITIES

Ruwanpura, Kanchana N. and Jane Humphries. 2004. "Mundane Heroines: Conflict, Ethnicity, Gender, and Female Headship in Eastern Sri Lanka." *Feminist Economics* 10(2): 173–205.

Salehi-Isfahani, Djavad. 2005. "Labor Force Participation of Women in Iran: 1987–2001." Unpublished manuscript, Department of Economics, Virginia Tech, Blacksburg, VA.

Strassmann, Diana. 1999. "Feminist Economics." In *The Elgar Companion to Feminist Economics*, edited by Janice Peterson and Margaret Lewis, 360–73. Cheltenham: Edward Elgar.

Tohidi, Nayereh. 2007. "Muslim Feminism and Islamic Reformation." In *Feminist Theologies: Legacy and Prospect*, edited by Rosemary Radford Ruether, 93–164. Minneapolis, MN: Fortress Press.

World Bank. 2004. *Gender and Development in the Middle East and North Africa: Women in the Public Sphere*. Washington, DC: World Bank.

AGENCY THROUGH DEVELOPMENT: HAUSA WOMEN'S NGOS AND CBOS IN KANO, NIGERIA

Adryan Wallace

ABSTRACT

Analyzing the participation of Hausa women in religiously influenced nongovernmental organizations (NGOs) devoted to development work provides critical insights into the complex intersection of gender, religion, class, culture, and politics and economics. Based on interviews with leaders and employees of various NGOs, including community-based organizations (CBOs), in Kano, Nigeria, in 2010–11, this in-depth case study provides important examples of how various types of NGOs navigate political pressures when it comes to funding; it recognizes the understudied importance of women's labor contributions in the context of the development apparatus in Africa; it highlights the role of women as progenitors rather than benefactors of economic development; and it illustrates the unique role that faith-based organizations (FBOs) can and do play in terms of reaching certain marginalized segments of the population.

INTRODUCTION

Analyzing the participation of devout West African Muslim women in development work – specifically, education, economic empowerment, and health – can provide crucial insights into the complex interactions of religion, culture, and politics with women's economic activities. The ways in which gender and development are framed by the state often cast women as beneficiaries of targeted development programming, which serves to further obscure their economic contributions. As several scholars have observed, dominant development paradigms have tended to ignore the contributions of Muslim women to development efforts in their communities (Amina Mama 1996, 2001; Ousennia D. Alidou 2005; Sherine Hafez 2011; Stephanie Williams Bordat, Susan Schaefer Davis, and Saida

Kouzzi 2011). This article aims to fill this lacuna by exploring examples where Hausa women in Kano, Nigeria, are contributing to the creation of a vibrant nongovernmental organization (NGO) community, with a particular focus on how Muslim women use their faith-based organizations (FBOs) and non-FBOs to provide a range of key development-related services, navigate the difficult terrain of funding, find creative ways to reach women who are in seclusion, and tap the labor resources of older devout women to contribute to the furthering of a particular development agenda.

Using interpretive methods, this research examines interactions between and within various faith-based and secular NGOs, including community-based organizations (CBOs) among Hausa women to, first, illustrate the impact of certain Hausa women's perspectives regarding their roles within the family and the state on the timing and nature of their labor choices and, second, outline how indigenous Muslim women's organizations strategically engage in development projects and thus further their own vision of development. This study examines the experiences of Hausa women in Kano, Nigeria within the context of feminist frameworks and makes three contributions. First, this work provides significant empirical data on Muslim women's faith-based and non-faith-based NGOs in Nigeria. Second, I show that women make strategic choices about when in their life cycles to engage more extensively in activities in the public sphere. Finally, I argue that Hausa women are engaged in NGOs and CBOs as "designers" of development rather than mere beneficiaries of donor or state-driven development paradigms.

Building on the work of Chandra Mohanty (1988) and Uma Narayan (1997), I argue that Hausa women resist externally constructed definitions of Muslim women both by the men in their communities and by foreign development organizations. By studying various faith-based NGOs in Kano, I uncover examples of the constant tension that African Muslim women experience by being subject to more conservative forms of Islam in their communities as well as the hegemony of Western feminists – and how they ultimately resist both (Ayesha Imam 1997; Oeronke Oyewumi 1998; Fatima Adamu 1999). Oyewumi (1998) contextualizes Mohanty's (1988) critique by arguing that assuming Western gender norms are valid in non-Western states homogenizes the experiences of women in African countries and obscures variations in gender constructs at the national level. Underscoring Narayan's (1997) argument, Adamu (1999) uses her concept of the "double-edged sword" to capture the constant tension African Muslim women working on gender equality encounter as they simultaneously push for women's inclusion while rejecting critiques that their approaches simply re-inscribe traditional gender norms. Imam (1997) speaks directly to this delicate balance when she argues that Muslim women in northern Nigeria do not use a monolithic definition of gender equality, and that instead they strategically choose to frame their struggle for equality in the context of

GENDER AND ECONOMICS IN MUSLIM COMMUNITIES

being good mothers, wives, and Muslims serving as the moral vanguard of their respective communities. It is important to understand how women are negotiating their identity in contexts where they face pressure both from their own societies and from larger development contexts – not only because such an understanding sheds light on how women are active, rather than passive, participants in the development "project," but also because it provides a more nuanced understanding of how women negotiate various development processes and how women emerge as development actors within a faith perspective. Much like Mohanty's (1988) disruption of the construction of non-Western women as a passive monolithic group, my study analyzes the varied experiences of Hausa women as development actors to illustrate their use of economic agency to challenge intersecting social and political power structures.

METHODOLOGY

In an effort to fill in some of the gaps in research about development-oriented NGOs in northern Nigeria, I collected ethnographic data and conducted thirty-five in-depth, semi-structured interviews over a period of five months (August 2010 to January 2011) in the Nigerian state of Kano, ten with women who participate in NGO activity, sixteen with women who participate in trading CBOs, and nine with members of traditional birth attendants' CBOs. The population of Kano is nearly entirely Hausa, the largest predominantly Muslim linguistic ethnic group in West Africa, with a history of institutionalized Islam since the eleventh century (Graham Furniss 1996).

Nigeria is a presidential federal republic in which three levels of government operate: federal, state, and local. Kano State has the largest population in Nigeria. Nationally, women comprise approximately 32 percent of the nonagricultural labor force in comparison to the 68 percent maintained by their male counterparts. However, in Kano State, women account for approximately 8 percent of the nonagricultural labor force while men represent 92 percent. There are also disparities in literacy rates in Kano, where roughly 71 percent of men are literate compared with around 50 percent of women. Additionally, the enrollment rates for boys in primary school are approximately 81 percent while for girls the figure is 66 percent, with the gap closing slightly at the secondary level. Gender and regional gaps in formal education are a legacy of colonialism, and efforts are being made to reduce this disparity (Nkechi Catherine Onwuameze 2013). Kano is one of nine states in northern Nigeria that have fully instituted a form of sharia law since 1999. It is important to also note that a very small percentage of the population in Kano practice *kulle* (seclusion).

I focused on seven CSOs that either explicitly or implicitly draw on Islamic principles in the work they do in the context of the Hausa

283

community. These include five larger, formally structured, NGOs: the Grassroots Health Organization of Nigeria (GHON), the Muslim Sisters Organization (MSO), the Federation of Muslim Women's Associations in Nigeria (FOMWAN), the Women and Development Network (WODEN), the Voices of Widows, Divorcées, and Orphans (VOWAN), and two CBOs, the Trading Cooperative and the Traditional Birth Attendants. These NGOs can be divided according to the type of work they engage in: (1) those that focus primarily on economic development, with special attention to economically vulnerable groups with limited financial resources or income that are vulnerable to shocks in local small scale trading markets; (2) those that focus primarily on political development; and (3) those that were established as Muslim women's umbrella groups and focus on working with women's CBOs and acting as intermediaries. Three of the NGOs – MSO, FOMWAN, and VOWAN – and both CBOs are membership groups, while the GHON and WODEN are not; this impacts upon the types of programming and intervention taken in development sectors. The two CBOs selected for this study are trading cooperatives and traditional birth attendants' groups. Both are clients of GHON, which provides mobilization training and equips them with tools with which to engage local leaders on microcredit, maternal health, and other issues. The types of diverse development activities in which these organizations were involved include infrastructural development, healthcare provision, support for women entrepreneurs, framing women's rights in the context of Islam, and election monitoring.

I relied on participant observation to analyze how women in these organizations related to one another, for example at programs conducted by GHON (the primary focus of this study), as well as their NGO and CBO networks. I observed two programming streams and five types of programs in each stream, conducted by GHON. The first initiative focused on increasing access to healthcare facilities of communities in four local government areas conducted in partnership with Pact Nigeria, and international health organization, and the Kano State Ministry of Health, which was funded by the Nigerian government. The other initiative, sponsored by the European Union, focused on access to clean water and sanitation.

In addition, I interviewed GHON officials, volunteers, and clients. Given the breadth of GHON's development work and the different women who come together through the organization, observing GHON closely revealed the ways in which privilege is constructed and contested by Hausa women and the variety of ways in which they conceptualize development on their own terms.

My outsider status as a non-Hausa, non-Muslim woman of African descent living in the United States underscored the importance of maintaining nuance in my analysis. By centering the experiences of Hausa women, I was

GENDER AND ECONOMICS IN MUSLIM COMMUNITIES

able to utilize their perspectives to speak back to the existing development policy assumptions and highlight the understudied role that religious women are playing in shaping development outcomes. This approach provided empirical data about NGO activities and women's involvement in shaping economic and political outcomes, which are often obscured in quantitative data analyses.

Since relying on statistical data alone can often provide a one-dimensional picture of women's development contributions, I drew primarily on feminist and interpretive ethnographic methods to create a textured picture of the dynamics and interactions among women and between women and the state (Barbara J. Callaway 1987; Martha MacDonald 1995; Gwendolyn Mikell 1997; Sherryl Kleinmon 2007; Richa Nager and Susan Geiger 2007; Jan Kubik 2009).

A multi-method approach allows this study to capture the experiences of diverse groups of African women as political, social, and economic actors, while avoiding essentializing their perspectives. I attempt to showcase the agency and perspectives of Hausa women, including how they define development, how they situate their work within the context of Islam, and their mobilization strategies around gender, which at times include engaging political structures. By emphasizing the role of NGOs that either explicitly or implicitly take Islam as their starting point, I am able to illustrate how these women are choosing a path that allows them to both maneuver within a context where religious conservatism and Western feminist ideas are being imposed, by rejecting both of these paths and choosing instead a third one. I am also able to illustrate how their unique positioning is particularly valuable when it comes to reaching certain populations.

DEVELOPMENT WORK IN WEST AFRICAN MUSLIM COMMUNITIES

Historically, the shifts in development paradigms from Women in Development (WID), to Women and Development (WAD), to Gender and Development (GAD) reflect the expansion of theoretical models to address structural impediments. An important aspect of evolving theorizing around issues related to gender and development is the focus on the importance of NGOs (Eva M. Rathgeber 1990; Hedayat Nikkhah, Ma'rof Redzuan, and Asnarulkhadi Abu-Samah 2012). Through their engagement with local populations and the development of programs and awareness campaigns, NGOs can transform individual levels of empowerment into collective efforts to challenge gendered power dynamics and cultural and institutional constraints (Vandana Desai 2005; Nikkhah, Redzuan, and Abu-Samah 2012). Furthermore, these groups can function as sites to reconstitute new gender norms by mainstreaming concerns of women into

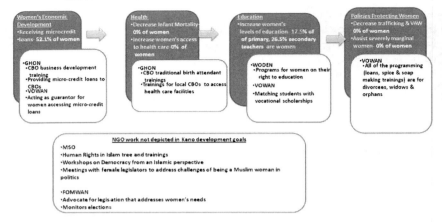

Figure 1 Hausa women's NGO and CBO activities uncaptured by labor data collected by Kano State

development approaches and policies and increasing their presence in public spaces (Andrea Cornwall, Elizabeth Harrison, and Ann Whitehead 2004; Caroline Moser and Annalise Moser 2005; Mats Alvesson and Yvonne Due Billing 2009). For example, in the education sector, women are the vast majority of teachers at the primary and secondary levels, but there are far fewer women at the tertiary level. However, organizations like WODEN and VOWAN also conduct programs on women's right to education using Islamic texts, VOWAN matches students with vocational scholarships, and FOWMAN actually helps build schools (see Figure 1). Additionally, NGOs are also active in areas where the presence of women is marginal. For example, FOMWAN engages in legislative advocacy on the maternal health bill and monitors elections (see Figure 1). While NGOs can potentially deconstruct gender hierarchies domestically within individual households and nationally, relationships between international and indigenous organizations are also capable of re-inscribing privilege given differentials in the ability to influence development agendas (Kanchana N. Ruwanpura 2007).

It is critical, though, also to note that NGOs take a myriad steps to address differences in programming agendas and priorities among members of the NGOs themselves, finding ways to challenge what Naila Kabeer, Simeen Mahmud, and Jairo G. Isaza Castro (2012: 2046) describe as the "homogenization of the NGO sector around service delivery" because the focus on the organizations becomes broader than mere "service delivery." They argue that this homogenization has caused NGOs to move away from social justice, social mobilization, and governance, to focus instead, with donor encouragement and support, on the delivery of specific services,

GENDER AND ECONOMICS IN MUSLIM COMMUNITIES

in particular, microcredit. My analysis suggests that NGOs may be able to balance the service delivery component with other activities that focus more on areas such as social mobilization.

Several feminist works have explored the relationship between domestic women's organizations and international donors. For instance, Christine Keating, Claire Rasmussen, and Pooja Rishi (2010) and Özlem Altan-Olcay (2014) disrupt narratives of microcredit that claim to enhance women's economic status and thereby increase their political and economic bargaining power. While their critiques are important, it is, at the same time, problematic to assume that indigenous NGOs invariably integrate women into the neoliberal economic systems in ways that make them additionally vulnerable. Because the indigenous organizations that are the focus of this study rely on multiple sources of domestic funding, they are often able, through specifically designed training programs, to avoid participation in some of the more overtly neoliberal models, such as those that rely heavily on the provision of microcredit. Development aid acquired from the World Bank, the International Monetary Fund, and other international donors is usually under the control of the state. Therefore, in many cases, the implementation of programs sourced with these funds can function as a form of global governance because they monitor and regulate women's economic activity. Consequently, the constraints imposed by donors have the potential to affect women – if women's organizations un-reflexively conduct programming (Marie L. Campbell and Kathy Teghtsoonian 2010).

In addition to the focus on international assistance, another strand of scholarship on Muslim NGOs in Africa focuses on the role of *zakat* (mandatory almsgiving in Islam) and the economic relationships between local organizations and transnational organizations (Holger Weiss 2002; Mayke Kaag 2008). Kaag (2008) explores the connections between neoliberalism and the increased influence of transnational Muslim organizations in Chad. Much of the funding for such projects comes from the Gulf States and is directed towards the building of mosques, wells, orphan support, healthcare, and education. While receiving external funding is essential to implement programs, the result is that, like the case of Western aid described above, these programs also reflect the priorities of donors and are not necessarily congruent with those of recipient organizations.

Pre-Islamic social-support systems among the Hausa serve a similar function to *zakat* and therefore reduce the need to formalize charitable financial contributions through Islamic institutions (Weiss 2002). It is important to note though that although they present their work within the framework of Islam, none of the organizations I studied reported receiving financial support from the Kano State Zakat Commission. Including indigenous Hausa women's organizations in the analysis expands the work of Weiss (2002) and Kaag (2008), who analyze the importance of institutional connections and strategies for revenue generation.

Hausa women's organizations in this study illustrate how acquiring multiple sources of funding, including from within their own social networks, at times partnering with international organizations or specific ministries within the government, allow them to maximize their autonomy. The organizations that participated in this study utilize creative methods of financing which prevent them from relying exclusive on any single international or domestic funding stream. These groups are cautious about the types of funding they accept because they are operating on the margins of both the development and faith-based communities. I am not arguing that they are completely autonomous rather that they have strategically placed themselves in a position to better negotiate which groups they work with on which programs. Their approach also helps insulate them from the shocks of donor grant cycles, allowing them to continue programming and to remain financially solvent between projects. Therefore their funding mechanisms include grants from Kano State, international organizations (USAID, EU, Pact Nigeria), and fundraising through the personal social networks of NGO leaders. CBOs also have successfully sourced small loans from local leaders in the community for their trading cooperatives.

Given that women's organizations often lack formalized fiscal-support mechanisms, including from the Zakat Commission established in 1982, it is important to understand how they conduct and finance their activities (Phillip Ostein 2007). While it is important to think about the implications of many of these development schemes, it is also essential that women's strategic decisions to lead NGOs, including CBOs, at a time when they are not dependent on revenue from their organizations for economic security is not overlooked. Economic autonomy provides the opportunity to retain local control of programs and priorities that are not determined by external funding mechanisms.

More generally, during the last decade, Muslim women in West Africa have increased their presence in development activities made available to them. And their unpaid work contributions have received more recognition. Badydai Sani and Sa'id Sulaiman, for example, have noted the significant contributions of women's work through civil society organizations and activities in Kano:

> Women in their matrimonial homes and in governmental and nongovernmental organizations (NGOs) also render many services which help the economy of Kano state. The services provided by women in their matrimonial homes to their families and neighbors, though very difficult to be measure [in] monetary terms, are very much appreciated and valued in the Islamic socio-economic system

GENDER AND ECONOMICS IN MUSLIM COMMUNITIES

cherished by almost 99 percent of the citizens of the Kano state. (2001: 36)

My research builds on existing accounts of Hausa women's contributions to development institutions by providing contextualized, detailed analysis of the ways in which Muslim women are participating in processes of social change and the potential longer-term impacts of their socioeconomic activities. Two points in this regard are worthy of further exploration. First, the relationship between CBOs and larger, more structured NGOs is important to development outcomes. CBOs often seek the support of larger NGOs to learn the best business practices and acquire small loans. NGOs using Islamic frames are able to successfully navigate the challenges of reaching women living in *kulle*. The institutional connections between CBOs and NGOs can provide a space where the labor of women in seclusion intersects with the labor of women outside seclusion (see also Enid Schildkrout [1982]). Writing in the early 1980s, Schildkrout (1982) highlighted the tensions that arose because of dependence on the children, particularly girls, to act as intermediaries for women who were in *kulle* and engaged in trading networks. Many development organizations emphasized the importance of girls' education, which placed them in direct conflict with conventional labor dynamics. As I show below, the experience of GHON illustrates how indigenous NGOs can help alleviate those specific tensions by facilitating contact with women in seclusion.

Women are very conscious of the fact that securing enough social capital, the "features of social life-networks, norms and trust that enable participants to act together more effectively to pursue shared objectives" (Robert Putnam 1996), to obtain the support of local religious and traditional leaders is an important factor in successful program implementation for women's groups. Additionally, there are other types of support women provide for one another beyond financial capital.

Similar to women in rural Bangladesh, Hausa women involved in both NGOs and CBOs see continuity in their conceptualization of their development agendas and their identities as Muslim women (Elora Shehabuddin 2008). The degree of institutional connection between NGOs and CBOs is analyzed in this study and provides insight into ways grassroots perspectives can be mainstreamed. Examining the relationships between NGOs and CBOs illuminates the ways in which women negotiate issues of privilege around development work and priorities (Ruwanpura 2007). Women use their agency to set programming agendas and articulate values through the sectors of the economy in which they choose to participate. Unfortunately many economic models oversimplify women's perspectives on value (economic, political, and social vitality) and fail to capture their contributions in the development sphere (Lourdes Benería 1981). Hausa women's development work illustrates the ways in which religious and nationalist strategies are deployed and how decisions around labor are situated within the context of ethno-nationalism, including that of Islam (Jean Baudrillard 1981; Jennifer Hyndman and Malathi de Alwis 2003; Kanchana N. Ruwanpura and Jane Humphries 2004; Kabeer, Mahmud, and Isaza Castro 2012; Damla Isik 2013). Self-defined identities as Muslim women influence decisions regarding when to participate in the labor market and in which sectors.

Women's perspectives on work and development

Hausa women reject standard development rhetoric and discourse and have found their own way of interpreting and contributing to development outcomes, framed within their understanding of what it means to be Muslim through their paid and unpaid labor contributions. Illustrating the tensions described by scholars such as Narayan (1997), in particular, a number of the leaders of more religious NGOs were careful to frame all of their actions in the context of Islam. For example, Haj. Auy of MSO and Excel College highlights her important economic role in development sanctioned by Islam:

> I am allowed [by Islam and it is outlined in the Quran] to engage in economic activities that do not compromise my position as a wife and a mother and a Muslim woman. I provide job opportunities for over 100 people which [makes me feel like] I am contributing something to the economy of the country. To the people around me and also no matter how small it is, it is pushing the wheel of progress forward.[1]

She also indicates the importance of waiting until children are an appropriate age before engaging in work, because the time you spend with them cannot be replicated or outsourced to someone else. She believes the first priority is adequate development of children, not financial gain. Haj. Auy explained how she ended up leading an NGO in terms of a life-cycle approach:

> For people who are my age who have already finished nurturing and the nest is now empty or virtually empty then you can indulge in some other activities even if takes up your time it doesn't matter ... But you jump trying to fix the world when your house is in disarray, ... your priorities are somehow amiss.

Women like Haj. Auy illustrate the interest even among women who in some ways advocate for somewhat rigid gender roles, a desire to mobilize around gender, disrupt narratives restricting women's contributions to the domestic sphere and the construction of development as a process of Westernization. Examples of this include GHON working with CBOs in

GENDER AND ECONOMICS IN MUSLIM COMMUNITIES

local government areas to increase women's access to healthcare facilities, VOWAN acting as a guarantor for women attempting to access microcredit loans, and MSO conducting training on human rights (see Figure 1).

While some women advocated for careers that followed childbearing, women like Haj. Jamila, engaged in NGO activities as part of volunteer work after retiring from a career that involved paid employment. Women such as Haj. Auy and Haj. Jamila had attended international conferences and worked with international organizations. Haj. Jamila, who had previously been a sociologist who worked in the Ministry of Health, when referring to her role within MSO, a faith-based NGO of which she is a member, stated: "Women like me [of my social status] ... did planning and going to international conferences, coming back with new ideas, try[ing] them on," suggesting that outside views were infiltrating these indigenous NGOs, but were then repackaged to fit local contexts.

Clear age and class differences separated the leaders of various NGOs and the women employed in the more and less formal NGOs, particularly the CBOs. The leaders, not surprisingly, were older and better educated. Haj. Jamila, Haj. Auy, Haj. Hassan, and Haj. Rakiya, Haj. Atine, and Haj. Hadiza represent a very elite group of women in Kano involved in faith-based and non-faith-based NGOs as leaders or members. While the amount of economic affluence and level of formal education are not representative of the majority of women in Kano, their perspectives are significant because they are the women that are best positioned to shape and define their own concepts of development including integrating perspectives and priorities of women in CBOs that are less privileged. Additionally these women are embarking upon changing gender norms and in many ways as Haj. Auy states that they have become the "gate-keepers" of promoting gender equality, particularly in Kano because they are able to work with all of the relevant stakeholders. Women working in NGOs had generally completed senior secondary school and many of them had gone on to earn additional teaching certifications, diplomas, degrees from polytechnic institutes, and undergraduate and graduate degrees. One participant obtained a Master's degree. Participants earned degrees in a myriad of disciplines, including education, social work, and zoology. Successful completion of Quranic schools and in-depth knowledge of the Koran was widespread among the women in NGOs. Women with less formal education concentrated primarily on providing fiscal support to the family and are members of CBOs. The quotations below highlight ways in which women in trading cooperatives see their economic contributions.

According to Haj. Ayana, a leader of a trading CBO:

[We are] working to provide food and according to Islamic goals. There are difficulties sometimes, mainly profits change, sometimes high sometimes low. It all depends on the marketability of the

GENDER AND ECONOMICS IN MUSLIM COMMUNITIES

food ... [which in turn depends] on the amount of capital available for food and so on. [...] There is one group and I am the leader of the group that works together. The group was formed by GHON because they worked with us before and they introduced the idea of forming the group. We are twenty-five and neighbors with each other.

Haj. Ayana also stated that as a result of the GHON creating the CBO they have been able to get loans from the local leaders to mitigate the shocks in the local food prices and the money is distributed to individual members of the group. Furthermore, the members pool their collective knowledge about the local market and diversify the foodstuffs they are selling.

Haj. Halima, a member of the same trading CBO that Haj. Ayana heads, indicates that she wants

to help take part in taking care of the children, including school fees, not just the husband. I also want to take part. My husband is very supportive. Yes there are more opportunities for women in business because the challenges of life have allowed them to come out.

She argues that the current economic conditions of the state have also created a space for women's economic activity and contributions to be valued at the familial level. While both of these women are members of CBO trading groups, women in NGOs also see their professions and nongovernmental work as part of fulfilling their societal responsibilities, not something they take on to meet economic and financial needs. Their NGO work, in other words, fulfills social and moral obligations rather than providing economic security.

The interviews depict the range of reasons why women chose to undertake NGO activities during particular periods of their lives. Some participants indicated that domestic labor, in terms of raising a family, was just as important as labor activities, which would reduce their time at home and away from their families. Because of their social location and access to formal education, they choose to participate in the external labor wage market once their children reach an age where they are self-sufficient, generally secondary school though this age can vary. Some women are also involved in their own economic endeavors and remain independent of any CSO activity. For example, Haj. Auy, a member of MSO, had established Excel College. Such endeavors allowed the women to engage in work through their NGOs without being dependent on the NGO as a source of revenue.

Given that the women married in their twenties, family commitments were generally fulfilled earlier, producing a more staggered allocation of labor first to the domestic sphere and then to the development sector. Hausa women engaged in NGO work have synthesized these two sets

GENDER AND ECONOMICS IN MUSLIM COMMUNITIES

of production requirements, domestic and remunerative labor, and have developed their own strategies to address gender inequality in an effort to contribute to their communities and toward the development goals of Kano State. The intense and demanding nature of development work requires that women have sufficient time to devote to projects. Being able to serve as a role model to their own children and other youth was also of great importance to them.

Furthermore, the elite women who headed these organizations often provided their labor on a volunteer basis and so were not dependent on the revenue from their NGO, which allowed them to be more selective about forging partnerships. As illustrated by authors such as Campbell and Teghtsoonian (2010), this is a critical form of resistance neglected by most feminist critiques.

Each participant highlights an example of the ways in which Hausa women in certain economic positions interpret their agency and the important role of Islam (more specifically, their contributions to the family in their capacities as mothers) in their decision making, and it drives the types of labor they pursue.

My interviews revealed that Hausa women see themselves as social developers with a serious commitment to solving development issues consistent with their roles as Muslim women. Their right to the self-definition of their roles is very important to them. Hausa women in this study identify Islam as a cross-cutting theme, regardless of their social status and level of education, to argue that their development and domestic labor are not mutually exclusive but are rather part of a coherent labor framework with contributions allocated across their lifespan. Hausa women have created a strategy for social and economic production, between familial and professional labor, that is more cooperative than conflicting. The cooperative approaches adopted by women participating in NGOs in this study include a sequential labor trajectory where motherhood (providing direct care for children until they reach an age where they are self-sufficient), professional career, and NGO development work are sequential with some overlap in the last two categories. Indeed, given their economic vulnerability, women in CBOs utilize a cooperative model where their development organizations are specifically created to expand and support the activities that function as the primary sources of income used to fulfill needs within their individual households. After understanding Hausa women's perceptions of familial and community roles, it is important to see how they translate into organizational mandates and structures.

RELIGIOUS WOMEN'S APPROACHES TO DEVELOPMENT

In the context of Northern Nigeria, a range of NGOs operate including those that have a more secular focus (for example, National Council of

Women's Societies [NCWS]), as well as the various NGOs included in this study, which all frame their work in the context of Islam, although the degree to which they are explicitly religious in their focus varies. NGO work provides a space where women can have a direct impact on development and policy priorities without being embedded within the formal political system. Much of NGO work in Kano focuses on assisting vulnerable populations (see Table 1).

A number of the elite women leaders I interviewed were particularly interested in the establishment of NGOs that reflect the Islamic framing of rights and discourses around education, political participation, economic security, health, and so on. FOMWAN, for example, was formed by members of MSO, such as Haj. Jamilia, who were interested in having an organization of Muslim women at the federal level that provided women with an experience distinct from that of the NCWS. While in some instances FOMWAN and NCWS collaborate on projects, in other ways they clearly see their main development aim as quite distinct. They do collaborate with Women in Nigeria (WIN), the International Federation of Women Lawyers in Nigeria (FIDA), and other organizations in areas such as HIV/AIDS prevention and sensitization, reproductive health, women's economic empowerment, and elections. One of the key differences between FOMWAN and NCWS, highlighted by Haj. Aisha – the *ameera* (leader, head) of the northern region of FOMWAN – was the specific period of child development when professional ambition can be placed on hold in favor of attaining goals around raising children and equipping them to be successful individuals in addition to not specifically advocating for women to contest to be head of state. Again though this did not preclude women from engaging in contributing labor (both paid and volunteer), it just shifted their strategies in terms of when to engage.

The types of projects that more faith-oriented organizations engage in are reflective of their conceptualization of development and the interaction of these frames with the state-centered macroeconomic approaches. For example, whereas a secular NGO might articulate their gender equality aims in terms of the secular human-rights discourse, MSO developed a rights-in-Islam tree for mass distribution and use in training. The tree outlines a total of twenty-seven rights that Islam affords specifically to women – among them rights around health, education, economic stability, and political inclusion – each supported by verses from religious texts providing extensive support for women's development work. For example, on the subject of women's right to vote and be nominated, MSO noted that in early Islamic history, "Every person was allowed to give his opinion. Decisions were usually taken on the basis of unanimity or sometimes by majority." MSO also supported the right to gender equality by citing the Quran: "I will not waste the work of a worker among you, whether male or female" with references to Quranic verse 3:195, while verses 40:40 and

GENDER AND ECONOMICS IN MUSLIM COMMUNITIES

Table 1 Indigenous Muslim women's NGOs' and CBOs' development work in Kano, Nigeria

Name	Type of organization	Development work	Institutional affiliations
Muslim Sisters Organization (MSO)	NGO – faith based	• Advisory council to FOMWAN • Human rights in Islam training • Democracy and good governance training	Trading CBOs Community CBOs
Federation of Muslim Women's Associations in Nigeria (FOMWAN)	NGO – faith based	• Maternal health bill • Polio vaccines • Community health outcomes • Monitor elections • Build schools • Girls' education	Trading CBOs Community CBOs
Grassroots Health Organization of Nigeria (GHON)	NGO	• Increase access to healthcare facilities • Clean water and sanitation • Women's reproductive health • HIV/AIDS • Training for women's trading cooperatives, business development, microcredit	Trading CBOs Traditional Birth Attendants' CBOs Community-Development CBOs
Voices of Widows, Divorcées, and Orphans (VOWAN)	NGO	• Scholarships for vocational students • Income-generating activity training • Loans • Mobilization around divorcées rights (organized protest march)	Individual women
Women and Development (WODEN)	NGO	• Women's right to education • Human rights	Individual women

(*Continued*)

GENDER AND ECONOMICS IN MUSLIM COMMUNITIES

Table 1 Continued.

	Type of organization	Development work	Institutional affiliations
Traditional Birth Attendants' CBO	CBO	• Share best practices • Referral system to local health centers	GHON
Trading Cooperative CBO	CBO	• Expand income-generating activities • Secure small loans from local leaders	GHON

4:125 were utilized to frame human rights and democracy training. MSO also developed a manual and workshops on democracy from an Islamic perspective aimed at targeting youth (Adryan R. Wallace 2012: 224).

FOMWAN, on the other hand, has carried out fairly standard political development activities, such as monitoring elections, voter registration, and worked on health issues. They also helped propose a bill in the state assembly on maternal health. But the particular way in which they approached these activities is worthy of further discussion as well. For example, one of the areas that FOMWAN had focused on is in the provision of polio vaccinations, and a particularly important role they have played has involved alleviating many male Muslim leaders' concerns the polio vaccines were tainted.

Another unique way that these organizations contribute to development objectives is through their ability to reach women practicing *kulle*. For example the larger NGOs work with smaller women's CBOs, including those involving trading cooperatives, some of which are founded by women in seclusion. More secularly oriented NGOs are less likely to develop and sustain relationships with such women unless, as Haj. Auy observed, they receive the backing of local leaders.

More generally, members of FOMWAN and other religiously based women's organizations are well positioned to bridge tensions that arise between international donors, state and local Islamic leaders, and members of the community. This allows them to engage in a wide range of development activities.

The current Executive Director of GHON, Haj. Hadiza, sees her work as critically important because Muslim Hausa women are often marginalized during the implementation phase of development programs by the state. Women are often left out of the discussions and programs that provide oversight for state projects and address issues related to access. Haj. Hadiza organizes programs centered primarily around reproductive health, income-generating activities and business

GENDER AND ECONOMICS IN MUSLIM COMMUNITIES

development, training for traditional birth attendants, increasing access to health facilities and services, in addition to clean water and sanitation funded by Kano State and the EU. The recent training on access to healthcare facilities targets local government areas in partnership with Pact Nigeria and the clean water and sanitation program sponsored by the EU. Haj. Hadiza, Executive Director of the NGO GHON, highlights the importance of helping women with less privilege when she states:

> Yes and you know the feeling that I can do something was so much and I could go a long length in helping others. Especially the grass roots people, you know ... that I could, you know, give some assistance to help the community ... Especially women not knowing their health right and, you know, how they are being sometimes, you know, even deprived of having access to health facilities.

CSO work can also address economic insecurity across age groups by improving the economic conditions of the parents and, in turn, their children and community. Haj. Atine, founder of VOWAN, articulates a similar rationale for her NGO addressing women's economic security by starting this membership organization focused on "becoming the voice of the voiceless." She states she created VOWAN to (1) raise societal awareness about the negative economic impacts of divorce on women; (2) assist orphans; and (3) address poverty for widows, divorcees, and orphans through income-generating activities. Haj. Atine's activities reflect a contemporary version of development efforts that began with the wives of the Prophet: "So this is the work we can do now, following the tradition of the development work of the women that were on the battlefield in the *jihad*. This is now our work." The emphasis placed on vulnerable populations is coupled with concerted efforts to have their clients' own interests frame programmatic agendas (Cornwall, Harrison, and Whitehead 2004). This also dovetails with concerns raised by political Islam around the need to address economic inequality in the context of religion.

NGOs also utilize rhetoric that interconnects women's empowerment, development, and Islam toward their own aims. Haj. Rakiya, the head of WODEN and NGO, selected "women's empowerment" as the motto for WODEN, a motto that transcends being a development buzzword because she emphasizes the ability of women to engage religious text and shape Islamic discourses around gender as a foundational component of empowerment. Rakiya believes women who have knowledge of the Quran and their rights under its teachings will "enhance the women folk economically to enable them to uphold their dignity, hence take part in decision making in their communities and nation at large."

GENDER AND ECONOMICS IN MUSLIM COMMUNITIES

Clearly, the Hausa women who participated in this study are not overly influenced by Western feminist approaches and international development organizations; instead, they define their own development. Avoiding these perceptions also impacts the women's decisions regarding when to participate in the wage market.

PROMOTING GENDER EQUALITY THROUGH COMPLIMENTARY DEVELOPMENT WORK OF NGOS AND CBOS

The larger NGOs that engage more directly with development partners were closely linked to smaller CBOs, but there were clear distinctions between NGOs and CBOs, and women engage with these development partners in different ways. NGOs worked directly with the donors and obtained funding, which was funneled into CBO programs. Analyzing the institutional relationships of GHON, MSO, and FOMWAN to CBOs is a valuable exercise for three reasons: (1) attention to the smaller CBOs increases the visibility of local women's groups, thus uncovering more detail concerning local economic and political networks; (2) the diverse sets of interests represented by NGOs can be further highlighted; and (3) the important ways these NGOs interact thus contributing to the creation of a collective action, and possibly a more coherent political voice, is also worthy of further exploration.

Larger NGOs and smaller CBOs have varying levels of connectivity to each other, to international organizations, and to the state. The relationship between NGOs and CBOs are often characterized as that of patron–client; in other instances, the CBOs are members of larger umbrella organizations in this study, MSO and FOMWAN. As has been argued by Ruwanpura (2007), there is the danger these interactions can reinscribe gendered power hierarchies; but I provide examples where these structural relationships have the potential to minimize these negative effects. NGOs can give women in CBOs a space to advocate for their interests directly to government officials and NGOs can integrate CBO priorities within the broader policy and legislative efforts NGOs undertake to address gender inequality. More specifically, the institutional relationships among NGOs and CBOs across social locations further serve to translate development programs into feedback mechanisms to the state. In addition to Hausa women's organizations addressing a myriad of development issues that are directly linked to the increased dismantling of normative systems of power, the relationships among NGOs and CBOs also provide a mechanism to incorporate the interests of women from different social locations and levels of economic security.

Among some of the women from the trading CBOs that worked with GHON (an NGO), women stated that economic issues were of primary

GENDER AND ECONOMICS IN MUSLIM COMMUNITIES

concern. For example the sixteen women in the marketing associations cited "helping their families financially" as their main motivation for trading and joining the cooperative, which enhanced their profit margins substantially. More generally, according to women, the main benefits of joining the CBOs included the fact that this allowed women to pool their financial resources, share ideas for marketing, and troubleshoot coping mechanisms to deal with fluctuations in capital and demand for their products. Almost all of the respondents indicated that being in a group allowed them to receive fiscal support from the group, an option that was not available to them when working independently. The primary goods traded are food, beverages, and packets of spices.

One of the most interesting aspects of the work one of the CBOs was doing was through their engagement with women practicing *kulle* who were involved in trading activities. Additionally, these NGOs help women in various CBOs, who come from different social and economic strata, by addressing their needs, while also understanding and having the social capital to navigate their religious constraints and contexts.

At the same time, direct economic motives were not the only driving factor in the case of CBO participation. In addition to trading cooperatives, GHON also works with traditional birth attendants. Traditional birth attendants were less focused on economic benefits and more on the information sharing value of the organization. The nine members interviewed stated they regularly were able to consult each other about maternal-health practices, and they felt more confident about their knowledge of maternity care. Additionally, they were able to receive training on new techniques as required from organizations such as GHON. More generally, Haj. Hadiza was instrumental in establishing a relationship between local hospitals and the traditional birth attendants' CBO. In the event of complications during childbirth, it is crucial that the woman can be transferred to a local hospital in order to prevent maternal deaths. Finally, participants reported that being affiliated with GHON brought them elevated status in their communities.

One of the key programs that GHON conducted recently with Pact Nigeria involved training community-development groups to identify obstacles that were preventing people in the community from accessing healthcare centers. The community-development groups were also tasked with proposing solutions and then monitoring the effectiveness of these implemented solutions in increasing access to the healthcare centers. The interaction I observed among GHON team members during training designed to increase community access to healthcare centers were marked by respect and demonstrated that the ideas and the input of the women was sincerely valued. During group presentations, GHON team members highlighted the problem-solving abilities of one of the women's groups and used the group's proposed solution as a model for the other groups to follow. With one exception, because they were nominated by community leaders who were usually men (with the exception of the women's groups), the ratio of men to women in the participating groups was 2:1 in the community-level development committees.

Sadia and Haladu, both employees of GHON, were vigilant about maintaining gender inclusion throughout the entire training process for the CBOs. They often insisted to local leaders that women represent themselves in the development communities rather than have their male counterparts represent the women's interests by proxy. This is an example of how women who are better positioned within the economic and political structure can create parallel spaces for other women within their respective communities. As a result, women's access to decision makers at the local and community level increases. After the training, GHON continued to follow up with women who were members of the community-development CBO. The participants expressed greater confidence, stated that they were taken more seriously, and that they maintained higher visibility in the community because they were members of the committee tasked with ensuring the community has access to health facilities. The potential long-term success of this CBO capacity-building model became clear when it was observed that women from various CBOs from previous programs for traditional birth attendants and trading cooperatives came to the GHON office freely to use the space for meetings.

According to Haj. Jamilia, women engaged in CBO work focus primarily on more practical issues, while women in NGOs take the lead on policy issues and in addressing gender equality. More generally, there is a clear link between women's social location and their institutional affiliation; women with more affluence tend to be members of NGOs, and women with less affluence typically work through CBOS, with women who occupy higher social locations being generally able to retain the social capital to occasionally work with international donors and engage directly with domestic political institutions. While this can be problematic because it could run the risk of relegating CBO women's input to practical issues rather than larger conceptualizations of gender equality at the policy level, in some ways the decision-making processes I observed involved consensus building, with women from the CBO and NGO sectors having equal numbers of representatives. This approach helps ensure all women's voices are heard, and they are able to represent their own interests while attaining collective goals.

Through this in-depth study of a small group of NGOs and CBOs that worked closely together, I was able to shed light on the complex networks that provide women with mutually beneficial support in a number of areas. For example, GHON trains traditional birth attendants, and uses their contacts to ensure traditional birth attendants' clients have access to local health centers. GHON also sponsors programs to empower

GENDER AND ECONOMICS IN MUSLIM COMMUNITIES

small-scale women's and community organizations to access their local medical facilities, which benefit not just women, but also men. CBOs for their part provide capacity training on key elements of business strategies and development for the trading cooperatives because they are key contributions to local economies and some increases in household income long term. Training sessions are designed to help women increase their market share and provide them with tools to help them diversify their products.

Similarly, the activities of MSO and FOMWAN in the political sphere created spaces for women to voice their concerns outside contemporary political institutions. FOMWAN's work on the maternal-health bill illustrates how organizations with social capital have the ability to move women's issues onto the political agenda with the right framing. Although passage of the bill has been delayed largely because the healthcare facilities lack the capacity to provide the maternal care required, advocacy efforts continue with the specific components of the bill proposing solutions to the logistical challenges.

Another key development issue, specified on the national development agenda rather than the state-level, is access to clean drinking water. The leader of one of the trading CBOs interviewed highlighted the groups' abilities to effectively lobby for fiscal support from community local leaders, suggesting that they were taken more seriously because of their affiliation with GHON. This provides just one example of the complex social relationships that emerged within and between NGOs, all facilitated by very dynamic and motivated Hausa women.

CONCLUSION

Utilizing ethnographic and qualitative methods, in this paper I contextualized the ways Hausa women involved in various NGOs, including CBOs, understand their social and economic production roles in the context of Nigerian development. This study also helps shape a stronger understanding of the ways in which Hausa women are key participants in development processes in Nigeria. As indicated by Narayan and others, women often face a challenging path in terms of navigating between nationalist men and Western feminists, not to mention international donors. The mixed-method approach I adopted generated data that created a more complete picture of the decision-making frames Hausa women are using to determine their economic activities through their civil-society groups. My analysis suggests that women leaders of NGOs, in Northern Nigeria in particular, carefully navigate these various challenges. A number of the women for example suggested they had made various strategic labor choices over the course of their lives in order to be able to actively contribute to the development needs of their families and

GENDER AND ECONOMICS IN MUSLIM COMMUNITIES

their broader communities. The Hausa women leaders I interviewed, while they participate in international conferences and accept various streams of outside funding, clearly defined themselves in terms of their roles as Muslim women, and defined development within a Islamic framework.

While I observed clear differences in the roles played by leaders and members among both NGOs and CBOs, the decision-making processes I noted also suggested a considerable degree of consensus-building and collaboration. Furthermore, the ways the NGOs and CBOs were linked created synergistic development benefits. Many of the contributions being made by women-led NGOs, particularly in the context of their acting as intermediaries for CBOs, are often overlooked; and yet these NGOs are positioned in such a way that they are beginning to change the relationship between women and the state by empowering and working with women across social strata. These organizations also play a key role in monitoring government delivery of services and therefore provide a number of benefits beyond just providing training. Finally, the faith-based organizations in particular are playing a critical role in reaching women in *kulle*, many of whom, despite being in seclusion, are active economic participants themselves. My analysis ultimately provides only a narrow glimpse of the rich dynamics unfolding in the context of NGOs in Northern Nigeria. Future studies are therefore required to further explore the political implications of Hausa NGOs facilitating interactions between women of various social and economic strata.

GENDER AND ECONOMICS IN MUSLIM COMMUNITIES

ACKNOWLEDGMENTS

This work was supported by the Fulbright-Hays Doctoral Dissertation Research Abroad (DDRA) award 2010–11 (grant number P022A0100026). This research would not have been possible without Haj. Hadiza, Haj. Jamila, Haj. Rakiya, Haj. Auy, and Haj. Atine being gracious enough to share their amazing development work with me. I confirm that the persons identified in this contribution have given permission for personal information to be published in *Feminist Economics*.

NOTE

[1] Excel College is a model science secondary school with an emphasis on Islamic identity.

REFERENCES

Adamu, Fatima. 1999. "A Double-Edged Sword: Challenging Women's Oppression Within Muslim Society in Northern Nigeria." *Gender and Development* 7(1): 56–61.

Alidou, Ousennia D. 2005. *Engaging Modernity: Muslim Women and the Politics of Agency in Postcolonial Niger*. Madison: University of Wisconsin Press.

Altan-Olcay, Özlem. 2014. "Entrepreneurial Subjectivities and Gendered Complexities: Neoliberal Citizenship in Turkey." *Feminist Economics* doi:13545701.2014.950978.

Alvesson, Mats and Yvonne Due Billing. 2009. *Understanding Gender and Organizations*. London: SAGE.

Baudrillard, Jean. 1981. *For a Critique of the Political Economy of the Sign*. St. Louis: Telos Press.

Benería, Lourdes. 1981. "Conceptualizing the Labor Force: The Underestimation of Women's Economic Activities." *Journal of Development Studies* 17(3): 10–28.

Bordat, Stephanie Williams, Susan Schaefer Davis, and Saida Kouzzi. 2011. "Women as Agents of Grassroots Change: Illustrating Micro-Empowerment in Morocco." *Journal of Middle East Women's Studies* 7(1): 90–119.

Callaway, Barbara J. 1987. *Muslim Hausa Women in Nigeria: Tradition and Change*. Syracuse, NY: Syracuse University Press.

Campbell, Marie L. and Kathy Teghtsoonian. 2010. "Aid Effectiveness and Women's Empowerment: Practices of Governance in the Funding of International Development." *Signs* 36(1): 177–202.

Cornwall, Andrea, Elizabeth Harrison, and Ann Whitehead. 2004. "Introduction: Repositioning Feminisms in Gender and Development." *IDS Bulletin* 35(4): 1–10.

Desai, Vandana. 2005. "NGOs, Gender Mainstreaming, and Urban Poor Communities in Mumbai." *Gender and Development* 13(2): 90–8.

Furniss, Graham. 1996. *Poetry, Prose and Popular Culture in Hausa*. Washington, DC: Smithsonian Institution Press.

Hafez, Sherine. 2011. "Women Developing Women: Islamic Approaches for Poverty Alleviation in Rural Egypt." *Feminist Review* 97: 56–73.

Hyndman, Jennifer and Malathi de Alwis. 2003. "Towards a Feminist Analysis of Humanitarianism and Development in Sri Lanka." *Women's Studies Quarterly* 31(3/4): 212–26.

GENDER AND ECONOMICS IN MUSLIM COMMUNITIES

Imam, Ayesha. 1997. "The Dynamics of WINing." In *Feminist Genealogies, Colonial Legacies, Democratic Futures*, edited by M. Jacqui Alexander and Chandra Talpade Mohanty, 280–307. New York: Routledge.

Isik, Damla. 2013. "'Just like the Prophet Mohammad Preached': Labor, Piety, and Charity in Contemporary Turkey." *Feminist Economics* doi:1345701.2013.825376.

Kaag, Mayke. 2008. "Transnational Islamic NGOs in Chad: Islamic Solidarity in the Age of Neoliberalism." *Africa Today* 54(3): 3–18.

Kabeer, Naila, Simeen Mahmud, and Jairo G. Isaza Castro. 2012. "NGOs and the Political Empowerment of Poor People in Rural Bangladesh: Cultivating the Habits of Democracy?" *World Development* 40(10): 2044–62.

Keating, Christine, Claire Rasmussen and Pooja Rishi. 2010. "The Rationality of Empowerment: Microcredit, Accumulation by Dispossession, and the Gendered Economy." *Signs* 36(1): 153–76.

Kleinmon, Sherryl. 2007. *Feminist Fieldwork Analysis: Qualitative Research Methods.* London: SAGE.

Kubik, Jan. 2009. "Ethnography of Politics: Foundations, Applications, Prospects." In *Political Ethnography: What Immersion Contributes to the Study of Politics*, edited by Edward Schatz, 25–52. Chicago: University of Chicago Press.

MacDonald, Martha. 1995. "Feminist Economics: from Theory to Research." *Canadian Journal of Economics* 28(1): 159–76.

Mama, Amina. 1996. *Women's Studies and Studies of African Women during the 1990s.* Working Paper Series 5/96. CODESRIA, Dakar.

——— . 2001. "Challenging Subjects: Gender and Power in African Contexts." *African Sociological Review* 5(2): 63–73.

Mikell, Gwendolyn. 1997. *African Feminism: The Politics of Survival in Sub-Saharan Africa.* Philadelphia: University of Pennsylvania Press.

Mohanty, Chandra. 1988. "Under Western Eyes: Feminist Scholarship and Colonial Discourses." *Feminist Review* 30: 61–88.

Moser, Caroline and Annalise Moser. 2005. "Gender Mainstreaming Since Beijing: A Review of Success and Limitations in International Institutions." *Gender and Development* 13(2): 11–22.

Nager, Richa and Susan Geiger. 2007. "Reflexivity and Positionality in Feminist Fieldwork Revisited." In *Politics and Practice in Economic Geography*, edited by Adam Ticklell, Eric Sheppard, Jamie Peck and Trevor Barnes, 267–78. London: SAGE.

Narayan, Uma. 1997. *Dislocating Cultures: Identities, Traditions, and Third World Feminism.* New York: Routledge.

Nikkhah, Hedayat, Ma'rof Redzuan, and Asnarulkhadi Abu-Samah. 2012. "Development of 'Power within' among the Women: A Road to Empowerment." *Asian Social Science* 8(1): 39–46.

Onwuameze, Nkechi Catherine. 2013. "Educational Opportunity and Inequality in Nigeria: Assessing Social Background, Gender and Regional Effects." PhD diss., University of Iowa.

Ostein, Phillip, ed. 2007. *Sharia Implementation in Northern Nigeria 1999–2006: A Sourcebook.* Ibadan, Nigeria: Spectrum Books Limited.

Oyewumi, Oeronke. 1998. "De-confounding Gender: Feminist Theorizing and Western Culture, a Comment on Hawkesworth's 'Confounding Gender'." *Signs* 23(4): 1049–62.

Putnam, Robert. 1996. "The Strange Disappearance of Civic America." *American Prospect* 7(24): 34–48.

Rasmussen, Claire and Rishi, Pooja. 2010. "The Rationality of Empowerment: Microcredit, Accumulation by Dispossession and the Gendered Economy." *Signs* 36(1): 153–76.

GENDER AND ECONOMICS IN MUSLIM COMMUNITIES

Rathgeber, Eva M. 1990. "WID, WAD, GAD: Trends in Research and Practice." *Journal of Developing Areas* 24(4): 489–502.

Ruwanpura, Kanchana N. 2007. "Awareness and Action: The Ethno-gender Dynamics of Sri Lankan NGOs." *Gender, Place Culture: A Journal of Feminist Geography* 14(3): 317–33.

Ruwanpura, Kanchana N. and Jane Humphries. 2004. "Mundane Heroines: Incorporating Gender and Ethnicity into Female-Headship." *Feminist Economics* 10(2): 173–205.

Sani, Badydai and Sa'id Sulaiman. 2001. "The Structure of the Kano Economy." Unpublished paper. Bayero University, Kano, Nigeria. http://kanoonline.com/jmqs/index.php/component/content/article/37-economy/72-structure-of-kano-economy.

Schildkrout, Enid. 1982. "Dependence and Autonomy: The Economic Activities of Secluded Hausa Women in Kano, Nigeria." In *Women and Work in Africa*, edited by Edna G. Bay, 55–81. Boulder, CO: Westview Press.

Shehabuddin, Elora. 2008. *Reshaping the Holy: Democracy, Development, and Muslim Women in Bangladesh*. New York: Columbia University Press.

Wallace, Adryan R. 2012. "Transforming Production Roles into Political Inclusion: A Comparative Study of Hausa Women's Agency through Civil Society Organizations in Kano, Nigeria and Tamale, Ghana." PhD diss., Rutgers University.

Weiss, Holger. 2002. "Reorganizing Social Welfare Among Muslims: Islamic Voluntarism and Other Forms of Communal Support in Northern Ghana." *Journal of Religion in Africa* 32(1): 83–109.

Index

Entries in *italics* denote figures; entries in **bold** denote tables.

2SLS (two-stage least squares) 74, 77, 82
9/11, and Orientalism 2–3

abortion: access to safe 22; female-selective 138–41, 145, 155–6, 158
Abu-Lughod, Lila 36, 177
abuse, language of 248
Adnan, Shapan 145–6
adoption 94
Afghanistan, US invasion of 4–5, 38, 177
Afyon 212, 214
Ahmadinejad, Mahmoud 262
Ahmed, Leila 36
AKP (Adalet ve Kalkınma Partisi) 22, 222–3, 226, 254n5
Algeria, family law in 123–4
altruistic-head household model 117, 187, 189–90, 193–7, 205–7
apparel industry 8, 12
Arab countries: family law in 7, 17; gender inequality in 62
Arabic language, in Israel 173–4
Arab Spring 21–2, 33, 37
Arab women: culturalist depiction of 165, 177; in Israel 169, 172 (*see also* Bedouin women)
Al-Araqib 170, 181
area studies, hostility to 34, 41
Armenia 139, 159
assemblages 212–14, 216–17, 222, 229–30n5, 246
Atatürk, Mustafa Kemal 63
authoritarianism 22, 37–8, 42–5
axiomatization 34, 39
Azerbaijan, Republic of 139, 159
Azerbaijan province, Iran 267

bad jobs 261, 268
Baliamoune-Lutz, Mina 62
Bangladesh: fertility decline in 140; globalization in 8; household gender norms in 192–3; marital quality in 16–17, 187–9, 198–205; marriage market in 158–9; neoliberalism in xx, 11; regional variations in **147**; rural households in 188, 192; rural oral traditions of 193–7; sex ratios in 138, 140, 143–6, 155–6, 159; social development in 7–8, 157, 191; son preference in 146–55, **150**; state religion in 6; women's entrepreneurship in 191, 199–201, 203, 205, 208n2, 250; women's paid employment in 221
Bangladesh NGO activity: and labor force participation 145, 149, 151, 157–8; and microcredit 188, 191, 193; and neoliberal development xx; women leaving 197
bargaining-based household model 117, 187, 189–90, 193–7, 205–7, 209n21; *see also* bargaining power
bargaining power: and child custody 124; and children's education 155; and divorce laws 16, 113–15, 118–19, 132; and gender norms 106, 120; in intrahousehold relations 189, 195–6; and women's well-being 15–16
Bates, Robert 41
Becker, Gary 116, 189–90, 194, 207
Bedouin: and creation of Israel 26n17; de-development of 171–2;

307

INDEX

forced relocation of 170–1, 174; health status of 174; and NGOs 12; socioeconomic status of 8, 168–9; Zionist narrative of 165–6, 174–5

Bedouin women: and aid donors 176–82; interviews with 167–8; Orientalist discourse about 165–6, 175–6; paid employment of 172–3; and poverty 169–70

behavioralist revolution 40

Benería, Lourdes 238

Bengali language 192

birth attendants, traditional *see* Traditional Birth Attendants CBO

Blaydes, Lisa and Linzer, Drew 42, 45–9, 53n16

Boko Haram 22

Boone, Peter 62–3

bootstrapped-improved critical values 122, 127, 129–30

bride-wealth *see* dower

British colonial heritage 52n10

Bush, George W. 38

capabilities approach 13

capitalism, Weberian 212–14

capitalist exploitation 15, 218–19, 228

Caregiver Parity Model 20

care work: and gender roles 91, 240; home-based 95, 109n17, 238; market economy's reliance on 242; multiple women involved in 105; social recognition of 20; and women's employment 92, 94–5, 102; and women's entrepreneurship 240, 245

carpet-weaving: in Iran 263, 274; in Turkey 212–17, 220–5, 227–9

caste system: marriage within 140–3, 159; resistance within 195; and sex ratios 157–8

CBOs (community-based organizations) in Nigeria 283–4, *286*, **295–6**; capacity training by 301; cooperative model of 293; economic value of 292; funding of 288; gender inclusion in 299–300; and larger NGOs 281–2, 289–91, 296, 298–9, 302

CEDAW (Convention of Elimination of all Kinds of Discrimination against Women) 10, 262

ceteris paribus 94–5, 243

Chad 99, 287

charity, in Turkey 213–14, 216, 228

childcare, and women's employment 87–8, 92–5, 102, 104–5

children: custody of 115, 118–19, 123–4, 132, 133n3, 134n14; gender discrimination among 141, 144–5, 156; mother's role in socializing 48

China, SRBs in 139–40

citizenship, gendered meanings of 236, 239, 248, 250; *see also* neoliberal citizenship

civilizing mission 4, 178

civil liberties 11, 61, 69, 72

civil society organizations: in Nigeria 283–4, 288; in Turkey 212–14, 216, 223, 235–6, 241–2, 250

Clinton, Hillary 37–8

colonialism: and development 18; and Muslim countries 7, 9, 35–6

colonized women 164, 177–9

Comilla 144, 146, 152–3

community-development groups 299–300

comparative statics 39–40, 42

complementarity, invisible 251

composition, fallacy of 52n13

constrained choice 261

context dependency 90, 95, 106

contraception 27

cooperative conflict household model 187, 189, 193–4, 206

Cromer, Lord 35, 38

CSRs (child sex ratios) 109n16, 138, 140–2, 155, 158, 161n2

culturalism: and methodological formalism 42, 44–5; in scholarship about Muslims 2, 33–4, 36–8

culturalization, in Israel/Palestine 165, 174, 178, 180–2

cultural regions 64

curiosity, voyeuristic 176, 179

daughter aversion 142–3, 153, 156, 159

daughters-in-law 191, 200, 204

DAWN (Development Alternatives for Women for a New Era) 10

DDW (Database Developing World) 89, 96

decision making, joint household 199, 201–2, 205, 270

de-development 166, 171–2, 174–5, 181

308

INDEX

democracy: from Islamic perspective 296; quantitative measurements of 42–3; Western promotion of 35

democratization: of economic policy 13; in Muslim societies 42; and women's interests 37

dependency theory 9–10

development: hegemonic discourses of 166; and modernization theory 9; women as designers of 282

development aid 287

development policies, neoliberal xx, 14

development programs: in Nigeria 296, 298; and women's entrepreneurship 237, 239–40, 242, 250, 252

DF (Deniz Feneri) 213, 216, 225–6

DHS (Demographic and Health Surveys) 89, 96, 144–5

division, fallacy of 52n13

division of labor, traditional gendered 91–2, 95, 104–5, 236–8, 250–1; *see also* male breadwinner/female homemaker model

divorce: in Bengali syncretic Islam 192; initiated by women *see khul*; maintenance after 159; and patriarchal risk 144, 189; social acceptability of 120; value of 133n5

divorced women 131–2, 284, 297

divorce laws: Islamic 62; reform of 19, 117–18; and religion 7; and women's labor force participation 16, 113–15

divorce rates 116–17, 119, *125–6*, 131–2, 133n2

domestic violence: in Bangladesh 191, 193, 196, 204–5; and divorce laws 118; laws against 69–70

double burden of work 14–15, 133, 196, 261, 266

dower 114, 117, 141, 144

dowry 141–4, 153, 156, 158

dress codes 172–3, 181, 262

dressmaking 270–1

Duflo, Esther 114

Easton, David 40

East/West binary 25nn3,4

economic determinism 39

education: of daughters 143, 202–3, 289; and economic growth 62, 66, 77; financing one's own 271–2; gender inequality in 59–60, 72, 74, 77, 80–3,

283; and modernity 9; in Naqab area 150–2, 172; in Nigeria 286; and son preference 149; women's attainment in 90, 97, 106, 109, 221, 291; and women's labor force participation 46

Egypt, divorce laws in 123

elderly people, caregiving for 87, 90, 93–5, 98, 105

endogeneity 52n12, 65, 69, 72, 74

England, Paula 199, 238

entrepreneurial subject xix–xx

entrepreneurship: in development discourse 235–7, 239–40, 252–3; family support for 251; and neoliberal discourse 243, 246–8; as obligation 249; *see also* women's entrepreneurship

Escobar, Arturo 9

Ethiopia 26n7

ethnography, feminist and interpretive 285

ethno-nationalism 290

exit threat 117

factor analysis 40, 109n10

factory workers, women 12

false consciousness 194–5

family law 7, 11, 16, 69, 123

family wage 20

Faridpur 144, 146, 153–5

fatherhood, investment in 199, 202–3, 205

FBOs (faith-based organizations) 281–2, 291, 294, 302

female genital mutilation 69

feminism: and alternatives to neoliberalism 12–14; anti-imperial 1, 3–4, 10; imperialistic 5, 23, 38 (*see also* Western feminism); Islamic 36

feminist economics: and double burden of work 14–15; and economic positivism 215, 217–18; household theories in 189–90, 193–4, 206–7 (*see also* household models); methodological diversity in 14; and neoclassical theory 34, 237–9; and Orientalism 18–19

fertility, and son preference 148

fertility rates: declining 138, 141, 144–6, 155; variations in 8

FIDA (International Federation of Women Lawyers) 294

INDEX

Fish, Steven 42–5, 52nn10,12, 53n13
Folbre, Nancy 7, 189–90, 193–6, 199, 206, 209n21, 238
FOMWAN (Federation of Muslim Women's Associations in Nigeria) 284, 286, 294, 296, 298, 301
formalism, methodological 33–4, 39–42, 50
Foucault, Michel 208, 230n8
France: colonial empire of 4; Muslim populations in 21
Fraser, Nancy 19–20, 26n16
Freedom House 43–4

game theory 63, 189, 193, 207
Gaza Strip 172
GEM (Gender Empowerment Measure) 44–5, 52n12, 69
Gender and Development (GAD), shift to paradigm of 10, 285
Gender Development Index 61
gender equality: attitudes to 63–4; and child welfare 133n9; deconstructive model of 20; in education 81; and entrepreneurship 235; indicators of 72; and Islam 42; NGOs and 151; in Nigeria 298; and North-South divide 10; in South Asian countries 157
gender hierarchies xx, 60, 92, 240, 286, 298
gender inequality: and authoritarianism 42, 45; and economic growth 59–61, 63; in education and income 74, 77, 80–3; and macroeconomic policies 10–11; measures of 52n12, 58–9, 65–9, **67–8**; and patriarchy 88; women as responsible for 196
Gender Inequality Index 157
gender justice 196, 205
gender norms: and economic development 18, 239, 249–50; evolution of 16, 20, 291; and inequalities 10; local-level 106; and NGOs 12; traditional 46, 262–3, 282
gender roles: and Arab uprisings 21; and divorce laws 114; in Iran 274–5; in Muslim communities 6; in Nigeria 290; in rural Bangladesh 192–3; in Turkey 215–16
gender segregation 224, 272; see also kulle
Georgia 139, 159

Ghana 139, 227
GHON (Grassroots Health Organization of Nigeria) 284, 289–90, 292, 296–301
GID (Gender, Institutions and Development) 58, 69, 83n2, 96, 98, 109n11
globalization: impact on women of 218, 228, 238; and Muslim countries 7–8, 213–14, 219; and pious conduct 216, 218–19, 230n7
Global North: Muslims in 21; and South 9
Global South: legal traditions in 6; Muslims in 5, 9; neoliberalism in 237–8, 241; population control in 26n12; women in 4, 10
governmentality studies 239
Grameen Bank: men's opposition to 203, 208n16; promoting entrepreneurship 242; women borrowers from 197, 201
Gramsci, Antonio 190, 195
Green Movement 22
Grewal, Inderpal 4, 12
grounded theory 197
Gulf emirates 7, 287

hairdressers, in Iran 264–5, 270
hairdressers, in Turkey 243, 246
hard work, discourse of 222–3, 243, 245, 252
harmonious optimal division household model 187, 193, 206
Harvey, David xix
Haryana 141–2
Hausa people 283, 287; see also Nigeria
Hausa women: centering experiences of 284–5; development work of 289–90, 292–3, 296–8, 301–2; NGOs and CBOs of 282–3, 286; retaining autonomy from funders 286–7
heads of household: children not related to 90, 94, 98, 102, 109n13; female 88, 94, 97, 102, 104–5, 197; and sex ratios 148
healthcare facilities, in Nigeria 284, 291, 297, 299, 301
helal 224, 230n11
Himachal Pradesh 142
Hindu communities: in Bangladesh 6, 149; and economic growth 80;

310

INDEX

and gender inequality 64; marriage in 159; and sex ratios 142, 158; son preference in 151; and women's education 61

Hinduism, stages of life in 192, 208n7

Hindu nationalism 22, 227

HIPC (highly indebted poor countries) 5, 9

household composition 87–9, 92–5, 97–8, 101–2, **103**, 105–7

household models 117, 187, 189–90, 193–7, 205–7, 209n21; *see also* male breadwinner/female homemaker model

household wealth 145, 148–9, 151

housework 240; division of 91–2, 95, 240, 251; inability to postpone 200; and paid work 208–9n20, 255n12, 261, 292–3; *see also* care work; unpaid work

human capital 108n8; measurement of 65–6, 77; women investing in 115

Human Development Index 36

human rights: Bedouin activism for 167; and gender oppression 63; government compliance with 13; in Islamic framework 291, 295; in Turkey 222

Huntington, Samuel P. 35, 43, 45

hypergamy 141

IBS (charitable organization) 216

IDRC (International Development Research Centre) 140, 142, 146, 157

IGLS (Iterative Generalized Least Squares) 97

IHH (charitable organization) 216, 223–4, 226

illiteracy *see* literacy

IMF (International Monetary Fund) xix, 11, 36, 241, 287

income uncertainty *see* precarity

India: regional variations in 140–1; resistance to patriarchy in 195; sex ratios in 138–43, 155–6; women's work in 145; *see also* caste system

individualism 218–19, 238–9, 248

inequalities, global 5, 10, 13, 20

informal economy: in Iran 264; in MENA 124–5; personal networks supporting 227–8; in Turkey 213, 220–2, 227, 229n4, 242; women's participation in 97

information asymmetry 202

Inglehart, Ronald 48, 63

intersectionality 1, 3, 17, 19

IPUMS (Integrated Public Use Microdata Series) 89, 96

Iran: Afghan women in 277n1; developmental indicators in 7–8; doing field work in 264–5; gender norms in 17; as Islamic Republic 6, 22, 262–3; location of paid work 272, **273**; men's duties to women in 278n7; reasons for women working 265–7, **266**, 271–4; sanctions against 8, 262–3, 274–5, 278n11; shameful work in 268–71; women's paid employment in 260–4, 274–6

Iraq, US invasion of 4–5, 38

Islam: and authoritarianism 42–5; as "dummy variable" xix, 2–3, 14, 18, 43, 53n13, 62–3, 89; formalist approaches to 41–2, 49; heterogeneity of xvii, 5–6, 120; and labor decisions 290; NGOs working within 12, 283–5, 287, 289–91, 294, 297, 302 (*see also* FBOs); patriarchal versions of 203, 208n6, 282; as state religion 6–7; support for radical 26n18 (*see also* Islamic fundamentalism); syncretic Bengali 191–3; Western stereotypes about 3–4, 19, 35, 83, 177; women's rights in 201, 267, 294–6; and women's wellbeing 25n1, 26n14, 33–4; and women's work 260, 267, 275, 290, 293; *see also* Prophet Muhammad

Islamic banking 230n7

Islamic exceptionalism 1–2, 91

Islamic fundamentalism 45–6, 48, 53n15

Islamic law 7, 49, 62, 99, 114, 283

Islamist politics: in Afghanistan 38; after Arab Spring 22; in different countries 6–7; in Iran xxin1, 262; theological approach to 48–9; in Turkey 223; and women 36–7, 46–7, 188

Israel/Palestine: Arab populations of 8, 12, 38, 164–6, 168–9, 172 (*see also* Bedouin); colonial logics in 164–6, 175, 178, 180–2; health inequalities in 8, 174; house demolition in 170; religion and state in 7, 22

INDEX

İstanbul: NGOs promoting entrepreneurship in 254n1; pious women in 15, 213–14, 225–6

İzmir 212–14, 216, 223

Jordan, family law in 133n7, 134n13

Kabeer, Naila 8, 195

KAGİDER 236, 242, 254nn1,3

Kandiyoti, Deniz: on patriarchy 34–6, 91, 107; and violence against women 21

Kano 12, 281–4, *286*, 287–9, 291, 293–4, 297; *see also* Hausa women

KEDV (Kadın Emeğini Değerlendirme Vakfı) 236, 242, 254nn1,3

Khamenei, Ayatollah 263

kharghi 267, 275, 278n7

Khatami, Mohammad 262

Khomeini, Ayatollah 262–3

khul: and bargaining power 118–19, 132; and divorce rates 117, *125–6*, 127, 133n2; introduction of 16–17, 122, **123**; limits to impact of 119–20; and women's labor participation 113–16, 120–2, 124–32, *127*, **128**, **130**

KILM (Key Indicators of Labor Market) 116, 124

kinship systems, and sex ratios 139–41, 143, 158

knowledge: naive 208n8; subaltern 187, 190, 193–4, 196

knowledge production: about Muslims 1, 36; of Bedouin women 164–5; and lives of producers 215

Konya: gender roles in 215–16, 221; weavers in 212, 214–15, 222, 229n4

Krueger, Anne 60

Krugman, Paul 50

kulle 283, 289, 296, 299, 302

Kurigram district 148

labor force: feminization of 238; women leaving 119, 265; women's reluctance to join 220–1; *see also* women's labor force participation

labor market: gender discrimination in 59, 72; women's participation in *see* women's labor force participation

labor politics 216–17

labor trajectory, sequential 293

liberal democracy 35, 43, 51n2

Libya: divorce laws in 122; NATO air strikes on 38

life-cycle effects 262, 273–5

life expectancy 7–8, 138–9, 141

literacy: among Bedouin women 173; and gender 44–5, 62

Ma'an - The Coalition of Bedouin Women 167–8

Madhya Pradesh 142

mahr see dower

mahram 92

male breadwinner/female homemaker model: feminist study of 217; in Iran 17, 260, 267, 275–6; and patriarchy 87–8, 92; and sex ratios 143; and women's labor force participation 15, 261

male dominance 45, 60, 69, 72

marital quality: and bargaining power 194–5; and intrahousehold relations 189–91, 206–7; local measures of 187–9, 193, 198–205

marital status, and employment 17, 88, 92–3, 102, 109n17

market capacity 236, 239–40

market logics 237, 240, 247

marriage: Becker's theory of 116; and daughter aversion 142–3; and ease of divorce 119; and employment 91; processes in 195; quality of *see* marital quality; refusing proposal of 202; regional differences in India 140–1; wealth transfers at 144 (*see also* dower; dowry); women's empowerment in 16, 19

marriage contracts 117–18, 124, 133n7

marriage market 46, 142–3, 158

married women: and other women in household 109n17; paid work of 102, 114, 265, 274–5; and religion 165

Marxism 9, 39, 189, 194

masculinity xix–xx, 6, 16, 187, 198, 206

masseuses 264–5, 269, 275

maternal health, in Nigeria 286, 301

mathematization 34, 39–41

Maya Enterprise 242

MCMC (Markov chain Monte Carlo) 97

MENA (Middle East and North Africa): child custody in 115; family law in 116–17, 120, **123** (*see also khul*); gender inequality in 84n7; marriage

312

INDEX

norms in 118–19; patriarchy in 91; women's employment in 113–14, 124–5, 131

microcredit: in Bangladesh 161n5, 191; as disciplining women 243–4; and marital quality 188, 190, 193, 199, 202–3; and neoliberalism 240–1, 252–3; NGOs providing 287; in Nigeria 284, 291; in Turkey 242, 246, 254n6; women's access to 15, 196

microenterprises 190, 245, 251

microfinance *see* microcredit

MICS (Multiple Indicator Cluster Survey) 144–5

Middle East: conflated with Arabs and Muslims 5; culturalist accounts of 34–5, 37–8, 49–50; formalistic approaches to 34, 41, 49; use of term 26; wars in xx; women's status in 36; *see also* MENA

migration xviii, 21–2, 241

missing women 69, 138–40

Moallem, Minoo xxin1

modernism, in development economics 18

modernization theory 9

Moghadam, Valentine M. 21–2, 36, 63, 91

moral economy: of the household 187, 190, 205–6, 208n2; and religion 218

mortality: gender gap in 138–9, 144, 156; infant 174; maternal 7, 141, 145, 191, 194

Moshiri, Zahra Sadat 278n9

motherhood: sacrificial 14, 250–1; sequential to paid work 293

MSO (Muslim Sisters Organization) 284, 290–2, 294, 296, 298, 301

Mubarak, Hosni 22, 37

muhtar 213, 229n2

multicollinearity 74, 82

multi-method approach 285, 301

Muslim Brotherhood 38

Muslim communities: in Bangladesh 158–9, 188; divorce in 16, 132 (*see also khul*); as Eastern 25n3; gender inequality in 34–6; heterogeneity of 3, 5–6, 8, 48; neoliberalism and gender in 14; sex ratios in 142; social safety nets in 21; use of term 25n1; women's work in 15, 19–20; *see also* Muslim-majority countries

Muslim-majority countries: authoritarianism in 42–5; comparing to other countries 109n11; development in 18; diversity of xviii; in Global South 9; number of 5; patriarchy in 88–9, 91–2, 98–9, 104–6; secular law in 49; use of term 25; women's labor in 62

Muslim minorities xviii, xx, 6, 21, 25n1, 43

Muslim organizations, transnational 287

Muslims: gender-equitable views among 18; global population of 5–6; moderate 36

Muslim women: activism by 22–3, 36; conception of good husband 187–8, 199; development work of 289–90, 295, **296**, 302; essentializing 26n14; everyday lives of 3; in formalist arguments 44–6; heterogeneity of xvii–xviii, xxin1, 14; and marital quality 187–9; and meaningful work 20, 226–8; in Muslim-minority contexts 21; and neoliberalism 11; Orientalist narratives of 1–2, 4–5, 17, 33–4, 36–7, 175, 177, 238–9; son preference by 151; West African 281–3, 288 (*see also* Hausa women)

Muslim youth 21

mutuality 189, 195, 198, 203

nafagheh 278n7

Naqab area: Bedouin settlements in 164–5 (*see also* unrecognized villages); de-development in 166–7, 174–5, 181; educational institutions in 173; Judaization of 171, 175, 178; NGO activity in 176–9, 182; poverty in 169–70

Nash, John 189, 194, 207

natal home: proximity of 141, 208n14; visiting 200–1, 204

NCWS (National Council of Women's Societies) 293–4

needs, opportunities and values framework 89–92

neoclassical economics: and development paradigms 237–8; gender in 253; of the household 189, 194; and political science 33–4, 38–41, 53n16; relation to reality 50

INDEX

neoliberal citizenship 235–6, 239–42, 246, 248, 251–3

neoliberalism: challenges to 13; gendered implications of 10–11, 20, 36, 237–40, 248–52; and globalization 213–14; impact on paid employment 220; and methodological formalism 50; and Muslim communities 14; and NGOs 287; and Orientalism 5; and pious conduct 216, 218, 222, 227–8, 230n7

Netanyahu, Binyamin 170, 174

NGOs (non-governmental organizations): African developmental 214, 281–6 (*see also* Nigeria); in Bangladesh *see* Bangladesh NGO activity; conservative Christian 22; faith-based *see* FBOs; and gender 10–12, 23; and globalization 219; indigenous 287, 289, 291; in Israel/Palestine 12, 167, 175–6, 179; secular and faith-based 293–6; and social mobilization 286–7; in Turkey 213, 241

Nigeria: development indicators in 7–8; Islamism in 7; neoliberalism in 11; women's NGOs in 12, 281–2, 290–301, **295–6** (*see also* Hausa women)

nonlabor income 133n6

Norris, Pippa 63

Nussbaum, Martha C. 13

Obama, Barack 37–8

oil production 8, 63, 81–2, 122, 131

older women: and divorce laws 113, 115–16, 119, 122, 132; and gender norms 17; labor force participation 128–31, 268, 272–4, 276

OLS (ordinary least squares) 63, 74, 82, 120, 149

Oman, family law in 122–4

OPEC countries 116, 122, 131

Oporajito 197

organic intellectuals 190

Orientalism: and the Bedouin 166, 176–7; and global inequalities 6, 13; in scholarship 1–5, 14, 17–18, 61

orphans 224, 284, 297

Othered women 165

Pact Nigeria 284, 288, 297, 299

pain, funding 166, 176, 179–82

Pakistan 102, 140, 157, 159

Palestinians *see* Bedouin; Israel/Palestine

PAPFam (Pan Arab Project for Family Health) 89, 96

participant observation: in Bangladesh 197–8; in Iran 17

Patai, Raphael 3

patriarchal institutions 10, 72; measurement of 58–9, 61–2, 83, 98

patriarchal legal structures 7

patriarchal norms 108n9; and oil production 63; variables representing 98

patriarchal preferences 58, 60–1, 82, 84n6

patriarchal rent-seeking 11, 59–60, 63, 69

patriarchal risk 144, 148–9, 151–2

patriarchy: Brahmanical 140; classic concept of 88, 91–2, 107, 139–40; dimensions of 88, 106; and household composition 95, **103**, 106; Islam as proxy for 15, 58–64, 82–3, 84n6; macro/micro-level interactions 104; and sex ratios 139; sources of power 63; as Third World problem 165, 175–6, 181

patrilineality 88, 91–2, 94, 102, 104, 139, 189

patrilocality 91, 139, 158, 189, 201

patron-client relationships 218, 222, 298

PD (patriarchal dominance) index 11, 65, 83; calculation of 69–72, **70–1**; correlations of 72–4, **73**; and economic growth **78–80**, 81–2

peace-in-the-household model 187, 206

per capita GDP, model of growth 65, **66**, 69, 74–81, **75–80**

per capita income 7–8, 83n1

personal status laws 6

pious economies 15, 212–14, 216–19, 227–8

pluralism, methodological 50

Polanyi, Karl 217, 238

Polity scores 43

poor women: and entrepreneurship 235, 242, 247; in Iran 260, 274, 276; and marriage 191, 194–6, 206; *see also* village women

population control 26n12

INDEX

postcolonial economics 238
postcolonial studies 36, 91
post-materialism 48
post-Washington Consensus 237
poverty: and gender oppression 62–3;
individual responsibility for 246; in
Israel/Palestine 166, 169; in Turkey
213; women's vulnerability to 21
poverty rates 7–8, 145
practices of care 238
Prawer Plan 170–1, 174–5
precarity xix, 213, 243, 245–6, 251, 269,
275
private and intimate spaces 180, 191,
218
property rights: patriarchal 7, 60, 72;
women's 69, 92, 98, 118, 188, 201
Prophet Muhammad: as model
husband 199, 204–5; and pious work
221, 223, 225; wives of 297
prosperity effect, negative 141, 149
Protestant Christianity 61, 64, 214,
230n8
proverbs 157, 193–4, 197, 200
provisioning 238, 252
pseudo-development 175
public institutions, quality of 66
public mobility: and equal-status
marriage 141; and marital quality
199, 201, 203–5; and sex ratios 139;
and women's work 144, 158, 263,
268–9, 274
public sphere: male dominance of 90,
92, 95, 98–9, 106, 108n3, 139; and
private sphere 217; women's mobility
in *see* public mobility
public transport, in Israel/Palestine
172–3
Punjab 141–2

qualitative research: in economics 215;
formalist hostility to 41; on women's
experience 190
quantitative analyses 3, 18, 40, 42, 285
Qur'an 23, 205, 225, 290–1, 294, 297

Rajasthan 141–2
Ramadan 213, 269
rational choice theory 40, 53n16
rationality assumption 46–7, 235–8,
252
reciprocity 195, 217–18, 238

regression analyses: in formalist
analyses 44–5; on Islam and
patriarchy 59; in neoclassical
economics 39–40
relational selves 218
religion: and economic behavior
217 (*see also* pious economies);
importance to women of 18–19, 218,
275; instrumentalization by power
xviii–xix, xxi; and sex ratios 142, 159;
and son preference 151–2, 158; *see
also* Hinduism; Islam
religiosity: and authoritarianism 44;
and feminist economics 18; and
globalization/neoliberalization
230n7
religious affiliation: and economic
growth **75–6**, 77, **78–80**, 81–2; and
gender inequality 58–9, 61–4, 72–4;
use of term 83
religious ceremonies, all-women 265
rent-seeking behavior 60; *see also*
patriarchal rent-seeking
reproductive labor: men's respect
for 198–200; and women's paid
employment 278n10
responsibility: gendering 236, 248–50;
in neoliberal discourse 239–40, 243,
246–8, 252
rest, respecting women's need for
200–1
Rouhani, Hassan 274, 277n2
rule of law 66, 77
Rwandan genocide 179

safety nets *see* social safety nets
Said, Edward 3, 36, 176
Sanskritization 158
SAPs (structural adjustment policies)
xix, 7, 10–11, 237
savings, compulsory 244
secularism 9, 44, 46
secular law 49
secular states 26n9, 223
Seguino, Stephanie 18, 59, 64
self-development 219
self-discipline 222
self-employment 143, 145, 156, 264
self-governance 222, 238–9, 241, 252
self-help 239
selfhood: and family 248; modern
230n8, 238

INDEX

self-interest 47, 52n6, 53n16, 60, 217, 247–8
self-sufficiency 235–6, 253
semiformal sector 213, 220, 228, 229n4
Sen, Amartya 13, 138, 188, 194, 196
sex ratios: changes in 16; of children *see* CSRs; determinants of 139, 159; divergence between India and Bangladesh 155–6; in formalist analyses 44–5; regional variations in 138–41; religious variations in 142; use of term 53n14; *see also* SRBs
sexual assault 69
sexual harassment 69
shalish 191, 193, 208n18
shameful work 261, 264, 268–9, 276
shangshar 192
shangshare shanti 187–8, 192
sharecropper women, in Bangladesh 188–90, 198, 205–6
Shari'a *see* Islamic law
Smith, Adam 52n6, 60
snowballing 197, 265
social capital 289, 299–301
social exclusion, in Turkey 240–2
social safety nets 7, 12, 15, 21, 223, 227, 237
social security systems 220, 242, 246–8, 252, 255n10
sohbet sessions 213, 223–6, 228, 229n3
son preference 16–17; and abortion 140; determinants of 146, 148–54, **150**; in South Asia 138–9, 142–4, 159
South Korea 139–40
spacio-cide 170, 182
spirituality, importance for women of 16, 18, 205
SRBs (sex ratios at birth) 138–41, 145, 156, 158–9, 161n1
SSA (Sub-Saharan Africa): lack of social safety nets in 21; literacy gaps in 62; PD in 74
standard errors, robust 75, 128, 130
subjectivities: economic xx, 236–8, 240, 253; neoliberal 14, 236, 243, 249–52

Tanzania 26n7, 67
Tehran 260, 268, 277n5, 278n9
textile industries *see* carpet-weaving
Third World women 4, 165–6, 177–8, 180, 182
time horizon 115, 132

time-use data 15, 26n13
TİSVA (Türkiye İsrafı Önemle Vakfı) 246, 254n6
togetherness 208n1; *see also* marital quality
tourism, in Turkey 222
Trading Cooperative 284, 288, 291, 299–301
Traditional Birth Attendants CBO 283–4, 297, 299–300
tropics, land area in 65, 77, 84n3
trust, interpersonal 44–5
Tunisia, family law in 124
Turkey: developmental indicators in 8; family planning access in 22; Islamism in 7; neoliberalism and work in 11, 220–3, 227–8, 230n10, 241–2, 252; passive revolution in 223; pious economies in 212, 219; unemployment in 230n9; women's employment in 223–6; women's entrepreneurship in 235–6, 240–6, 250, 254n3

UAE (United Arab Emirates) 123, 134n13
ugroponthi 193, 203
ultrasound scanning 139, 155–6
UNDP (United Nation Development Program) 36, 140, 161n1, 242, 254n6, 255n7
Universal Breadwinner Model 20
unpaid work: and access to resources 14–15; in India and Bangladesh 143–5, 156; necessity of 20; and paid work 17; recognition of value 8, 199; *see also* care work; reproductive labor
unrecognized villages: demolition of 170; education in 173; health in 174; NGO activity in 175–6, 179, 181; poverty in 169–70; use of term 165
US Supreme Court, *Hobby Lobby* decision 22
utility function 39, 46, 52n6, 116–17, 189, 194

vaccination 296
vakifs 213
values, traditional and modern 48, 172
variance inflation factors 74, 84n4
veiling: compulsory 69, 262–3; forbidden 277n4; *see also* dress codes

INDEX

vendors, in Iran 265, 268–9, 271, 275, 278n9

Vietnam 139, 159

village women, in Bangladesh 188–9, 191, 193–5, 198–201, 206, 208n2

violence: against women 21; Muslim support for 26n18; *see also* domestic violence

volunteer work 216, 291

VOWAN (Voices of Widows, Divorcées and Orphans) 284, 286, 291, 297

voyeurism 176, 179

WAD (Women and Development) 10, 284–5

wage gaps, gender-based 59, 81

water supply 170–1, 174, 224, 284, 297, 301

Weber, Max xix, 214, 230n8

the West, use of term 51n2

West Bengal 142, 195; *see also* Bangladesh

Western bias and privilege 19

Western feminism 4, 282, 285, 298, 301

Western imperialism: and Arab authoritarians 22; and Muslim women xviii, 33, 35, 37–8, 51n4; and Orientalism 3, 36; and Third World women 4, 26n12; and the *ummat* xxin1

Western women, self-representation of 4–5

white privilege 19, 179

WID (Women in Development) 10, 281, 285

widowed women: in Bangladesh 148–52; in India 195; in Iran 261, 265; Islamic provision for 133n1, 159, 297; and patriarchal risk 144

WIN (Women in Nigeria) 294

WODEN (Women and Development Network) 284, 286, 297

women: access to resources 95, 196; household bargaining position of *see* bargaining power; knowledge traditions of 193–4; meanings of work for 218; mobility of *see* public mobility; as objects of development 178; parallel spaces for 300; spending on families 250

women's agency 190, 196, 206, 217, 261, 275, 289

women's cooperatives 191, 239, 242, 247

women's empowerment: and bargaining model of households 196; in developing countries 118; and dislocation from community 177; intersecting factors influencing 23, 276; and marriage 16; and Nigerian NGOs 297; and paid employment 19, 221, 239, 241

women's entrepreneurship: and family responsibility 248–53; and gender equality 14; in Iran 271; programs promoting 235–6, 240, 242–8, 254n3, 255n7

women's labor force participation: and age 128, 272–5; as choice and constraint 260–1; determinants of 15–17, 90–1; and divorce laws 113, 116–19, 131–2 (*see also khul*); and household composition 92–5, 101–2, 105; and housework 255n12 (*see also* double burden of work); increasing 20; in India and Bangladesh 141, 145, 156; and intrahousehold relations 190, 199; in Iran 263–4; measuring 26n10, 89, 96–7, **100–1**, 124; men's consent for 124, 203–4; in Nigeria 283, 292; and patriarchy 87–92, **93**, 99, 104, 106–7; as proxy for empowerment 14, 19, 196, 236, 239–40, 260; regional comparisons *115*; and religion 62; and sex ratios 139, 148; in Turkey 221, 241–2; variations in 7–8; and years of schooling 128–9, 134n18

women's organizations: funding and autonomy of 287–8; in Iran 262; in Naqab area 173, 178; in Nigeria 282, 287, 296 (*see also* Hausa women)

World Bank 255n7, 287; World Development Indicators 116

WVS (World Values Survey) 44, 46, 48, 53n19, 63–4

younger women: and divorce laws 16, 113, 115–16, 119, 122; labor force participation 128–31, 261–2, 271–2; and son preference 151

zakat 12, 287–8

Zionism 165–6, 171, 176